WRITING STAGES AND STRATEGIES

| Issues | THE COLLEGE WORLD | | | THE WORKING WORLD |
	Research papers	Essay examinations	Critical papers	Reports
52–154	192–194	244–245	262–266	296–298
54–167	199–222	246–251	270–280	301–308
67–169	223–224	253–254	280–281	308–309
69–172	197–199	251–253	266–270	298–300
72–174, 185, 87–188	221–222, 227–228, 238	254–256	281, 291, 292	309–312, 323–324
69, 172–175, 85	194–195	251	266–267	
	194–197, 227–228, 229–230, 238	251	267, 281	298
74–175, 185–86, 188	224–226, 228, 239	254–256, 238–239	282	309–312, 324–325
36–137	225	255	282, 292	
	226	255		
		256	282, 293	309–312
75–176, 177–78, 173–174, 85–186	225	254–256	282	
85, 187	237–238	260–261	291, 292	323
76, 185–186, 88	225–226, 228	254–256	292	
77, 177–180, 86–187, 188	228–231	256–257	283–284, 292	313–321, 325–326
77–180, 186–87	221–222, 228–229	256–257, 261	283–284	313–314, 325–326
80–184, 186–87, 188	221–222	256–257	284–288, 281	317–321, 325–326
85–191	236–242	260–261	290–295	322–327

FOUR WORLDS OF WRITING

JANICE M. LAUER
Purdue University

GENE MONTAGUE
University of Detroit

ANDREA LUNSFORD
The University of British Columbia

JANET EMIG
Rutgers University

HARPER & ROW, PUBLISHERS, New York
Cambridge, Hagerstown, Philadelphia, San Francisco,
London, Mexico City, São Paulo, Sydney

1817

Consulting Editor
GARY TATE
Texas Christian University

FOUR WORLDS OF WRITING

CREDITS

Exploration beginning on p. 33.: "Perspectives on Writing" by Janice Lauer, from *Retrospectives and Perspectives: A Symposium in Rhetoric* by Turner S. Kobler, William E. Tanner, and J. Dean Bishop, eds.

p. 65: from *The Book of Nightmares* by Galway Kinnell, published by Houghton Mifflin Company. Copyright © 1971 by Galway Kinnell. Reprinted by permission of the publisher.

p. 210: Reprinted by permission from *The Progressive,* 408 West Gorham Street, Madison, Wisconsin 53703. Copyright © 1977, The Progressive, Inc.

p. 263: "Wires" by Philip Larkin from *The Less Deceived.* Copyright © The Marvell Press, 1955, 1960. Used by permission of The Marvell Press, England.

p. 265: "Finding a Teacher," by W. S. Merwin, from *Writings to an Unfinished Accompaniment,* by W. S. Merwin. Copyright © 1973 by W. S. Merwin. Reprinted by permission of Atheneum Publishers.

p. 270: "Bess," by William Stafford, from *Stories That Could Be True: New and Collected Poems,* by William Stafford. Copyright © 1966 by William Stafford. Reprinted by permission of Harper & Row, Publishers, Inc.

p. 279: "Losing Track," by Denise Levertov, from *O Taste and See.* "Losing Track" was first published in *Poetry.* Copyright © 1963 by Denise Levertov Goodman. Reprinted by permission of New Directions Publishers.

p. 414: "The Whore of Mensa", copyright © 1974 by Woody Allen. Reprinted from *Without Feathers* by Woody Allen, p. 33, by permission of Random House Inc.

Sponsoring Editor: Phillip Leininger
Special Projects Editor: Ann Torbert
Project Editor: Claudia Kohner
Text and Cover Designer: Gayle Jaeger
Production Manager: Marion Palen
Compositor: York Graphic Services, Inc.
Printer and Binder: Halliday Lithographic Corporation

FOUR WORLDS OF WRITING

Copyright © 1981 by Janice M. Lauer, Gene Montague, Andrea Lunsford, and Janet Emig

Library of Congress Cataloging in Publication Data

Main entry under title:
Four world s of writing.

  Includes index.
  1. English language—Rhetoric.   2. English
language—Grammar—1950-   I. Lauer, Janice M.
II. Tate, Gary.
PE1408.F547   808′.042   80-26826
ISBN 0-06-388635-9

BRIEF CONTENTS

v

II / GUIDE TO EDITING AND SENTENCE-COMBINING

Front endpaper: Table of writing stages and strategies
Back endpaper: Editing symbols

DETAILED CONTENTS

Writing with a Persuasive Aim
THE PUBLIC WORLD

4 / Issues 151

Writing with an Expository Aim
THE COLLEGE WORLD

5 / Research papers 192

Writing with an Expository Aim
THE COLLEGE WORLD

6 / Essay examinations 243

II / GUIDE TO EDITING
AND SENTENCE-COMBINING

9 / Editing 331

PREFACE

We set out to build *Four Worlds of Writing* around the composing process, basing our approach on premises derived from rhetorical theory of the last decade:

–that writing is a unique way of learning

–that meaningful writing grows from a writer's own pressing questions

–that the composing process is a series of stages that can vary in sequence and are often recursive, even though they must be ordered in certain ways in a text

–that primary to meaningful writing is the discovery and communication of a significant focus to which aims and modes are subordinate

–that specific skills such as sentence-combining, paragraph building, and conventions of usage are best developed within the framework of the whole composing process

Throughout, we have merged theory with the practical experience of college instructors who have developed, tested, and refined that theory in their classrooms. Numerous samples of student work exemplify all stages of the composing process, and present the struggles and achievements of many kinds of students attempting many different types of writing.

In developing this approach, we have been aware always of the difference between *stages* of writing and *strategies* that guide writers through stages. Alternative strategies can be helpful at a given stage. For example, our Exploratory Guide does not preclude the use of others. We adopted this model, however, because it worked well for our students, is easily understood, easily remembered, and applicable to all writing situations.

Our general approach in each chapter has been this:

1. To identify for the student the writing situation the chapter poses and to differentiate it from the situation in the preceding chapter or chapters.
2. To explain the stages of the writing process as they bear on the unique writing situation, stressing always the sameness of the stages.
3. To explain at each stage the strategy a writer can use to complete the stage.
4. To exemplify, by copious display and analysis of student work, the movement through the stages and the use of particular strategies.
5. To supply class exercises so that students may practice the strategies.
6. To assign specific tasks at each stage so that students, while learning from principles, examples, and exercises, are required to develop their own papers, stage by stage.

Taken in sequence, the chapters move the student from the expressive paper to the expository, from the inward to the outward, both in subject matter and audience. The order in one sense is arbitrary, in another logical and desirable. But the instructor who wishes to change the sequence can do so easily by using the Table of Writing Stages and Strategies on the front endpaper, which permits the use of sections of chapters the instructor may not wish to deal with as wholes. Thus *Four Worlds of Writing* can be adapted for either a one-term or two-term course; our arrangement permits the instructor to limit the course by aim, by type of writing, or by subject matter.

The Table of Writing Stages and Strategies also allows the instructor to choose the emphasis to be placed on developing editing skills. Part II of the book deals with the conventions and includes assignments in sentence-combining and editing checklists, followed by a convenient glossary of terms. The chapters themselves contain introductions to sentence-combining, choosing appropriate diction and syntax, and paragraphing at stages where instruction in these matters is most profitable. All of these sections are cross referenced.

Our concern for producing a book that is "adjustable" grows out of a practical, unavoidable fact: a book that can be used by all students must be flexible enough to provide practice material for students who need a good deal of work in the conventions, but it must not burden all students with the same work. On the other hand, there are limits to flexibility. This book is deliberately arranged to discourage the notion that students must wait to write until they have eliminated their problems with the conventions of language. Fundamentally, this book directs the attention of the student and the instructor to the composing process, and puts the acquisition of conventional skills in perspective as only one part of that process.

That view manifests itself in the organization of the book. Janet Emig's introduction emphasizes the necessity of conscious control of the writing process at the college level, the importance of understanding what the writer is doing, and why he or she is doing it. The center of the book—the eight chapters by Janice M. Lauer and Gene Montague—stresses the pedagogical importance of the repetition of the process, the pedagogical necessity of mastering one aim at a time, the pedagogical advisability of not pestering the student with concerns irrelevant to the stage he or she is working in. The final section, by Andrea Lunsford, addresses itself to self-instruction in self-editing skills. Among other things, the book attempts to reduce the confusion between matters rhetorical and matters grammatical and to put the emphasis where it belongs.

We wish to acknowledge the aid we received from Harper & Row and a corps of editors. It was not easy to coordinate the work of four people, especially when one lives on the west coast of Canada, another on the east coast of the United States, and the remaining two in the American midwest. The largess of Harper & Row permitted us to come together at critical times for planning and revision. We are grateful to the three teams of reviewers who corrected our excesses and helped refine the organization of the book, but we are most grateful to them for supporting our belief that a careful concentration on process, not product, and a strong emphasis on the determining role of aim in the writing process was not only proper but true and, above all, needed to be said at book length. We are indebted to Gary Tate, the original convenor of the group; to the students whose work runs through our pages; to Richard E. Young and James Kinneavy, whose rhetorical work underlies several key features of our text; to Virginia Patek, whose help in the chapters on the research paper and the essay exam was invaluable; to Angela Garnetti, who typed with accuracy and equanimity the versions of the manuscript; and to our families and friends whose support sustained us through three years of effort.

Janice M. Lauer
Gene Montague
Andrea Lunsford
Janet Emig

FOUR WORLDS OF WRITING

INTRODUCTION
Understanding writing

Writing is one way of making meaning from experience for ourselves and for others. For many of us, writing serves as the most available and the most compelling way because the outcome, visible language, is a satisfyingly permanent record of thought and feeling. We are consequently willing to engage in a process that is often long and complex so we can render meaning as a sequence of words on a page. Can others help us as we actually move through the process of writing? Can others strengthen our abilities to write effectively and well?

The authors of *Four Worlds of Writing* believe that the response to both questions is *yes* and that this text offers direct help to writers of all ages. We have spent many years finding out how writers work. We have examined and analyzed statements made over the centuries by many of the world's noted writers. We have asked student writers about their practices and have observed them as they write. We have asked ourselves how we write.

WRITING AS PROCESS

In this text we stress certain points about writing as process. These points are generalizations based on research by ourselves and others as well as on our experience as teachers and writers.

In the text, we will examine each of the following statements about the writing process:

1. Writing represents a way of making meaning of our experience. Generally defined, that process by which we make meaning of experience is called *learning*. Writing provides us with a unique way of learning, a way of learning unlike any other.

2. Writing occurs as a chain of processes. It is a series of interactions with words and ideas that develop and change over time.

3. These interactions may sometimes be complicated and difficult to describe. They are complicated because we engage in so many activities almost at the same time: We try to remember past or ongoing experiences. We plan what we intend to write, from the next word, phrase, or concept to the shape that the entire piece of writing will take. We put down on paper the selections we have made from the range of available possibilities. We read and reread what we have written. We change and revise parts or even the whole. We try to convey large concepts and themes, as well as supplying supporting evidence and detail. We consider who our audiences will be; how each audience will respond to what has been written; and how we can direct words effectively to the audience.

4. The process of writing can differ from text to text. For example, most of us require different lengths of time for writing an original story from writing a letter to a friend. Usually, however, when we have written regularly over a period of time, we tend to develop somewhat consistent patterns and strategies of working.

5. External factors affect us. These factors include what aspect of experience we are dealing with, how much time we have for doing the writing, whom it is we are writing for, and how much the writing will count.

6. Internal factors also affect our writing processes. These factors include how deeply we care about the writing we are doing and how certain we are of our abilities to do it well.

7. Many writers write differently in and out of the college classroom. Outside the classroom they tend not to be so limited by deadlines. Outside the classroom, readers usually concentrate on the message conveyed, rather than on the way it is conveyed. When writers do not have

deadlines or grades or teachers' comments to worry about, many of them are willing to spend more time writing, rather than less. Often, perhaps consequently, writers do higher quality writing outside the classroom than they do within it.

8. Another reason that writing done outside the classroom is different from writing done in the classroom is that students discover that descriptions some teachers have given them about how people write are too simple or downright inaccurate. Planning what we want to write, for example, is much more complicated than making any kind of outline, even a sentence outline. We do not plan only when we begin: we plan, and replan, as we write.

9. Perhaps a third reason for differences in writing in and out of the classroom is that students' experiences with learning to write in school, exclusively for teachers, are often negative. Teachers often do not concentrate on what is most central about writing—the meaning the writer is trying to convey. Instead, instructors are distracted by a forgotten comma or a misspelled word. Part of the problem is that teachers seldom share in the writing process from the outset. Instead, they wait until writers hand in papers before commenting on what should have been done differently during the writing of those papers. The method is neither helpful nor efficient, for teachers or for writers.

10. There is no doubt, however, that teachers can help you learn to write. In fact, a *variety* of persons can help you write more skillfully and successfully; friends and other students, as well as teachers, can make useful comments about your writing. Teachers and peers tend to make different contributions. You can learn to balance what each group gives and profit from both.

Obviously, as these descriptions make clear, the authors and editors of this book believe that writing can be taught. What do we mean when we make that statement? We believe that teachers and peers can provide you with helpful and even powerful methods for dealing with the writing process. That process is one that begins with a puzzlement, a curiosity, with a telling word or phrase, and ends with a feeling of satisfaction that comes as a result of having made meaning of your experiences.

There are many methods and strategies that teachers can suggest to students for enhancing the quality and strength of their writing. We have chosen the ones in this text because in our experience they provide the most help to the greatest number of students, regardless of their abilities and prior experiences with writing. We believe you will find in this text helpful ways of developing your skills and powers as writers.

WHY WRITING?

We have said that writing is a process by which we make meaning of our experiences. One of the chief ways of responding to experience is, of course, by speaking and writing—by using language to express yourself. Are there special advantages to using language when responding to experiences in contrast to other kinds of responses? In order to find an answer to this question, we asked students like yourselves to perform the following experiments, which you can try if you wish to check the results for yourselves.

For the first experiment they chose an emotion they felt, like joy, sorrow, or anger, and described it in two ways. First, they described it in ways that did not use words: they painted pictures that expressed the emotion or made tapes using classical, jazz, or rock music. Second, they described the emotion in words. Then they divided into groups of four to six people within the class and compared the two versions they had made, listing the advantages and disadvantages of each of the versions of expressing their emotion. They asked what the advantages were in presenting that emotion in a form other than words and what the advantages were to the version that used words.

As a second experiment they each recalled an experience when they thought that they had learned something. (Learning occurs outside as well as inside schools, as you know.) They again described this experience in two versions—the first, as a painting, a sculpture, a dance, or a taped piece of music; the other, using words. Again they divided into groups and compared the two, asking whether one version was more satisfactory than the other.

In the third experiment they described the emotion from the first experiment in the form of either a mathematical equation or a scientific formula and then compared these to the verbal description of the emotion, trying to decide which version the members of their group understood more readily, which described the emotion to others more exactly. They asked whether there were advantages to the verbal description.

As a fourth experiment they described the experience in which they thought they had learned something, this time presenting it as a mathematical equation or a scientific formula. They then contrasted this version with the verbal version produced for the second experiment, discussing which description was more readily understood by members of their group, which was more exact in describing the experience.

When they did these experiments, they came to the following conclusions about the verbal versions:

1. The verbal version was the medium most available for communicating to themselves and to others; it also was the one most widely and readily understood by others.

2. Most of them could best set out the relations among the major tenses of their experiences—past, present, and future—using the verbal version. With the other versions, they could not so readily specify *what* was happening *when,* nor could they clearly express the interplay among past, present, and future tenses. Conditional (if . . . then) or imaginary statements also proved difficult to express in the nonverbal versions.
3. The verbal version was fuller, more elaborated. Using it, they could make more extensive and more qualified comments, descriptions, statements, and even propositions and hypotheses.
4. The verbal version was more reflexive. That is, they could make it refer to itself and comment on itself in ways most of them could not do with, say, painting, music, or dance.
5. The verbal version best conveyed to others, as well as to themselves, their view or understanding of the world. In a sense, it gave the most information.

They found, then, many advantages to using language when dealing with representations of experience. As we will show next, there are particular advantages in using *writing* over talking, listening, and reading, the three other processes that use language. To test this statement, our students conducted a fifth experiment.

First, they noted down their opinions of a current local, national, or world event that interested them. Then they experienced this event in the following ways:

1. They *read* everything they could about the event in newspapers, magazines, and journals.
2. They *listened* on radio and *watched* on television everything they could about the event.
3. They *talked* with friends or members of their class about it.
4. They *wrote* their responses to the event in any form they chose: a list of random thoughts, a journal entry, a letter to a friend or editor, an essay.

In groups, they then compared these four ways of responding to the event, considering the following questions: (1) Which way gave them the greatest understanding of the event? (2) Through which means did they experience the greatest involvement? (3) By which means could they possibly *affect* the event?

They came to the following conclusions:

1. Their understanding of the event was greatest through writing, although for some of them, talking and reading provided as much.
2. Their *involvement* and *engagement* with the event was greatest through talking and writing.

3. Writing provided the most opportunity for *affecting* the event; talking was next; listening, watching, and reading provided no opportunity at all.

In other words, among the processes that use language, only writing provided *all at the same time*, understanding, involvement, and the power to affect experience and events.

WRITING AS LEARNING

We said earlier that writing is unique as a way of learning. The very nature of the writing process requires that you perform several activities simultaneously; for instance, you observe as you write.

The process of writing is multimodal

Psychologists who study cognition—the process of learning—have found that we learn best when we learn in several ways or modes at the same time. Psychologists like Jerome Bruner and Jean Piaget point out that we learn in three basic ways: (1) "on the muscle" (*motoric*); (2) "by the image" (*iconic*); and (3) "by restatement in words" (*representational* or *symbolic*). What is unusual, if not unique, about writing is that the process requires that we make use of all three modes at once. Literally putting words on paper—writing or typing them—is a physical act (motoric). The piece of writing represents an image (iconic). This image is composed of words that represent verbal symbols (symbolic). In other words, when we write, all three modes are involved and, very likely, reinforce one another.

Using words as symbols to describe experience has certain special features. It requires that we assign an order to experiences and set them out as linear sequences, one word (one graphic symbol) after another. In this process, we make explicit to ourselves and others the relationships we find among words, meanings, and concepts. We indicate, through the verbal symbols we use, when one event causes another; the words *because* and *since* are signals that we use when we believe a causal connection exists. We must also make clear whether one element is larger than another, whether it is a generalization of which the second element is an example; the phrases *for example* and *that is* are common signals of this relationship between thoughts. As another psychologist Lev Vygotsky put it, we are required "to elaborate our webs of meaning."

The process of writing results in a record of meaning

The value of setting out one's understanding fully and graphically is immense. We have a visual and steadily available record of our thinking, one that can be shared by others. It can be rescanned, reread, reviewed, revised. Such a record shows, in graphic form, the evolution of our thinking and feeling, from the first few words tentatively jotted on a page to the final version that sets out the limits and shape of our comprehension.

Most people profit from having available such temporary fixes on experience as writing provides. We learn best, it seems, when we can assess our understanding or lack of it. A written record helps to prevent self-deception and fosters honest appraisal. We learn best when we ourselves have the opportunity to evaluate the quality of our learning. Writing provides such an evaluation.

The process of writing is a whole-brained activity

The process of writing engages hand, eye, and brain. Scientists have found that as we mature, the two spheres of our brain develop certain special functions. The dominant sphere (for those who are strongly right-handed, the left sphere) deals with what is linear, logical, sequential. The minor sphere (for right-handers, the right sphere) receives and interprets wholes, such as the visual, the spatial, the emotional. The process of writing requires integration of the functions of both spheres of the brain. In the process of writing, experiences that come to our right sphere as wholes must be rendered by our left sphere into linear sequences of verbal symbols with explicit logical and psychological connections.

Does this division of functions mean that we could not write successfully if an accident or stroke were to occur to one of our spheres, or if the spheres were surgically separated from each other? The ability to write does seem always to be impaired initially by such changes, although factors of age, sex, and environment, along with other individual differences, may also be responsible for such different long-term effects. The fact that writing is impaired suggests that, for the reasons given above, both spheres of the brain must make major contributions to the process of writing. In other words, writing is a whole-brained activity.

Two of our higher learning processes are analysis and synthesis. *Analysis* is the process of breaking or dividing wholes into coherent parts; *synthesis* is the process of combining parts to form coherent and, often, fresh wholes. The dominant sphere of the brain proceeds by analysis; the minor sphere, by synthesis.

The act of writing requires the double action of analysis and synthesis. The process seems to work this way: Experience comes to us as a whole; the outcome of even what seems a linear experience such as reading a book still results in our having a whole response. A way to comprehend an experience and then to communicate its meanings to ourselves and to others is to write— that is, to organize a response or account in a linear sequence that, in its turn, becomes a whole. The cycle seems to be:

WHOLE $\longrightarrow$ Analysis $\longrightarrow$ **PARTS** $\longrightarrow$ Analysis $\longrightarrow$ **WHOLE**

Experience,   Linear   Account, such
direct or   rendering   as a letter,
vicarious   theme or essay

Writing and learning, then, are integrative processes. For the purposes of understanding and communicating, they translate wholes into parts. These parts are then reformed into new wholes, the finished written accounts.

Since writing is so powerful, it is understandable that we want it to be a part of all the worlds of experience in which we live.

FOUR WORLDS OF WRITING

What are those worlds? We live in at least four:

1. *The private world:* the world of meaningful places and environments, peopled with families, friends, and others we care about and find significant
2. *The public world:* the world of the media—television, radio, magazines, books, newspapers, and films, and of shared issues that connect us with our society and with others in the world
3. *The college world:* the world of classes, courses, and diplomas; of class notes, laboratory reports, research papers, and essay examinations
4. *The working world:* the world of jobs, careers, and professions; of memos, reports, applications, evaluations, and studies

We respond to experience in all of these worlds. In fact, it could be said that the more we respond to all of the worlds, the more we are alive.

The private world: places and persons

To describe in detail the private worlds in which we live is, of course, impossible. They are too diverse and too individual. But individual and diverse as these worlds are, they are also alike in major and important ways. Perhaps the most important is that, in our private worlds, if we are at all thoughtful, we try to understand ourselves and our connections with others, particularly those closest to us. We also try to understand our connections with places that are parts of our past and present.

Places can shape experiences for us as significantly as persons can. In fact, as we scan our pasts, we realize that persons and places are often closely connected in our memories. We remember certain people in given settings that affect the ways they act and respond and the ways we respond in turn.

Places do not serve merely as backgrounds, however. They can become the foreground of interest, as happens when we travel. In some cases, places even become central characters, as they have for great travel writers: Greece, for Henry Miller; the Hebrides, for Samuel Johnson; Alaska for John McPhee.

New places are inherently intriguing for many of us. They have the value of providing a contrast to settings that have become so overfamiliar that we no longer experience them. New places can help us see, hear, taste, and smell the worlds in which we lead our daily lives; they often make familiar places grow fresh and alive once more. "Coming to our senses" is not a trite saying where writing is concerned: it is solid advice to observe when experiencing, and writing about, places and persons.

Some people as they get older lament that life seems to have passed them by, that they have been caught up in the superficial. Most of us at some time experience this sense of having missed something in the past, of having lived so fast that we don't remember or understand what happened to us. But writers sense this loss less than most. Why? Because each piece of writing has given them the chance to catch those swiftly passing moments of loving, encountering, wondering, and fearing and to hold them long enough to find personal meaning by writing about them. Writers save the meaning of their lives by dealing with that meaning in writing. They *act* on experiences and events through their writing. Writing is one of the most active ways we can engage in and with the world.

When we write in our private worlds, we may find what is unique in our personal experiences. We may also find patterns and structures in our own lives similar to those we have heard or read about from others. Most likely, we will find a mix of what is unique and what is shared: what makes us unlike anyone else who has ever lived, as well as what makes us like all others who have ever lived. Writing about the private world can even prove a form of preservation and renewal. The philosopher George Gusdorf puts these values eloquently:

> *To speak, to write, to express is to act, to survive crisis, to begin living again, even when one thinks it is only to relive one's sorrow.*[1]

What forms does writing about the private world take? To discover these forms for yourself, over a given period of, say, one or two weeks, collect all private writing that you do. Forget nothing. Include every fragment, every piece of writing. Into what categories do these writings fall? Compare what you wrote with what other members of your group wrote, and make a master list.

Did you find what we found? Although the writings within our private

---

[1] George Gusdorf, *Speaking* (Evanston, Ill.: Northwestern University Press, 1965), p. 59.

worlds divided into writings produced exclusively for ourselves and those directed toward intimates, the forms were common to both audiences:

autobiographies	journals	lists	notes	poems
diaries		letters	memoirs	personal essays	stories

Who is it, again, that we write for in the private world? Chiefly, we write for ourselves and for those close to us. If there is a reader outside this intimate group, it is someone we have decided to treat as an intimate. What this usually means is that we establish an unspoken contract with the outside reader to respond as an intimate would: to focus upon message and meaning above form. Such a contract may apply to teachers as well as to peers. It requires the outside reader to behave like a listener in an intimate conversation. We know that when we listen to someone close to us, we usually pay close attention to what is being said. We are generous, often supplying what is not yet stated, since the speaker may be expressing certain feelings and thoughts for the very first time. We are understanding, since we know from our own experience that sharing our feelings and thoughts is one of the most difficult forms of expression. We try not to judge the message prematurely or recast the experience in terms that make meaning only to *us*. Nor do we initially criticize the language in which the speaker casts the experience.

Examine again all the writing you did for your private world over that two-week period. Recall now how you wrote; how much time you spent on various forms of your private writing; how you divided your time among phases of the process. Is it not true that

your starting point was often a puzzle, an enigma in your private life that you wanted to solve?
you spent little time planning what you wanted to say?
your central concern was to convey as exactly as you could how you felt and thought about your subject?
you did not worry at first about any audience but yourself?

The public world of shared issues and the media

The private world is not, of course, the only world in which we move and have our being: we live in larger, more public worlds as well. We experience these larger worlds in two ways: (1) what we know directly because things happen to us and to those we know; and (2) what we perceive through the media—radio, television, tapes, newspapers, magazines. We respond to events that come to us vicariously as well as directly. One powerful and effective way to respond to events as well as to affect them is through writing about them, as we suggested earlier in the fifth experiment (pp. 5–6).

If you polled your group to learn what kinds of writing you did in order to respond to and to affect your immediate world, your block, your neighborhood, or your country, you probably found that the forms of writing included posters, signs, notices, petitions, and hand-outs. The purpose of these was probably to correct a wrong or to get action on an issue.

As you attempted to affect or influence an audience farther away, someone you did not know and were unlikely to have encountered personally, you probably added other forms of writing, as the following list suggests:

> posters, signs, notices
> petitions and hand-outs
> letters to individuals and groups with particular responsibility and power
>> directors and administrators of social, civic, and religious groups
>> editors of newspapers and magazines
>> announcers, producers, and sponsors of radio and television programs
>> political representatives and spokespersons
>> consumer advocates and agencies
>> individual businesses and corporations
>> original tracts, newsletters, magazines, radio and television programs

An important form of writing that we found through our own search in the world of shared issues is what could be called *consumer writing*. Why? The reason is not difficult to discover. In our society, we often find that the products we use are as unsatisfactory as they are expensive. What are we to do, for example, about a $7000 car with a $7 part that cannot be obtained for three weeks, three months, or at all? Beyond citing warranties and guarantees, is there any written action we can take?

When we looked into the effect we could have as consumer writers, we were heartened by what we found. We had long known that certain consumer advocate writers like Ralph Nader had affected policies and products in our society. For example, as a result of Nader's being bumped from an airline, there is now a law to recompense us for the inconvenience if the same thing happens to us. But we did not know the power of just one well-written and well-directed letter until we had interviewed people in consumer affairs, radio and TV station managers, and executives of some large corporations. The president of a large manufacturer of automobile parts, for example, told us that when a consumer writes to complain about a specific product or problem, every person with any major responsibility for that product must write an explanatory memo detailing a response and a solution. The president or a member of his staff then combines these memos into a personal letter of response, which is sent to the consumer. Such a system of memo writing and accountability is common practice in many individual businesses and corporations. In other words, through skillful letter writing, we may be able to affect the products, programs, and policies that touch on our daily lives.

Consumer writing affects our lives in the economic realm. Another form of writing, which might be called *citizen writing*, can affect our lives in the political realm. A well-written and well-directed letter or campaign of letters can affect and even change political events, as well as the laws under which we live. Examples are frequent and easy to cite. A well-known recent example is the letter Allan Bakke wrote to the Board of Regents at The University of California, a letter that led to the reformulation of affirmative action programs for colleges and universities through a Supreme Court decision.

The college world

A world in which you now write most frequently is the college world—the world of courses, classes, and seminars, of papers, research reports, and essay examinations.

Like other bureaucracies, schools also require the filling out of forms, and more forms. The way you present yourself in writing on an application form, for example, is the first encounter a college has with you. The most significant portion of that application can be the writing of an autobiography and a statement of your academic intentions and ambitions. Admissions counselors, committees, and deans often regard these presentations as the most revealing portion of the admissions packet, and the most predictive of college and postcollege success.

School may also be the world in which you will be expected to observe the most fixed and formal sets of writing conventions that you will ever experience. In what other world, for example, are you asked to describe to others in elaborate written essays what you and they already know and have demonstrated through other forms of expression (such as class discussion)? Unless you become an editor, critic, or professor, you will not again be asked to respond to a book with an analysis of its stone or bird symbolism, or with a discussion of how the minor characters develop in contrast to the major characters. We are not suggesting that the writing you are asked to do in your English, psychology, history, music appreciation, or chemistry classes should not be appropriate, even unique, to the discipline. One way a discipline is distinguished from others is in the writing conventions it observes.

One virtue of this text is that such kinds of special responses are not stressed. The writing assignments in the book stress, instead, your making meaning in many kinds of texts in all four worlds of writing. The book shows how engaging in the full writing process, which starts with a question significant to you, can turn outside assignments, which may seem artificial, into genuine learning experiences. The forms of writing that you will encounter in the world of school include:

class-related forms	college-related forms
bibliographies	applications
essay examinations	continuations
journals	graduation
lecture notes and outlines	registrations
lists	
précis	
prospectus and proposals	
reports	
reviews	
research and critical papers	

There is now some research about the processes of writing in and for school that is interesting, if not necessarily surprising. When college students are given the opportunity to participate in the selection of subject, they tend to write pieces of higher quality according to evaluations both of their instructors and of outside judges. This generalization also holds true if students participate in choosing writing topics for entrance or placement examinations. In other words, your involvement or engagement with what is to be written enhances the quality of your writing.

Whether or not you can choose or help choose your own topics can also affect the amount you write, at least if you are like your younger counterparts. Donald Graves, now of the University of New Hampshire, contrasted two groups of second graders.[2] Those who wrote whenever they wanted to wrote *four times* as much as did children whose teachers assigned all the writing they did. High school seniors, when interviewed by Emig, revealed that they did much more writing outside of school because there they did not have deadlines to worry about and because their friends and families, unlike their teachers, focused on what they were trying to say, not on how they were saying it.[3]

Other research suggests that the abler the college writer, the more time that writer spends on a given piece of writing. As Pianko has shown, college writers who are deeply engaged in their writing processes spend more time planning, more time writing, and far more time revising and reformulating. Also, when they finish, they spend time contemplating what they have written—that is, they like what they have done.[4]

Which comes first: Does lengthening and intensifying your processes of writing increase your abilities as a writer? Or do your abilities lengthen and

---

[2] Donald Graves, "An Examination of the Writing Processes of Seven Year Old Children," *Research in the Teaching of English* (Winter 1975), 227–241.

[3] Janet Emig, *The Composing Processes of Twelfth Graders* (Champaign, Ill.: National Council of Teachers of English, 1971).

[4] Sharon Pianko, "Reflection: A Critical Component of the Composing Process," *College Composition and Communication Journal* (October 1979), 275–278.

intensify your processes? We don't know. We do know, however, that length and complexity of your writing process are correlated with establishing the quality and success of what is written.

The working world

"You do not need to write in order to survive and to succeed in the working world." Such is the curious, if powerful, myth that has grown up over the last decade or two within the United States. According to this myth, a person can engage in most kinds of work, even the most significant and high-salaried work, without ever writing a sentence. People believe that secretaries, clerks, and other kinds of assistants are hired to do most of the writing within businesses and corporations. Only a handful of professions, like law, teaching, the ministry, publishing, and journalism, requires that their members write with any regularity and seriousness.

Recently large-scale studies have begun to assess the amount of writing done in government offices and labor unions. Such a study describing and analyzing who writes what, to whom, when, and why in a given social group is called an *ethnography;* a term that comes from the field of anthropology. It refers to a detailed descriptive examination of the customary behaviors and beliefs of a particular social group. Their initial findings indicated that almost all Americans write on the job.

Writing in the world of work takes a wide variety of forms.

> resumés and applications
> personnel records
>   personal (i.e., job evaluations)
>   medical
>   insurance, pension, and other benefits
> expense and travel requests, forms accounts
> diaries, logs, and journals
> letters
> memos
> outlines
> presentations and evaluations of concepts, products, programs,
>   within and outside the company
>   studies
>   reports
> in-house journals, newspapers, magazines, and summary sheets
> professional, career, and business journals
> media releases

The audiences for writing in the working world are perhaps more diverse than those in the other three worlds. In-house audiences include peers, superiors, special offices, and units. Outside, they include work affiliates, work rivals, the public as individuals, the public en masse, and the media.

Much writing in the working world consists of record keeping. Even when computers keep the records, programs must be written. Particularly in smaller businesses and units other than data processing units, a very large number of records are written by individuals. Much writing in the working world also consists of justification: explanations to a range of audiences as to why an individual or group has taken a particular course of action or made a certain decision; why a unit did not show a profit or why management should promote or abandon existing policies or programs of action.

Initial pieces of research suggest that, despite the myth that secretaries and other kinds of scribes write the memos and letters in the working world, the person whose name appears on that memo or letter usually composes it, no matter who types and transcribes it. Quite soon, the working world will use voice-actuating typewriters that will type letter-perfect copy directly from dictation. Whether or not such technology eliminates the role of secretary, it assuredly eliminates the myth that people do not do their own writing in the working world.

CONCLUSION

In a powerful essay Marjorie Kirrie, a professor of writing from Oregon, makes the argument that all of us live in a world that writing built:

> Once we had writing, we could exploit the hitherto unattainable possibilities of language, and that exploitation led to an acceleration of change—we usually call it progress—undreamed of in the purely oral millenia of our ascent to dominance. Writing made possible science and technology; it made possible educational systems, bureaucracy, corporate structures, complex philosophies, and even the fine arts as we know them. Writing made possible our forms of government, space exploration, and today's struggle for human rights. Writing is ultimately responsible for nearly all of the man-created aspects of our rapidly changing world.[5]

In this text the authors suggest that all of us live in four worlds that writing can help to shape and to make understandable since writing either serves or actually represents so many of the functions that make us human, that make us civilized. Through writing we can record, describe, explain, argue, justify, codify, discover, create, reflect, destroy, and build our own lives and the four worlds in which we live.

[5]Marjorie Kirrie, "Writing in the World That Writing Built," *The College Board Review* (Spring 1978), 23.

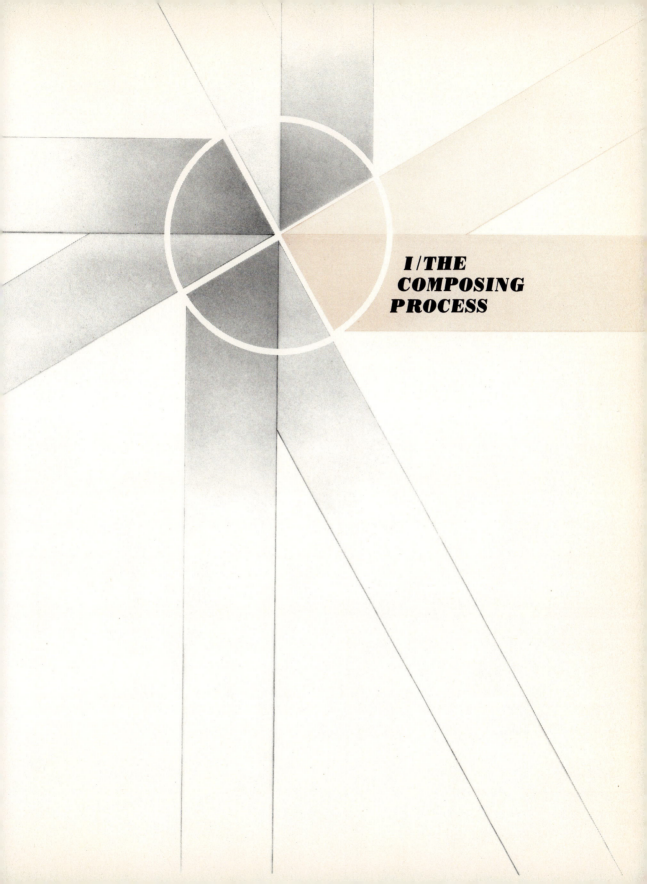

I/THE COMPOSING PROCESS

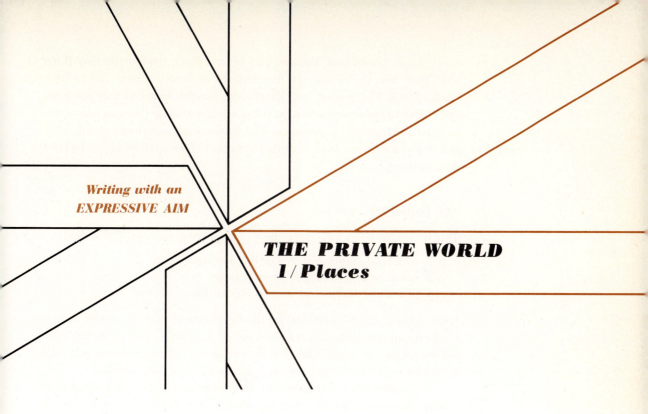

THE PRIVATE WORLD
1 / Places

We start with writing in your private world because a primary function of writing is to help you know yourself and to share yourself with others. Have you ever been in situations in which someone's actions implied: "I'd like to get to know you better," or in which a person asked: "What are you into?" or "What turns you on?" Have you ever posed the same questions to yourself?

The desire to understand oneself is basic and intensifies through contact with others. But how do you deepen knowledge of yourself? Writing is a key way because it allows you to withdraw from the whirl of your activities to the quiet center of yourself, where you can spend time understanding yourself and your world. Two factors in your background help answer the question "Who am I?": the environment or "places" that have been a part of your life and the relationships you have had.

THE WRITING CONTEXT

As the writing context for your first paper, therefore, Chapter 1 sets the following area of investigation: a place that has influenced your development. Many places have become part of you. Even though you may think you "just" live in Chicago or Birmingham or Seattle, these places have changed you. The houses, neighborhoods, and job locations that you have spent time in have crept into a part of yourself so quietly that you may never have puzzled over their influence. The first writing experience in this book will give you a chance to investigate the impact of one of these places on your development.

THE COMPOSING PROCESS

This book also offers you three ways of improving your writing ability:

1. *understanding* the *stages* of the writing process
2. *using* helpful *strategies* at each stage
3. *practicing* these *strategies* in the *worlds of writing*

Each of these ways is essential for the development of a competent writer. Understanding without practice does not work; practice without understanding leaves you at a lower level of development. Writing without powerful strategies is like building a piston engine with your bare hands.

We cannot offer you help with two important factors that affect your writing: those acts that are not conscious and your physical habits. For example, you may need a quiet room in which to write, or you may need the noise of a stereo in order to write. You may compose in short segments separated by interruptions or in long periods. You may need pen or pencil or typewriter, long pads or notebooks. You may compose orally or work in silence, writing fluently and later crossing out a great deal or writing haltingly and scratching out phrases often. This book will not deal with these physical habits nor with acts that are not conscious but will concentrate on the *conscious* stages, helping you build better habits of thinking, imagining, inquiring, and symbolizing.

The first chapter, then, will explain and engage you in such *conscious* stages of the writing process as

1. Finding and Expressing the Starting Point
2. Exploring
3. Discovering and Stating the Focus
4. Planning for Aim and Audience
5. Developing, Organizing, and Refining Your Paper
6. Critiquing and Rewriting

Although the first chapter will examine these stages in order, we do not wish to imply that they provide you with a mechanical formula for a paper. You may weave back and forth between the stages, be in several at once, or at times even meet a dead end. For example, planning for your audience and aim may occur earlier for some types of writing, later for others. Exploring may prompt you to reformulate your starting question. But while you are learning the proposed writing strategies, it might be helpful to follow the order of the stages as presented, writing your first paper in slow motion.

If writing is to be more than a finger exercise or a game, the way you start is crucial. What is a genuine starting point? The trigger to writing is an intriguing question, sparked by a puzzle, a wonder, a curiosity you meet in your personal life, your reading, or your research. A writer is basically a *questioner*. However, you may have been discouraged from questioning by a world that rewards right answers rather than uneasy questions. Even if you have been educated to be an answer person, you can learn to be a questioner, but you have to be your own trainer, your own coach. You must start tuning in to the questions that arise when your expectations or your values are challenged, when the image of the world you grew up with does not fit the world you meet.

For example, if your two values of equal opportunity and job security clash with your employer's discrimination against women, you can ignore one of the values and remain uncomfortable. Or you can engage in a writing process to resolve your tension and even to change your work situation. If you expect a teacher to be difficult to work with and you discover, instead, a noble and inspiring friend, you can write, exploring this gap between your expectation and the reality. If you are puzzled by an image in a poem, you can struggle for an insight into its function, or you can claim a temporary peace resting in partial understanding.

A starting point, then, is a sense of *dissonance*, a gap, between your present way of looking at things and whatever challenges that view. Note here that dissonance is not necessarily negative. When something exceeds your expectations—goes beyond what you have known—your dissonance takes the form of wonder, often of great pleasure.

FINDING THE SUBJECT

To discover a place that has had significant influence on you, start with your feelings. Ask yourself questions like: Is there some place that I would or did regret leaving? Is there a place in the present or past that I despise or fear or have nightmares about? Is there a place that provides surprising or puzzling or conflicting reactions? Is there a place I get excited about returning to? The following are examples of places that five students chose in answer to these questions.

When Writer 1 encountered dorm living for the first time, she was overwhelmed with conflicting feelings. Writer 2 had a hatred for a clinical institution in which she had been forced to stay. She had feared examining the impact the place had on her. Writer 3 had returned from a trip to Rio with mixed emotions that had stayed with her for a couple of years. She sensed her trip had somehow changed her but she didn't know how. Writer 4 often thought of the small city in which he had grown up, wishing to return yet reluctant to do so. Writer 5 was disillusioned with his job at a car dealership. He wondered why. Notice that these writers chose places vibrant with feelings, places whose significance they wanted to understand.

EXPRESSING THE STARTING POINT

Identifying a place resonant with feelings does not yet constitute a sharp enough starting point. We suggest a two-part strategy for doing some pointing.

First, identify an aspect of your place that challenged your expectations or caused you to raise questions about some of your values.

Second, formulate a question expressing what you want to learn to satisfy your curiosity or resolve your tension. Your question should spring from the dissonance you sense between an aspect of your subject and your values or expectations.

These two parts of the strategy interact. A meaningful question comes from a sense of challenge, of incongruity between some aspect of your place and your expectations or values; it does not arise from the subject itself. You may try stating several questions before you find the one that captures your dissonance. A starting question, however, is only that, a useful beginning. You may change, refine, or reject your question as the rest of the process moves along. Finding a question significant to you, however, makes writing worth pursuing . Study the Starting Points of the five student writers.

STARTING POINTS

Writer 1* **MY VALUES OR EXPECTATIONS** **ASPECTS OF THE DORM**
—neatness and order —messiness
—financial and personal security —decisions about money and living

*The student writing displayed throughout this book is the work of the following students, whom we hereby acknowledge: J. Ballew, S. Bickford, I. DeSloover, J. DuBose, J. Hassell, L. Hullum, A. Humbert, G. Hungerman, H. Maksym, M. Massaron, M. Rabaut, J. Reed, P. Southlea, M. Spriggs, J. Tully, M. Wheatley, and R. Wheatley.

Question: What kinds of changes is dorm life bringing in me? Are they for the better?

Writer 2 MY VALUES OR EXPECTATIONS

—freedom

—pleasant surroundings

ASPECTS OF THE INSTITUTION

—the smell and artificiality of the place

—sense of confinement

Question: What impact has a stay in a clinical institution had on me?

Writer 3 MY VALUES OR EXPECTATIONS

—natural beauty

—excitement of a jet set city

ASPECTS OF RIO

—the ugliness of the surrounding huts

—the richness and glamour of the city

Question: Why did Rio disappoint me, somehow change me?

Writer 4 MY VALUES OR EXPECTATIONS

—culture and nightlife of a big city

—memories of childhood security in G.R.

ASPECTS OF GRAND RAPIDS

—smaller city limitations

—reality of present day G.R.

Question: Why do I dream of going back to Grand Rapids to live when I like a big city?

Writer 5 MY VALUES OR EXPECTATIONS

—high pay

—drive sports cars

—regular hours

—no maintenance work

—friendly atmosphere

—strict boss

—regular breaks

ASPECTS OF THE DEALERSHIP

—minimum wage

—drove more Impalas than Corvettes

—long hours, no overtime pay

—washing cars, mopping floors

—many cordial acquaintances

—professional, firm, hardworking boss

—no breaks

Question: When taking on a job, why do I neglect to consider the harsh realities of it and see only the superficial benefits?

Commentary Writer 1's question commits her to exploring dorm life as a whole, a task that is too broad and doesn't reflect the dissonance she feels between dorm and home life. But her need to understand and evaluate changes in herself will be a compelling start for the writing process. The writer revised her starting point:

How are the differences between dorm and home life changing me? Are they for the better?

Writer 2 could sharpen her question by asking "What impact on my need for freedom has a stay in the institution had?"

CLASS EXERCISES

For each stage of the process, this book provides two kinds of exercises designed to give you practice with the writing strategies under the guidance of your teacher and classmates before you use them in writing your own paper. The first kind of exercise involves *discussion* of the student examples in the book. By examining the way in which other students have worked at each stage, you can benefit from their efforts. The second kind of exercise offers *practice sessions* in which the class as a whole uses the writing strategies on sample subjects. Even though this kind of exercise is artificial because you are not writing on *your* subject, it gives you valuable practice in using the strategies.

CLASS EXERCISES

1. Discuss the Starting Points of Writers 3, 4, and 5 above.
   - How do the aspects of their places either clash with their values or exceed their expectations?
   - In what ways do their questions capture these dissonances?
   - How might their questions have been better formulated?
2. Select a place familiar to the entire class.
   - Share the emotions that the place provokes.
   - Identify values or expectations you have had in relation to the place.
   - Write down (on the board or paper) ways in which the place either exceeds those expectations or clashes with those values.
   - Formulate questions that ask what understanding you seek about the place.

ASSIGNMENTS

The out-of-class assignments constitute the most important parts of each chapter because they engage you in the stages of writing leading to a finished paper. Using a strategy during an assignment differs from working with it in class exercises. When doing the assignment, you employ the strategy as a tool to help you create your actual paper. In the class exercises, you use the strategy to learn how it operates. The *assignments* are stages of a genuine writing experience; the *exercises* are the practice sessions. If you can obtain commentary on each completed assignment before proceeding to the next stage, you will find such guidance invaluable during the complex act of writing and useful in steering you from wrong directions before you have gone too far.

Stage 1 Toward a Paper on Place: Finding and Expressing the Starting Point

1. Identify a place that you wish to investigate to find its impact on you.
2. Express the aspects of the place that challenge your values or exceed your expectations.
3. Write a question to guide your search for that understanding.
4. Seek comments on your starting point from your teacher or classmates or both.

Now that you have formulated your starting point, you need to explore your subject, seeking a broad view of it. You already have many stored memories, but you must retrieve them. The Exploratory Guide will help you *recall* and also *discover* ideas about your place; it will increase your flexibility of mind, prompting you to examine your subject from several points of view to avoid single-mindedness. The Exploratory Guide will direct you to take three views of your subject.[1] The first view, labeled *static*, directs you to recall those relatively unchanging features, details, definitions of your subject that differentiate it from similar subjects. The static features of a place serving as subject, for example, might include sensory impressions (sights, sounds, scents, tastes), distinguishing elements (aspects that it shares with no other place), and its parts, or layout.

The second view, labeled *dynamic*, directs you to see your place as a *process*, noting its movements and its physical and historical changes. The third view, labeled *relative*, prompts you to discover new connections between your subject and other realities by *classifying*—relating your subject to larger groups within which it fits; *comparing and contrasting*—relating your subject to other subjects in the same category; and *analogizing*—relating your subject to apparently unlike subjects. This relative view is the most free-wheeling, carrying you beyond the subject itself, stimulating you to create rich associations that often reveal your deepest feelings.

EXPLORATORY GUIDE

Static view (see student examples below)

–Recall and record as many features as you can about your place–

---

[1] These three views are adapted from a writing theory of Young, Becker, and Pike, based on a linguistic theory called TAGMEMICS, which in turn borrows its ideas from physics. See Richard E. Young, Alton Becker, and Kenneth Pike, *Rhetoric: Discovery and Change* (New York: Harcourt, Brace, Jovanovich, 1970).

aspects that describe and define your place so that anyone can distinguish it from other places.

—Note down as many of your attitudes toward your place as you can.

—Identify the parts that make up the whole of your place.

Dynamic view   (*see student examples below*)

—Recall and record the processes (changes, physical movements) that the place has undergone in the past, is experiencing in the present and will probably face in the future.

—Trace your involvement with the place through one day or over a long period of time.

—Think about where your place fits into the larger history of similar places.

Relative view   (*see student examples below*)

—Classify your place, locating it in larger groups.

—Examine how your place relates to the other things in those classifications.

—Compare and contrast your place with other places, noting the similarities and differences.

—Let your imagination create analogies for your place (unusual things with which your place can be identified). Explore the bases for such analogies.

In this chapter we will show you the explorations of all five student writers so that you can see the individual ways each writer recorded ideas.

Writing down the ideas that each view generates plays an important role in your planning:

1. It starts your search for the personal words and phrases that help you understand experiences that you have never verbalized.
2. It records your ideas so that you won't forget them and so that you can rearrange, organize, and play with them.

This exploratory activity is freer than drafting because you are not struggling with sentence or paragraph patterns.

Although the five student explorations may suggest that the writers discovered all their static features first and then went on to look at the dynamic and relative aspects of their "places," the process of exploring is not necessarily so rigid. While it helps to see a subject in a more static sense first, you should be flexible enough to move back and forth among the views if your mind is so prompted. Keeping separate lists may help you. The three ways of looking are, after all, *means* of recalling and discovering ideas; they are not ends in themselves. What is important to you as a writer are the quality and number of ideas you gather by taking the three views.

Notice also that the writers felt free to generate ideas without concern for grammar, spelling, and punctuation, without worry if some of their ideas seemed unconventional or apparently irrelevant to an outsider, because exploring is not the time for being critical. Later they could reject some of these ideas as inaccurate or irrelevant.

EXPLORATION

Writer 1   DORM

STATIC VIEW

Features of the dorm
—long-haired girls clustered around the front desk
—muffled stereo sounds through fifteen identical doors
—long, half-dusted hallways
—starry-eyed freshmen easily impressed
—heavy woolen sweaters hanging unevenly over the stiff backs of dorm chairs
—one blue argyle sock turned inside-out hidden underneath one of Mother's faded rugs
—not-so-crunchy cookies
—corroded shower ceilings
—sleepy-eyed seniors
—fuzzy blankets
—food-filled milk crates
—rippled Campbell soup lids tossed into half-folded bags
—an elegant showcase piano out of place in the modern setting of the dorm lounge
—artificial home
—prickly curlers
—individuality personified

DYNAMIC VIEW

Movements in the dorm
—the irritating sound of telephone brrings competing
—massive trade market, "let me borrow it please, you can borrow anything of mine"
—the nervous ticking of an aging alarm clock
—everybody's buying "earth shoes"
—the echoing of laughter through the cold granite

Contrast

Dorm	Home
half-dusted	clean enough to eat off the floors
usage of old tacky furniture	relatively new upholstered furnishings
boxed potatoes, soft (mushed in spots), apples, aging crackers and crunchy peanut butter	well-balanced fresh food . . . steak, crisp red apples
gray-green granite walls	blue and white flowered wallpaper
monotonous off-white on black tile	sinking my toes in soft plush, baby-blue carpeting
clothes washed without a softener	pajamas that smell sweetly flower-like
a cluster of food trays and books on a round, unwashed table for ten	sharing a meal with the seven members of my family
forcing yourself out of a bed to attend a 9:00 a.m. class	waking up when you have had enough sleep
withdrawing hard-earned dollars	saving money in the bank
listening to the radio station of your choice	constantly hearing my parents telling me to change the dial
"the chill"	sitting at my vanity, feeling the blowing heat billowing my pant legs
stuffed animals . . . Raggedy Andy	live, breathing English pointer running loose in the back yard
the need to make more decisions on your own	parent-oriented decisions
never a spare minute	quiet hours without many demanding deadlines
beer	seven-up
a slight, round callous on the third finger of your writing hand	pampered fingers
an awareness of the way you dress	faded sweatshirts, patched blue jeans, slippers
sharing a bedroom with three goofy girls	sharing a room with my sister
the tendency to gain weight due to the starchy food	slim, lean waistline

Analogy

Spaceship	Dorm
a spaceship takes people physically away from their homes	a place to stay away from the loved ones at home

a spaceship is a means of discovering new places	by living in a dorm, one is able to meet new friends, and friends are always full of suggestions for places to go
exciting, bizarre, educational and dynamic	a wild (also educational) fresh experience
encounter unusual experiences	at the door one never can tell what to expect
a spaceship rises upward	a hair-raising experience

Commentary Through the static view, Writer 1 records sensory details of dorm living, sights, sounds, and so on, expressing these features specifically. The writer does not, however, identify many elements that distinguish her dorm life from other colleges or from other group living. The dynamic view is very limited, listing isolated movements rather than tracing a typical dorm day or exploring changes in the writer, lines of thinking that would have responded more directly to her starting question. Within the relative view, the contrast between dorm and home life may suggest an answer while her analogy reveals positive feelings about dorm life.

EXPLORATION

Writer 2   A STATE HOME

STATIC VIEW

Sensory impressions of the home
—a loud clatter   unknown, distant voices, mingling, a low hum
—a gray clock set into the cement block wall . . it lingers over endless minutes, then pulled reluctantly, jerks ahead with a loud flat click
—a hoarse female whine: "please mis wells"
—arid smell   disinfectant
—dirty socks
—faded tile, ceiling and floor   walls green—dull institutional green
—florescent lights, cruel   a harsh whitish glare
—bathroom darker green door with half legible obscenities scratched into it, always locked
—"Keep your hands to yourself. There are some girls who *like* to touch other girls."
—green plastic and metal chairs
—girls in faded jumpers sit, tipped back against the wall
—gray underwear   grayish tennis shoes   gray oatmeal
—"I wouldn't if I were you. They pulled a rat out of the tureen once."
—brown mats pulled out at night, lined up along the floor.
—a gray tennis shoe tapping, tapping behind the girls . . . brilliant yellow and pink seclusion rooms, pure, unscarred, unscratched paint

–hoarse female cry rising from behind the yellow door, heavy,
   weighted down in the air   "miz wells: Please: Oh, God help me!"
–the hands of the clock jump forward—a click

DYNAMIC VIEW

Public attitudes (Fortas) vs. present reality
–Fortas' opinion attached firmly the prevailing view that because juvenile courts were virtually therapy clinics, children who came before
   them did not need the protection of the Bill of Rights of the American
   Constitution (case of *Gault* vs US, from *The Throwaway Children*, by
   Lisa Richette)
–a huge brick structure with long steel screens over its windows and a
   high brick wall which ran in waves down Fort Street and turned the
   block—a castle, a fortress we would pass on the way to school and
   laugh. "WASPS: There's the Youth Home!"
–"Witness Gerald Gault's sentence of six years for a crime which for
   adults carried a five-to-fifty dollar fine and a maximum sentence of
   two months." *The Throwaway Children.*
–By standing close to the mesh screen and craning my neck, I could see
   the snow falling outside. I pushed my fingers into the metal screen and
   pressed against it. A child pulled his sled across the snow, and two
   schoolgirls, in plaid skirts, hurried down the street. I could just make
   out the lettering on the brown metal sign facing me a hundred miles
   below—Wayne County Youth Home. Established 19–
–"How many Gerald Gaults had been here? How many   Croziers?"
   Ibid.
–putting my own wrinkled clothes on again, throwing the faded jumper
   and the old socks into a hamper, I was led back up to the ward to wait
   for release. I went back into the room not seeing or feeling the buzz
   of excitement that surrounded me. "You're going home? Karen's going
   home! I'll miss you kid. You're going home . . ."
–"There is nothing worse that the smell of a dirty female. You will take
   a shower every day and clean yourselves thoroughly." God, yes, let
   me get the sound of you out of my pores.
–"you're going home Karen? I hope I do too soon."
–"What kind of hearing should a child receive in a juvenile court." *Ibid.*
–Waiting on a wooden bench, pink and blue jumpers, scared, tapping
   feet. Braids, Afros half picked out, stringly dyed hair; slept-in curls.
   "Don't cry, they don't feel sorry for you and it only goes worse on you."
–moving . . . but not all stagnant   trapped in their small circular environment going through the notions like the hands of the clock on the
   wall

RELATIVE VIEW

Analogy
–the children move about as the hands of the gray metal clock

steady   numbly   sluggishly
crawling about routine tasks
    routine which cannot vary
dragging their chairs behind them down the hall.
tipped back against the wall   fingers drumming against the metal legs
    of the chairs   feet tapping   tennis-clad   muffled   like the toneless
    noisy clicks of the clock
—day is highlighted by feedings everyone awaits eyes glancing up push-
    ing the hands of the clock forward from breakfast   waiting for lunch
    from lunch waiting for dinner   after dinner waiting until the garish
    lights are turned off and fanciful dreams begin
—time   clicking   an endless, toneless whisper of a scream
    inside heads of the girls
    muffled by dirty cotton tennis shoes that muffle the angry
    pounding of feet against the floor
—the muted anguish of the clock   black hands jerking forward caught
    suspended in its black cage
        some frightened black insect trapped under the glass face
    impaled on a slender rod   its legs kicking in the air   its
        antennae jerk convulsively while the rod moves slowly in its cycle
    unable to escape—impaled and waiting for death—oblivion
        blackness which hides in the corner of the brains of all the girls
—the soft whispered screams   watching the quiet anguish of the clock
—cockroach under glass

Contrast

do not pity	cindy . . . throws
mehitabel	back her head
she is having	her breasts, too
her own kind of	large for a 14 yr
a good time	old rest on her
in her own way	protuding stomach
she would not	"God: you lost your
understand any other	navel kid—
sort of life	a bitter cry—
but the life	You're all whores.
she has chosen	just because I'm
to lead	the only one who
she was predestined	got caught."
to it as the	poor mehitabel . . .
sparks fly upward	"all marriage is
chacunad son gout	is one damn
as they say in france	kitten after
start her in	another," (archy)
as a kitten	spotted
and she would	mulatis kitten

repeat the same story
and do not overlook
the fact that
mehitabel is really
proud of herself
she enjoys
her own sufferings
(archy's life of mehitabel—don marquis)

another litter
for grandma
to look after
poor baby.

Commentary Through the static view, Writer 2 remembers painful sights, sounds, and smells, recording these in vivid language. She does not mention features that distinguish this place from other institutions. In the dynamic view, she concentrates on past attitudes toward children in institutions (Supreme Court Justice Fortas) in relation to the present reality of the home with its ironic movements: the wall running in waves, craning her neck to see snow falling, pressing against the screen, and the dull routine of dressing, washing, and undressing. The writer sums up these movements as "stagnant," trapped like the hands of the clock in a circular pattern. The relative view pursues the analogy of the children as hands of the clock and adds the cockroach analogy, another trap. Through the contrast, Writer 2 again symbolizes her anger at the outside view versus the inside reality.

*CLASS
EXERCISES*

1. Read the Explorations of Writers 3, 4, and 5, which follow.
2. Discuss the Explorations of Writers 3, 4, and 5.
   Static
   • What distinctive features of the places do the writers provide?
   • How specific are the details that the writers recall? What other aspects could have been noted?
   • How much does the language give you a clear and vivid sense of the place?
   Dynamic
   • What movements have the writers captured?
   • What physical or historical changes have been noted? Are there other processes that could have been explored?
   Relative
   • In what categories do the writers place their subject? What reasons are given for such classification? Are there others that could have been made?
   • How fully have the writers explored the comparisons or contrasts that were made?

- What kinds of feelings about the subject are expressed through the analogies?
- How will the relationships discovered through this perspective help the writers to answer the starting question?

3. Select a place familiar to the class (perhaps the sample topic used for the class exercise on the starting point). Using the Exploratory Guide, discover as a class as many ideas under each perspective as you can. Record these either on the board or on paper. Work to make the language as specific as possible.

EXPLORATION

Writer 3   RIO

STATIC VIEW

The beach
—harsh, white sand
—brown, lean bodies
—the smell of gasoline mixed with the salty air
—the ocean salty clear
—soccer games on the beaches   men yelling & the sand scrunching underfoot
—old cars and horns that are never quiet
—Volkswagen taxis
—long beaches lined with hotels
—the hotels casting shadows on Copacabana beach, leaving small spaces of sunlight between them, looking out of the window & seeing sunbathers arrange themselves into those irregular rectangles
—hot oppressive heat
—greasy sun-tan lotion, sticky sand
—young men and their soccer games
—different schools of fish visit the beaches, sharks & jellyfish
—kite and cake vendors
—little   black boys & girls from the apartment buildings

The city
—mosaic sidewalks, the Moors & the Portuguese
—the vendors, kites & coconuts
—the Brazilian people and thier rhythm
—hundreds of caterpillar buses, new, proud drivers, weary passengers

The hotel
—busy, frantic, disorganized
—people lifting luggage and arranging packages

—uniformed men
—brown sweating bodies
—baths with sand in the bottom, wet bathing suits, soggy towels
—the slap of the keys on the wood desk

DYNAMIC VIEW

—movements in:
   early morning
—digging a hole in the sand, wriggling into it & watching people arrive
—the vendors getting set up
—buses, traffic jams, honking
—people eating rolls & fruit, looking out of their hotel windows onto the
   beach
—mountains crowding in on the city, appearing to move in the night and
   pushing the city slowly ahead of them into the ocean
—movements in:
   late afternoon
—squinting to find the right windows & waving to my parents
—hot, sweating office workers, shedding clothes & cares, relaxing
—tourists sunning & protecting themselves from the fierce sun with lotion
—movements in:
   night
—car doors slamming, people talking, laughing
—walking on the beach sidewalk
—laughing young men shouting at pretty girls
—people holding hands
—beggars returning from a day's foraging in the city
—new surfers, some drowned today, some will die tomorrow

Inner change—the city
—the mountains temperamentally shedding the favelas that hug them
—feeling sad when the stricken jumble of tin and paper cartons slides
   down and leaves them uncovered and cold
—poverty-ridden shacks are redecorated with a new piece of cardboard
   to shield the owners from the rain
—tiny corners in parks & empty lots are settled by destitute mountain
   people
—new shacks go up
—huge, dreary concrete apartment buildings are being constructed in
   the little space left in the city
—a beggar stakes out a corner—territory once belonging to a different
   emaciated face
—new advertisements come with the arrival of a new import—Japanese
   radios—American Coke

—eager, young men & brown-eyed girls meeting in bars & leaving together
—street markets: farmers & their little boys arriving 4 a.m. Saturday
  and leaving 9 p.m. Sunday
—flowers and fruit change hands
—young, unskilled men, maybe drought-stricken farmers from the North
  flock to Rio to help in the construction of the concrete dominos
—government changes:
  coup d'etat last night—generals & newspaper censorship this morning
—rich Brazilians & their families leaving their hot city apartments for
  their houses in the country
—poor families leaving their shacks to visit their relatives in the mountain forests
—taxis scuttle between the airport & the hotels

The beach
—new, translucent, multi-colored shells are daily washed onto the
  beaches, little boys & girls redistribute them with their toes & new
  shells come tomorrow to replace the old
—the sand—unshifting, still in the morning, at the end of the day
  marked & hilly, after a rain—brown, damp, cold with tiny little craters
—people shifting between beaches: Copacabana today, Ipanema tomorrow
—scalding in the afternoon, covered by towels & mats
—bums awakening

Outer change

    Past
—Cabral—discoverer, rich clothes, Portuguese settlers
—years of Portuguese rule & exploitation
—Rio, once capital of Brazil: kings, queens, slaves
—agricultural marketplace surrounded by coffee fazendas, rubber plan-
  tations
—primitive tribes
—wealthy Europeans, poor Cariocas
—remote, isolated

    Today
—Brazil—the sleeping giant stirs & yawns
—effect on cities like Rio is tremendous
—foreign enterprise & industry booming
—international tourist playground
—Rio will continue in exactly the same fashion, unchangeable
—character of the Brazilians, particularly the Cariocas, works against
  progress

–poor will get poorer, favelas will continue to be washed off the mountainsides

Future
–rich will remain rich, their grandchildren will inherit millions & be sent to Europe for their education

RELATIVE VIEW

Classification

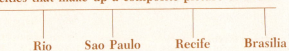

1. places that remain suspended in time — the industrial & political events of the rest of the world have little effect on the people & their strong cultures

Rio

tiny villages in Iraq & Lebanon

India—the caste system

small cities in Africa starting to emerge industrially like Rio

2. cities that make up a composite picture of Brazil

Rio   Sao Paulo   Recife   Brasilia

3. big South American cities

Rio   Buenos Aires   Caracas   Santiago   Sao Paulo

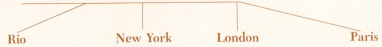

4. countries where people love and enjoy children, reflecting their own love of life

Brazil (Rio)   Mexico   Italy

5. one of the international "jet set" cities

Rio   New York   London   Paris

6. places that have been settled by Europeans and still demonstrate
signs of European influence

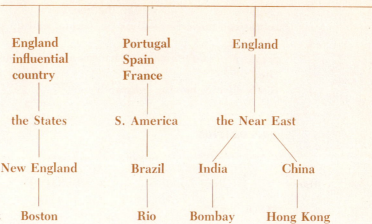

England influential country	Portugal Spain France	England
the States	S. America	the Near East
New England	Brazil	India	China
Boston	Rio	Bombay	Hong Kong

Comparison/Contrast

São Paulo	*Rio*
Brazil's largest city—huge population	not too many people
flat on a plateau, can devour more land from the jungle as it needs it	naturally bounded by the mountains on one side and the Atlantic on the other
fast, energetic people	slower pace of life

the sea—one main difference

the sea helps to slow people down; they stop to look, smell & hear the
  roar

S.P. is a few miles from the Atlantic	Rio is a coastal city
architectural beauty created by man	natural beauty
not many tourists	a shifting population of tourists
few cultural events	a cultural center (for Brazil)
industrial city	not much industry—tourism
no Carnival	Carnival!

Analogy

Rio is like a zebra

the zebra's stripes remind me of the black & white mosaic sidewalks of
  Rio

a zebra can graze slowly, resting often just like the Cariocas
  they take their time & stop to rest often in the day

a sleek animal—the wealthy men & women of Rio are smooth & polished

an unusual animal—Rio is unique

an animal of hot climates—Rio is hot, Brazil is hot

a zebra gallops at night—a part of Rio, silent in the day, comes alive at
  night—the city gallops like the zebra

zebras can move fast—Rio's beat can speed up to fever pitch at carni-
  val time

zebras are wild animals—Cariocas are free, spirited people—uninhib-
  ited

Rio is alive & moving constantly

EXPLORATION

Writer 4   GRAND RAPIDS

STATIC VIEW

—old-fashioned green frame house with a big front porch

—a tree-lined street filled with children playing

—an attic filled with treasures hidden in boxes, books which had been
  my mother's like *Little Women* and *Black Beauty*, old dolls with a broken leg or arm that someone had carefully packed away to be fixed
  and never did, clothes, pictures

—our backyard—large lawn with an overgrown rock garden and an
  empty goldfish pool at the back

—a mammoth fallen tree which stretched from end to end behind our
  lot blocking the view of the field beyond—filled with crevices for hiding in or making into secret mailboxes

—the "field" about five acres of undeveloped land in the middle of the
  city

  —wild grass which grew as tall as I was

  —weatherbeaten tree-stumps with branches still protruding here and
    there (we used for riding on)

  —a swamp with its musty smell, green moss, mud, snakes and polli-
    wogs

  —a steep hill over which children swung from ropes tied to tree
    branches like Tarzan and in winter sledding

—the library, an old stone building with the smell of bookbindings and
  cool quiet aisles filled with books of every kind—a park across the
  street that had a fountain with cool splashing water

—stores with names like Herpelsheimer's and Steketee's and hospitals
  named Sunshine, Mary Freebed and Butterworth

—the museum—small and not intimidating, its exhibits seen so often they
  became like old friends—the doll collection, china dolls and rag dolls—
  the room filled with rocks and gems which had a little booth you could
  go into like a photo booth to see certain stones which lit up in the

dark, a history exhibit with an Indian hunter crouched near the ground, camoflaged in an animal skin, arrow poised, his unsuspecting prey nearby

—the art gallery—at Christmas a tree for every country each with its own decoration

DYNAMIC VIEW

Activities

—walking to Booth's Dairy on summer evenings—real old-fashioned ice cream and spinning on stools by the soda-fountain

—children laughing and playing on front porches during summer rain storms

—public parks where families had picinics—hot dogs and marshmallows roasting on sticks, lovers holding hands strolling through the formal rose gardens while children raced in and out on the paths playing tag, a stream, dark and cool in the woods, wading pools where children played "Sally sitting in the water" and other games

—sparklers, parades, picnics and fireworks on the fourth of July with flags neatly hanging on nearly every house

—grown-ups raking leaves into piles by the curbs and watching them burn while children played Mother-may-I and tag until the last embers burned out

Going back to Grand Rapids

—my old house, now smaller and less impressive—the front porch gone and a garage stood where the goldfish pond was once

—the swamp used as a landfill by the city was gone

—the field, its grass all neatly cut, fallen trees sawed up and cleared away stood empty now

—park—a victim of city budget cuts—unkempt now, grass filled with bare dirt patches, overgrown roses, and a wading pool with cracked cement and not a drop of water

—articles written in newspapers about urban problems, slums and crime followed by optimistic reports of rebuilding efforts

—staying at the Pantlind, a downtown hotel, its graceful elegance now faded into peeling paint and threadbare carpets

—a once grand downtown movie house now showing pornography

RELATIVE VIEW

Classifying

—medium-sized Midwestern city

—city with strong religious influence Dutch-Reform and German Catholic

—hometown—place of roots and family

Compare/contrast with Detroit
–slower pace to life of a smaller town
–friendlier, more neighborly people
–more homogenous population
–both towns (although Detroit's image may be changing) where people
  seem to enjoy living more than out-of-towners want to visit
–both towns where most people want to live in single-family homes with
  their own lots
–both have had suburban malls and other things which led to deterio-
  rating downtowns which are being rebuilt

Analogy
like a snapshot taken in black and white—when looked at by the people
in it, it calls to mind the feelings of that moment, long since gone in
time and yet still there in memory—to a stranger the photo seems drab
and poorly taken when I see Grand Rapids now, I don't see the physical reality as much as I recall the happy, carefree days of childhood
when I was surrounded by people who loved me and convinced that
nothing bad or hurtful could ever happen to me—to a stranger Grand
Rapids seems like an industrial town of medium size with most of the
big city problems and few of the advantages

EXPLORATION

Writer 5   THE CAR DEALERSHIP

STATIC VIEW

large body shop surface area, pungent aroma of paint in body shop,
deafening din of power tools, various car parts scattered about, oblivi-
ous mechanics working on wrecks, dimly lit shop, dust and grit in the
air, tool boxes, paint cans, cigarette butts strewn on the floor, heavy
scent of turpentine stings the eyes, workers in blue uniforms, small
glass enclosed office within the body shop, complaining customers, file
cabinets, desk and chairs, adding machines and typewriters well worn
carpet, cigarette smoke, phones ringing, outside in the massive parking
lot the air is fresh and clean, a barbed wire fence surrounds the lot,
endless rows of cars, car wash, gas pump, tow trucks, new car dealers
trying to make a sale.

DYNAMIC VIEW

rush to the time clock, stroll into the office, greet my fellow workers,
lean against the wall and wait for a command, receive an order, proceed to drive a wreck in to be repaired, go back in office, stand around

somemore, told to drive a car through the wash, drive carefully checking around corners, walk back to office to get a fresh set of directions,
walk from building to parking lot and back to building and so it goes all
day, legs get weary and a big thirst builds up as day nears completion,
sweep up the dirt in the shop with clouds of dust floating up, cart out
jagged metal body parts, hose down the floor, brush grime and water
down the drain, drive the next days cars in, relief as you make your
way to the time clock and punch out.

RELATIVE VIEW

Classify

Bad aspects of the job

sweeping the floors	all the dust
carrying heavy objects	low pay
hand washing cars	too much walking
loud noises	long hours
	dull work

Good aspects of the job

meet new friends
opportunity to drive expensive cars
encourages good driving habits
learn how to follow directions

Enjoyable cars to drive

new cars   sports cars
cars with air conditioning
easy to park small cars
autos with plenty of glass for good vision

Comparison

Reality of job	Expect from job
minimum wage	high pay
drove more Impalas than Cor-vettes	drive sports cars
long hours, no overtime pay	regular hours
washing cars, mopping floors	no maintenance work
many cordial acquaintances	friendly atmosphere
professional, firm, hardworking boss	strict boss
no breaks	regular breaks

Auto job	Gas station job
low pay	low pay
lot of cleanup work	lot of cleanup work
too much walking	too much walking
friendly people	unfriendly people
bad hours	bad hours

Analogy
When I take on a job, it's like a person who buys a used car for the paint color rather than looking under the hood.

Stage 2 Toward a Paper on Place: Exploring

1. **Explore the question you formulated in the first assignment (p. 25), discovering as many ideas under each view as you can.**
2. **Record these ideas in the most personal and vivid words you can find.**
3. **Seek commentary on your exploration from your teacher.**

DISCOVERING AND STATING THE FOCUS

INCUBATING

During writing, your mind engages in activity that is not conscious but plays an important role in composing. But because you are unaware of this activity, you often get in its way or fail to stimulate it. Three important facets of this activity will help you as a writer:

1. It uses what your conscious explorations supply.
2. It takes time for ideas to associate.
3. It is the source of your insights.

If you prepare yourself with a rich stock of ideas during your exploration, your chances for finding the answer to your starting question increase. You need time (at least a good night's sleep) after your conscious searching. Even though you are pressured, you can still pace yourself by starting the writing process early enough to give yourself some incubating time. Finally, you should understand that meaningful answers are more likely to spring from complete explorations.

DISCOVERING THE INSIGHT

Insight is the spark of understanding that holds promise for resolving your original tension. You see an answer or sometimes several possible answers to your question. Or perhaps you begin to sense a deeper meaning in your subject than you had started out to find. But insights are as yet unexpressed in words, untested.

STATING THE FOCUS

Recording insights in two parts helps you to test them, to see them more clearly. We will call an expressed insight a *focus*.

A well-stated focus has two parts: *aspect* and *point of significance*. The aspect is the part of the subject you find important. The point of significance is either your best answer to the original question or a deeper meaning you have discovered. Below are the writers' insights, formulated into focuses. (See pp. 22–23 for their starting questions.)

FOCUSES

	SUBJECT	POINT OF SIGNIFICANCE
Writer 1	The contrast between my first experience of dorm living and my life at home	changed me from a person who had played the "child" role to one who was more mature and independent, a painful but giant step.
Writer 2	Being confined in a state home	oppressed me but could not wipe out my sense of inner freedom.
Writer 3	Rio, with its extremes of poverty and wealth,	will remain oblivious to the sufferings of the poor, a horror I had never experienced before.
Writer 4	The Grand Rapids of my childhood	is not so much a place I want to return to as a lifestyle with more security and sense of permanence.
Writer 5	The realities of the job at the car dealership	caused me to become much more suspicious of low skill job offers and to make intensive inquiries before applying for a job.

Commentary Writer 1's *point of significance* has answered both her starting questions, discovering the kind of impact dorm living has had on her and evaluating that impact. Her *aspect of the subject* (contrast between dorm and home life) reflects her revised starting point and her exploration, limiting her paper to the points of contrast.

CLASS EXERCISES

1. Discuss the Focuses of Writers 2, 3, 4, and 5.
   - Does the first half of each focus indicate the aspect the writer wants to concentrate on? If the writer has chosen to deal with the subject as a whole, how long will such a paper be?
   - How do the points of significance respond to the writers' starting questions (pp. 22–23)?
   - How could the writers have better formulated their focuses?

2. Discuss the way in which the following alternative focuses are formulated. Will these formulations work for the writers? Why or why not?
   a. My experience of dorm living is good.
   b. Clinical institutions are poor places in which to live.
   c. My vacation to Rio.
   d. The history of Grand Rapids.
   e. I disliked working at the car dealership.
3. Using the ideas from the sample exploration you did in class, work at formulating some focuses.

ASSIGNMENT

Stage 3 Toward a Paper on Place: Discovering and Stating the Focus
1. After allowing time for incubation, express your insight as a focus.
2. Seek comments on your focus from your instructor and the class.

PLANNING FOR AIM AND AUDIENCE

Two questions that need answering early in the process are: What aim does this writing involve? Who is my audience? In many writing situations, your aim and even your audience are set by the type of writing required. This course will offer you several chances to choose your audience. Your aim will be designated in each chapter. Even when your aim and audience are established, you still need to understand their implications for later work in the process. In this chapter, we are introducing these two factors after you have discovered and stated a focus. Other chapters will consider them earlier.

OVERVIEW OF AIMS[2]

Every unfinished piece of writing has four components: writer, audience, subject, and language-form. Your aim is a question of emphasis. If you emphasize yourself as writer, expressing your feelings, hopes, fears, or beliefs, you have an *expressive* aim. If you emphasize the audience, desiring to concentrate on changing it, you have a *persuasive* aim. If you emphasize the subject, concentrating on giving information about it, you have an *expository* aim. If you emphasize the beauty of the language and form, as in poetry, fiction, or drama, you have a *literary* aim. Every piece of writing has all these components, but the one you stress determines your aim.

It would be foolish to pretend that these aims exist in a state of complete separation, in airtight chambers. For example, a biologist reporting the results of a revolutionary experiment will have both an expository and a persuasive aim. The biologist wants to give the reader information, but also

[2]James Kinneavy, *A Theory of Discourse* (Englewood Cliffs, N.J.: Prentice-Hall, 1971).

wants to change the opinion of the reader. A short-story writer whose story illustrates the theme that crime sometimes does pay has both a literary and a persuasive purpose. But one purpose almost always dominates the other, and you should be clear in your own mind about which aim you wish to emphasize.

Why? Because each aim offers its own method of selecting material and of refining style. Some aims also offer patterns of organization. We do not write prayers (expressive) as if they were legal contracts (expository), nor short stories (literary) as if they were deodorant commercials (persuasive). Before this book ends, you will have the opportunity to write with all the aims, except the literary. For now, we again note that each aim requires an emphasis on one of four elements present in any writing situation: The expressive concentrates on the *writer*, the persuasive on the *audience*, the expository on the *subject matter*, the literary on the *language and form*.

THE EXPRESSIVE AIM

This chapter will explain and illustrate writers working with the expressive aim. Writer 1 wanted to share her insight into the positive changes the dorm had worked in her. She was not out to write a sales brochure for her college. Writer 2 wished to release the dread and fear that a hellhole had imprinted on her fearful self.

CLASS EXERCISES

1. Share with the class any previous writing you may have done with an expressive aim.
2. Discuss why the expressive aim might often be the emphasis of writing in the private world.

CHOOSING AN AUDIENCE

Whether the piece of writing is an essay, a diary, a letter, a poem, or a report, it always has an audience. Sometimes your audience is simply you, the writer. More often, the audience is someone whose thoughts or feelings you wish to shape. You should fashion your writing so that the audience can *reconstruct* and *experience* the focus that you intended to communicate. In order to do so, you must know your audience, be sensitive to its attitudes and convictions. That means you must consciously, at some point during the planning stages, identify and analyze your audience.

Some writing situations seem to permit you to choose your audience freely while others do not. Writing in the private world, for example, seems to allow you to choose audiences, whereas a paper assignment from a history professor on some aspect of contemporary economic policy would seem to allow no choice. The choice of audience lies hidden in each case, however, because you always face two choices. The first choice is: Who will be the audience? An editor, a publisher, an employer, a teacher can make this choice for you. The second choice is: What role will the audience be asked to play? Take the history professor as an example. Assume the professor is a male. What roles does he play? First of all, he's obviously a history professor. But he is probably also a taxpayer, probably a Republican, a Democrat, or an independent, possibly a husband, possibly a father—and so on. The approach you take in your writing asks the reader to assume a role. For example, when the history professor is reading the *Journal of American History* he is playing one role; when he reads *Parent's Magazine,* another; when he reads *Runner's World,* yet another. A paper on some aspect of contemporary economic policy could be addressed to him, for example, in his role as an expert on recent economic history, in his role as taxpayer, in his role as a Republican voter, or in a combination of roles. Notice that readers not only can play a variety of roles, but they have the option of refusing to play a role. The history professor who refuses to read *Runner's World* refuses to play the role of a *Runner's World* reader—and hence rejects the attitudes and values that underlie *Runner's World.* It is important, therefore, that you choose roles that your audience can play; otherwise, the audience will stop playing an active role.

In this writing experience on place, you as writer will make both choices. How do you know what audience to choose? Try applying this principle: The best audience will be the one that will find the focus you have arrived at most helpful. Ask yourself who will profit most from the focus you will share. That's your audience.

Writer 1 chose next year's freshman class in order to prepare them for some of the same shocks she underwent. The choice of audience was good because the writer's insights will be put to use and it is an audience the writer can easily define and identify with. Writer 2 selected herself because she said: "Someone else might profit from it, but I know that it will be most helpful to me. I am exorcising demons, trying to rid my present self of the dread and fear that hellhole imprinted on me. I'm the one who needs to understand the experience so that I can grow beyond it." An older self looking at a younger self for a specific purpose may allow the writer to focus the paper precisely. But writing for oneself in this fashion is an ambitious, challenging task, since the writer must conceive of herself as basically different from what she is now. We will follow Writer 2 through the entire writing process in this chapter.

Writer 3 chose the teacher of her writing class as audience because she felt this teacher was more likely to have traveled abroad than her classmates; she hoped her comparisons might cause her to reflect on her foreign experiences. This is a good choice because it takes into account the possible similarity in experiences and the dissimilarity in what came out of those experiences. The writer is seeking a use for her insight beyond her own needs. Writer 4 wanted to write for families who have moved from one kind of city to another, perhaps because of a job change. Writer 5 chose young people of 16–18 who were considering their first jobs.

ANALYZING THE AUDIENCE

After you have identified your audience, it is time to get to know it (i.e., him/her/them). Most writers know more about their audiences than they are consciously aware of. The task is to bring the knowledge to the surface. How?

First, by asking yourself a series of pertinent questions. Pertinent to what? Remember that you want to establish a role the audience can play. That means that the questions must pertain to the knowledge, values, and attitudes that the audience possesses or professes.

Second, by thinking carefully and answering those questions realistically. It is fatal to fantasize an audience. We'd all like to write for the audience that loves us from the first word because it shares our knowledge, values, and attitudes. Audiences like that are rare.

Following is a two-part guide for audience analysis.

AUDIENCE GUIDE

A. Analyze the audience in relation to itself.
   1. What are the levels and types of experiences that my audience has had (cultural, professional, recreational, educational, and so on)?
   2. What hierarchy of values does my audience possess or profess (money making and power, friendship, security, intellectual growth, and so on)? It is important to distinguish, if possible, between what an audience holds dear and what it professes to hold dear, if indeed there is a difference. Does the audience hide one set of values under another? If so, the writer's task grows more complicated.
B. Analyze the audience in relation to the subject.
   1. What opinion does my audience have on my subject?
   2. How strongly does my audience hold that opinion?
   3. How willing to act on its opinion is my audience—if acting is appropriate?
C. Considering what you have learned from your answers to A and B, determine what role your audience should play in relation to

your voice as writer (peer, authority, subordinate, familiar, and so on).

Step C is the most challenging because it requires you to create the relationship with your reader that you will maintain throughout your paper. In order to create the relationship, you should understand two terms: *role* and *voice*.

Audience role

We discussed role briefly on p. 46. A reader can be asked to play a *specific* or a *relational* role or both. When readers are asked to play a *specific* role, they are asked to act as if one part of their total characters were the whole; that is, they are asked to read as if they were only (or at least primarily) mothers, fathers, baseball fans, Republicans, nuclear physicists, and so on. Often there is no reason to assign so specific a role to readers. When readers are asked to play a *relational* role, they are being asked to accept a certain relationship to the writer: equals, subordinates, or superiors; opponents, friends, or disinterested observers. Because this kind of role is unavoidable, it is the one any writer must be able to control.

Writer's voice

The writer suggests to the reader the relational role the reader should play by means of the writer's *voice*, another term for the role the writer has chosen to play in relation to the reader. If that seems confusing, consider a situation in which you are approached by someone who blurts out loudly, "What the heck do you think you're doing?" That voice has defined the roles that the person wants the two of you to play. Consider the difference in suggested roles if the person had approached you and said, "May I help you?" Voice is the expression of a choice of writer's role.

The *choice* of voice rests on two considerations: what you know of the audience in itself and what you know of the audience in relation to the subject matter.

AUDIENCE ANALYSIS

Writer 2   **AUDIENCE: SELF**

A. Audience in itself
   1. –lower middle class, white neighborhood
      –experience of being in a psychiatric clinic
      –my father deserted my family
      –private city high school

2. I value security, concern for others, ability to write, freedom from fear and confinement.
3. I have a difficult time relating well to my mother but I value my relationship with my sister.

B. Audience in relation to the subject

My two selves—the demon-tormented, fearful self vs. the free, loved, secure self.

1. My fearful self hates the institution and dreads remembering it.
2. My fearful self clings to that dread.
3. —Doesn't apply.

C. My fearful self feels estranged from my free self; the two selves are both strangers and intimates, but I can't write as if that were true. It will be best to treat the audience as a stranger and to speak to her from a distance but as an equal. My voice should be calm and reflective and friendly.

Commentary The strain of the starting question that led to the focus shows through in the answers to A; the answers are limited and even occasionally hesitant. The answers to B are more definite, and the answer to C is very perceptive. One has to read between the lines in dealing with a sensitive subject like this, but it appears that the writer is trying to solve the problem of self as audience by putting some distance between the two persons, while at the same time maintaining an even, balanced relationship. The writer is struggling with a very complicated writing situation.

AUDIENCE ANALYSIS

Writer 4 A. Audience: Families who have participated in corporate moves

1. Most of these people are well educated, middle class and have lived in large urban areas. They often live in middle class suburbs which are usually quite transient.
2. These people often believe that America's history is one of almost uninterrupted progress. Corporate families place a high value on intellectual growth, position and influence and material well-being. Families, while important, are often secondary to the corporate family.

B. I believe that most corporate families feel the conflict between permanence, security and family ties and adventure, new people & places and ever upward mobility. They have made a choice and are living with it, but I think they sometimes regret some of the things they've given up.

C. I think the audience would be peers of mine. My story is a reflection on and remembrance of, a place & time which I left. Many of them have had similar feelings. My voice, therefore, will be of an equal.

1. Discuss the audience choices of Writers 4 and 5 (pp. 46–47) and the Audience Analysis of Writer 4.
   - In what way will these audiences stand to profit from the writers' focuses?
   - What other aspects of the audiences' backgrounds and values could have been noted?
   - Why has Writer 4 chosen a peer role for the audience to play and a voice as an equal?
   - What other audiences could have been chosen? Why?
2. Select an audience for one of the sample focuses you formulated in the class exercise. Using the Audience Guide, analyze this audience.

Stage 4 Toward a Paper on Place: Planning for Aim and Audience

1. **Choose your audience by asking yourself this question: Who will profit most from sharing my focus? Write down your choice, along with your reason for making it.**
2. **Analyze your audience by answering the questions in the Audience Guide.**
3. **Seek commentary on your choice and analysis of audience.**
4. **Keep your expressive aim in mind.**

In this stage you will move from planning to writing the paper. We will reserve until Chapter 2 a discussion of refining your *style* to allow you here to concentrate on the tasks of developing and organizing your paper.

DEVELOPING THE EXPRESSIVE AIM

Effective writers write from abundance; they do not use everything they generate as raw material. Instead, they tuck it away for future use. Developing a paper is a matter of (1) selecting material generated in earlier steps in the process and (2) adding useful material as it occurs to you during this stage of the process. But what should be selected and what can be usefully added depends on your aim and focus.

The expressive aim requires that the writer select on these principles:

1. Exclude material that is not personal, except on very good grounds. Appealing to books, other people's experiences or popular truths tends to shift the aim to persuasive; you will seem to be trying to justify your perceptions or feelings. The expressive aim does not require the writer to be absolutely right, only open, honest, and sincere about private feelings.

2. Include as much as possible the language of feeling; avoid the language of flat statement. The language of feeling abounds in images and metaphors (see Defining Terms) and in concrete diction (see Defining Terms). Emotion is not conveyed by abstract or general statements. The reader shares your feelings not by reading statements about your feelings—"I felt sad"—but by sharing the concrete situation that generated your feeling, or by perceiving, through an image or metaphor, a comparable situation in his or her own experience.

For example, the exploratory list that Writer 2 will work from looks promising (see pp. 29–32). She has amassed a good many descriptive details that don't state but imply an emotional attitude. The use of "arid [acrid] smell," "disinfectant," and "dirty socks" in conjunction with "dirty cotton tennis shoes that muffle the angry pounding of feet against the floor" conveys an emotional attitude that would be very hard to state directly. Suppose we tried to paraphrase those perceptions. To say that the place was dirty and it smelled bad is expository rather than expressive, but misses the point as well. So we would say something like, "We felt that we were dirt, something to be disinfected (but without much care or enthusiasm) and it made us feel dirty and angry and frustrated." But the statement still doesn't convey the feeling; it only summarizes inaccurately and turns the feeling into information. The items on the list, however, are useful and appropriate because they invite the reader to recreate and share the perceptions and the feeling.

On the other hand, there are other items, particularly in the dynamic view, that probably should not be used. The writer has researched her own case, so to speak; she has read Lisa Richette's *The Throwaway Children*, probably in an effort to understand better her own difficulties. It's doubtful that the material can be used because the issue here is not one of convincing an audience by appeal to external authority, as it might be in expository or persuasive writing. Introducing Lisa Richette's study might break the focus.

That is not to say that reading *The Throwaway Children* and noting its contents were not useful to the writer. Richette may have helped the writer understand her own plight. But there is a difference between what a writer has available and what a writer uses in a paper. Although this is a principle common to all the aims, it is particularly important to the writer of expressive discourse because of the temptation to turn away from the painful exploration of feelings to other things, external, objective, and neutral.

ORGANIZING A PAPER

Writing your paper not only requires having an *aim* that guides your choice of material, but also requires a pattern of organization. *Modes* are patterns of organization, ways of putting together material. The four modes that you will eventually work with are *description, narration, classification,* and *evaluation.*[3] Choosing your mode before writing saves you endless meandering drafts that grope for organization.

The four modes offer different ways of arranging material. A pet cat, a person, a poem, a building, an idea can all be discussed in any of the modes. But in each mode different aspects of the subject will be selected, and the aspects will be organized differently. This chapter will discuss the descriptive and narrative modes.

The descriptive mode

The *descriptive mode* implies a movement from whole to parts or from parts to whole. If the subject is physical, like a place, the mode involves a sequence in space: left to right, right to left, far to near, near to far, up to down, down to up, clockwise or counterclockwise. If, instead, you are using the descriptive mode to organize a research paper on a scientific theory or to organize a critical paper on a poem, you divide your subject into its parts and discuss these parts, one by one. In the subsequent chapters we will discuss and exemplify the use of the descriptive mode for different kinds of subjects. This chapter illustrates physical description.

The narrative mode

The *narrative mode* implies a sequence in time, basically chronological, as one o'clock is followed by two o'clock. The sequence can be altered by rearranging significant units of time (i.e., incidents, events, happenings) so that they fit more closely with other units. A "flashback," a unit from the past suddenly inserted in the present sequence, may appear in order to help the audience understand the unit in the present sequence. The basic chronological sequence—one, two, three, four—is altered only for reasons of *audience,* or of *emphasis.* That is, the writer breaks the basic chronological sequence only so that the audience may understand more clearly a unit in the present time sequence or be alerted to something that has happened in the past. Audiences expect certain sequences, whether they occur in time, space, or the mixed realm of thought. After a subject in a sentence, the audience expects a verb; after one, two; after an argument, a conclusion; after a question, an answer. If those expectations are not satisfied, *emphasis* occurs. That is, the unexpected takes on great importance.

[3] James Kinneavy, John Cope, and John Campbell, *Writing—Basic Modes of Organization* (Dubuque, Iowa: Kendall/Hunt, 1976).

Choosing a mode of organization

Previous choices of audience and aim by Writer 2 indicate that she wants to show her audience that a "demon" has been "exorcised"; that her present self understands the past self, the fearful self is understood and accepted by the free self. Narration is a distinct possibility; the writer could show the deadly round of a day in the prison of a state home. Description is also a distinct possibility; the exploratory list is crammed with descriptive details. Writer 2 chose to use a descriptive mode of organization.

FIRST VERSION

Writer 2

THE CAVERN

The room draws itself into a triangle. It spreads out from the wide glass-enclosed booth that holds the guards, and runs into a long narrowing corridor, walls tucking themselves under, past the rows of bright pink and yellow doors until they meet together, in a brief green corner. The low ceiling, as well as the floor is tiled, in a dull beige. It traps the odors that rise out of the floor and holds them in the air, the disinfectant from the mop pail mingling with the sweat from graying tennis shoes. The walls are dull green concrete blocks, broken by the lines of steel doors in the corridor. Painted by a sure, hard hand, their enamel coats are smooth and shiny, unmarred by graffiti scratches and usage. They have a gaiety inappropriate to the room. A small, high window in each door out into the hall; so many eyes watching over the children.

The girls, in loose jumpers sit, tipped back in green plastic and metal chairs lined up along the hall. Muffled in cotton tennis shoes, feet bang against the concrete, the girls watch the grey metal clock set into the wall above the guards' station. He holds back, languidly, hoarding over precious minutes, until pulled, against his will, he jerks forward with a loud click. A clattering, followed by distant shouting rises promisingly in the air, then dies down. Music from a local radio station, piped into the room, settles, mixing with the dirty disinfectant smell. Fingers drumming against the seat of the chairs, the girls watch the miser clock give up his minutes.

Behind the steel doors, in the dark, there is life still. There is no need of paint on this side of the door. The close walls are green-tiled and bare. It has a thick, dark odor all its own. In the corner, on the cement floor, a young girl sits in a white nightgown, rocking back and forth. She is far away, riding her horse through an English meadow, sweet yellow-green dotted with flowers.

CLASS EXERCISES

1. Read the First Versions of Writers 4 and 5 below.
2. Reexamine the Explorations of Writers 4 (pp. 38–40) and 5 (pp. 40–42).

- What material was useful for developing an expressive aim?
- What material was put aside?
3. Study the First Versions of Writers 4 and 5.
   - Does the material fit the expressive aim?
   - Is there enough development?
   - What mode of organization is used? Why?

FIRST VERSION

Writer 4

LOOKING BACK

My family became corporate nomads when I was eight. Each year in the spring as other people looked forward to new flowers blooming in their gardens, we looked forward to a new house, new school, new people in a new and different city. It was, we assured each other in later years, a "broadening upbringing." It made us tolerant of other life-styles.

Still I often think back to Grand Rapids, the city where I was born, the city of my parents and of their parents before them. I dream of returning, of experiencing again the sense of belonging that I knew there, but the Grand Rapids of my childhood no longer exists except in my memory.

We lived in an old-fashioned green frame house with a big front porch. In the back of our house was a large lawn, an overgrown rock garden, and an empty goldfish pool at the back. A mammoth fallen tree which stretched from end to end behind our lot blocked the view of the field beyond which consisted of about five acres of undeveloped land right there in the middle of the city.

The seasons seemed more vivid then, each with its own sights, sounds, smells, and activities.

In summer we would go exploring in the field, wandering through the wild grass which grew as tall as me. Some days we found weather-beaten tree stumps with branches still protruding here and there. These became horses and we would ride. Some days we spent at the swamp with its musty smell, green moss, mud, snakes, and polliwogs. There was a steep hill nearby and sometimes we swung off it from ropes tied to tree branches like Tarzan. On summer evenings my father walked with us to Booth's Dairy where we would spin on stools by the soda fountain licking our ice cream cones. Or sometimes he and my mother took us to the library. My father watched the younger ones at a park across the street. They played by the fountain with its cool splashing water while we older ones were allowed to accompany my mother across to the old stone library building with its smells of bookbindings.

We tiptoed up and down the quiet aisles filled with books of every kind carefully choosing one book from the children's room to take home. My grandparents lived no more than a mile away as did most of my dad's seven brothers and sisters. Frequently we met at the public park in our neighborhood for a picnic. We roasted hotdogs and marshmallows on sticks. The children would then race off to play tag, or change into bathing suits and play "Sally sitting in the water" at the wading pool. Lovers, holding hands, strolled through the formal rose gardens or down cool dark paths in the woods. On the fourth of July we celebrated with sparklers, parades, picnics, and fireworks. There was a flag neatly hanging from nearly every house. In autumn the grown-ups raked leaves into piles by the curb and stood watching them burn while we children played "mother-may-I" or tag until the last embers burned out.

When winter came there were other things to do. We would climb the stairs to the attic filled with treasures hidden in boxes. We never knew what we might find. There were books which had been my mother's like *Little Women* or *Black Beauty*, old dolls with a broken leg or arm that someone had packed carefully away to be fixed and never did, strangely styled clothes we dressed up in playing grown-up, and faded pictures of people posed stiffly in front of a camera. Sometimes we visited the museum, its exhibits seen so often they became like old friends. There was a doll collection with china dolls, rag dolls, dolls filled with sawdust and dolls made of wood. One room, filled with rocks and gems, had a little booth you could go into like a photo booth to see certain stones which lit up in the dark. There was a history exhibit with an Indian hunter crouched near the ground, camouflaged in an animal skin, arrow poised, his unsuspecting prey nearby. At Christmastime, we trudged through the snow to the art gallery to see the Christmas trees each decorated in a different country's style. There were also trips downtown to stores named Herpelsheimer's (which I pronounced purple-shiners and thought of black-eyes) and Steketee's.

There were many out-of-the-ordinary names there, a part of what made the city unique. No Grand Rapids Municipal or Kent County General to name their hospitals. Instead they were called Mary Freebed, which I was sure meant no charge, and Butterworth and Sunshine which is still the most cheerful name for a hospital I've ever heard.

I went on my own tour of Grand Rapids not long ago. I stayed at the Pantlind, a downtown hotel, its graceful elegance now faded into peeling paint and threadbare carpets. Across the street was a once grand downtown movie house now showing pornography. My old house seemed smaller, less impressive now. The front porch was gone and a garage stood where the goldfish pond was once. The swamp, used as a landfull by the city, was gone now. The field, its grass neatly cut, fallen trees sawed up and cleared away, stood empty. The park, a victim of city budget cuts, looked unkempt. The grass was filled with bare dirt patches, the roses overgrown, and the wading pool had cracked cement and not a drop of water.

For me Grand Rapids is like a snapshot taken in black and white. To someone who was there when the picture was taken it calls to mind all the colors, sounds, smells, and emotions of that moment even though the picture may be faded and poorly taken. What I see in Grand Rapids is a life-style of permanence where families lived and died in close proximity and life seemed somehow simpler and roles more easily defined.

Writer 5   THE HARD WAY

School is out for the summer, and the hot months drag on. Boredom sets in quickly so I reach for a nearby newspaper and start to scan the help wanted ads looking for something to occupy myself. I run my eyes over the thousands of little boxes on the classified page. Most ads are for career positions for which I have neither the time nor skill. I run my finger down the first column, "auto machinest, auto mechanic, auto painter, auto porter." My finger suddenly stops. That sounds interesting, so I read the details provided. "Auto porter wanted for body shop, apply Smith's Chevrolet.

As I am sitting thinking about the job, exciting ideas start to glide through my imagination, spending hot summer days driving around in air conditioned Corvettes, picking up a sizeable paycheck weekly and best of all no more afternoons spent watching "Wheel of Fortune" and the "20,000 Dollar Pyramid." Seems great, so I snap myself out of my euphoric daydream and rush down to Smith's to apply.

I arrive. Darn! No place to park. I leave my car in a no parking zone and walk quickly, almost jog, into the main office; constantly repeating to myself, "hurry in, get there before they give the job to somebody else." At the personnel office the secretary gives me a form to fill out. Upon completing this, I am ushered in to see the personnel director, a middle aged man in a three-piece suit. I tell him all about my perfect driving record, and what a hard worker I am. He explains to me that the job is "mostly" driving and parking cars, as I expected. Then, he hit me with a roundhouse punch I hadn't expected. The job requires an eight hour day five days a week with earnings of $3.10 an hour. I am temporarily stunned but recover to reason that the weekly pay will be about what I originally want I'll just have to sacrifice a lot of free time, and I rationalize that there isn't anything to do at home anyway. With that out of the way, I am told to report at eight A.M. tomorrow. I depart from the office, my original vision shaken a little, but feeling lucky I landed this job and saying to myself everything will be fine.

I arrive at eight sharp the next morning, punch in, and then get my first glimpse of where I'll be spending most of my days. The body shop work area is rather large, about the size of a basketball court. The floor is dirty and gray with numerous paint stains. A lane separates the mechanics' stalls, which are located in two rows against the long walls and are stuffed with tall red tool boxes, various car body parts, paint cans, dirty rags and stacks of hoses. The walls and windows above the stalls are coated with dirt and grime, letting little sunlight enter. The high ceiling contains several light fixtures that try in vain to keep the place bright. The two things, though, I notice first are the incessant noises and the large amount of dust in the air. The power sanders, grinders, air hoses and hammers work overtime to keep the place in an almost never ending racket. The dust particles floating about in the air make breathing trying. It's a guaranteed headache for the first couple of days. In a corner of the work area the supervisors assemble in a small glass enclosed office. The furnishings are spartan, a long desk, three chairs and file cabinets against the back wall. Outside is a huge parking lot surrounded by a barbed wire fence; the body shop wrecks are in a long row against one side of the fence, the rest of the area is occupied by new cars.

I walk into the little office and stand against the wall waiting for the boss, a small energetic man of fifty, to give me a task to carry out. I don't have to wait long before he hands me a set of keys and tells me to drive a car into a mechanic's stall. I walk outside, down the long row of cars until I find the wreck I am looking for, a 1973 Impala. My illusion of driving sports cars is quickly dashed, and I realize that most of the cars I will drive are beat up old family sedans. I drive the car into the stall, go back to the office, and I wait for another direction which isn't long in coming as they are understaffed with porters. I get the order and walk out again, find the car, drive it in, go back to the office. This is the constant pattern throughout the day. There is seldom time for a lunch break as I have to work straight through. The day wears on; my legs ache, I have a huge thirst and my head hurts from the deafening noise. I even feel sick from breathing all the garbage in the air.

Relief comes as the clock approaches quitting time and just when I think it is time to leave, the boss informs me that it's the porters' responsibility to clean the place up. I am too weak to argue so I and one other armed with brooms take on the mess. What follows is one gigantic cloud of dust. After the sweeping, heavy, awkward, body parts with jagged metal edges are carried out to the trash bin. I finish and punch out two hours later than anticipated.

As I'm driving home, reflecting on the days happenings, I raise my right hand and solemnly swear to let investigation rather than imagination be my guide when it comes to choosing another job.

Stage 5 Toward a Paper on Place: Developing, Organizing, and Refining the Paper

1. Write a first version of your paper that
   a. communicates your focus
   b. to the audience
   c. using either a descriptive or narrative mode of organization.

Effective writers are rewriters. A first version is never as good as a second version, a second as good as a third, and so on, *so long as the changes from version to version are made for good reasons.* But how do we arrive at good reasons?

Professional writers hold three seemingly contradicting opinions. In rewriting, they say:

1. There is no substitute for advice from another professional (editor, teacher, publisher, successful writer, and so on).
2. There is no substitute for advice from your audience.
3. There is no substitute for self-criticism.

All three are true. If you can obtain all three, your writing has a greater chance of improving. Let us examine some ways in which classrooms can provide such criticism:

1. Using the Critical Guide (p. 59), instructors can provide you with either written critiques or oral ones, if time permits conferences. Many teachers prefer to reserve grading for the revision.
2. Using the Critical Guide, other students, playing the role of audience, can provide you with both written critiques and oral group criticism. Some writers find that they receive the most help when their classmates have prepared written critiques before group sessions.
3. Although it is often difficult for you to get enough distance from your own work for effective self-criticism, you can develop the power of self-criticism by critiquing others' papers. Another useful practice is to read your work aloud.

THE CRITICAL GUIDE

The Critical Guide (shown on p. 59) will help you review five important facets of your first version. Each facet contributes to the success of the whole paper. Because as a developing writer you have strengths in some facets of writing and weaknesses in others, isolating areas for revision can be very helpful.

CRITICAL GUIDE

NAME _____
(Writer)

NAME _____
(Critic)

1. Focus

2. Development

3. Organization

4. Style

5. Conventions: Grammar, Spelling, Punctuation

Answering the following questions will help you apply the guide.

1. Focus

What is the writer's focus?
In what ways has the writer maintained the focus?
Where has the writer strayed from the focus?

2. Development

What material has the writer used to develop the aim and focus?
In what ways can the audience *experience* the writer's focus?
What voice and audience role are created?
What other material does the audience need?

3. Organization

What mode of organization is the writer following?
How does the writer follow that mode?
What sections, if any, break the organization?

4. Style

(Questions on style will be added in Chapter 2.)

5. Conventions: Grammar, Spelling, Punctuation

In what places has the writer failed to follow the conventions?
What impact does this have on the audience?

CRITIQUE:
Writer 2

Focus

The draft now has a title, "The Cavern" (p. 53). "A state home," the topic, has changed to a metaphor. When a writer is ready to give a title to a piece, it usually means that the writer feels firmly in control and sees the implications and focus of the material. A cavern is a carved-out passage with a dead end.

Development

Two perhaps surprising things work well here:

1. The amount of material the writer has discarded, considering the size of her Exploration (pp. 29–32). All those impressions have come down to about 300 words.
2. The absence of first-person pronouns common to expressive writing. Here she seems to have tried to objectify the experience, to understand it "from outside." This fits exactly with her Audience Analysis (pp. 48–49).

The first paragraph suggests a prison; the second, girls waiting to get out. But the clock cannot release them, nor can the guards. It isn't as if at the stroke of whatever o'clock they will all be free; they won't be. The question becomes, If you are not free in time or space, in what way can you be free?

The first sentence of the third paragraph answers the question: "Behind the steel doors, in the dark, there is life still." The implication of the statement is that to be in the hall (space), watching the clock (time), is not to be alive. But back in a solitary confinement room, with its lack of gay paint, its bareness, its cement floor, there is someone who has solved the problem.

She imagines herself "riding her horse through an English meadow, sweet yellow-green dotted with flowers." By an effort of imagination and will, she has transcended time and space and has escaped. Even the yellow of the imprisoning doors and the deadly institutional green have been transmuted by her imagination into the colors of sunlight, sweetness, and growth—the colors of a meadow.

The use of *understatement* (see Defining Terms) is remarkable here. The sense of something imprisoning everyone in the home, something almost suprahuman or subhuman, is conveyed in a series of dependent constructions. The guards themselves are imprisoned in the "booth that holds the guards"; the doors have been "[p]ainted by a sure, hard hand"; "the girls watch the miser clock give up his minutes"; the windows suggest "so many eyes watching over the children."

Organization

The organization is basically descriptive. It moves from the whole to the parts, in that the first paragraph supplies a total floor plan of "the cavern," and succeeding paragraphs address details of the plan. Furthermore, there is a logical movement both in the summary and in the succeeding paragraphs from the guard booth to the corridor into the one room. But if the strength of the first version is its sensory details, its weaknesses lie there also. Any reader may be confused by the early visual description. If the room is or seems to be a triangle, how can it then run "into a long narrowing corridor," if the tip of the triangle is the guards' booth? Where is the observer or at least the observation point that can see a triangle both spreading and narrowing? Is the room a reception room? Is the corridor also the hall where the girls sit? What exactly are the spatial relationships of booth, room, hall corridor? Is the room where the girl sits rocking simply another of those rooms behind a steel door? And why does the writer say, "Behind the steel doors, there is life still"? Behind what other doors than that one is there life still? Repairs are necessary.

Conventions

Punctuation problems are the only difficulties this writer has. But punctuation is important here for the reader because the movement and syntax are complex. The writer should examine the punctuation for mistakes, after reviewing the conventions of punctuation, in Chapter 9 (pp. 345–352) in Part II, Guide to Editing and Sentence-Combining.

REWRITING

After weighing the criticism from the instructor and the class, Writer 2 revised the paper.

REVISED VERSION

Writer 2

THE CAVERN

The room draws itself into a triangle. From the wide, glass-enclosed booth that holds the guards, it narrows into a long corridor, walls tucking themselves under, past the rows of bright pink and yellow doors until they meet sharply in a dead end.

The low ceiling, like the floor, is tiled a dull beige. It traps the odors that rise out of the floor and holds them in the air, the disinfectant from the mop pail mingling with the sweat from graying tennis shoes.

The walls are dull green concrete blocks, broken by the lines of steel doors. Painted by a sure, hard hand, their enamel coats, smooth and shiny, are unmarred by graffiti scratches. They have a gaiety inappropriate to the room. A small, high window in each door looks into the hall: so many eyes watching over the children.

The girls in loose jumpers sit, tipped back in green plastic and metal chairs lined up along the hall. Muffled in cotton tennis shoes, feet thump against the concrete. The girls watch the gray metal clock set into the wall above the guards' station. He holds back languidly, hoarding precious minutes, until, pulled against his will, he jerks forward with a loud click. A clattering, followed by distant shouting, rises promisingly in the air, then dies down. Music from a local radio station, piped into the room, settles, mixing with the dirty disinfectant smell. Fingers drumming against the seats of the chairs, the girls watch the miser clock give up his minutes.

Behind the steel door, in the dark, there is life still. No need of paint on this side of the door; the close walls are green-tiled and bare. The room has a thick, dark odor all its own. In the corner, on the cement floor, a young girl in a white nightgown sits rocking back and forth. She is far away, riding her horse through an English meadow, sweet yellow-green dotted with flowers.

CLASS EXERCISES

1. Using the Critical Guide, do a class critique of Writer 4's First Version (pp. 54–56).
2. Using the Critical Guide and working in groups, critique each other's first versions.
3. Compare Writer 2's Revised Version with her First Version. How has she responded to the advice of the critic?

ASSIGNMENT

Stage 6 Toward a Paper on Place: Critiquing and Rewriting
1. **Use the Critical Guide to critique your own paper. (Written or oral critiques from your instructor and classmates are invaluable in guiding your self-critique.)**
2. **Guided by your critiques, rewrite your paper.**

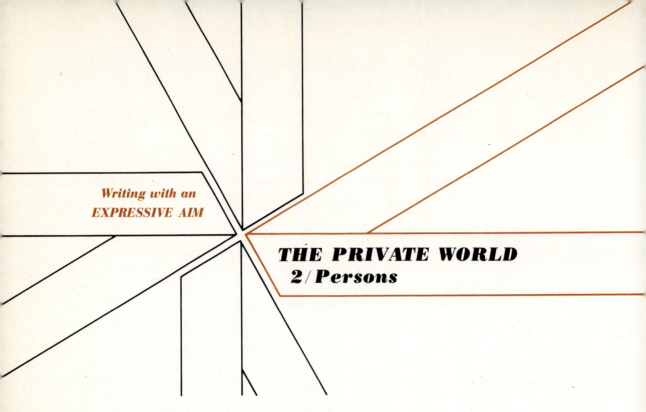

Writing with an EXPRESSIVE AIM

THE PRIVATE WORLD
2/Persons

THE WRITING CONTEXT

We come to know ourselves in the mirror of other people. In their reactions, we see reflected our own ways of behaving, our personalities, our aspirations. But other people are more than mirrors. Every close relationship we have allows us to step through the looking glass. The special persons in our private worlds live at the core of us. Our relationships with the members of our families, our friends, some of our teachers, an employer, or a neighbor can strike deep roots in us and turn our lives in new directions, quickening our deepest emotions. Because the impact of "our people" is so strong in us, we often want to talk or sing or write about these persons. Recall how many poems and songs and paintings are their creators' celebrations of persons in their lives.

In the following poem from Galway Kinnell's *Book of Nightmares*, note the healing power of the "we" over the speaker.

You scream, waking from a nightmare.
When I sleepwalk
into your room, and pick you up,
and hold you up in the moonlight, you cling to me
hard,
as if clinging could save us. I think
you think
I will never die, I think I exude
to you the permanence of smoke or scars,
even as
my broken arms heal themselves around you.[1]

Chapter 2's area of investigation, as the writing context of your second paper, is a relationship that has had strong impact on you.

THE COMPOSING PROCESS

1. Perhaps you discovered how much pondering it takes to find a genuine *starting point* (pp. 21–25) and how easy it is to settle for something superficial.

2. Did you find exploring to be another challenge? If you felt more comfortable using one of the three perspectives (pp. 25–42), you probably tend to see the world more often from that vantage point. But the purpose of the exploratory guide is to expand your vision into new directions.

3. After your exploration, did you allow enough time for incubation (p. 42)? Only you can pace yourself while writing. In this second piece of writing, therefore, you should have a better estimate of how soon you need to start to give your ideas time to germinate. Did you notice that the more extensive your exploration, the more resources you had for insight? If you had trouble *stating your focus* (pp. 42–44), you may need more practice in precise thinking, which always requires great effort.

4. You will again be working with an *audience* (pp. 45–50), *aim* (pp. 44–51), and *mode* (pp. 51–53). The more careful your planning here, the easier your paper will be to write and the better you can criticize the final version.

The following pages will describe students working in each stage of the writing process as they strive to understand the meaning of important relationships.

[1]Galway Kinnell, Part 1 of "Little Sleep—Head Sprouting Hair in the Moonlight," *The Book of Nightmares* (Boston: Houghton Mifflin, 1971), p. 49.

FINDING THE SUBJECT

To choose the relationship you write about, examine your feelings. Ask yourself questions like: Does a past relationship still cause me to tingle or shudder? Does some current relationship excite me, challenge me, irritate me, give me a sense of security?

The following choices were made by five student writers. Writer 1 had been struggling with her confused feelings about her 17-year-old brother's death. Writer 2 felt a strong comfort from a long-time friendship. She wanted to understand how this relationship had affected her development. Writer 3 felt a disappointment and bitterness about her relationship with her mother. Writer 4 admired a high school friend. He wondered why. Writer 5 felt that he had been strongly influenced by an eighth-grade teacher. In each of these cases, the writers followed their emotions to identify relationships that they suspected had somehow shaped a part of themselves. Not until they had completed the entire composing process, however, would they more fully understand those influences.

EXPRESSING THE STARTING POINT

After you have selected the relationship you wish to explore, hone your starting point by two strategies:

1. Identify an aspect of your relationship which challenges one or more of your values or exceeds your expectations.
2. Formulate a question that asks what you would like to understand about this relationship.

STARTING POINTS

Writer 1

MY VALUES OR EXPECTATIONS
—my love of my family, esp. my brother
—my sense that life was secure

ASPECT OF MY RELATIONSHIP WITH MY BROTHER
—the news of my brother's coming death

Question: How did the news of my brother's death influence my outlook on life and my sense of security?

Writer 2

MY VALUES OR EXPECTATIONS
—my need for security and guidance

ASPECT OF MY RELATIONSHIP WITH RHONDA
—the marvelous gift of a friend like Rhonda

Question: To what extent does my friendship with Rhonda exceed or satisfy my need for security and guidance?

Writer 3

MY VALUES OR EXPECTATIONS
—my need for my mother's attention
—my sympathy with woman's liberation

ASPECT OF MY RELATIONSHIP WITH MY MOTHER
—my mother's job

Question: What impact did my mother's job have on my development?

Writer 4

MY VALUES OR EXPECTATIONS
—most kids in high school were into a lot of trouble

ASPECT OF MY RELATIONSHIP WITH JAMES
—James was popular but different

Question: What was so different about James? Why did I admire him?

Writer 5

MY VALUES OR EXPECTATIONS
—a teacher who respects students and helps them

ASPECT OF MY RELATIONSHIP WITH ONE OF MY TEACHERS
—his belligerence and humiliation of members of the class.

Question: How did my eighth-grade teacher help or hinder my growth?

Commentary Writer 1 has identified two deeply rooted values that are challenged by the news of her brother's death. Her question incorporates this challenge and seeks to understand the extent of its impact. The writer already senses that her brother's death did influence her sense of security. What she wants to discover through writing is the precise nature of that influence.

CLASS EXERCISES

1. Examine the Starting Points of Writers 2, 3, 4, and 5.
   • What values or expectations does the writer identify? What dissonances exist for the writers?
   • In what ways do the questions reflect those dissonances?
   • What kind of understanding does each question seek?
2. In order to practice formulating a starting point, select a relationship that is known to the entire class (e.g., historical couple: Franklin and Eleanor Roosevelt; TV characters: Mork and Mindy; literary relationship: Romeo and Juliet).
   • Identify a characteristic of one of the pair that clashes with the values of the other or exceeds the other's expectations.
   • Formulate a question that seeks to understand this dissonance.

ASSIGNMENT

Stage 1 Toward a Paper on Relationship: Finding and Expressing the Starting Point

1. Select a relationship whose impact you want to investigate.
2. Identify an aspect(s) of that relationship that either challenges your values or exceeds your expectations.

3. Write a question that points you toward an eventual understanding or resolution.
4. Seek comments on your starting point from your instructor and classmates.

EXPLORING

To explore your relationship, use the following Exploratory Guide:

EXPLORATORY GUIDE

Static view

—Recall and record the nature of your relationship: what makes it different from all others.
—Describe the other person's physical and personality traits.

Dynamic view

—Trace the stages of your relationship from its beginning to its current state and then speculate on its future potential.
—Analyze the changes that have occurred in both of you as the relationship has developed.

Relative view

—Determine in what classification (personality type, role player) the other person fits as an individual and in relation to you (nurturer, competitor, and so on). Note down your reasons for these classifications.
—Compare and contrast this person with others, or this relationship with other relationships, analyzing the likeness or differences.
—Create at least one analogy for your relationship (something other than another person) with which you can connect your person or your relationship.
—Probe the basis for the analogy.

Writer 1 followed the directions to explore her relationship with her brother.

EXPLORATION

Writer 1

MY BROTHER

STATIC VIEW

—details of learning about my brother's illness
—increasingly frequent visits with my 17 year old brother, Paul, to Children's Hospital
—a worn expression on my father's face

—my mother, at time, seemed depressed and preoccupied
—a gathering of the family in the basement, 5:30 in the evening
  —hesitance
  —my mother's trembling voice—"Paul has leukemia."
  —shock
  —bewilderment
  —a MacDonald's hamburger turning to dust in my mouth
  —spontaneous racking, sobbing
  —a sense of disbelief and unreality
  —the stern facade melting from my father's face, being replaced by
    a soft, vulnerable expression
  —pressing queries filling our minds
  —"Does Paul know what he has?"
  —"What are the doctors doing to alleviate progression of the dis-
    ease?"
  —all medication has been exhausted
  —a fresh effusion of tears
  —anger and bitterness
  —helplessness
  —a realization of the loss at stake—the preciousness and rarity of our
    relationship
  —numbness
  —an attempt to regain lost composure
  —soothing hands comforting exhausted bodies and spent minds
  —an acceptance of our fate
  —a swelling of strength and determination within each of us
  —a release of tension

DYNAMIC VIEW

—Changes
  —a release as family progresses from tension to relief
  —a concerted family will to rise above our burden
  —a whole new perspective on life around me—an aligning of my val-
    ues and priorities
  —a desire to revert back to the "way we were"
  —a strong, overwhelming desire to live each day to the fullest
  —a reluctant sense of acceptance

RELATIVE VIEW

Comparison

The stages we went through to accept the illness were similar to
the stages my brother experienced. He, also, had to cope with denial,
anger and frustration, severe depression, and finally, acceptance, after
learning of the nature of his illness.

Commentary In the static view, the writer concentrates on the details of the family's gathering to confront her brother's death. In this recall, she has indirectly expressed some of her feelings about Paul and noted her family's closeness. She needs to explore her own relationship with her brother, as well as his personality and appearance. Although the dynamic view lists general changes in the family attitude, it makes little note of changes in the writer, lacking examples of "aligning my values and priorities." What values? What priorities? The relative view makes a short comparison between the family's and Paul's stages of acceptance. In what ways did these stages manifest themselves in behavior? Because *analogies* (see Defining Terms) reveal strong feelings, Writer 1 should try to create some for her brother (Paul was like *X*), for her relationship with him (my brother was like *X* to me), or for her process of acceptance (learning to live with my brother's death was like *X*). Writer 1's additions to her Exploration are shown below.

EXPLORATION

Writer 1 **STATIC VIEW**

    —relationship with my brother
        —one year apart
           common interests, friends, experiences
        —no petty rivalries
        —would seek him out for counsel, friendship, pass the time of day
        —shared fears and anxieties
        —liked introducing him as my brother
—Paul's attitude toward death
        —took pleasure in a sunny day
        —never complained
        —relished talking with friends
        —worked to improve his mind & body

DYNAMIC VIEW

—changes in priorities & values
        —spent more time with my family
        —worried less about boyfriends or dates
        —concerned more about compassionate aspect to personality

RELATIVE VIEW

—Paul was like a bridge between me and what I valued

1. Read Writer 2's Exploration.
2. Discuss Writer 2's Exploration.
   - How many specifics about the relationship or the other person are noted?
   - What feelings about the relationship emerge through these details?
   - What other aspects of the relationship could be recalled?
   - What stages of the relationship does the writer remember?
   - What changes are examined?
   - In what ways will the activities noted help the writer to understand the relationship's impact?
   - What classifications, comparisons/contrasts and analogies are made? What do they reveal about the relationships?
3. Using the Exploratory Guide, examine the relationship which the class used for practice in expressing a starting point.

EXPLORATION

Writer 2   **RHONDA**

STATIC VIEW

Features of my friend and our relationship
–female, met in grade school, went to high school together, now both attending college
–reliable, trusting, loving
–stable, strong-willed, secure
–my other half
–impulsive, lively
–an unending explosion of excitement
–overwhelming, amusing
–straightforward and honest—when I seem to be neglecting her or others, she lets me know
–dancing, laughing, poking, joking
–nervous laughter and shrieks of anxiety among frantic ramblings
–anxiety caused by a dance class
–someone to hang around with—discuss classes, movies, guys
–a familiar face in class—makes a class more relaxing to me
–someone to share secrets with—knowing it was safe and secure
–a source of insight to a puzzling problem—how should I break up with this guy that keeps calling me
–a reliable art critic—I'm never satisfied with my work—she helps me see good and bad points
–a source of confidence and comfort

DYNAMIC VIEW

Activities
–holding up walls together at a dance—if we were bored, it was boring
  together
–fighting and forgiving
–a crutch to lean on after a broken heart—suddenly never hearing
  from a guy again
–someone to get me on my tracks after slipping off—loafing all weekend, she helps me see the need to crack down during the week

RELATIVE VIEW

Analogy
–a beacon of light during a dreary day
–a supporting beam to a crumbling bridge
    My friend is like a cat—
    –napping when the craving arises—a finicky fussy feline
    –full of vigor and ready to flare up and lash out at any threatening
      foe—a sometimes sneaky sidekick
    –ready to pounce on obstacles preventing her coveted course
    –faithful companion capable of many fascinating hours

ASSIGNMENT

Stage 2 Toward a Paper on Place: Exploring
1. Examine your relationship from the static, dynamic, and relative perspectives.
2. Record your ideas in specific language.
3. Seek comments on your exploration from your teacher.

**DISCOVERING
AND STATING
THE FOCUS**

INCUBATING

Lack of time creates a major block to finding a significant insight. Even
though you are distracted by many academic demands, if you want to increase your chances for a good focus, you need time for incubation, time to
mull over the ideas you have discovered through exploration.

STATING THE FOCUS

The sharpness of your starting point and the fullness of your exploration
increase your ability to discover an insight. When you find a possible answer
to your starting question, state it in two parts:

1. the *aspect of the relationship* that you decided was important
   (you may want to deal with the relationship as a whole)
2. the *point of significance* that best answers your original question
   or expresses new meaning you have discovered

	SUBJECT	POINT OF SIGNIFICANCE
Writer 1	My family's sharing of grief over my brother's death	helped me to accept it and caused me to realign my values.
Writer 2	My friendship with Rhonda	offered me guidance, security and love.
Writer 3	My mother's job	had a bad influence on me.
Writer 4	My friendship with James	enabled me to pick up many good traits he possessed.
Writer 5	My eighth-grade teacher's unusual style	eventually caused us to learn a great deal.

Commentary Writer 2's Focus goes little beyond her starting question, which asked: "To what extent does my friendship with Rhonda exceed or satisfy my need for security and guidance?" The first part commits the writer to discussing the friendship as a whole, possible but perhaps too ambitious. The second part does not resolve the dissonance, which suggested that the friendship might have exceeded her expectations.

Writer 3's point of significance is too vague. What kind of "bad influence"?

Writer 3's revised focus read:

My mother's job	burdened me with adult responsibilities and never allowed me to have a close relationship with her.

CLASS EXERCISES

1. Review the Focuses of Writers 1, 4, and 5.
   • What aspects of the subject have been selected? Why?
   • How do the points of significance answer their starting questions?
2. Consider the following alternative statements of focus:
   a. The news of my brother's death was troubling.
   b. James's good traits.
   c. One of my teachers was great.
   d. I value my friendship with Rhonda.
   • In what ways do they compare with the ones above?
   • Are they better formulations? Why or why not?

3. From your class exploration of a public relationship, practice formulating some focuses.

ASSIGNMENT

Stage 3 **Toward a Paper on Relationship: Discovering and Stating the Focus**
1. After allowing time for incubation, state your focus in two parts:
   a. The aspect (or whole) of the relationship that you are going to focus on.
   b. The point of significance that answers your original question.
2. Seek comments on your focus from your instructor.

PLANNING FOR AIM AND AUDIENCE

THE EXPRESSIVE AIM

Writing that concentrates on relationships can adopt any of the aims. You can, for example, adopt the literary aim and turn personal experience into a short story or poem. Or you can adopt the expository aim and write a paper on, say, "The Working Mother." The latter choice would, of course, require a good deal of outside reading at the very least; your own core experience could not furnish all the information an audience would rightly expect from such a paper. In this chapter, you will see students again working with the *expressive aim*, emphasizing their feelings, beliefs, insights into their relationships. In order to gain experience in writing with the expressive aim, we ask you to assume it again in this paper on a relationship.

CHOOSING AN AUDIENCE

If you had difficulties in choosing an audience for the last paper, remember that you are learning to juggle several balls at the same time; if one bounced on your toe or banged your shins, don't be discouraged. Practice may not make perfect, but it makes things easier each succeeding time.

When you write about relationships, you may find the choice of audience easier. Recall that the principle by which you chose an audience before was, "Who would benefit most from sharing my focus?" As some of the student examples will illustrate, that question can be easier to answer here because we tend to cast people into the roles they play for us. Turn back to p. 73 and look at the statements of focus. Notice how each writer has defined the other person in the relationship as playing either a supporting or a threatening role.

This pattern can be seen more clearly if we cast the relationships into a framework:

Writer	Voice of the writer	Role of the other person	Function of the other person
1	One who needs to be a member of a permanent family unit	My brother as a dying boy	A threat
2	One who needs a model and helper	Rhonda as my friend	A support
3	One who needs love & guidance	My mother as a worker	A threat
4	One who needs a role model	James as superior	A support
5	One who needs guidance & inspiration	My teacher as challenger	A support

Even the framework is deceptive; all five writers are working with a threat. Three are writing about people who reduced the threats the writers felt (the threat to Writer 2's need for a model and helper, to Writer 4's need for identity, to Writer 5's need for guidance and inspiration).

If we follow the principle that an audience should be those who will profit most from sharing a focus, then the best audience for each paper will be those who see themselves in these situations. The second column defines the audiences.

Our writers did, more or less, choose their audiences in this fashion. For example, Writer 1 said, "I want to write for anyone who faces or will face the death of a member of his or her family." That's a very large audience; everyone will face a death in the family sometime. The choice will not help the writer select and develop material. Writer 2 said, "I write for all lonely teenage girls." That's a vague choice; not all lonely teenage girls can or should solve their problem with a consuming friendship. The choice doesn't seem helpful. Writer 4 said, "I will write for people my age [18] who are floundering, unsure of their own attitudes because they have no one left that they admire to imitate." That's an exact choice—people with the same problem, not just people in the same situation. It's a good guess that 18-year-olds who *have had* his problem will be the largest group; 18-year-olds who still have the problem are, one would think, less numerous. This means that he and the bulk of his audience will be looking back together, not facing a current problem in which the writer is expected to prescribe an immediate cure.

ANALYZING THE AUDIENCE

Analysis of the audience can be easier this time, not only because you have been through it once, but because the choice of audience has narrowed the possibilities. If the proper audience for your paper in this chapter is one that shares your role relationship to the other person, then there cannot be much difference between your values in this kind of relationship and the audience's values.

At the risk of repetition, we point out that you can complicate the analysis by choosing what we called above a *secondary* audience—for example, the working mother instead of the son or daughter of the working mother. We urge you not to do so because you would be unnecessarily complicating the writing process—*unnecessarily* because the secondary audience will be affected anyway by overhearing what you say to the primary audience. If a writer, playing the role of dependent son or daughter, writes to a primary audience of dependent sons and daughters and writes well, the secondary audience of working mothers will be affected, even though it is not the target audience.

You probably learned from your audience analysis in Chapter 1 that the most important question in the Audience Guide (reviewed below) is the one in which you determine the role of your audience and your voice. This time, if you have made a reasonably narrow and exact choice of audience, A and B will be easy. But C will be as difficult as ever because you are going to have to choose a role that suits speaking to someone who is much like you and yet a stranger.

AUDIENCE GUIDE

A. Analyze the audience in relation to itself.
  1. What are the levels and types of experiences that my audience has had (cultural, professional, recreational, educational, and so on)?
  2. What hierarchy of values does my audience possess or profess (money making and power, friendship, security, intellectual growth, and so on)? It is important to distinguish, if possible, between what an audience holds dear and what it professes to hold dear, if indeed there is a difference. Does the audience hide one set of values under another? If so, the writer's task grows more complicated.
B. Analyze the audience in relation to the subject.
  1. What opinion does my audience have on my subject?
  2. How strongly does my audience hold that opinion?
  3. How willing to act on its opinion is my audience—if acting is appropriate?
C. Considering what you have learned from your answers to A and B, determine what role your audience should play in relation to your voice as writer (peer, authority, subordinate, familiar, and so on).

The key question here is whether you will try to instruct the members of your audience (and, therefore, appear superior to them) or simply share your experience and let them profit as they may (and, therefore, appear as an equal). Bear in mind that readers don't generally like to be preached at and that moralizing is foreign to the expressive aim.

Writer 1   THOSE WHO FACE THE DEATH OF LOVED ONES

A. **Audience in itself**
   1. **All kinds of experience, but most important, they face the experience of death of a loved one.**
   2. **All kinds of values, but in this case they have two constant values: They value human life and they don't want to lose a loved one.**
B. **Audience in relation to subject**
   1. **They are frightened and bewildered by the subject.**
   2. **Very strongly.**
   3. **Very strongly.**
C. **The audience should listen to my advice, since I coped with their problem. They will play the role of one not experienced. My voice will be as an expert.**

Commentary What the writer says is probably true. But the too large choice of audience begins to take its toll here. All the list really says is that no one likes to lose someone he or she loves; that is so obvious as to be useless. Answer C is an invitation to failure: does the writer really have a universal cure for fear and grief? Unlikely.

The writer seems to be looking forward to a persuasive aim—"should listen to my advice."

Writer 2   LONELY TEENAGE GIRLS

A. **Audience in itself**
   1. **The same as mine.**
   2. **That loneliness is bad.**
B. **Audience in relation to subject**
   1. **They don't know Rhonda so they can't hold an opinion about her, but they must believe that friendship is better than loneliness.**

2. They will hold that opinion about friendship very strongly.

3. I think they would be willing to act.

C. I will tell them, as a friend, what a friend can do for a lonely teen-ager.

Commentary   The analysis shows the defects of a bad choice of audience. Not all lonely teenagers hold the values of all other lonely teenagers, and our writer is not even a lonely teenager; she has Rhonda, after all.

The exploratory list Writer 2 generated doesn't seem to offer any advice about how to obtain a friend like Rhonda; it simply lists the glories of having a friend like Rhonda. Praise of a relationship with Rhonda is likely to make another lonely teenager even more lonely because she doesn't have a Rhonda.

The writer is not really using the guide. She's going through the motions mechanically. That's a waste of time—and usually a sign that the writer ought to go back a step in the process and review earlier choices. When a writer gives empty answers, it means that he or she has already made up his or her mind, consciously or unconsciously, what that paper is going to look like, without the benefit of any later step.

AUDIENCE ANALYSIS

Writer 4   PEOPLE MY AGE WHO LACK ROLE MODELS

A. Audience in itself
   1. All types and levels, but they will know that they spent a lot of time looking for answers to questions that confused them.
   2. They have to believe, just because they share my problem, that nobody should have to live without a sense of identity, without some sort of core idea of who you are and how you should act.

B. Audience in relation to subject
   1. As I said above, they have to believe that nobody should have to live as a zero.
   2. Very strongly because it is a painful state to be in.
   3. They would be willing to do almost anything to find an answer that would suggest positive action.

C. Only a peer relationship will work here. If the audience are strangers, they aren't strangers to the problem, and I'm not going to gain anything by pretending to be superior to them. I just got lucky and found a solution. I will discuss the solution, showing what benefits I received.

The analysis already points to an aim (expressive) and to a mode (descriptive); notice that the writer says that he will show "what benefits I received," suggesting a division into specific parts, the method of description. In his answer to C, the writer seems to have narrowed his audience to those who have not solved the common problem. There's nothing wrong with that. The effectiveness of a piece of writing cannot be judged by the number of people who will be affected by it immediately. Furthermore, the narrower the audience, the easier it is to write effectively. A child of 12 knows that it is easier to explain a problem to one parent than to two and easier to explain to two parents than to every parent in town, and so on.

CLASS EXERCISES

1. Study Writer 5's Audience Analysis.
2. Discuss the Audience Analysis of Writer 5.
   • Why was the choice of audience a good or poor one?
   • What other background information or values could have been noted?
   • What information is missing from the audience's attitude toward the subject?
   • What voice will the writer assume?
3. As a class, choose a suitable audience for a focus on the public relationship you have been analyzing. Practice using the Audience Guide.

AUDIENCE ANALYSIS

Writer 5   **CLASSMATES**

A. **Audience in itself**
   1. They all had good heads.
   2. They wanted to learn.
B. **Audience in relation to the subject**
   1. All had their own opinions of Mr. B.
   2. They held those very strongly.
   3. They were very willing to act.
C. **They will listen to me as a peer who went through the same experience.**

ASSIGNMENT

Stage 4 Toward a Paper on Relationship: Planning for Aim and Audience
1. **Choose your audience by selecting the person or group who would profit most from sharing your focus.**
2. **Using the Audience Guide, analyze your audience.**
3. **Seek comments on your analysis from your instructor.**
4. **Keep your expressive aim in mind.**

CHOOSING A MODE OF ORGANIZATION

Although writing about relationships can adopt any of the modes, narrative often works well. We all know that relationships are changing, dynamic. How, for example, do you deal with a dying brother as a static relationship? Or a teacher whom you *suspect* on the first day, *like* on the tenth, *trust* on the thirtieth, and *regard as a guide and inspiration* on the fortieth?

The students writing in this chapter used either the narrative or the descriptive mode, as one would expect. A relationship, from one point of view, has a history; tracing the history calls for the narrative mode. On the other hand, in some relationships the history has little significance, the importance lying in perhaps widely spaced moments or sudden insights that emerged when the writer looked back over the course of the relationship. In that case the descriptive mode is appropriate. The writer divides the relationship into its major phases or effects and treats them as separate parts, the product of reflection on the whole. In either mode the parts or the events must be connected so that the account flows smoothly.

MAINTAINING UNITY AND COHERENCE

Any mode of organization requires unity and coherence, virtues that manifest themselves in orderly sentences and paragraphs that connect neatly with one another. Let's examine how the ideas of unity and coherence appear in sentences and paragraphs.

Crucial to both unity and coherence is the *focus* that you have worked toward. A focus is a planned route on which your sentences and paragraphs will travel; the focus sets a direction and it sets boundaries for the selection of ideas, examples, and lines of reasoning. A focus is a commitment you make to the members of your audience; it sets up their expectations. When you maintain that commitment, satisfy their expectations, the paper has *unity*.

Whenever an idea, example, or fact wanders beyond the boundaries of the first or second part of the focus, unity vanishes. If Writer 2, for example, writes of Rhonda's childhood, she violates her commitment to write about their friendship. If she writes of Rhonda's influence on other people, she violates her pledge to discuss Rhonda's gifts to her. Unity, in other words, is a matter of selecting material.

Coherence is a matter of putting the selected material in the right order with the right connectives. *Coherence* means literally "to stick together." The basic elements of the written piece are so clearly related that (1) the reader is never confused and (2) the paper moves forward in an orderly fashion. Thus, the total paper is like a chain, each unit interlinking with the one before it.

Repetition

The simplest device for tying both sentences and paragraphs together is *repetition:* something in the preceding unit is repeated in the succeeding unit. That something is usually a single word. You move from one unit to another by

1. repeating an important word, or
2. substituting a pronoun for an important word, or
3. using a synonym for an important word

If you have difficulty in tying the units together, perhaps the ideas are not really related. Then it's time to reexamine the order.

Why is there any need to tie sentences and paragraphs together? Because when you construct a sentence or paragraph, you are practicing *division*. To put a period at the end of a sentence or to indent for a new paragraph is to say to the reader, "Here ends this idea or set of ideas. What follows is different." But, of course, it is not completely different or it wouldn't follow. After dividing, you must join.

If we look back at the final version of "The Cavern" (pp. 62–63), we can see the writer developing coherence. Inside the paragraphs, sentences are tied together by repetition. In the first paragraph, for example, the subject of the sentence, *it*, repeats the subject of the first sentence, *room*. The same practice links the two sentences of the second paragraph. In the third paragraph, the last phrase of the first sentence, *steel door,* is echoed in *their enamel coats, they,* and *each door* in succeeding sentences. In addition, paragraphs that might not seem to be closely related are tied together by repetition. The "hall" in the last sentence of the third paragraph appears again in the first sentence of the fourth paragraph.

Writers' desires to get where they want to go often destroy coherence. They know where their papers are going; their readers do not. Anxious to get on, writers sometimes ignore the fact that the readers know only what has gone before and that they need to be shown continually how what is now appearing relates to what has gone before.

The most obvious type of repetition—one so common that we often overlook it—is grammatical. A piece of writing flows smoothly and coherently when there are no abrupt shifts in *number, person,* or *tense* to confuse the reader. There are only two grammatical numbers in English—singular and plural. The flow breaks down most frequently when a pronoun and its antecedent do not agree, as when singular antecedents like *everyone, one,* and *none* are followed by a plural pronoun, most commonly *they.* There are three grammatical persons: the first stands for the writer (*I, we*); the second for the person spoken to (*you*); and the third for the person or thing spoken of (all other pronouns and all nouns). The common problem here is forgetting who is talking to whom about what: "You start out right, but then you forget, even though we know that one should not . . . ." The writer's point of view should be consistent. A tense sequence should also be consistent. A narrative paper that begins in the present tense should stay there and not shift to the past tense. The common problem with tense, however, lies not in shifts occurring between but *inside* sentences, as in "Being convinced of the corruption, he resigned his office." The writer means, "Convinced of the corruption, he resigned his office." If you don't know why the second version is better, consult Defining Terms (pp. 403–416) and discover the difference between present and perfect participles.

Paragraphing

The problem of continuity is most apparent in the *paragraph*, a series of statements (sentences) about a central idea. A good paragraph, like an entire paper, will adhere to a focus and therefore will show unity; to the unity it will add coherence. Let's take those points one at a time:

1. *Unity of paragraphs.* There should be nothing in the paragraph that does not deal directly with the focus of the paper. In addition, there should be nothing in the paragraph that does not deal with the *aspect* of the focus addressed in the paragraph, which is really a subsection, one division of the subject matter the focus encompasses. In a paragraph that discusses Rhonda's loyalty, for example, a statement about Rhonda's intelligence would be out of place.
2. *Coherence in paragraphs.* Obviously, there is no coherence without unity. First, select for unity, then write for coherence. To achieve coherence, keep always in mind the basic structure of a paragraph: a series of related sentences that includes:
   a. a core sentence of greater generality than any other sentence, often the first sentence;
   b. a number of sentences of lesser generality supporting the core sentence.

Here, for example, is a paragraph from *Guide to Women's Publishing:*

> *[1] There is no one phrase, not even a short paragraph, that can capture the essence of* Earth's Daughters, *a feminist literary and art periodical. [2] It comes in all shapes, contains all manner of art, and is published at all times. [3] Issue No. 4 was a little anthology of one woman: "Robinson on the Woman Question": short poems in a 6 × 4 format. [4] Double issue No. 5/6 was a heady collection of poetry and some rather interesting art work, which featured xerox reproduction of common household objects. [5]* Earth's Daughters *specializes in surprise and unusual formats.*[2]

[2] Polly Joan and Andrea Chesman, *Guide to Women's Publishing* (Paradise, Calif.: Dust Books, 1978), pp. 25–26.

The five sentences exist at three levels of generality:

Sentence 1. This is the core sentence, the statement of broadest generality.

Sentence 2. This sentence comments on sentence 1; it is, therefore, on a lower level of generality—that is, it is *subordinate* to sentence 1.

Sentence 3. This sentence illustrates sentence 2 and is, therefore, on a lower level of generality than sentence 2; by now we have reached the lowest level of generality—the most concrete level—that this paragraph offers.

Sentence 4. This sentence also illustrates sentence 2; it is, therefore, subordinate to sentence 2 but coordinate with sentence 3.

Sentence 5. This sentence is coordinate with sentence 2; that is, it exists on the same level of generality as sentence 2, a higher level than sentences 3 and 4.

In outline form, the paragraph would look like this:

1 Highest level of generality
   2 Middle level of generality
      3 Lowest level of generality
      4 Lowest level of generality
   5 Middle level of generality

Notice that all the sentences are related. Sentence 2 is a development of sentence 1; sentences 3 and 4 are developments of sentence 2; sentence 5 generalizes from sentences 3 and 4. No sentence stands alone.

Transitions in paragraphs

The sentences in a good paragraph are tied together by a third element: *transitions*. On pp. 81–82, in suggesting that *repetition* is the simplest device for tying sentences and paragraphs together, we were speaking of *transition*, which means "getting across," that is, bridging gaps. Transitions are important for the entire piece of writing as well as individual paragraphs.

Notice the transitions in our sample paragraph:

1. Sentence 2 connects with sentence 1 by using the pronoun *It* to repeat a noun, *Earth's Daughters*, from the first sentence.
2. Sentences 3 and 4 are linked by the same beginning grammatical construction (indicating that they are coordinate):

   Issue No. 4 was . . .
   Double issue No. 5/6 was . . .

3. Sentence 5 links with sentence 2 by beginning with the noun, *Earth's Daughters*, that sentence 2 refers to in its opening pronoun.

These internal signals tell the reader where the writer is going and remind the reader where writer and reader have been. There are also "external" signals, links that the writer may insert to indicate direction of movement. A simple *then* at the beginning of a sentence signals a forward movement in time. *Therefore* signals a movement from a limited statement to a larger one, usually to a conclusion. *However* signals a reversal. With the aid of such signals, the writer can construct a unified, coherent paragraph, as well as an entire essay.

CLASS
EXERCISES
1. Read Writer 5's First Version.
2. Examine Writer 5's First Version for unity, coherence, and paragraphing.
   - What mode of organization is used? Has it been maintained? If not, how has the pattern been broken? How could it be restored?
   - What techniques to maintain coherence has the writer used? For example, show how full paragraphs and individual sentences are tied together by repetition. Where is coherence lacking?
   - How is the paragraphing structured? How many levels of generality has the writer used in his paragraphs?
   - How does the paper maintain unity? What sentences, if any, violate the commitment of the focus?

FIRST VERSION

Writer 5

TYRANT

We were in a peculiar state of shock that second day of classes, and for good reason. Mr. B. stood in front of us, drumming his broad fingers on the podium, beaming his sinester satisfied grin over our anxious faces. Just what he was up to no one knew, but he was up to something; he scraped his fingers through that full black beard of his to let you know that. All eyes were upon him, all ears attuned to his footsteps as slowly he began circling the room. Some pretended to be searching through their notes to avoid eye contact, just as I was when the footsteps came to a casual halt just behind my back.

A huge hand came over my shoulder and flipped through the pages of my homework. It traced certain words, paused over a few passages, rubbed the paper as if checking the thickness, and finally resumed the tedious drumming on the top of my desk. Except for the deadly looks I shot at those who saw humor in my situation I didn't move a muscle. I could feel him breathing on my back. The hand stopped drumming its fingers and picked up my notebook by the corner of one page of my homework. Holding it aloft long enough to build a suitable dramatic tension, in a deep voice that always had a hint of sarcasm in it, he spoke his first words to me, "What is this, Mr. Humbert?" I replied timidly that it was my homework assignment. "No, Mr. Humbert," (apparently I had misunderstood the question.) "This is chicken scratching, Mr. Humbert, chicken scratching." (He was talking about my handwriting.) After one last vain attempt to make out what I had written, he shook the page loose sending my notebook flying across the room, crumpled it up, and casually tossed it in the other direction. He then informed me that I could retrieve my homework. I sat motionless trying to contain my anger. When he asked why I hadn't gone to get my notebook, I explained that he had indicated no specific time I should do so, and not wishing to appear presumptuous, I didn't. Having made my point I got up. To my surprise, nothing more was ever said about my handwriting.

The rest of the year continued in much the same manner, extended periods of silence just before the hammer fell on some unsuspecting victim, and abusive treatment for those who had committed some small indiscretion or who had the catastrophic misfortune of being caught. It wasn't long before the eighth grade, tired of this unwarrented persecution, turned its thoughts to revenge. We reasoned that the best way to shoot him down would be to catch him making mistakes in class. We'd hit him in his home territiory; nobody got the best of the eighth grade.

So we all studied like hell and even assigned specialists to certain fields; dates to Mike, battles to Steve, opinion and press to Earl, and foreign policy to Pete. The moments we caught him were few and far between, but when we did everybody felt a great sense of satisfaction. Justice had been reckoned.

On the day of the Civil War debate class morale was low. We all had the third quarter blues and as if that wasn't enough, Mr. B. was on a rampage. The day before, he had thrown Steve out of class for not doing his homework. (He had drop-kicked Steve's book out into the hall. When Steve went out to get it, Mr. B. closed the door behind him and locked it.) Now it was decided that Mr. B. would take a seat on the North side of the debate. He was killing us. Everything the South came up with he had a counter for. Just when it seemed all was lost, he made one little mistake. The debate was supposedly to take place in 1860, but Mr. B. quoted from Lincoln's Emancipation Proclamation (1863). Mike rose from his desk and remained standing until Mr. B. recognized him; then he pointed out the mistake. We were allowed to carry on the debate by ourselves from that point on. Mr. B. also began treating us a little more like human beings and student teacher relations improved almost to normal.

We learned a lot from Mr. B.; a lot more than most of us were willing to give him credit for until the last day of class when he actually apologized for any hard feelings his unorthodox methods of teaching may have caused. He went on to say he was proud of the way we refused to knuckle under to his tyranny and he regretted he wouldn't be back next year to have us as ninth graders. We weren't sorry to see him go then, but what a time we would have had in ninth grade.

REFINING THE EXPRESSIVE STYLE

When we talk of constructing sentences and paragraphs, we are talking of *style*. Style is another name for the results of a series of choices you have made in selecting words and ways of arranging them in sentences and paragraphs. Many make those choices unconsciously; knowing aim and audience brings those choices to the surface, enabling the writer to make more and better choices.

Stylistic choices are an inescapable fact of language. If you choose to write *steal* instead of *rip off*, that's a stylistic choice; knowing your audience helps you to make the choice. If you choose to refer to the reader as *you*, instead of linking yourself with him and writing *we*, or impersonalizing your relationship and referring to him, you, and the world as *one* ("One should note that . . ."), those are stylistic choices that should have been determined by considerations of aim and audience. Each choice shapes in some way the voice you project. We will deal here with the stylistic characteristics of the expressive aim.

Expressive writing uses many first-person pronouns—*I*, *me*, *mine*, *us*, *our*, and so on. In harmony with this, the expressive writer often emphasizes his or her *idiolect*, a language unique to the writer. All of us have habits of speech that enable our friends to identify us; it is these habits that the expressive writer indulges. In addition, the expressive writer searches for figures of speech (see Defining Terms), for imaginative comparisons; the writer is dealing with feelings, and feelings are difficult to convey adequately in literal statements. The expressive writer leans heavily on concrete diction, for reasons that follow.

If your aim in writing about a relationship is expressive, the voice you project must imply to the members of the audience that you and they share, have shared, or will share a common experience, and that you are about to outline that experience and share with them an insight that offers a point of view, a solution, or a consolation. If you set out to do that, then you will write to the audience not as a superior or an inferior but as one who has been through a common experience. The danger here is "talking down" to your audience. Remember that your advantage is not one of greater wisdom or strength but of *time:* you have lived through what some of them are living through or will live through. And if part of your audience has already lived through the common experience, you haven't even that advantage.

INFLATED DICTION

"Talking down" to an audience manifests itself as inflated diction.

1. The writer falls into this trap by using words that are outside the vocabulary of the audience—not just "big" words but rare words.

2. The writer uses words that may seem common enough but appear to have technical meanings when they occur in combination. For example, there's nothing wrong with the word *individual* by itself so long as it is used precisely. *Individual* is not a synonym for *person;* it means one person set off from all groups and considered as unique. If that's what you mean, use the word. But notice what happens when the word occurs in a combination such as "An individual raised in an environment that . . . ." If you write like that in an expressive paper, the voice you project is that of a sociologist; suddenly whatever contact you had with your audience may evaporate because you are implying a clinical, detached, superior, "scientific," perhaps even a statistical approach to a common human experience. You have, so to speak, gone expository.

3. The writer chooses words that are too general, too abstract, or too grand for the idea or emotion they attempt to capture. Inflated diction makes the writer look foolish. For example, Writer 1's First Version is afflicted with inflated diction:

a sharing of grievous emotions
when anxieties were soon substantiated
the crushing news engulfed us
to eliminate a sense of disbelief and unreality
to alleviate the progression
a fresh effusion of tears
a total realignment of my values and priorities

CLICHÉS

Clichés also mar any style but especially the expressive. Probably no one deliberately tries to sound like everyone else (and, therefore, like no one in particular), but many writers do so by using clichés, that is, trite, stale, overworked expressions:

wise as an owl
last but not least
it was an experience I will never forget
the passing scene

You can use these phrases without thinking—or, more exactly, when you use them you are *not* thinking. Clichés have usually been emptied of content by overuse, and their use has the fatal effect of making you sound like nobody. This is especially dangerous in the expressive aim, in which you must establish a believable and individual, if not unique, voice. The diction of the expressive aim in particular needs to be not only clear but vigorous and attractive. Trite expressions come up to none of these three standards.

Writer 1's use of clichés makes her sound like a stranger to her own experience:

impending death	meant the world to me
loved one	petty rivalries
hurting more than helping	wise counsel
sense of foreboding	broke my spirit
complete shock	burst of swelling pride
racking sobbing	continued effort
stern facade	the fate that had befallen us
torturing my mind	release of tension
filled with panic	heavy burden

CLASS
EXERCISE

1. Study the list of inflated phrases and clichés above in the context of Writer 1's First Version below.
   • Discuss ways in which these undesirable phrases and clichés can be turned into concrete diction (see below).

FIRST VERSION

Writer 1

LEARNING OF THE NATURE OF MY BROTHER'S ILLNESS

Every family, at one time or another, is confronted with the impending death of one of its members, and must learn to cope with the situation in their own way. Some families try to escape from the inevitable separation from their loved one by running from doctor to doctor in an effort to secure a favorable diagnosis. Others try to ignore the knowledge of the illness, and hope that it will "go away." These unrealistic approaches usually end up hurting more than helping. My family was faced with the imminent death of my seventeen year old brother, Paul, almost two years ago. Through a sharing of grievous emotions, we were gradually able to face the reality of his terminal illness, and come to an acceptance of it together.

For three years, my sister, Donna, and I had not been forced to deal with the exact nature of Paul's illness. He had been diagnosed with leukemia on June 30, 1970, but my parents simply told us that he had a "blood disorder." Outside of Paul's frequent hospital visits, our lives, from the time of the diagnosis, hadn't changed significantly. Occasionally, I experienced an unfounded sense of foreboding, but I wanted to remain ignorant of my qualms. These anxieties were soon substantiated. One evening about 5:30, my parents returned home with Paul from Children's Hospital. Paul was not feeling well, and immediately went to bed. My parents explained that they had something very important to discuss with my sister and me. We gathered together at a table in the basement. We sat in silence for a moment as my mother hesitated to speak, and then, suddenly, her voice broke, and trembled that my older brother was fighting a losing battle with leukemia. The complete shock that was registered in my sister's face must have been echoed in my own. I was eating at the time, and was aware of a MacDonald's hamburger turning to dust in my mouth. Looks of bewilderment passed between Donna and I as the crushing news engulfed us. We were spontaneously filled with racking sobbing, and desperately wished that someone would tell us the prognosis was wrong, that the whole thing was a terrible mistake. I couldn't seem to eliminate a sense of disbelief and unreality. My mother appeared exhausted and defeated after having made this revelation. The stern facade had melted from my father's face, and was replaced by a look of tenderness and vulnerability. We then began to question our parents. Did Paul know what he had? What were the doctors doing to alleviate the progression of the disease? I whispered the question that was torturing my mind, "Aren't they going to do *anything* to help him?" My father sighed as he explained that every available medication had been exhausted. His words brought a fresh effusion of tears as my sister and I were consumed with anger and overwhelming bitterness that my brother should have to suffer with this illness, and that we could do nothing to help him. I was filled with panic at the realization of the loss that was at stake. My close relationship with Paul meant the world to me. Being only a year apart, we enjoyed so many common interests—school, friends, experiences. We never engaged in the petty rivalries characteristic of many brothers and sisters. Instead, I would often seek him out for wise counsel, friendship, or just to pass the time of day. Our relationship was precious and rare. It broke my spirit to think that there would come a time when I could no longer feel that burst of swelling pride I had always felt in introducing him as my brother.

A moment of numbness preceded a communal effort to regain lost composure after the discovery. My mother's hands attempted to comfort our exhausted bodies, and to soothe our spent minds. We knew that we had no choice but to reluctantly accept the fate that had befallen us. A swelling of strength and determination emerged from each of us as a result of our commitment, and we could all sense the tremendous release of tension in the atmosphere now that things were out in the open. We had acquired a heavy burden, but the concerted family will to rise above it made the load seem lighter.

It was as though I was seeing the world with different eyes as a result of this revelation. My perspective on life around me had changed drastically. I experienced a total realignment of my values and priorities, and was stunned by the realization of how very precious my family was to me. Even though I would always be able to allot time to homework and friends, I realized that moments spent with my family created memories that were irretrievable. I cannot say that I didn't wish every day that we could revert back to the "way we were." We couldn't be carefree and lighthearted as we were before Paul was stricken with leukemia. We had a great concern to deal with, and it added a deeper, more compassionate aspect to our personalities. Paul taught us how to make the best of the situation, and never complained of his misfortune. Instead, he took pleasure in a sunny day, relished talking with his friends, and he continually worked to improve his mind and body. He was our constant source of strength, support, and comfort. He truly lived each day to the fullest, and left us a beautiful philosophy to live by.

The stages that our family passed through in learning to accept Paul's terminal illness were similar to those that Paul, himself, had to cope with. Shock and bewilderment are usually characteristic of both the patient's and the family's initial reaction to the revelation. The next stage seems to be denial, followed by anger and frustration, severe depression, and finally, when both parties realize there is no other choice, acceptance. Being able to talk and cry together at times will make the family much more comfortable about the impending separation. The more the grief can be expressed before death, the less unbearable it becomes afterward.

CONCRETE DICTION

Expressive writing usually depends on *concrete diction* for its effectiveness. When you choose the most specific and evocative word or phrase from among your available choices, your diction is concrete. For example, in each of the following lists, the last item is the most concrete:

> vehicle, car, old car, old Oldsmobile, 1938 Oldsmobile, a 1938 Oldsmobile sedan with a broken right headlight
> light, dim light, glow

The two examples illustrate the two different ways of making a relatively abstract word or phrase more concrete:

1. adding words to more sharply define the image or concept
2. choosing a more specific word

Words that more sharply define the image are *evocative;* that is, they evoke things that simple specificity does not. It is possible to be specific without being concrete. Relentlessly specific prose by itself can produce endless inventories that only seem to convey ideas and images clearly to the reader: "I, John Jones, a white male, 20 years old, was walking down Main Street in Cleveland, Ohio, at 6:30 P.M., on August 15, 1978." Specific but not evocative. Here are concrete versions of that sentence:

One steamy afternoon last summer I was sauntering down Main
Street.

I sloshed down Main Street late one rainy afternoon last summer.

On August 15, 1978, I was running down Main Street in Cleveland,
frantic to reach home before dark.

There are dozens of other possibilities. Notice that in each version the concreteness issues from offering the reader a relatively exact notion of who was doing what, where, when, under what conditions, and in what manner—perhaps even for what reason. But not all parts of the sentences are equally concrete. The principle is that what the writer wishes to emphasize should be expressed as concretely as possible.

In the versions above, we arbitrarily assumed that the manner of walking was important; therefore, we selected more specific and evocative verbs: *sauntering, sloshed, running.* In the first two versions we assumed that the date and place were not important; in the last version we assumed it was. Making the date specific, you will notice, conveys to the reader that the date *is* important; the reader becomes curious about the date.

Specificity and evocativeness spring from careful attention to (1) concrete nouns and verbs and (2) modifiers that will make the nouns and verbs even more concrete. You choose the best noun or verb available for your purpose and then make it better by additions, if necessary:

I climbed over the fence into the alley.

There is nothing wrong with that sentence so long as all it is intended to do in the paper is indicate that you went from one place to another, over an obstacle. There is, however, very little for the readers to see exactly; the readers simply note that you say you went over a fence to get to an alley. If you want the readers to see and, therefore, become engaged in the experience, there are three units in that sentence that could be made more concrete: two nouns and a verb.

The verb *climbed* is very vague. Did you leap or scramble or claw or inch your way over? (Notice that the more exact verb helps define the following noun more clearly—a person cannot leap the fence that he must scramble over; the verb suggests the height of the fence.)

The first noun is *fence.* Was it tall or low, made of pickets, chain links, bricks, concrete blocks? The second noun is *alley.* Was it wide or narrow, light or dark, clean or littered? If littered, littered with what?

In a sentence in which the nouns and verbs are the most concrete available to you, increased concreteness can be achieved by adding words that do one of three things:

1. add a detail (fence $\longrightarrow$ a picket fence)

2. add a quality (fence $\longrightarrow$ a picket fence $\longrightarrow$ a rotting picket fence)
3. add a comparison (fence $\longrightarrow$ a picket fence $\longrightarrow$ a rotting picket fence $\longrightarrow$ a rotting picket fence leaning toward me at a drunken angle)

Using concrete diction can help solve one very troublesome problem that all writers face: adjusting their diction to the reader. If concreteness were simply a matter of selecting the absolutely specific word for an idea or concept, there would be no problem. Perfect writers would communicate perfectly with perfect readers. But neither writers nor readers are perfect. Concrete diction offers a solution to that dilemma.

For example, suppose you are trying to describe a roommate who is driving you crazy with constant compulsive neatness. You might do it with one word: *meticulous*. It's a "perfect" word: based on the Latin root *metus* (fear), it means a person who is compelled to be neat out of a fear of being found wanting. But suppose your audience doesn't know what *meticulous* means? Then it simply looks like a big word, perhaps an insult to the readers. You could, of course, try *neat*, but that isn't what you mean totally. The solution is to be concrete: Describe what it is your roommate *does*. Whatever your readers' vocabulary, they will understand the concrete details at their own level of diction.

CLASS EXERCISES

1. Examine the diction in the First Versions of Writers 2 and 4.
2. Compare and contrast the diction of Writers 2 and 4.
   • What concrete diction do the writers use?
   • Which words could be made more concrete?
   • What inflated diction or clichés do you find?
3. Rewrite one of the papers using more concrete diction. Compare your version with those of others in the class.

FIRST VERSION

Writer 2

RHONDA

The world is a mass of interactions. The earth needs something to produce and a flower needs earth to grow. Likewise people need to share with others and need feedback in return. Friendship offers an exchange of these needs. Through my relationship with my best friend, Rhonda, I fulfill my incentive to be needed and she offers me guidance, security, and love in return.

Throughout high school Rhonda gave me security and guidance. Since we attended an all girl high school we had to meet guys on the weekends at dances, which were the only events happening. Although our main objective at dances was to meet some guys and have a good time, we also formed a security plan. If Rhonda or I met someone we didn't like and he wanted one of us to go to McDonald's after the dance we had the excuse that we had to stay together. If there were two guys, it presented a problem but we just insisted on a double date. Not only did we make our mothers happy but we accomplished getting both of us dates. Dating ended quite abruptly with some guys. One week I'd hear from him every day and then suddenly he would disappear. Rhonda was a crutch to lean on after a broken heart. We often used each other as sounding boards for our agressions. When a guy stopped calling, I'd ask Rhonda repeatedly "what happened and why me?" We'd spend hours talking and gradually I'd find comfort in just having someone who cared to listen.

Drawing can be an emotional experience and Rhonda's guidance has been a supporting beam to my crumbling bridge. After spending hours drawing a pencil sketch of a white marble stairway and totally despising the end product, I would submit it to Rhonda. Once her initial eye squints and brow wrinklings subsided she quickly decided whether she liked it. She pointed out that my perspective of the stair edges were slightly slanted and I realized that it needed more work. She then emphasized that the worm's eye point of view was especially appealing to my sketch, which gave me an incentive to continue.

Having Rhonda as a roommate at college helped me to fulfill my incentive to be needed. Last semester she slept overtime whenever I left for classes before her; she needed me to make sure she got up. Another problem that occurred was the anxiousness and fear provoked by college classes. Although Rhonda had taken previous dance courses elsewhere she was unsure about a college level class. As the time approached for her to leave for class she started expressing her anxiety with bits of nervous laughter amidst frantic ramblings. I had to reassure her that she wasn't that lost because she was a talented dancer. When Rhonda left for class she seemed more sure of her abilities and I felt gratified that I had helped her.

Love leaves no regrets or jealousy between Rhonda and I. She has had a six month lead on me since birth, and I've never quite caught up. She started dating, learned to drive, and began working before me. She was also able to drink first, registered to vote first, and got her ears pierced first. Though I seem to be behind I don't reget it because there's a sense of security knowing that someone has walked ahead of me.

Writer 4   LEARNING FROM A FRIENDSHIP

When I first saw James on a spring afternoon at the high school that we both attended, he was tall, dark, powerfully built, and casually dressed. He had a rounded nose in a ruggedly handsome face. His closely cut brown hair brought out his slightly scornful eyes. I was not prepared for his gentle courtesy and relaxed humor when he asked questions about the motorcycle that I was riding. From that point on, we became friends. My friendship with James enabled me to pick up many of the good traits that he possessed.

James had a rapid-fire conversation that made me believe that it was not necessary to ask him questions. He was always trying to get to the "inside" or "the bottom" of something—a clock, a lock, an idea. It was James who showed me the insides of a telephone and took a car engine apart to show me how it worked. The result of his teaching was the fact that I started to inquire about the things around me.

James felt that happiness was obtained through kindness and good deeds to others. He worked at a drug store and, as a result, had extra money that he gave to people who claimed that they were in need. When I told him that he was probably being taken advantage of, he said that he was "giving to mankind." On another occasion, he shoveled the snow for a widowed neighbor and insisted that silence be his only payment. Soon, I found myself helping others and receiving satisfaction from it.

Eventhough he was still an adolescent, James proved to be a logical and coherent thinker. While most of the fellas in our age group judged girls by their physical appearance, he looked at their personalities saying that "to know a person is more important." Once James and I were expressing how we felt about people who were receiving public assistance, when he said, with dignity, that he felt sorry for those people but, that he would never feel that way about himself. I wanted to see things the way he did so I started to tap the resources of my own mind.

The profound effect that James had on children was beyond my understanding. Wherever he went, children seemed to love him. When the neighborhood children saw him coming, they would run to meet him. He would give the children money, take them to the circus, play ball with them, and remember their birthdays. I found out that a child wanted love and attention; and when I applied the methods that James used, children responded to me in the same manner.

He had the ability to see others, including children, as people with individuality; this made him a giant at understanding people, and a friend who helped bring out some good qualities in me.

SENTENCE PATTERNS

Certain sentence patterns also weaken expressive writing. You "talk down" to the reader by using an order of words that is not above but *below* the reading capability of the audience. Unfortunately for the writer, most people are better readers than they are writers; that is, they can comprehend (and they *expect* to comprehend) more complex patterns than they can reproduce in their own writing.

The previous sentence, for example, could have been broken down into simpler units:

Most people are better readers than they are writers.
They can comprehend complex patterns.
They can't write the same complex patterns.
So the writer is in an unfortunate position.

Instead, as a combination of these short examples, the sentence came out "Unfortunately for the writer, most people are better readers than they are writers; that is, they can comprehend (and they *expect* to comprehend) more complex patterns than they can reproduce in their own writing." You, as reader, would have been insulted by the other sequence.

An overuse of the *passive voice* can also weaken the expressive paper. "Their grief was shared by me" (passive) instead of "I shared their grief" (active). Another example of Writer 1's use of the passive is "every family is confronted by."

CLASS
EXERCISES

Sentence-combining

1. Study the simple expansion patterns below. Notice that each sentence is a combination of several sentences. Practice combining each set of sentences into one sentence matching the pattern above it.
2. Examine the First Versions of Writers 1 (pp. 88–90), 2 (pp. 92–93), 4 (p. 94), and 5 (pp. 84–85), identifying the writers' uses of the simple expansion patterns. Indicate places in their essays where sentences could have been combined. Combine these sentences.

I. SIMPLE EXPANSION PATTERNS

Pattern A The lean, muscular stunt man leapt onto a narrow, icy precipice.

1. The student just passed the test.
2. The student was relaxed.
3. The student was carefree.
4. The test lasted three hours.
5. The test was in physics.

1. The chimp demanded a candy bar.
2. The chimp was playful.
3. The chimp was aggressive.
4. The candy bar was chocolate nut.

----

1. The coach whipped his team into shape.
2. The coach was tough.
3. He was an ex-professional.
4. He coached football.
5. The team was from a small college.

Pattern B **The General Motors assembly line grinds out cars** swiftly, smoothly, **and almost** effortlessly.

1. The cat eyed its prey.
2. The cat was scruffy.
3. The cat was yellow.
4. The prey was imaginary.
5. The cat eyed it craftily.
6. It eyed it tauntingly.
7. It even eyed it murderously.

----

1. Oil massages you.
2. The oil is bath oil.
3. It is Beauty's oil.
4. The massaging is gentle.
5. The massaging is soothing.
6. The massaging is almost loving.

Pattern B1 **She studied** diligently **so that she could answer the examiner's questions very** quickly **and very** accurately.

1. The boys argued.
2. The arguing was loud.
3. The arguing was so that they could avoid the call.
4. The call came from their mother.
5. Their avoiding was very efficient.
6. Their avoiding was very effective.

----

1. Geoff played the game.
2. His playing was cautious.
3. He played so that he might meet the challenge.
4. The challenge was his opponent's.
5. His meeting of the challenge would be convincing.
6. It would be overwhelming.

Stage 5 Toward a Paper on Relationship: Developing, Organizing, and Refining the Paper

1. Write a first version of your paper
   a. developing your focus
   b. for your audience
   c. according to your aim and mode.
2. Refine your style.

USING THE CRITICAL GUIDE

Below we repeat the questions to guide your critique, adding some that apply new understandings discussed in this chapter.

1. Focus

What is the writer's focus?
In what ways has the writer maintained the focus?
Where has the writer strayed from the focus?
How has the writer maintained unity?

2. Development

What material has the writer used to develop the aim and focus?
In what ways can the audience *experience* the writer's focus?
What voice and audience role are created?
What other material does the audience need?

3. Organization

What mode of organization is the writer following?
How does the writer follow that mode?
What sections, if any, break the organization?
What means of maintaining coherence has the writer used?
How does the paragraphing work?

4. Style

What kind of diction has the writer used?
How do the sentence patterns help the reader?

5. Conventions: Grammar, Spelling, Punctuation

In what places has the writer failed to follow the conventions?
What impact does this have on the audience?

The following critiques use these questions to examine the First Versions of Writers 1 and 2.

This is a promising paper (pp. 88–90) in which some unfortunate choices have been made.

Focus

Her original statement of focus was "my family's sharing of grief over my brother's death helped me to accept it and caused me to realign my values" (p. 73). Here the focus is clearly on the writer, but the paper does not maintain this focus. First, the writer has to get rid of the distracting discussions of Donna, the parents, and "every family." Second, she has to dig out the subject of her paper—her relationship with Paul—and give it prominence. In this first version, it was buried in the middle, 500 words into the narrative. This mistake in the beginning afflicts the rest of the paper. Nowhere does the paper illustrate that the *family* changed; only *she* changed. The paper vacillates between the singular *I* and the plural *we*. The focus is blurred in the first paragraph.

Development

The expressive aim is also badly bent by the vacillation between *I* and *we*. Besides Paul, the only other person named is Donna, the sister. She appears twice in the second paragraph and then disappears. There is no sign in the paper that Donna or either or both of the parents went through the change that the writer says she went through. The voice of the writer varies throughout the piece. Read the last paragraph only. That is the voice of a clinical psychologist analyzing the situation and prescribing: "The more the grief can be expressed before death, the less unbearable it becomes afterward."

Now read the third paragraph only. What voice speaks there? What did the mother's hands do to "comfort our exhausted bodies"? What could those hands have done to "soothe our spent minds"? What voice moves from a personal "moment of numbness" to "a communal effort to regain lost composure"? And who could see and know that a "swelling of strength and determination emerged from each of us as a result of our commitment"?

Now read the second paragraph only. How many voices are there?

Now consider two sentences in the same paragraph:

His words brought about a fresh effusion of tears as my sister and I were consumed with anger and overwhelming bitterness that my brother should have to suffer with this illness, and that we could do nothing to help him.

I was eating at the time, and was aware of a MacDonald's hamburger turning to dust in my mouth.

Those two sentences are not in the same voice. What we are seeing is the result of trying to write for everyone. Such an attempt is especially dangerous in expressive writing, which places on the writer the primary difficulty of writing honestly and adequately about feeling. This writer wants both to show the experience and not to show it, and therefore, tends not to narrate and describe her feelings but the feelings of others, which, of course, she can only infer. That's a thoroughly understandable human failing, but it's an obstacle to good writing.

Flaws like these result from a failure to use audience, aims, and modes efficiently. What did the writer use instead of audience, aims, and modes? Only her list of ideas in the exploration. Turn back to pp. 68–69 and look at the list. She simply began at the top and turned the fragments into sentences. The material in the lists is raw material, unorganized and unfocused, nothing more. The writer also has to begin developing for a narrower audience; that narrowing will correct statements such as "I experienced a total realignment of my values and priorities [audience: a teacher of clinical psychology] and was stunned by the realization of how very precious my family was to me [audience: a family member who feels a sense of loss or the prospect of loss]." As we said before, the selection of a too-wide audience begins to damage the paper at the onset. Why is it necessary to talk about "Every family" when the focus should be on *me?*

Organization

The narrative mode is faithfully carried out through paragraphs two and three. Then it disappears. The writer needs to concentrate on chronological order. The narrative mode never requires an introductory paragraph that summarizes the chronology or the insight that arises from a series of events. The writer also has to recall more exact detail so that she can *narrate* a sequence, *describe* the actions, and *imply* the feelings. As we have said under the discussion of focus, the shifting between *you* and *I* causes many problems.

Style

Some of the mixtures of diction have already been noted. General terms like "confronted," "impending," "inevitable separation," "loved one," "imminent," "grievous emotion," and "terminal illness" are better suited to a referential aim. The writer establishes an undesirable sense of detachment from the experience with such phrases as "unfounded sense of foreboding," "ignorant of my qualms," "anxieties substantiated," and "fresh effusion of tears." The reader cannot experience the narrative but only learn about it. Mixed in with these terms are clichés that violate the personal sense of grief that the writer is trying to convey—"her voice broke," "crushing news," "filled with panic," and "broke my spirit." The sentence patterns are varied but on occasion do not work for the writer. For example, in the sentence "I was eating at the time, and was aware of a MacDonald's hamburger turning to dust in my mouth," the coordinate structure with "and" suggests that both experiences are equally important. A similar problem exists with the sentence "His words . . . nothing to help him."

Conventions

The grammer, spelling, and punctuation are adequate. The lapses include:

> superfluous commas, as in the first paragraph ("illness, and come") and the second paragraph ("at the time, and was")
> wrong case, as in the second paragraph: "between Donna and I"
> wrong tense, as in the third paragraph: "Even though I would always be able"

CRITIQUE:
Writer 2

Focus

Even though the writer works from the focus "My friendship with Rhonda offered me guidance, security, and love" (p. 43), the paper (pp. 92–93) begins oddly—"The world is a mass of interactions." Why is it necessary to talk about "the world"? The subject is a relationship between Rhonda and the writer. It is always unnecessary, generally superfluous, and usually disconcerting to an audience to begin expressive writing with generalizations about the world, the universe, society, and so on. The First Version does not begin as expressive discourse. Why didn't it begin with the second paragraph? That's the subject.

The fourth paragraph bears little relationship to anything that has gone before. Consciously or unconsciously, the writer was aware of that flaw, as the introductory sentence shows: "Love leaves no regrets or jealousy between Rhonda and I [i.e., me]." What does that mean? As we saw in the last chapter, when a writer sets down *an unusually bad sentence,* something besides grammar is usually wrong.

Development

Writer 2 elected an audience of peers who, like her, needs guidance, security, and love. She writes with the expressive aim, trying to use the narrative mode,

And ends up, alas, with a jumble.

"Rhonda" is probably beyond repair, unless the writer is willing to go back almost to the beginning. That process went off the track back in the exploratory stage. Perhaps the writer did not face the relationship squarely at the outset. The impression a dogged reader will carry away from the First

Version is that Rhonda is not a friend but a mother—the writer does little things like waking her in exchange for enormous gifts of love and support; that is not friendship, an equal trade, but almost absolute dependence. And thus arises the question of whether the writer has solved the problem or is simply postponing a solution. You can't write about a subject unless you understand it, and there are few signs that this writer has progressed beyond simply feeling snug in a comforting relationship. The problem was forecast at the time of focusing, but the writer did not remedy the problem then.

Most damaging of all, the paper says nothing to that lonely teenager the writer has selected as audience, except possibly, "I'm happy and secure; why aren't you?" That is writing down to the chosen audience.

Organization

The mode is not narrative. There is a superficial "high school to college" sequence implied, but the paragraph on "drawing" breaks that sequence; was the drawing in high school or college? The last paragraph also breaks the sequence; it is an *evaluative* paragraph.

Behind the organization—or lack of it—seems to be some concept of writing that dictates that no matter what the audience, aim, or mode, one writes a five-paragraph paper with a one-paragraph Introduction, a three-paragraph Body, and a one-paragraph Conclusion. But even that mistaken theory is not carried out. Notice that there is a focus set up in the last sentence of the first paragraph: "Through my relationship with my best friend, Rhonda, I fulfill my incentive to be needed and she offers me guidance, security, and love in return." A conclusion has been offered; now we wait for the supporting evidence.

And we wait for it in the order it was predicted:

1. my incentive to be needed
2. guidance
3. security
4. love in return

But it doesn't appear in that order; item 2 appears first (paragraph 1). Then item 2 again in paragraph 2, and after it, item 1; item 4 never appears at all.

Style

You will already have done a class exercise on the style of this paper (pp. 92–95).

Conventions

The writer has observed most conventions. However, this correctness does not make it a good paper. Probably the writer should start over rather than tinker with the present paper.

Focus

The focus (p. 73) is implied in the title (p. 94) and clearly stated in the last sentence of the first paragraph: "My friendship with James enabled me to pick up many of the good traits that he possessed." That focus is at the core of every paragraph.

Development

The focus is two-sided; it refers to the traits of two people. The writer has apparently decided to be specific about James's traits and to be general about those traits as they appear in the writer. All but the last sentence of each paragraph describes a valuable trait in James. The last sentence in each paragraph generalizes; that is, it simply asserts that the trait in question appeared in the writer. There is no attempt to develop the assertion by examples or details. This leads to vagueness and occasional confusion. For example, the concluding sentence of the fourth paragraph is unclear without illustration: "I wanted to see things the way he did [,] so I started to tap the resources of my own mind." Without more detail, the sentence sounds contradictory. Adding an example of tapping "the resources of my own mind" would yield the writer one of two dividends:

1. reassure the audience that the writer indeed was not simply imitating James's opinions *or*
2. show the writer that the statement is wrong, that he was imitating, not tapping his own resources

Aims are always developed for specific audiences. Writer 4 may be in trouble with his audience, 18-year-olds who have not had an easy time of it. James emerges from this paper as almost a patron saint of humankind. There are such people, but the task of the writer is to make one of them believable to a very skeptical audience. The danger is overstatement, claiming too much. Overstatement generally exists where there is lack of development. The details, examples, and illustrations that make up development tend to pull generalizations back into line with reality simply because they are the evidence that supports the generalization. Let's take just one example of overstatement in this paper, the fifth paragraph.

1. The first sentence cannot be exactly true. The writer does understand the effect because he describes it in the paragraph; the effect is hardly *profound* in view of the details of the third sentence.
2. The second sentence is overstated; the writer can't possibly testify to a generalization that sweeping.
3. The third sentence may be true, but an audience that has been through two suspect sentences will by now doubt anything.
4. The fourth sentence is overstated. *Would* is an auxiliary verb that

denotes habitual action. Taken with the preceding sentence, this sentence says that after the children habitually swarmed to James, he habitually gave them money, took them to the circus, played ball with them, and so on. What is probably meant and what is believable is that James has been known to take them to the circus, to give them money occasionally, to play ball with them when he can, and to remember some of their birthdays. These actualities need to be separated into concrete examples. Separate acts performed over a long period cannot be condensed without falsifying the whole and losing the confidence of the audience.

The scaling down of James's charity would also help to harmonize another very delicate touch the writer has inserted in the paper. In the first paragraph we read of James's "slightly scornful eyes," and the idea is echoed in the fourth paragraph when James says that he feels sorry for people on welfare, but "he would never feel that way about himself." These two sentences hint at a feeling of superiority in James which does not fit well with the total self-sacrifice outlined in the rest of the paper.

Organization

The writer has chosen the descriptive mode. The focus refers to "good traits" James possesses. The writer has divided the good traits into four:

1. curiosity
2. kindness
3. logicality
4. love of children

He addresses each quality in a separate paragraph, describing James's actions that illustrate the quality. He adds a concluding paragraph that summarizes the common element in the traits: "the ability to see others, including children, as people with individuality."

The organization is good, but it could be improved. The first sentence of the second paragraph suggests a quality that is not developed in the paragraph—self-confidence. The topic of the paragraph is curiosity.

Style

We have already noted the problems with *would* and *profound* and the consequent problems with overstatement. What is most remarkable stylistically is the formality of the diction and sentence structure, given the audience analysis done by the writer (p. 78) and the subject, a close friendship. When the writer has had a choice he seems (except once, *fellas*) to have elected formal diction and sentence structure. Thus we read "many of the good traits he possessed" instead of "many of his good traits"; "it was James who showed me" instead of "James showed me"; "receiving public assistance" rather than "welfare"; "people with individuality" instead of "individuals." The writer communicates with his formality a distance between his subject and himself, perhaps even an awe of James. Although excessive formality in expressive writing can dampen the sense of authenticity, it may be appropriate here, in this guru-and-novice relationship.

The writer connects his sentences well with simple transitions. In the third paragraph, for example, the first two sentences are connected by the noun and pronoun occurring in the subject position, *James* and *he*. In the second sentence, *as a result* is inserted to indicate the relationship between the two ideas, that he worked and that he had extra money. The rest of the sentences in the paragraph are prefaced with time indicators—*when, on another occasion, soon*—that move the reader smoothly through the sequence.

Conventions

The writer has a good command of spelling, grammar, and punctuation. There are only a few problems: In the fourth paragraph, the second sentence requires a comma after *personalities;* in the following sentence the comma after *but* should be removed; in the next sentence a comma is required after *did.* For discussion of proper use of the comma, see pp. 346–347.

REWRITING

Rewriting is another name for *improving*. A good rewriter looks at five aspects of the paper, just as the informed reader will:

1. Focus
2. Development
3. Organization
4. Style
5. Conventions: Grammar, Spelling, Punctuation

As a rewriter, you always benefit from getting as many reactions as possible to your first version, but that is not to say that you take every suggestion. However, if several readers see the same flaw in the paper, it's a good bet that the flaw exists. And there's another benefit: if you are able to collect four or five reactions to three or four of your papers and the same flaws keep popping up in the reactions, you know that you have ingrained, habitual problems because you keep repeating them in paper after paper.

The point of rewriting is not just to produce a better paper but to discover what faults *you*, not others, have so that you can correct them. We are urging, in other words, that you seek out your instructor's or your class's critiques (preferably both) on the strengths and weaknesses of any paper you write.

Assuming, then, that you accumulate some useful criticism, how do you improve the paper?

1. If the flaws in the paper rest in Style and Conventions: Grammar, Spelling, Punctuation, you are facing a relatively simple repair job. As we have said before, the real "basics" of writing do not lie in conventions; conventional mistakes can be remedied in editing after some concentrated attention.

2. If the paper is flawed in Organization, you are in for a larger repair job—as if your car had thrown a rod in the engine and dropped its transmission. In the first case, you have no power, and, in the second, even if you had power you couldn't go anywhere. Repair at this level means a lot of work, since it means going back and reassessing your choice (or understanding) of aim and mode. But the repairs can be made.

3. If flaws rest in Focus or Development, you ought to consider junking the paper and beginning again. In this case the problems lie so far back in the writing process that by repairing you would in effect be almost beginning again. Junk the paper—unless, of course, you are one of those determined souls who may be bloody but unbowed, determined to see this thing through, unwilling to be defeated except on your own terms, convinced that a thing worth doing is worth doing well (or worth doing badly), in short, despite those dreadful clichés, someone who wants to get this right before moving on. If you are, you have our admiration. But we repeat, it isn't *better* to start again; it's only *easier*.

Even though Writer 1 had problems with Focus and Development, she wanted to rewrite her paper. Here is her revision.

REVISED VERSION

Writer 1

PAUL

For three years I had lived with a lie or at best a half-truth. My parents had known that my seventeen-year-old brother Paul had leukemia since June, 1970. But, wanting to spare us, they had told my sister Donna and me only that he had a "blood disorder."

Over those three years, except for Paul's frequent visits to the hospital, our lives, and mine in particular, changed almost not at all. Occasionally I would feel a sense of foreboding and depression, but I pushed those feelings away. I did not want to know.

But one evening about two years ago the truth came home. My parents returned with Paul from Children's Hospital; Paul, who was not feeling well, went immediately to bed. Dad, Mom, Donna, and I trooped down to the basement where we gathered around a small table on which I had spread out a meal from MacDonald's. Still acting as if this were a normal day, we began to eat. Suddenly Mom blurted out that Paul was fighting a losing battle with leukemia. I was aware of a hamburger turning to dust in my mouth. I began to cry. Inside I was whispering, "It's a mistake, it has to be a mistake," but the exhaustion I could see in my mother and the way my father's face seemed to have gone slack—he looked so vulnerable, my strong father—told me that there was no mistake. And the way Donna's eyes, smeary with tears, shifted away from mine told me something else: that we had known it all the time. Only now the fact was loose there in the room.

We talked and we wept through a series of necessary questions, necessary because I was still pretending that this new reality was new. "Aren't they going to do anything to help him?" I asked, and my father patiently explained that everything available had been tried.

Sitting there, alone among my family, I went through the normal feelings that are grief. Rage and bitterness at my brother's fate and also at my own helplessness. Panic because Paul had been my mainstay. We were only a year apart; he had been my friend and counselor and, I now realized, my bridge to people and things I valued, and I thought bleakly of the time when I would no longer feel that burst of swelling pride when someone said, "Paul's sister." Then came the guilt for the selfishness.

Those feelings stayed with me in the weeks that followed, but another, more positive feeling began to emerge, for all of us, I think. I began to realize how very precious to me were the days and hours I had with my family. As a hedge against the darkness, we began to spend more time together, and in that time we were more gentle with one another, as if we were storing up memories, not only of Paul but of the family.

I can't say that I didn't wish every day that we could revert to the "way we were." But we had gained something because of what we were about to lose. Paul, of course, went on being Paul. He laughed on good days, worked hard at being healthy, and never complained. And then he died.

CLASS EXERCISES

1. Using the Critical Guide, critique Writer 5's First Version (pp. 84–85) as a class.
2. Using the Critical Guide and working in groups, critique each other's papers.
3. Compare Writer 1's Revised Version with her First Version (pp. 89–90). How has she responded to the advice of the critics?

ASSIGNMENT

Stage 6 Toward a Paper on Relationships: Critiquing and Rewriting

1. Using the Critical Guide, critique your own paper. (Written or oral critiques from the instructor and your classmates can be invaluable guides for your self-critique.)
2. Rewrite your paper, guided by your critiques.

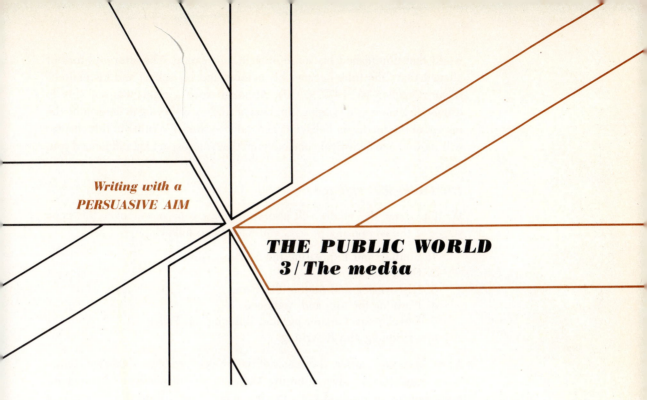

Writing with a
PERSUASIVE AIM

THE PUBLIC WORLD
3 / The media

THE WRITING CONTEXT

You have been writing in your private world, exploring the meaning of places and relationships. This chapter sets as the writing context a part of the public world, the mass media you share with millions of others, as you watch TV programs and commercials, listen to the radio, read magazines and newspapers. Even though you have devoted hours to the media, you may never have realized their impact, because they work hard at being unobtrusive, playing to the corners of your mind, costumed as entertainment. Many television programs or magazines do not want to be caught off guard with their influences showing. A striking attempt to prove their power was made in Florida.

You may recall the case of 15-year-old Ronald Zamora, who was accused of murdering an 82-year-old Miami Beach widow. His defense attorneys claimed that he was suffering from and acted under the influence of prolonged, intense, involuntary, subliminal television intoxication. They claimed that he was "electronically brainwashed" by a fantasy television world that diminished his sense of right and wrong. The attorneys further alleged that "the tube became his parents and his school and his church" (*Time*, October 10, 1977, p. 87). Although such a claim was not able to exonerate Zamora, increasing numbers of studies are trying to determine the impact of the media on behaviors and value systems. Writing in this chapter will allow you to investigate one medium that you suspect has influenced you.

THE COMPOSING PROCESS

Writing about the media will also strengthen your power over the same stages of the composing process you have been following:

1. Finding and Expressing the Starting Point
2. Exploring
3. Discovering and Stating the Focus
4. Planning for Aim and Audience
5. Developing, Organizing, and Refining the Paper
6. Critiquing and Rewriting

As we have said earlier, the stages of the process are often recursive, sometimes simultaneous, always untidy. The examples displayed in this text are work the students turned in for teacher commentary. With the exception of the explorations, which should be spontaneous records, the examples were probably reworked often before being submitted.

FINDING AND EXPRESSING THE STARTING POINT

FINDING THE SUBJECT

To select a medium for scrutiny, ask yourself questions like: Is there some television program that I have mixed emotions about, feeling addicted yet disliking some aspect? Am I ever torn between watching a certain kind of program and spending time with family or friends? Do I pay good money for a magazine and feel frustrated when reading it? Do I hate commercials and yet buy certain products? Have I eagerly read about crime in the newspaper and yet been torn by seeing how it harmed someone close to me?

Five student writers selected a range of media. Writer 1 was curious as to why he preferred watching Monday Night Football to the Sunday games. Writer 2 was angered by commercials but felt influenced by the values they propagated. Writer 3 had subscribed to a fashion magazine for years but was becoming disillusioned with it. Writer 4 had read comic books since he was small but felt guilty about it. Writer 5 had loved the TV family shows of the fifties and sixties when she was growing up but now felt disturbed about their view of family life. All of the writers chose media with which they had a great deal of contact and about which they had strong feelings.

EXPRESSING THE STARTING POINT

To move beyond feelings to a sharper beginning, the writers used the two-part strategy for expressing starting points:

1. Identify aspects of your medium that appear to challenge your values or seem to have influenced your interpretation of the world.
2. Ask a question to point your inquiry toward understanding.

STARTING POINTS

Writer 1

MY VALUES OR EXPECTATIONS	ASPECTS OF MONDAY NIGHT FOOTBALL
—two good teams playing each other	—most games are between top teams
—good camera work	—camera angles and instant replays good
—accurate announcing	—semi-accurate announcing
—truthful analysis not cover up or double talk	—announcers who tell it like it is
—game to come before entertainment	—ABC guilty of occasionally putting show biz before game
—don't want to spend whole afternoon viewing game	—Monday night format ideal
—good half-time show	—exciting half-time high-lights

Question: Why do I enjoy watching ABC's Monday Night Football so much more than Sunday afternoon football on the other networks?

Writer 2

MY VALUES OR EXPECTATIONS	ASPECTS OF BODY PRODUCT COMMERCIALS
—I respect the woman as a whole	—Ads for body products exploit the woman's body and ignore her intelligence and capability
—People should accept themselves and others for what they are	—The ads tell us to reject somebody or be ashamed of ourselves if we don't make use of all the available products
—A person should be valued by their personality and not by what type of body product one uses	—These ads tell us our popularity will be determined by our choice of body products

Question: What can I do to keep myself from becoming so emotionally angered while watching body product ads that subliminally or blatantly take advantage of the psychological weaknesses and insecurities of men and women, specifically with the use of sexual references?

Writer 3 MY VALUES OR EXPECTATIONS

ASPECTS OF FASHION MAGAZINES

—looking fashionable

—unreal look-a-like models

—being economical

—high prices of fashion clothes

Question: What real benefit do fashion magazines offer an average American girl like me?

Writer 4 MY VALUES OR EXPECTATIONS

ASPECTS OF THE COMICS

—the sophistication of the imagination

—seem to many parents to be a waste of time, if not harmful

Question: What advantages can be gained from reading comics which seem to adults to be harmful wastes of time?

Writer 5 MY VALUES OR EXPECTATIONS

ASPECTS OF TV SHOWS

—close supportive family

—ideal family life on shows in '50s and '60s

—variety of lifestyle

—family lifestyle on shows of today

Question: How have changes in TV Family Shows influenced my view of family life?

Commentary Writer 2 captures clashes between her values and the commercials but doesn't take note of the obvious dissonance that she watches these commercials despite her dislike. Her question will also focus her investigations on herself, rather than on the commercials. Her revised question read:

How do body product ads, especially those using sexual references, subliminally or blatantly take advantage of our psychological weaknesses and insecurities?

Although Writer 3 has noted two aspects of fashion magazines, "high prices" and "unreal look-a-like models," that conflict with her values, her question does not reflect that dissonance. Her revised question read:

What real benefit do fashion magazines, with their high prices and ideal models, offer an average American girl like me?

CLASS EXERCISES

1. Discuss the Starting Points of Writers 1, 4, and 5.
   • How have the statements of values and aspects of the subject helped the writers to ask questions?
   • To what kinds of explorations will the questions lead?
2. Select a medium the class wishes to use for practice (a TV program, a newspaper, a radio show, a magazine).
   • Identify aspects of that medium that clash with or that fit strongly with the class' values.
   • Formulate a question to guide further investigation.

Stage 1 Toward a Paper on the Media: Finding and Expressing the Starting Point

1. **Identify a medium whose impact you want to investigate.**
2. **Express the aspect(s) of that medium that challenges or corresponds with your values.**
3. **Write a question to direct your further investigation.**
4. **Seek comments on your starting point from your instructor and classmates.**

The Exploratory Guide will again be helpful in directing your inquiry into the medium you have selected. Following are some questions under each view to help you apply the guide to the media.

EXPLORATORY GUIDE

Static view

–Recall and record as many features of your subject as you can, noticing what distinguishes it from others like it.
–Examine its parts: the characters, settings, themes of TV shows, the types of articles and sections in magazines, the type of music on radio shows.

Dynamic view

–Trace the history of that medium from its start (if you can), or through your past experience with it, to its present stage, to speculations about its future.
–Determine how it has changed.
–Trace your changing attitudes toward it.
–Trace the sequence of a typical single program, or describe the format of a magazine.

Relative view

–Classify your subject.
–Indicate the reasons for your classification.
–Compare and contrast the program or magazine with others, recording the likenesses and differences.
–Create at least one analogy for your subject, explaining its basis.
–Evaluate your subject, relating it to criteria you select for a good TV program, a good magazine, a good radio program or whatever medium you have chosen.

Here is Writer 3's Exploration.

Writer 3   FASHION MAGAZINES

STATIC VIEW

Parts of the magazine:
–pages and pages of ads
    –makeup ads
    –cigarette ads
    –sterling silver ads
    –shampoo ads
    –perfume ads
    –jewelry ads
    –vacation ads
    –toiletry ads for women
–beautiful models with:
    –perfect figures
    –straight teeth
    –peaches 'n cream complexions
    –long fingernails
    –manageable hair that looks good in a variety of styles
    –big, beautiful eyes
    –little feet
–stylish clothes, meaning "faddish"
    –styles are not lasting
    –expensive outfits
    –average outfit consists of:
        –longer skirts
        –woolen sweaters either short, long, slinky or big (large knit)
        –patterned shirts, full blouses
        –scarf
        –argyle knee socks
        –platform shoes, spike heels
        –head-hugging hats
        –skinny belts
        –accessories such as:
            –bangles
            –earrings
            –gold necklaces
            –stick pins
            –small leather bags
            –mod watches
            –sexy evening wear

–hair-coloring techniques are shown
–various articles that appear in fashion magazines are:
    –dieting tips
    –exercise hints for a slim, trim figure
    –marriage advice
    –recipes for delicious snacks
    –letters to the editor or an expert on such topics as:
        –beauty problems
        –sexual problems
        –boyfriend and girlfriend problems
–many fashion magazines have a horoscope section
–"shop by mail" sections in the back of fashion magazines advertising
  things that you can send away for as:
    –rings, bracelets, earrings
    –purses
    –smock-tops
    –shoes
    –body shapers
–these magazines also include articles with travel tips

DYNAMIC VIEW

–process of production
    –alot of camera magic involved in photographing these models
    –photographers only choose the best one of their pictures
    –girls are of a very highly select group, not your average girl
–fashion magazines save you alot of time by giving you a preview of the
  clothes and accessories carried at the department stores
–sometimes articles are written by experts in a particular field such as
  doctors, marriage counselors
–ads consume over half of the fashion magazine
–in special issues celebrities write articles on some crafts or hobbies
  that they enjoy
–the average person can't trust this kind of information on handling
  life's problems, college advice, etc.
–many fashion magazines show the person how to conform to their fashions in clothes, their hairstyles, accessories and their advice on how to
  act and what to think on today's current problems
–sophisticated reader would not take everything at face value that is
  pictured or written about in these fashion magazines
–these styles pictured in fashion magazines are often impractical for the
  average person's budget, figure and taste
–there doesn't seem to be any individuality in these fashion magazines,
  everybody looks the same

Comparison

Fashion magazines are alot like college. Fashion magazines do not pertain to, or cannot be of value to everyone. Unless the reader has a perfect figure and alot of money I don't believe the fashion magazines can be of any help to them. Some of the articles are written to a very liberal audience and they can't relate to the conservative reader who doesn't believe in pre-marital sex or some of the other current problems. Since a reader may not be able to relate with these articles, she is left without much of a variety in the magazine, fashion world.

College doesn't apply to everyone. Only the select few who want to study and learn some more in order to succeed in the profession of their choice go on to college. For some, trade-school or an early start in a job. But at least he does have an alternate route.

Analogy—Fashion magazines are like fad diets.

Fashion magazines do not pertain to the average American girl. The girls chosen for these pictures are of a very select group, they do not portray the average girl, because most average girls do not have perfect figures, straight teeth and cute smiles.

Fad diets such as grapefruit diets and water diets cannot hardly apply to the average person who is working hard, either mentally, or physically, for how can he survive on such a small amount of calories all day. Maybe these diets work wonders for celebrities or people who rest all day but not for the average person who works hard.

Evaluation

Criteria for a good fashion magazine: it should offer practical advice on fashions for average girls, it should advertise clothes that are affordable and not too faddish
—Most fashion magazines do not meet the criteria.

Commentary Writer 3 has recorded under the static view a catalog of features common to most fashion magazines. But she has not selected very concrete language, using such phrases as "jewelry ads," "makeup ads," which present little that can be seen or felt or heard. Her exploration would improve if she added specific examples for each feature, as she does occasionally with "argyle knee socks" and "head-hugging hats." Most of the ideas under the dynamic view are actually static. Although this writer needs help using the dynamic perspective, more important is that she has discovered some useful ideas, even though misplaced. A dynamic exploration would have speculated on past fashion magazines, the changes the writer has noted since she began to read the magazine, and the typical way the contents are sequenced in a single issue. Although the connection made between colleges and fashion magazines is not a comparison but an analogy because the two are of unlike order, her idea that fashion magazines are not for all may lead to an insight. The Exploratory Guide is a tool, not an end in itself.

1. Examine the Explorations of Writers 1 and 5.
   - What distinctive descriptions do they give of their subjects? Could you identify the subjects from the features they record?
   - What parts of the subject are explored? What kind of language is used to record the ideas?
   - What changes in the subject, sequences or history have been analyzed?
   - What do the comparisons and contrasts or analogies reveal about the subject? About the attitude of the writer toward the subject?
   - What other aspects of the subject could be explored?
2. As a class, explore the subject you chose in the class exercise on the starting point.
   - Record as many ideas under each perspective as the class can generate.

EXPLORATION

Writer 1

MONDAY NIGHT FOOTBALL

STATIC VIEW

—the upbeat theme song
—ariel view from Goodyear Blimp of the "alive" well-lit stadium in the middle of a darkened "dead" city
—the bowl-shaped arena jampacked with frenzied fans
—high atop the stadium in the pressbox are the three announcers wearing yellow blazers
—headphones, microphones and monitors surround the announcers
—Frank Gifford does play by play, former star running back of the fifties with the N.Y. Giants, medium build, short blond hair graying around the edges, blue eyes, an even sane voice, error prone on play by play, occasionly slips in good football insight
—Don Meredith analyzes replays, star quarterback of the Dallas Cowboys in the sixties, 6.1″ tall, light brown hair, slow Texan drawl, good country wit, offers intelligent, amusing analysis, exhibits amazing clairvoyance at predicting upcoming plays
—Howard Cosell supplies background information on players and the game, looks in his sixties, six ft. tall, on the stocky side, dark eyes, large nose, hand shakes when he holds microphone, no football experience, legal background, low nasal voice, uses polysyllabic words, tell it like it is presentation, prides himself on controversial remarks

—Keith Jackson did first season play by play, in his fifties, chubby, offered smooth consistant commentary
—Fred "The Hammer" Williamson did analysis in Merediths absence, fourty years old, black, former Kansas City Chief star, average analysis
—Alex Karras, hefty ex-Detroit Lion player, wears glasses, amusing analysis
—ABC camera work good
—quality of games good
—half-time highlights exciting
—games last till well after midnight

DYNAMIC VIEW

—Monday Night Football evolved in 1970 as pet idea of football comissioner Pete Rozelle
—televised on ABC, they adopt a show-biz approach
—ratings a big hit
—unfavorable to players at first, not as many days preparation for next weeks game
—original announcers Keith Jackson, Howard Cosell and Don Meredith
—Jackson departed next season to broadcast college football
—replaced by Frank Gifford
—ratings continue to climb in '71
—players enjoy game, like being showcased on prime time television
—Cosell emerges as fullfledged star, people love to hate him
—'72–'73 ratings level out but are still good
—after '74 season Meredith is lured to NBC with promises of acting in television movies
—Fred Williamson is given a try out for Meredith's job during '75 exhibition season, he and Cosell don't get along, Williamson is fired after two preseason games
—Alex Karras is then given the job
—ratings slide during Karras' tenure
—mismatches between teams are more numerous than previous years
—Meredith's acting career fizzles, he agrees to rejoin ABC Karras is fired
—ratings are immediately revived
—a typical game is started at nine o'clock
—the show is opened with a theme song
—announcers discuss the upcoming game
—the first half of action is intersperced with constant chatter by the announcers and celebrity appearances in the broadcast booth
—Cosell's half-time highlights are witty but don't include all games
—the second half follows the hollywood approach of the first half.

Comparison

Football on ABC	*Football on NBC*
–Monday night rather then spending whole Sunday viewing	–Sunday afternoon
–good announcing	–excellent announcing crews
–good replays and camera angles	–even though NBC has more than one game to telecast each Sunday
–half-time highlights are exciting	
–show biz approach to football, interesting, fun	–boring half-time announcers and show
	–NBC makes football dull

Football on ABC	*Football on CBS*
–Monday night	–Sunday afternoon
–good announcing	–too many unqualified ex-athletes in the booth broadcasting
–good replays and camera angles	–camera work is way below ABC and NBC
–half-time high lights are exciting	–again hindered by unqualified personnel
–full approach to game	–for the most part dull

Classification

Interesting announcers

Frank Gifford	Pat Sumerall	Keith Jackson
Dick Enberg	Don Meredith	
Merlin Olsen	Howard Cosell	
John Brodie	Hank Stram	

Dull announcers

Curt Gowdy	Bryant Gumbel
Chris Schenkel	Alex Karras
Jim Brown	Fred Williamson
Irv Cross	

Analogy

Watching ABC's Monday Night Football is like eating stew. With stew you get a variety of different things to eat, with the game one gets variety also, a little football, a little outspokeness all thrown into one pot.

Evaluation

Criteria for a good sports show: action, great personalities, fast presentation

Monday Night Football meets them all.

Writer 5   FAMILY COMEDY SHOWS IN 50's AND EARLY 60's

STATIC VIEW

—*The Adventures of Ozzie & Harriet*
   —underplayed situation comedy revolving around the domestic life of
     one "ideal family"
   —Ozzie—crinkly eyes, wide smile, self-deprecating humor, wore
     shirts with button-down collars, a narrow tie and cardigan sweater;
     week after week wandering in and out of Harriet's kitchen at all
     hours of the day, always available to help solve any domestic
     crisis—I don't recall that his job-work was ever discussed on the
     show.
   —Harriet—brown hair always neatly combed and simple shirtwaist
     housedresses
   —David—the older brother, blond hair
   —Ricky—the show went on the air in 1952 (I was not much more than
     1 yr old) I knew him so well he was almost like a brother first get-
     ting into scrapes quickly solved before the end of the show by an
     ever patient mother or a father conspiratorially entering into the
     fun; later—singing rock-and-roll songs, brushing back his curly
     brown hair sheepishly as teen-age girls screamed; and finally fall-
     ing in love, getting married to beautiful Kris—all continued from
     week to week. I felt shock, disbelief when I read in the paper that
     he & Kris were separating
—*The Dick Van Dyke Show*
   —situation comedy showing life in New Rochelle for a comedy writer
     Rob and Laura his wife
   —Rob—tall, gangly head comedy writer for the Allen Brady Show
   —Laura—bright dark eyes, vulnerable smile, beautifully coiffed
     hair wearing blouses, capri pants with black flats on her feet.

DYNAMIC VIEW

Sequences on shows
—*The Adventures of Ozzie & Harriet*
   —gentle humor—not a trace of the insults, masquerading as jokes
     on the Norman Lear comedies
   —I can't recall the plots of the shows—images of a family almost
     more real to me than my own
—*The Dick Van Dyke Show*
   —Laura & Rob buying a suburban home in New Rochelle next door
     to their old friends Jerry, the dentist and Milly; then worrying
     about money to buy furniture

–Laura & Rob having a baby boy—Ritchie; Laura thinking Rob is jealous says "that Dr. Spock just knows everything"
–Laura—the ideal wife & mother—standing by the stove each morning, dressed, hair neatly combed, make-up on, asking Rob how he wanted his eggs; Laura took a week long job as a replacement for a dancer on the Allen Brady show; Rob worried that she'd go back to work full time; Both content at the end of the show that Laura was back home

RELATIVE VIEW

Classify
–both situation comedies about middle-class family life

Compare
–very much like
     Leave It to Beaver
     Father Knows Best
     The Donna Reed Show
–each with loving fathers who worked hard but were home a great deal with their families, wise, patient mothers happy to be at home, keeping perfectly clean houses, cooking three delicious meals a day; cute children who got into periodic scrapes or minor spats with siblings which were always resolved by the end of the show

Contrast
–One Day at a Time
 a divorced mother of two girls
–Family
–Jeffersons

Analogy
–shows were like blowing soap bubbles so round and beautiful but when you reach out to catch them, make them your own, they disappear

ASSIGNMENT

Stage 2 Toward a Paper on the Media: Exploring
1. **Using the Exploratory Guide, explore your starting point.**
2. **Find the most concrete words that express your perspective on your subject.**
3. **Seek commentary on your exploration from your instructor.**

DISCOVERING
AND STATING
THE FOCUS

INCUBATING

Even though you may feel as if you are in a pressure cooker, with assignments and exams piling up, allow your mind a rest so that the ideas can germinate, combining with one another. A greater number of significant insights spring from a good night's sleep than from an all-night vigil.

STATING THE FOCUS

The focus that you formulate must stand the test not only of your past experience but also of others' encounters with the same medium. You must decide whether a part or the whole subject has emerged as important. Has Writer 1, for example, found Monday Night Football as a whole necessary to answer his starting questions? Or will he limit his focus to the announcers or the format? The second half of the focus expresses whatever understanding you have gained of your subject—the answer to your starting question or a solution to a new question that has emerged along the way.

FOCUSES

	SUBJECT	POINT OF SIGNIFICANCE
Writer 1	Monday Night Football	is more enjoyable than Sunday afternoon football because of the quality of the action, magnetism of the personalities, and the show biz approach, all combining to make it a happening.
Writer 2	Advertisers' manipulative techniques for body product commercials	should be understood by the viewer in order to defy their power.
Writer 3	Some fashion magazines	are not practical guides for the American girl.
Writer 4	Comic books	relax the reader, develop the imagination and reading skills, and provide hero models.
Writer 5	T.V. shows of the 50's and 60's	gave an image of family life so perfect that it could never be matched.

Commentary Writer 3 is careful not to make a universal claim about "all" magazines, one that a short paper would be unable to support. The writer does, however, make an ambitious judgment that may get her into trouble. She assumes that (1) there is a "typical American girl" and (2) that she is it. Her point of significance should be qualified.

Writer 5's focus needs limiting to "T.V. [family] shows of the '50's and '60's." Notice that she has shifted away from changes in TV family life because she wishes to emphasize the fifties and sixties. Her point of significance answers her question.

1. Study the Focuses of Writers 1, 2, and 4.
   - To what do the writers commit themselves in the first half of the focuses?
   - What responses do the second halves make to the writers' starting points (pp. 109–110)?
2. Formulate focuses for the subject you explored as a class.

ASSIGNMENT

Stage 3 Toward a Paper on the Media: Discovering and Stating the Focus

1. **After allowing time for incubation, state your focus, formulating it into two parts:**
   a. **the aspect (or whole) of the subject that you are going to focus on and**
   b. **the point of significance that answers your original question.**
2. **Get advice on your focus from your instructor.**

PLANNING FOR AIM AND AUDIENCE

THE PERSUASIVE AIM

The writing in this chapter illustrates the persuasive aim, which emphasizes the audience. In the public world of the media the writers share the same experiences: watching television, reading magazines, and so on. The primary aim of these writers is to persuade the members of the audience of some impact of the media on them.

Writer 1 wants to persuade an audience that Monday Night Football will be more enjoyable than watching games on Sunday afternoon. Writer 2 is interested in convincing an audience that recognizing and understanding the manipulative techniques of advertisers will give the audience power to defy such seduction. Writer 3 desires to persuade an audience that fashion magazines do not give practical advice. Writer 4 chooses to convince an audience of the value of comics. Writer 5 wants her audience to understand the idealistic view of family life portrayed by the shows of the fifties and sixties.

In the paper you write on the media, we ask that you adopt a persuasive aim to gain command of working with this emphasis. Let us consider what a persuasive aim requires of you as a writer:

1. Establishing your credibility as a writer. Credibility rests generally on your ability to show sufficient knowledge of the subject, concern for the good of the audience, and lack of deception. By displaying these qualities, you project a personality that, in general, audiences respect and, therefore, accept. But particular audiences require you to think more exactly about how those qualities are to be projected in terms of *style and subject matter*. It is, for example, safe to say that the officers of the

Salvation Army will require a different voice than the officers of the U.S. Army, even though both groups can be expected to look for knowledge of the problem, concern for the good of the audience, and lack of deception. The voice you choose sets your image of credibility. The role you play must convince the reader that you have had much experience with the medium you are discussing, that you are aware of the audience members' attitudes, and that you have their good in mind. How do you prepare and carry out this attempt to establish credibility?

When you develop your paper, your introduction and conclusion, your choice of examples and diction, all contribute to building the image you wish your reader to accept. These means will be discussed further in the section on development. What can you do in the planning stages to prepare to establish credibility? Three important things: (1) When you analyze your audience, probe deeply into the values, especially the kind of speaker or writer its members value, and analyze carefully their attitude toward the subject; (2) choose your role in accordance with the above analysis; and (3) look back on your exploration to determine what ideas and information will work best for this audience. You may have to generate more material.

Finally, persuasive writers realize that there is only one basic need of every audience whether that audience is one person or a million people: the need to be esteemed, that is, to be respected, to be judged as of a high order, to be prized. Nothing in the argument should damage the self-image of the audience as being worthy of esteem.

2. Establishing the plausibility of the argument. This is an appeal to the audience's reason, to its sense of "logic." But persuasive writing differs from expository writing in providing only the logic that the audience requires in order to be convinced. In persuasion you avoid forcing your audience to go through rigorous logical procedures, unless, of course, you are writing for an audience of logicians. In the next section on development, we will discuss the three types of logic you have available for persuading your audience.

3. Appealing to the audience's emotions. Audience members are influenced far more by what they feel than by their logical abilities. You are concerned about feelings because the audience is. But by the same token, you have to have some sense of the audience's emotional state. An audience apathetic toward the subject cannot be treated in the same way as an audience angry over the subject.

When you analyze your audience, make careful note of its emotional state. Think about what emotions you need to play down and which to arouse. In the stage of refining the style, we will discuss how your choices of diction control audience emotion.

CHOOSING AN AUDIENCE

Choosing an audience for a paper dealing with mass media is simple if you keep one principle in mind. As always, the best audience is the one that will profit the most from sharing your insight. Specific audiences will vary from writer to writer, but generally two audiences may be selected from: the people who, like you, view the mass media (the consumers) and the people who create the material in the mass media (the producers). You should decide in the beginning which one of those audiences you will focus on since you cannot write for both simultaneously.

Let's look at the principle in practice. Writer 3 has stated as her focus, "Some fashion magazines are not practical guides for the American girl." Writer 3 has two general audiences to choose from:

1. actual and potential readers of the magazines
2. publishers and editors of the magazines

Which should she choose? Let's apply the principle that the best audience is the one that will profit most:

1. If she chose the first, she would be setting out to warn readers that the content of some fashion magazines is unreliable as a model for their own lives. If she chose the second, she would be setting out to persuade the publishers of those magazines to correct their ways.

2. If she chose the first, she would be writing for an audience that may or may not be aware of the impracticality of the magazines; hence, there is potential profit for that audience. If she chose the second, she would be writing for an audience whose members doubtless are fully aware of the nature of their publication. The publishers know quite well that they are not offering "practical guides for the American girl," and they are successful precisely because they are consciously selling something else—a romantic illusion.

Therefore, the logical choice should be the readers, not the publishers. But which readers? Not "the American girl" or even American girls who read fashion magazines, but American girls of limited means who think that they will find practical advice in fashion magazines applicable to their appearances, incomes, and lifestyles.

The student writers chose the following audiences: Writer 1 selected "Men and women with no extensive knowledge of football." Writer 2 chose "Poor to middle class housewives and high school students (the biggest market of body product consumption)." Writer 3 chose "Two girlfriends of mine, avid readers of fashion magazines, that I went to high school with; they spend more money than they can afford on outfits that the magazines display." (This is a relatively narrow audience, but the choice could very well prove to be an advantage.) Writer 4 chose "The distressed mothers of children who read comics." Writer 5 chose "T.V. viewers of the '50s and '60s." (This is a large audience but not necessarily broad; those who grew up with the TV of the fifties and sixties have a common base of experience and interest that should make the choice workable.)

ANALYZING THE AUDIENCE

Analyzing the audience for a persuasive paper again employs the full Audience Guide.

AUDIENCE GUIDE

A. Analyze the audience in relation to itself.
  1. What are the levels and types of experiences that my audience has had (cultural, professional, recreational, educational, and so on)?
  2. What hierarchy of values does my audience possess or profess (money making and power, friendship, security, intellectual growth, and so on)? It is important to distinguish, if possible, between what an audience holds dear and what it professes to hold dear, if indeed there is a difference. Does the audience hide one set of values under another? If so, the writer's task grows more complicated.
B. Analyze the audience in relation to the subject.
  1. What opinion does my audience have on my subject?
  2. How strongly does my audience hold that opinion?
  3. How willing to act on its opinion is my audience—if acting is appropriate.
C. Considering what you have learned from your answers to A and B, determine what role your audience should play in relation to your voice as writer (peer, authority, subordinate, familiar, and so on).

By concentrating heavily on the values the audience holds, the writer can define the audience's image of itself. Once the writer has defined that image, he or she can select the proper voice with which to address the reader. Knowing the values and, therefore, the self-image of the audience is so important because a persuasive writer tries to avoid attacking the audience head on. An audience is rarely persuaded to change its ways by a writer who attacks the image the audience holds of itself; the writer must find a role for the reader that does not threaten the audience's self-esteem. If, for example, you want to convince a winning Little League baseball coach that his methods are harmful to the children he coaches, you might try finding a role other than coach for him to play. Chances are that he is also a parent, a role he could play with pride. And you might choose then to project the voice of another parent, a concerned equal. Study Writer 3's analysis below.

Writer 3　　AUDIENCE: TWO FRIENDS OF MINE, BOTH WHOM ARE VERY DIFFERENT, BUT WHO LOVE TO READ FASHION MAGAZINES

A.1. Background of my audience
  –both went to high school with me
  –both live in the suburbs & come from middle to upper middle class families
  –both were fairly active in school activities
  –both are attending X University, as freshmen this fall and they are both in occupational therapy as their career
  –both have volunteered in many hospitals and schools, where they have had an opportunity to get an idea of their future career
  –one friend, Julie, worked this summer for 6 weeks in a car factory and as a waitress so she could pay for her room & board at college
  –both of these girls would go into the library and before doing any studying would glance over the latest issue of "Seventeen" or "Glamour"
  –Julie is not quite as glamorous as my other friend
    –she wears jeans, overalls, smock tops, tennis shoes, earthshoes, little, or no jewelry, her hair hangs straight & is rarely curled, which is certainly not the latest style, but just right for her
  –Julie comes from a very religous family and so many of their current articles on living together, pre-marital sex & abortions really don't interest her
  –She is a little plump, so many of the fashions shown on the pencil-thin models arn't right for her
  –My other friend, Karen, is more the glamorous type, she always wears fancy clothes & she loves jewelry. She is very thin & so many of the fashions in magazines don't flatter her either.
  –Even though she loves these things in the magazines she will not pay their high prices & get many of her clothes at budget stores.
  –Although not coming from such a deeply religious family as Julie, Karen still holds many of the values that her parents have, and she also finds many of the articles unhelpful, since she can't relate to marriage, etc., at this time in her life
A.2. Values that my audience holds
  –both of these girls value their college life, and try to do their best, since they have found the field that interests them

       –they value the new friendships they have made at college, and
         the old ones from the high school years
       –they value a good career in which they are happy
       –they value being an individual in their thoughts, actions & clothes
       –since they are away at college they value practical advice & in-
         formation on all aspects of life to make their stay away from
         home as pleasant as possible

B. How do they feel about the subject
       –I think both of my friends like to read these magazines and
         maybe wish, as we all do that we had that perfect figure or that
         much money so we could afford those things
       –I think if they examined themselves as I have, they would find
         that truly these magazines have been very impractical for them

C. My audience's relationship to me
       –these girls are two of my best friends
       –we correspond to each other by letters
       –I am always interested in their life styles at college & they enjoy
         hearing about my college
       –We respect each others individualism in dress, mannerisms, &
         background and because we are so different we have so much
         fun together

Commentary Writer 3 has set down the history of two relationships without actually defining roles, but her last sentence implies them: She will be the wiser friend.
There is no reason why this should not work well, if indeed the friends do
"respect each others individualism."

CLASS
EXERCISES
1. Discuss Writer 1's Audience Analysis below.
   • Was his choice a good one? Why or why not?
   • What emotions does he discover that govern his audience?
   • What voice will he assume to establish credibility?
   • What values will he appeal to in his audience?
   • What more information should the writer have gathered?
2. Select a good audience for the medium the class chose to explore.
   • Analyze the audience's background.
   • Decide on the voice necessary to establish the writer's credibility.
   • Analyze carefully the emotions of the audience.

AUDIENCE ANALYSIS

Writer 1   **AUDIENCE:**

A. Sixteen and older, high school education or above, men and women
    with no extensive knowledge of football, people not familiar with tel-**

evision football presentations, people not offended by television advertising or innane comentary, persons who like to see good competition, people who value their time, people who want a big spectacular

B. The audience's attitude toward my focus is lukewarm because of limited knowledge of football on television, but I hope to persuade them to look in on a game some Monday night.

C. I want the audience to listen sympathetically to the reasons why Monday night football may be the most enjoyable sports happening on television and therefore worth their time. I, therefore, will assume the voice of a viewer thoroughly familiar with the program over a long period of time. I am an expert viewer. The audience will play the role of those who are indifferent, not hostile.

ASSIGNMENT

Stage 4 Toward a Paper on the Media: Planning for Aim and Audience

1. Choose your audience, applying the principle of "best audience" and add a brief statement explaining your reasons for thinking that your choice is best for a persuasive aim.
2. Using the Audience Guide, analyze your audience.
3. Seek commentary on your audience analysis from your instructor.

DEVELOPING, ORGANIZING, AND REFINING THE PAPER

DEVELOPING THE PERSUASIVE AIM

You can develop a persuasive aim by induction, deduction, and analogy.

Proof by induction

Inductive development expands the focus by providing many instances or examples or data or by using one powerful extended example. The number of instances depends on the audience; persuasion uses enough development to sway the reader. As you read Writer 1's First Version below, pay particular attention to the inductive development.

FIRST VERSION

Writer 1

MONDAY NIGHT SPECTACULAR

It is a typical Monday evening in early October. An uninitiated viewer goes to his television set and flips it on. What he sees next is a shot of 80,000 crazed maniacs packed into a football stadium. He immediately thinks to himself "not another football game; I saw two yesterday;" as he reaches out and switches channels. That viewer is just unwittingly depriving himself of a night of pure entertainment and sheer fun that won't be found on any other channel. "The Monday Night Football Show" is not just another football game! It is a comedy, slapstick and burlesque. The broadcasters interwoven with the overall Hollywood dazzle almost relegate the usually fine game to a subplot role. "Monday Night Football" is more enjoyable than Sunday afternoon football because of the quality of the action, magnetism of the personalities and the show biz approach all combining to make it a happening.

In order to appreciate the show he must know about the birth and development of this program. When ABC executives first acquired the Monday night package in 1970, they made a decision then that this was not going to be a typical football show. It was going to be snazzy, a mixture of show biz, humor and controversy. The selection of announcers was the integral decision in keeping with this idea. The executive producer of sports at ABC, Roone Arledge and his associates, decided to break with the tradition of only two broadcasters in the booth and go with the then-unheard of three. They wanted a professional play-by-play man who would act as a balancing force, or the only sane person sandwiched between two irreverent crazies. Keith Jackson was chosen to broadcast the game account for that first season. The chubby, articulate and accurate fifty-year old had an impressive list of credentials for sports coverage at ABC. Most importantly he was a low-key person who wouldn't try to steal the limelight or interfere with his future partners.

With one down, Arledge went after another person who would analyze replays and provide insights into the game. It was decided that a former player would be the best pick since he would have the most knowledge of the game. Arledge was well aware of the dangers of unqualified ex-jocks in the booth. They either wouldn't talk clearly or would put half the audience to sleep with over technical explanations of football strategy. The person selected would have to have a quick wit, someone who could appeal to the middle class working man viewing the game. Of the candidates a tall, blond Texan named Don Meredith seemed to best fit the qualifications needed. He had football experience as a quaterback of the Dallas Cowboys during the sixties. In addition he displayed a good natured country charm that endeared him to many. That added to his ability to think quickly made him the definitive choice.

So far Arledge had a strong team, but he still lacked someone to really make it the most talked about football show on television. He refered back to his original edict of never wanting to be dull and so opted for a controversial spokesman who could stir people up, cause the emotions to work, a person people could love to hate. He had his long-time friend, Howard Cosell, in mind as the third vital member of the team, Cosell, a sixty-year-old man of medium build, had already gained prominence as an outspoken proponent of Cassius Clay. He arrived on the Monday night scene high aloft many people's enemy lists.

Now that Arledge had departed from the football mainstream with his announcer selections he decided to go Hollywood all out, turn the game into an event. Cheerleaders in skimpy outfits were to be given extra attention by ABC cameramen during lulls in the show. Around the stadium fans were going to be encouraged to hang signs and banners with outrageous comments on them; they, too, would be thrust on the home viewers' screen. Arledge had created a circus atmosphere, and to top it off, big name celebrities would be invited to stop by the broadcast booth to chatter with the announcers; in return they could plug their upcoming specials.

Arledge knew he could have all the hoop-la in the world, but without quality games he'd run the risk of losing a segment of his audience. Football czar Pete Rozelle was more than happy to oblige Arledge with good competition. Rozelle could see the benefits of showcasing his product before such a wide audience, including people who didn't watch Sunday football because it cut up their whole day. So the NFL schedule makers chose the best teams based on the previous years' results and matched them against one another.

Needless to say, the show became an instant hit. The zany announcers, rowdiness of the fans and good action on the field caused millions to rave. During the years of the show's existence Arledge was forced by circumstances to make changes. Some changes were not drastic, like Frank Gifford replacing Keith Jackson on play-by-play when Jackson departed to broadcast college football in 1971. Gifford was from the same announcing mold as Jackson so his addition caused few ripples. Bigger problems ocurred in 1974 when Don Meredith was lured to greener pastures by NBC. He was replaced first by Fred Williamson, an ex-Kansas City Chief star who didn't make it through the exhibition season, and then by former Detroit Lion player-turned-actor, Alex Karras. Karras added occasional humor but had a weakness of not researching the teams playing on a given night and therefore offered spotty analysis. The ratings slipped during his two year tenure. Meredith, who viewers had grown close to over the years was hard to replace. However, when his movie career fizzled he rejoined the Monday night team. Another low spot occurred this year when in addition to the sixteen Monday night games, four other similar extravaganzas were telecast on selected Sunday and Thursday nights spread over the season. While the Thursday night games received good ratings, the Sunday night ones bombed. Oversaturation of football on Sundays appeared to be the obvious cause so these games will most likely be left off future schedules.

The amazing thing about the Monday night telecasts, though, is that they are still as fun to watch as the first show was. They've been through eight seasons but continue to cling to the original plan of being trendsetters rather than imitators of their Sunday counterparts. The viewer still feels like he is looking in on an event and if he doesn't watch he will miss something his friends or the papers will be talking about Tuesday morning.

Proof by analogy

In each exploration, you have been encouraged to create analogies for your subject. Sometimes you can use one or more of these to develop your entire essay or a section of it. The use of analogy gives the writer two peculiar advantages. It often relates the unfamiliar to the familiar, providing the reader with a comfortable, secure base. In addition, it is concrete in a unique way. Development by analogy is generally a matter of working progressively deeper into the similarities of the two things being compared. The more superficial the analogy, the less persuasive it will be. The more strict the analogy, the greater the possible development.

In reading Writer 5's First Version, pay particular attention to her use of one analogy.

FIRST VERSION

Writer 5

BUBBLES

The American entertainment industry has created many heroes, movie stars of the '30's and '40's like Clark Gable, Humphrey Bogart, and Greta Garbo, sports stars like Joe DiMaggio, music stars like Mick Jagger, Bob Dylan, and Linda Ronstadt but none seemed so near at hand as the families in the '50's and '60's who came into our living rooms each week on television. Watching these shows was like blowing soap bubbles as a child. The bubbles floated through the air so round and beautifully translucent but when we reached out to touch them they would disappear leaving only wet sticky hands behind. They were lovely, those bubbles like the TV images, but they were never solid enough to build a life on.

Those families had a profound effect on the children who watched them. Patrice, a 28 year old friend, recalled that "when I watched them I felt uncomfortable. My mother worked and there seemed to be something wrong with that." But for those of us with mothers at home the shows confirmed what we'd been taught, that this was the way things were "supposed to be." One bubble was Laura Petrie on the *Dick Van Dyke Show* replacing a sick dancer one week. She danced all day, scurried home to clean on her lunch hour, and served gourmet candlelit dinners to Rob each evening. She worried that she might not be satisfied "just being a wife and mother" after this, but at the end of the week she was happily settled back into her role. Each morning Laura stood in the kitchen, wide awake, hair combed, make-up on, fully dressed, ready to pour Rob's coffee and cook his eggs while he read the newspaper. In the morning I sit at the kitchen table, my old bathrobe wrapped around me, my eyes red and not fully open, slogging down three cups of coffee in a vain attempt to get going. My husband cooks his own breakfast while I sit feeling vaguely guilty.

In contrast to the family shows of today, *Family, One Day at a Time, Jeffersons,* and *the Fitzpatricks,* with mothers going back to school, a divorced mother raising children alone, black families, white families, lawyers, businessmen, and a steelworker, we viewed *Leave It to Beaver* wearing a plaid shirt, sweater, and a baseball cap, with a grimace on his freckled face because a little girl had kissed him, or Danny on *Make Room for Daddy* with his dark heavy eyebrows raised, listening to his precocious son, Rusty, or Ozzie wearing a cardigan sweater, oxford shirt and narrow tie, talking with Harriet about their children, Ricky and David, who grew up on television just as we did at home. Like soap bubbles from a pipe these shows were a constant stream of mothers in aprons, all-knowing fathers, and freshly scrubbed children. Still we never thought of them as television characters or actors playing roles; they were images of family life almost more real to us than our own—but when we tried to catch them, they disappeared.

Proof by deduction

Deductive development is especially useful when the writer is trying to persuade an audience of a highly controversial focus. Because deductive development moves from a general principle to a conclusion that validly follows, it operates well as a way of indirectly leading an audience to a conclusion, especially one that is threatening.

Deduction involves combining three ideas, such as

1. threat (a subject)
2. something the writer should try to eliminate (a point of significance)
3. anything that blocks communication (a linking idea)

into three kinds of statements:

1. a principle or standard:

    Anything that blocks communication *is* something the writer should try to eliminate.
            3   2

2. a linking statement (joining the writer's subject to the principle):

    Threat *is* something that blocks communication.
       1   3

3. a conclusion (often the writer's focus):

<u>Threat</u> is <u>something the writer should try to eliminate.</u>
  1   2

Constructing a deductive chain

How, then, does a writer construct such a deductive chain of statements?

1. Make your focus the third statement in your chain. Notice that you now have ideas 1 and 2. Below is a student writer's focus following an exploration of crime coverage in the news.

   <u>The sensationalism of crime coverage in newspapers</u> is <u>a threat to civil rights.</u>
                      1   2

2. Find a linking idea. Because the audience for this paper was to be the local newspaper editors, a difficult audience, the writer decided to use a linking idea concerned with innocent citizens, to which he felt his audience would relate:

   <u>Anything that damages the reputation of innocent citizens.</u>
                                 3

3. Set up your deductive chain.
   With this third idea, he set up his chain.
   a. principle:

   <u>Anything that damages the reputation of innocent citizens</u> is <u>a threat to civil rights.</u>
                           3   2

   b. joining statement:

   <u>The sensationalism of crime coverage in newspapers</u> is <u>something that damages the reputation of innocent citizens.</u>
                       1   3

   c. conclusion:

   <u>The sensationalism of crime coverage in newspapers</u> is <u>a threat to civil rights.</u>
                       1   2

4. Express the chain in less formal terms wherever you intend to use it in your paper.
   Below is the writer's less formal statement:

   Because we value our reputation as one of our highest possessions, I think we would agree that anything that damages the reputation of any innocent citizen is a real threat to the civil liberties of all of us. I have been concerned for some time now about the damaging impact of sensational crime coverage on the reputation of some innocent citizens, one of whom was a friend of mine. I'm concerned that such coverage is becoming a threat to our civil liberties.

5. Shift your development to the joining statement. The writer then went on to explain the damages of sensational coverage to several citizen's reputations.

Study Writer 3's First Version, examining the use of deduction as a framework for development.

FIRST VERSION

Writer 3   FASHION MAGAZINES OFFER IMPRACTICAL FASHION ADVICE

Every young woman in today's American society cannot help but feel the pressures of having to be attractice, glamorous and sexy. Many popular fashion magazines such as, *Glamour, Seventeen, Mademoiselle, Teen, Vogue* and *Harper's Bazaar* portray how the ideal woman should look. Marlo Thomas, Cher, Ellen Burstyn, Cybill Shepherd, Princess Caroline of Monaco and even Susan Ford are just a few of the many popular celebrities who often appear in these magazines to model the very stylish clothes. But can the average American girl really relate to and identify with these fashionable models? Although many girls are pretty, they never seem to think of themselves as being as perfect as they would like to be; either they are too tall, too short, too skinny or too fat; their hair is unmanageable, or their complexion is blemished. Everyone would agree that only practical fashion advice is helpful to girls. But as the young reader anxiously looks through the latest monthly fashion magazine, hoping to find that one eye-catching outfit that would spark up her wardrobe and her season, she is frequently discouraged by the outrageous prices of the outfits and is doubtful as to whether she has that perfect figure needed to wear the latest fashions. For these reasons most fashion magazines do not offer practical fashion advice. It becomes apparent, after many years of subscribing, that most fashion magazines are not helpful to the average American girl.

In today's age of inflation, the career girl and the college girl definitely need practical fashion advice. Both require a variety of clothes that are stylishly and reasonably priced while browsing through a popular fashion magazine, *Glamour*, one will notice that the average outfit consists of a midi skirt or pants, a woolen sweater, a patterned shirt and crazy-colored argyle kneesocks. The outfits shown are never complete without such accessories as: a head hugging hat, scarves, skinny belts, bangles, earrings, gold necklaces, mod watches and leather bags.

Each outfit, excluding the accessories, comes to a staggering figure, considering that a variety of clothes is necessary for work or school. Evening dresses, also, come with a high price tag. The price of these formal dresses hardly seems worth it for one night.

Some of these expensive clothes tend to be very faddish. The most drastic change in fashions has occurred in the length of the woman's hemline, which has gone from one extreme, the mini, to the other extreme, the maxi and all lengths in between in a period of two or three years. Fashion changes, although not as apparent, have also occurred in the styles of shoes, sweaters and makeup. In one college issue, *Mademoiselle* magazine says that yesterday's classic blazer is being replaced by big, bulky sweaters, and high-heeled platform shoes are giving way to the lower, more confortable heels and fashionable "cowboy" boots. The new, brightly colored ankle-to-thigh leg warmers, which are worn over jeans, must be the most unusual new fad pictured this year in *Mademoiselle* magazine. Today, earthtones of browns and light oranges are common in lipstick and nailpolish instead of the pink pastels. Even that earthy fragrance is present in many perfumes where the scent of roses or lilie of the valley used to dominate. Some fashion changes are very impractical for everyday use, and some have even been surrounded by controversy. Experts argue about how unsafe platform shoes are for driving, and twisted ankles are not unheard of as a result of walking on these four inch heels. Also, many of the clothes shown in these fashion magazines seem impractical both in price and texture, for anything but special occasions. Today's girl definitely needs reasonable, comfortable and good-looking clothes for relaxation and other activities, such as attending football games, and going to school, work or shopping.

In addition to being expensive and faddish, a further limitation to the practicality of the fashion advice presented by these magazines is that the clothes are designed for the tall, pencil-thin girl. The models featured in these magazines are from a very highly select group, rather than an average girl. These beautiful models all appear to have perfect figures to complement all of these expensive clothes, gleaming, straight teeth, clear complexions, long fingernails, big eyes, little feet, and manageable hair that looks attractice in a variety of styles. One cannot help but wonder how much camera-magic is involved in these photographs, for it seems unrealistic that a person can be ever so perfect. It is widely known that many celebrities, whose photos appear in fashion magazines have had different types of cosmetic surgery. Marlo Thomas, who appeared as a special feature in *Teen* magazine, must have had a "nose-job" for she certainly doesn't look like her father, Danny Thomas. Many celebrities admit to having facelifts, and rumor has it that Cher Bono even went so far as to have her buttocks lifted. Clothes, on a model whose appearance has been improved by plastic surgery and camera tricks may look very peculiar on a girl with an average face and figure. Unable to physically relate to these fashion models, the young woman feels bewildered about the kind of clothes that are flattering to her.

The average American girl avidly reads a variety of these popular fashion magazines hoping to find information that will guide her to select clothes that are comfortable, flattering and affordable. But most fail the girl miserably because their fashion advice is so impractical. Experience proves that the clothes they portray are expensive, faddish and unbecoming to the average figure. Therefore, most fashion magazines are not helpful to the average American girl.

CLASS
EXERCISES

1. Recall the exploration you did as a class on some medium. Identify the material that could be used for inductive proof.
   • Determine the analogies that could work for a persuasive aim.
2. With one side of the class playing different audience roles and the other the role of writer, propose analogies that would work for those audiences.
3. Starting with a focus the class chooses, build a deductive chain around it. Try several chains with different focuses. Test each principle for class acceptance.

ORGANIZING A PERSUASIVE PAPER

Most persuasion has three or four large sections:

1. introduction
2. proof
3. refutation (not always present)
4. conclusion

Introduction

The introduction of a persuasive paper has three functions: (1) it establishes the image of the writer, (2) it appeals to the attitudes and emotions of the reader, and (3) it announces the issues that the writer will discuss (that is, it states the focus).

If you need to, return to pp. 121–122 and reread what is said there about establishing the credibility of the writer, the plausibility of the argument, and an appeal to the reader's emotions. The plausibility of the argument will be developed in the middle sections of the paper—proof and refutation— but developing the image of the writer—the voice—and the emotional appeal should begin in the introduction.

CLASS
EXERCISES

1. Examine the introduction of Writer 2 below.
   • What emotions and attitudes of the audience does the writer arouse?

- What voice does the writer project? Will this writer seem credible to the audience? Why or why not?
- What other voice could have been used?
- Where is the writer's focus?

FIRST VERSION

Writer 2

SUBLIMINAL SEDUCTION

What would you say if I were to tell you that you are emitting foul odors from a hundred forty seven different parts of your body; your teeth are yellow and scummy; your hair is snowing dandruff (that is the dandruff that survives drowning in the oil); your face is a scabby prune and your brain is plugged up because you don't use Q-tips? Hopefully, unless you are '70's latest creature feature, you would tell me to get lost, go fly a kite or go suck an egg. Why, then, are the men and women on body product commercials allowed to bombard us each T.V. evening with advertizing pitches designed to make us feel inferior, unattractive and undesirable unless we use what they are selling? When we are able to recognize and understand these manipulative, psychological techniques used by advertizers, we will have the power to defy Madison Avenue's subliminal seduction. Otherwise, we will remain computers, involuntarily fed data that programs us to obediently pay top dollar for pre-selected products.

Advertizing today, as a result of much research, practice and money, has developed precise and effective ways to suck our subconscious through a tunnel of garbage that we, in turn, pave with our hard earned paychecks. Close-up toothpaste is one of the top five sellers on the market today because when that toothy girl tells us to put our money where our mouth is, we do it. Close-Up guarantees that whiter teeth and fresher breath will turn Billy on, implying that using a gooey, red gel on our teeth will remarkably improve our love life. So rather than buying a product that might be advantageous to the health of our teeth, we are sold on the sex appeal image. Love's Baby Soft products say "You can try hard or you can try soft. Soft'll get 'em every time." The ads show before and after sequences. First, the girls are aggressive and get no response from the guys. Then, they are passive and sacharine sweet, which results in instant dates. This ad also follows the "product-man" routine; but implies that using X product will get the woman a man by changing her personality. Hmmm—simply a variation on a theme, but still a psychological trap that is very carefully set for us.

Another technique applied, is that by using product X you will be one of the select crowd, or even more simply, just one of the crowd. A breathy young woman selling English Leather cologne assures us that all her men wear English Leather or nothing at all. That means that a man either chooses to wear English Leather or suffers the consequences. Advertizers are pouncing directly on men's fears of rejection by women.

A woman on the Clorets' breath mints commercial is shown to be suffering from a horrible case of humiliation and anxiety before asking to buy a breath deodorant, which she even has to ask for in a whisper, because she is so embarrassed. After the friendly neighborhood drug store clerk gives her a breath deodorant, she is immediately relieved of all worry and is able to breathe easily again now that she has been given her fix. Before she bought the mints, she could hardly bring herself to speak, let alone face the world. Through the constant repetition of this type of advertizing, people are conditioned to feel like they must always be supplied with product X before leaving the house; thus, turning them into addicts who are psychologically dependent on a product. This is, once again, playing on the impending fear or rejection. Watching these ads can be like looking into the distorted mirrors at the circus because no matter which one is looked at, the reflection is unattractive and undesireable, according to the media's standards.

The proof

Your proof (induction, deduction, analogy), the longest section of most persuasive papers, often contains several paragraphs. To organize this section, you have alternatives. We have already discussed description and narration. If your material for proof contains a potential chronology, you can arrange your proof using the narrative mode. If you wish to take up parts of your subject one by one, you can use the descriptive mode. You can also employ the evaluative mode to organize your proof.

THE EVALUATIVE MODE

The pattern of the evaluative mode is similar to that of deduction:

1. setting standards or criteria by which something can be judged
2. relating your subject to the criteria
3. drawing the conclusions that follow

Anything can be evaluated. You can evaluate a rock so long as you state a standard. A standard often is based on a purpose you have in mind: A small, flat rock is better than a large round one, if you want to skip a rock across the water; if you want to kill a snake with a rock, the large round one is better. The center of value rests in the use you propose for the subject. The correctness of your conclusion, furthermore, does not rest on your opinion. It is a fact that snakes are more easily killed with large rocks than with small ones and that large rocks do not skip well, especially if they are round.

Using the evaluative mode lays on you the absolute burden of making clear to the reader what the standard is. If the standard is acceptable to the audience, the conclusion will generally be acceptable, supposing that the account of the subject is clear and exact. It is useless to argue to an audience of deer hunters, for example, that deer hunting is "bad" unless you have first convinced the hunters, for example, that the suffering of the deer outweighs the satisfaction of the hunter.

Hence, in the evaluative mode your business is to convince the audience of the correctness of your judgment by

1. persuading the audience of the reasonableness of the standard you have established and
2. describing the subject faithfully and accurately, showing how it meets or doesn't meet that standard

The evaluative mode, although it looks easy, has its peculiar dangers. You must distinguish standard from conclusions by being certain that the standard is not simply the conclusion in disguise. That is, if the underlying sequence is this:

A thing is good if I like it, bad if I don't.
I don't like this thing.
Therefore, it is bad.

there is no standard apart from the conclusion. The task is to find a standard external to your likes and dislikes that the audience will accept as objective and fair.

CLASS EXERCISES

1. Study Writer 1's First Version (pp. 127–130).
   - What mode does he use to organize his proof? How do the paragraphs correspond to that mode?
   - How does his introduction establish his credibility as a writer? If not, why not?
   - How does the introduction as well as the entire paper appeal to the emotions?
2. Examine Writer 2's and 3's First Versions (pp. 133–137).
   - What mode of organization is used for the proof? Explain why this organization works or doesn't work for the persuasive aim.
3. Reread Writer 5's First Version (pp. 130–131).
   - What mode of organization is used for the proof?
   - What emotional appeal does the paper make to the audience?

Refutation

An effective persuasive writer knows that the audience is not neutral on an issue it is interested in. Inevitably, the audience will object to some parts of a writer's argument; the wise writer anticipates these objections and brings them into the paper in order to answer them. Answering objections is called *refutation*.

In order to refute, you have to know what the objections are. Sometimes that is easy; your audience may have written something on the subject. But commonly you must construct those statements yourself by concentrating on what you know of your audience's values and opinions.

Drawing up such statements and using them in your paper can actually add to the persuasive force of your paper in several ways. First, you meet the very practical problem of not seeming to ignore opposing views; you enhance the plausibility of your argument. Second, if you state objections fairly and accurately, you add to your own credibility. Third, by acknowledging the audience's emotional involvement in the issue you will defuse some of the potential hostility.

How you refute statements of objection is obviously very important. Theories of formal argument teach that there are two means of refutation: direct and indirect. *Direct* means an attack on an audience's statements of fact or statements of proof. *Indirect* means an attack on the audience's character or method of reasoning.

There are three kinds of direct refutation:

1. *Denial.* You deny the audience's statement and maintain that something else, perhaps the opposite, is true, whether the statement is a matter of fact or a matter of proof. This becomes an important kind of refutation for writers using the evaluative mode. These generally are objections to the standard being employed, and that type of objection, because it is so basic, needs to be brought forward and dealt with. For example, in the statement "Philosophy isn't worth studying because it doesn't get you a job," the basic assumption is that one should only study what will produce a job. That's a statement of proof that can be denied. Of course, it's also possible to deny it as a statement of fact, since people who study philosophy do get jobs.

2. *Distinction.* You accept an audience's statement in one sense, but deny it in another, more important sense. Look, for example, at the very vulnerable statement "Poison should not be put into public water supplies, and fluoride is poison."

3. *Retort.* You use the audience's reasoning to draw a different conclusion. If, for example, a Republican argues that the Democrats risked higher inflation by selling gold internationally and raising the prime interest rate at home in November, 1978, a Democrat might reply that both practices raised the exchange rate of the dollar and prevented a depression in the United States.

There are two kinds of indirect refutation. They are effective in persuasive writing only when the objections being refuted can be attributed to someone other than the audience:

1. An attack on the objector's character. This kind of refutation is useful only if the objector can be shown to be biased or ignorant. A writer who asks his or her audience to play either of those roles is in trouble. A writer who maliciously attacks a third person is likewise in trouble.

2. An attack on an objector's methods of reasoning. Simply stated, you examine an objector's process of deduction or induction and point out flaws. This can amount to calling him or her stupid, a role the audience should never be asked to play, although it can be a suitable role for a third person.

The danger in using indirect refutation lies in the damage it can do to the credibility of the writer. It is better to accept and acknowledge a minor objection than to risk losing the sympathy and respect of the audience.

CLASS EXERCISE

1. Study Writer 4's First Version.
   • What kind of refutation does he offer?
   • How will the refutation help to persuade his audience? If not, why not?

FIRST VERSION

Writer 4

THE COMICS: NOT FUNNY

Johnny is not your average sixth grader. Although only eleven years of age, he has a list of accomplishments that range from breaking up infamous diamond smuggling rings to rescuing astronauts stranded on the moon, not to mention saving the world from certain destruction many times over. Widely admired and recognized as a citizen of all nations, he is somewhat of a recluse spending many hours a day shut away in his room. Some speculate he is deeply involved with critical research on some new device or some special super power to add to his already vast repertoire, but Johnny's mother has put an end to the controversy with her single explanation, "Johnny spends one-hundred-and-ten-percent of his allowance on comic books." Tell the truth now. How many of you have ever seriously considered that comics might have some value other than as an alternative to juvenile delinquency?

Some of you with little Johnny's of your own at home know what a peculiar feeling it is when the words your child speaks to you must often are not, "Can I go out to play." nor "But, I don't wanna go to bed." nor even (though wouldn't it be nice) "I love you" but rather the singularly disgusting phrase, "Ma, can I have some money for comic books?" Of course, the more industrious of you have turned this to your advantage by using it to get Johnny to take out the garbage or even, under unusual circumstances, to take his little sisters to the Saturday matinee. For those of you who still have your doubts, consider that while your child is eagerly engaged in the fight of right against wrong he is not sliding through your neighbor's rose garden, not throwing a baseball through the basement window, not trying to light kitty-kat's tail on fire, and most important of all, not trampling about underfoot.

How many of you have even stopped to think that while your child is wasting his time reading those dumb comic books that he is in fact reading, a skill once almost universally possessed before the advent of that most nonparticipatory medium, television. What is more, your impressionable youngster isn't reading some seedy rag that will age him too quickly. No he reads how Dr. Doom, caught up in his plan of world conquest, flees from capture by the Fantastic Four. He reads of the Black Panthers, an American super hero who is the ruler of prosperous and peaceful nation in Africa. Kids form hero images of characters like Black Panthers or the Fantastic Four. These hero images are a convenient place for a child to place his values of right and wrong both to work with those values and to have a place to store them intact when the more personal issues of adolesence begin to occupy his mind.

While it is true that a comic book habit does involve a certain cost, there are other hobbies that are equally expensive and much less advantageous. The notorious chemistry set is one such example. In addition, if your child didn't spend so much money on comics, he might spend it on candy. You can buy a lot of comics with the money it takes to pay one dentist bill. Anybody still not convinced can just turn her back on the situation in hope that maybe some day her little Johnny will grow out of it. Maybe. However, the really shrewd mother knows how to get hers. She saves all those old comics that her children have so carelessly tossed under the bed and takes good care of them because one day when little Johnny becomes big Johnny those old comics are going to be worth some good money. The first issue of Batman sold for ten cents and is now worth four-hundred dollars.

Conclusion

The ending of a persuasive paper requires the reader to do two things: to summarize the proof and to restate the major conclusion. In a short paper, the summary and the major conclusion may be included in a single sentence. In a longer paper, the two may require a paragraph if they involve both changing the audience's mind and urging action. However, the ending should be as brief as possible, for several reasons. A long summary may irritate readers who have paid close attention to your proof. Furthermore, the ending does not lend itself to the introduction of new issues, new arguments, or new tasks; whatever needs to be argued should have been argued earlier. In addition, if you have arranged your argument properly in the body of the paper, the conclusions will have been explicit or self-evident. The purpose of the ending is simply to draw together what you have said so that the reader cannot mistake your intentions; the fact that your ending is no more than a neat condensation is a virtue in the persuasive aim.

REFINING THE PERSUASIVE STYLE

Styles vary according to aims. In Chapter 2, we described the style of the expressive aim. We now will discuss the style of the persuasive aim.

Diction

1. Since persuasion concentrates on the audience, the language of persuasion takes on the dialect of the audience—that is, the diction and sentence structure conform to the audience's "natural" language.

2. The language of persuasion tends to be more highly repetitive than the language of other aims. Repetition is the simplest way of emphasizing.

3. The language of persuasion contains an abnormal amount of humor, wit, and satire, probably because humor pleases audiences and, therefore, makes them more receptive to the writer.

4. The language of persuasion is remarkably concrete, despite our universal acquaintance with the political orator's use of abstract references: God, country, love, patriotism, freedom. These abstract words in persuasion do not function so much as units of meaning as signals to the audience of a cultural myth; the terms do not so much contain meaning in the ordinary sense as they say "You and I share certain beliefs and attitudes."

5. The language of persuasion contains a high proportion of figures of speech, probably because figures of speech are highly *connotative* (see Defining Terms).

6. The language of persuasion contains a high proportion of categorical statements, statements that offer definite, inclusive generalizations about the classes they name. Categorical statements imply certainty instead of doubt or indecision on the part of writers; part of the credibility of writers rests on their appearing to be certain of what they are saying.

7. The language of persuasion includes an abnormally high proportion of terms that refer to logic, logicality, reason, reasonableness (and the opposites: illogicality, unreasonableness), probably in order to meet the criterion of plausibility.

Among the preceding list of seven items, the one most easily misunderstood is item 6. While it is true that categorical statements are frequent in persuasive writing, you should not make categorical statements that are untrue. It is easy to fall into sweeping generalizations, to say "all" when you mean "some," "everything" when you mean "very little." The wrong categorical statement can destroy the very credibility that valid categorical statements should establish.

CLASS EXERCISE

1. Examine the diction of Writers 2 (pp. 136–137), 4 (pp. 140–141), and 5 (pp. 130–131).
   - What examples of humor, wit, or satire do you find?
   - What repetitions occur?
   - What evidence of concrete diction and connotations is present?
   - What concreteness and connotations could be introduced?
   - What figures of speech are used?
   - Identify the use of categorical statements.

SENTENCE PATTERNS

A good persuasive writer commands a wide range of sentence patterns, possessing the ability to combine or expand them easily. If your repertoire of structures is limited, you can increase your fluency by studying and practicing different patterns, which we will continue to introduce in selected chapters. Only by effort and use can you incorporate them into your own style. If you need further work with a particular combination, we include additional exercises on pp. 368–401. If you discover when you try these imitating and generating exercises that you need even more practice, your teacher can suggest workbooks devoted to sentence-combining.

CLASS EXERCISES

Sentence-combining

1. Study the clausal expansion patterns below. Then combine each of the sets of sentences into one that imitates the pattern above it.
2. Examine the First Versions in this chapter for evidence of these patterns. Indicate places where the writers could have combined sentences. Rewrite such sentences.

Pattern A **Alfred the Great,** who was the most famous king of the West Saxons, **reigned in the second half of the ninth century.**

1. Roger Shuy has written articles.
2. There are many such articles.
3. Shuy is professor of linguistics.
4. The articles are on differences.
5. The differences are in dialects.
6. These dialects are regional.

---

1. The Inuit can teach us.
2. The Inuit are the native people of Alaska.
3. They can teach us this.
4. We can adapt to climates.
5. The climates are harsh.

Pattern A1 **The large folding screens,** which once decorated the houses in Kyoto and Edo, **give the most complete visual account of everyday life in old Japan** that has come down to us.

1. The language resists the controls.
2. The language is English.
3. The language is growing.
4. The language is also changing.
5. These things happen constantly.
6. The controls are of the standardizers.
7. The standardizers are among us.
8. They try to regulate the language.

---

1. "Star Wars" replaces the complexity.
2. It is a movie.
3. It uses simple names.
4. It uses simple plots.
5. The complexity is of life.
6. The life is everyday.
7. The complexity is replaced with polarization.
8. The polarization is sharp.
9. The polarization differentiates good from bad.
10. It does this rigidly.

Pattern A2 **The man** whom we feared **made us an offer** that we couldn't refuse.

1. The executive gave him a look.
2. He admired the executive.
3. The look was sharp.
4. The look was full of contempt.

_____

1. The child splashed us.
2. We teased the child.
3. The splashing was with water.
4. The water was in his bucket.

Pattern B **Mary Queen of Scots was beheaded** after Queen Elizabeth's chief spy intercepted and decoded Mary's letters.

1. The audience stomped.
2. The audience clapped.
3. The audience whistled.
4. The players reappeared.
5. They were bluegrass players.
6. Their reappearance was for an encore.

_____

1. Jonathan Swift usually published his works.
2. Swift was an eighteenth-century satirist.
3. The publishing was anonymous.
4. He did so although his authorship was known to many.

Pattern B1 While his friend sunbathed on a flat rock and the puppy slept beneath the alders, **Gene baited a red wriggler on a Number 8 hook and waded into the icy water.**

1. The band played the alma mater.
2. Her mother and father waited in the auditorium.
3. Janice donned the robe.
4. The robe was black.
5. She also donned the mortarboard.
6. The robe and mortarboard were of a university graduate.

_____

1. The cupboards were bare.
2. The fridge was empty.
3. The roommates pulled sweaters.
4. They did this over their shirts.
5. They also strapped baskets.
6. They put them onto their bikes.
7. They headed for the nearest grocery.

Pattern C *That the atmosphere of desperate failure grows steadily* makes the worn-out men and nervous, overworked women old before their time.

1. The team would lose.
2. This would happen eventually.
3. This left the players despondent.
4. It also left the coaches despondent.
5. Their despondency was about their record.
6. The record was of the season.

---

1. The vegetables of Anjou are probably the best in France.
2. The fruit of Anjou is also probably the best in France.
3. This made our mouths water.
4. The watering was in anticipation.
5. The anticipation was of our meal.
6. The meal would be our first.

Pattern C1 At bedtime we crawl into our sleeping bags and hope *that tomorrow's hike will be an easy one.*

1. The following happened in ancient Greece.
2. Citizens appeared.
3. The citizens were ordinary.
4. The appearance was in courts.
5. The courts were law courts.
6. The citizens appeared on their own behalf.
7. They argued the following.
8. They wanted the lands to be returned to them.
9. The lands were confiscated ones.

---

1. The following happened during lectures.
2. The lectures are three hours long.
3. We sit in seats.
4. The seats are ours.
5. We imagine the following.
6. The bell will never ring.

Pattern C2 One of the functions of the wilderness is to teach us *that constant activity is not the only way of life.*

1. The following happens at the end of the day.
2. Their bodies ached.
3. Their aching was to discover the following.
4. A pool waited.
5. The pool was still.

6. The pool was beyond the rapids.
7. The rapids were next.

---

1. The visitors need.
2. They are visitors at the zoo.
3. The zoo is a city zoo.
4. Their need is to remember the following.
5. They should not give food.
6. The food is junk.
7. Their giving is to the animals.

ASSIGNMENT

Stage 5 Toward a Paper on the Media: Developing, Organizing, and Refining the Paper

1. **Plan your paper with a persuasive aim and a subordinate mode of organization (descriptive, narrative, or evaluative).**
2. **Developing your focus in the light of your audience, write the first version of your paper.**
3. **Refine your style.**

CRITIQUING AND REWRITING

CRITIQUING PERSUASIVE PAPERS

In critiquing a persuasive paper, your best procedure is to read the paper first as if you were the intended audience (no very easy thing to do sometimes, but necessary) without trying to be analytical. Then ask the simple question, "Am I persuaded?" Whether the answer is "yes" or "no," you can then go back and try to isolate the features of the paper that led to the answer.

Role playing the audience for the paper can be done in two ways: (1) If you know the intended audience, you can then evaluate the persuasiveness of the paper, from the viewpoint of that audience. (2) If you do not know the intended audience, you can speculate on whom the writer intended as the audience and proceed from that point. If you can in no way determine the audience or if the audience turns out to be different from what you guess, the writer may find the root of several problems in the paper.

CRITIQUE:
Writer 3

Focus

The focus is announced in the first paragraph and then strictly adhered to in the remainder of the paper (pp. 133–135). A deductive chain is set up in the first paragraph as the focus, and in the deductive chain, the focus also serves as the conclusion of the paper. Here is the chain:

Only practical fashion advice is helpful to [average American] girls.
Most fashion magazines do not offer practical fashion advice.
[Therefore] Most fashion magazines are not helpful to the average
American girl.

Development

The paper is well tailored to its audience, the fashion conscious American
girl. Especially impressive is the writer's regard for the intelligence of her
audience; every generalization is illustrated (and, therefore, supported) by a
series of concrete examples that are stated exactly, without exaggeration.

Those generalizations are subdivisions of the linking statement; the
body of the paper consists of a series of criteria developed by illustrative
details that violate the criteria, therefore proving that fashion magazines that
put a premium on expense, faddishness, and an atypical figure are not practical.

By doing these things, she has satisfied the requirements of the persuasive aim. She has established her credibility as writer by showing her detailed knowledge of the problem, by her concern for the good of the audience, and by her lack of deception. She has, furthermore, established the
plausibility of her argument by, as we have noted, her profuse use of illustrations and by the reasonable standard of judgment that she has set up. She
has, finally, taken into account the emotional state of her audience by pointing out and sympathizing with the doubt and discouragement the advice in
fashion magazines may engender in the reader.

Organization

The paper uses the evaluative mode within the larger persuasive framework;
the writer is also faithful to her deductive chain throughout. Moreover, she
has maintained the third-person point of view. In addition, she has eased the
reader from paragraph to paragraph with careful transitions.

Style

The style is adequate, but it could be improved. Categorical statements, as
in the first sentence, are believable. And the writer knows when to back off
from sweeping generalizations—for example, "Many popular fashion magazines . . . ."

The diction could be improved. The paper is a bit wordy. Take the
first paragraph alone. The opening phrase, "Every young woman in today's
American society," could become "American young women." In the third
sentence, the phrase ". . . are just a few of the many popular celebrities who
often appear" is largely unnecessary. Consider the logic of language: if the
writer gives a list of famous people, then obviously they are "celebrities,"

and celebrities are by definition "popular"; and if they represent a "few," then obviously there must be "many." In the fourth sentence, "relate to and identify with" is redundant. In the fifth sentence, "being as perfect as they would like to be" can be nailed down to one word: "perfect."

Conventions

The writer has a good command of the conventions of Standard Written English. Occasionally her grasp of punctuation slips: "Many popular fashion magazines such as, . . ." ("Many popular fashion magazines, such as . . . ."). But there is no serious problem here.

REWRITING

After weighing the advice in the instructor's critique, Writer 3 revised her paper.

REVISED VERSION

Writer 3

LET THE READER BEWARE

American young women cannot help feeling pressed to be attractive, glamorous, and sexy. Many popular fashion magazines such as *Glamour, Seventeen, Mademoiselle, Teen, Vogue,* and *Harper's Bazaar* portray how the ideal woman should look. Marlo Thomas, Cher, Ellen Burstyn, Cybill Shepherd, Princess Caroline of Monaco, and even Susan Ford model in these magazines.

But can the average American girl really profit by identifying with these people? The only helpful fashion advice is practical. Since most American girls are neither rich nor gifted with perfect figures and flawless complexions, most fashion magazines are not very helpful to the average American girl.

With today's inflation, the career girl and the college girl need very practical fashion advice. Both require a variety of clothes that are stylish and reasonably priced. The most recent issue of *Glamour* features outfits consisting of midi skirts or pants, woolen sweaters, patterned shirts, and crazy-colored argyle knee socks. These outfits are incomplete without such accessories as head-hugging hats, scarves, skinny belts, bangles, earrings, gold necklaces, mod watches, and leather bags. Each outfit, excluding the accessories, costs a staggering figure, considering the variety of clothes necessary for work or school. Evening dresses also come with a high price tag. One issue of *Seventeen* features Susan Ford in formal dresses, the latest spring prom look. What those dresses cost hardly seems worth it for one night.

Some of the expensive clothes are faddish. In two years the hemline has gone form mini to maxi. *Mademoiselle* says that yesterday's classic blazer is being replaced by big bulky sweaters, and platform shoes are giving way to cowboy boots. Some outfits are appropriate for special occasions only—like the bizarre outfit *Seventeen* advised for a wine-tasting party. Today's girl needs reasonable, comfortable, attractive clothing for school, work, and recreation, and these are scarce in the popular fashion magazines.

In addition, the clothes shown are designed for a tall, pencil-thin figure. When one considers how unaverage that kind of figure is, then adds in the fact of plastic surgery—as when Cher had her breasts redesigned and her buttocks lifted, and compounds all of that with the magic thrills a camera can perform, she has to wonder what one has to be to wear these clothes well.

The American girl needs advice on how to select clothes that are comfortable, flattering, and affordable. In the popular fashion magazines, she is instead advised to buy clothes that are expensive, faddish, and unbecoming to the average figure. Let the reader—and the buyer—beware.

CLASS EXERCISES

1. Using the Critical Guide, critique the First Version of Writer 1 (pp. 127–130).
2. Working in groups, critique each other's papers.
3. Compare Writer 3's revision with her First Version. How has she responded to the advice?

ASSIGNMENT

Stage 6 Toward a Paper on the Media: Critiquing and Rewriting
1. **Guided by criticisms from your instructor and classmates, do a critique of your own work.**
2. **Revise your paper.**

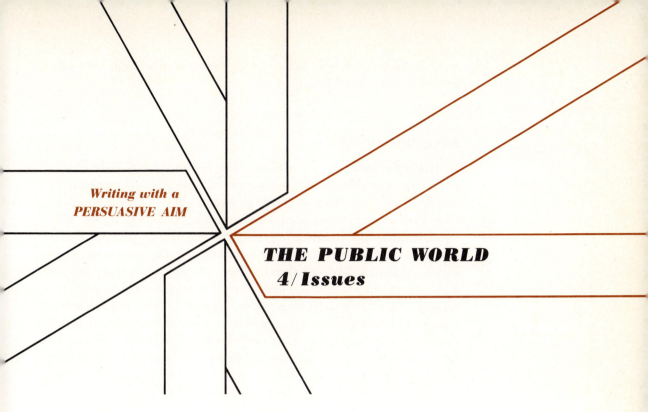

Writing with a
PERSUASIVE AIM

THE PUBLIC WORLD
4/Issues

THE WRITING CONTEXT

In the public world, you are surrounded by issues—social, political, economic, moral, cultural. Many only brush your lives, lightly touching you as you read the papers or listen to the news. But a few issues may strike you heavily, influencing your behavior, limiting your freedom, sometimes turning the course of your life. You may ignore the unemployment story on page three of the newspaper until you struggle to find a summer job. "Crime" may be merely an ominous word until it turns into someone grabbing your purse. Inflation may seem distant until you despair over your own budget.

When an issue strikes your life, you take a strong stand, but emotion often clouds your judgment, moving you from indifference to prejudice. How, then, can you find balance, a reasonable judgment, on your crucial issues? How can you step beyond passion toward a reasonable center in the midst of public debate? The writing process is one type of balancing act whose center is probability, the middle point between impassioned opinion and certainty. A reasonable judgment is a focus stabilized by good reasons, tested in the public world. As the writing context for this chapter, we set an issue that is important to you.

THE COMPOSING PROCESS

Writing in this public world will also provide further exercise in the stages of composing. Even though we have presented these stages in an order, you may find yourself working in several at once or weaving back and forth because they are neither totally separate nor mechanically lockstepped. When trying to formulate a starting question, you may decide to select another subject. As you begin to explore, your question may lose importance, so you have to begin again. As your ideas incubate, you may see the need for more exploring. In other words, you often operate in several stages at once or in varying order. But none of these phases is missing from a genuine writing process. Composing is not only complex; it demands time. Cramming the phases into one night or one hour rarely leads to a good focus. Learning to write demands the same patience and practice as mastering any art. Your efforts may often be awkward until you gain a mastery that blends your early deliberate labor in each stage into a powerful performance.

FINDING AND EXPRESSING THE STARTING POINT

FINDING THE SUBJECT

In the jungle of public issues in which you wander, keep two guidelines in mind when selecting an issue on which to write. Choose an issue:

1. that has entered your life or the lives of those close to you
2. that is open to your deeper investigation, not closed by your prejudice (that is, one on which you will be willing to come to a new focus, a deeper understanding)

Writer 1 selected the welfare issue because she had irritating problems with Aid to Dependent Children and wanted to see several sides to this issue. Writer 2 decided on the issue of care for the aging because his visits to his grandmother's house and a nursing home aroused strong conflicting feelings in him. Writer 3 chose to investigate the women's movement because her lifestyle as a homemaker conflicted with her sympathy for the movement. Writer 4 was concerned about the struggle in Northern Ireland because she had visited relatives in Ireland and England. Writer 5 had favored a lower drinking age until he saw its impact on students at his high school.

In each case, the writers chose issues with which they had had personal experience. The first three held conflicting attitudes toward the issue and, hence, were open to new understandings. Writer 4's "concern" doesn't indicate her dissonance. Writer 5 selected an issue whose dissonance seems in the past. He now appears to be against a lower drinking age.

EXPRESSING THE STARTING POINT

Because any public issue by its nature has endless dimensions, a sharpened starting point will better control your exploration. Recall the strategy used in the previous chapters:

1. Identify aspects of the issue that challenge your values or interpretation of the world.
2. Formulate a question that points your exploration toward the desired probable judgment.

STARTING POINTS

Writer 1 MY VALUES OR EXPECTATIONS
–my own dignity
–courtesy
–fairness

ASPECTS OF ADC
–I dislike the indignity of the process of getting aid
–the impersonality
–I need ADC

Question: What impact does being on ADC have on the recipient's values?

Writer 2 MY VALUES OR EXPECTATIONS
–respect for older people
–vitality and peacefulness
–good care for the elderly

ASPECTS OF CARE FOR THE AGED
–the ugliness of the nursing home
–the boredom of the older people at homes

Question: Is staying at home better for older people than staying in a nursing home?

Writer 3

MY VALUES OR EXPECTATIONS
–being a wife and mother
–developing my talents

ASPECTS OF THE WOMEN'S MOVEMENT
–emphasis on job rights
–looking down on "housewives"

Question: How has the women's movement affected housewives' attitudes toward themselves?

Writer 4 MY VALUES OR EXPECTATIONS
–peace and tolerance

ASPECTS OF NORTHERN IRELAND
–attitude of the Irish people I met
–continuous violence

Question: What has caused the struggle in Northern Ireland to continue on and on?

Writer 5 MY VALUES OR EXPECTATIONS   ASPECTS OF LEGAL DRINKING AGE

—18-year-olds should be treated like adults

—learning is important

—the behavior of some at my high school

Question: What impact on their education does drinking have on high school students?

Commentary   Writer 1 notes a personal conflict between economic need and values. Her question expresses this problem and points her inquiry toward ADC's impact on her values.

     Writer 2's aspects of the issue center on negative features of nursing homes. If he is already prejudiced against them, his question may not lead to an open investigation of the issue.

1. Examine the Starting Points of Writers 3, 4, and 5.
   • What dissonances do they express?
   • How will the starting questions guide their explorations?
2. Choose an issue for class examination.
   • Identify aspects of the issue that clash with the class's values.
   • Formulate a question to point toward a balanced answer.

ASSIGNMENT

Stage 1 Toward a Paper on an Issue: Finding and Expressing the Starting Point

1. **Identify an issue that has touched your life.**
2. **State the aspects of the issue that challenged one of your values or expectations.**
3. **Formulate a question to direct your exploration.**
4. **Seek comments on your starting point from your teacher and classmates.**

EXPLORING

     The Exploratory Guide will help you gain the distance needed to explore beyond feelings and prejudices. Your inquiry should probe both the issue's public dimension and your experience with it. The directives below suggest ways of adapting the guide to this writing context.

EXPLORATORY GUIDE

Static view
   —Define your issue, distinguishing it from other issues like it.
   —Record the details of your personal experience with it.
   —Determine the sides of the public debate on the issue.

Dynamic view
  –Trace the history of the issue, noting causes and effects, changes in its nature, and importance in the public sphere.
  –Speculate on the future of the issue.

Relative view
  –Classify your issue, defining the larger groups in which you place it.
  –Compare and contrast your issue with others.
  –Create at least one analogy for your issue.

EXPLORATION

Writer 1   ADC

STATIC VIEW

–long waits and working through red tape
–intimidating
–impersonal
  –state-of-mind trap for parents of small children
–not enough money to expand on—just enough to get into a penny-pinching, rather-spend-time-than-money (waiting for rummage sales, stores' specials and clearances, closely calculating food budget) bag
–nothing left over for mind-stimulating activities, or even amusement (getting out of the city, other entertainment & recreation)
–on the other hand
  –counter-intimidation working to turn it into a tool rather than an only alternative
  –example: single father demands, not asks aid, after being unemployed for a year. The crooked path is made straight, sudden abundance is heaped on him, instant food orders on demand, cab fare home, all accumulated bills paid, mortgage and utilities paid henceforth
–the myth of the flourishing ADC mother with twelve illegitimate children
–the stagnant state of mind to which the ADC mother is susceptible
–the indignity of trying to obtain help of any kind (even the phone lines are always busy) from social services

DYNAMIC VIEW

–compliant, meek recipient will struggle on, slowly putting herself through school, fearful of spending an unnecessary penny
–powerful independent fellow (whom social services has decided to put through ceramics school or something—he's already a master electri-

cian) will turn the aid to his benefit without suffering its degradations, and do as he pleases

RELATIVE VIEW

Analogy

—ADC is a trap. The poor and unready (for instance the unwed mother types unable to handle the practical world) are bailed out, provided with enough for subsistence in inadequate housing, etc.

—ADC is a ladder: The clever in temporary distress can get themselves on their feet again without sullying their self-respect, jeopardizing their children, or kow-towing to the bureaucracy.

Commentary The exploration is limited. The writer records only a few features from her personal experience with the issue. She should expand to note the public dimensions of the system: Who is eligible for aid? What are the regulations? What is the source of funds? and so on. The writer should also more fully examine the sides of the ADC issue. The dynamic view makes a brief mention of two means of getting aid. A fuller exploration would probe the writer's knowledge of ADC's beginning, current status, and future. The analogies for two types of recipients may be fruitful for insight. Classifying the issue and comparing it to other welfare programs would have enriched the writer's exploration.

EXPLORATION

Writer 2   CARE FOR THE AGING

STATIC VIEW

—old people
  —slow, but competent
  —mobile and self-serving
  —need help with strenuous work

—Grandmother's home sights:
  —worn, beautifully carved antiques
  —pink blossoms of a crab apple tree
  —old-fashioned rockers
  —old, faded pictures
  —a victorian loveseat
  —an old cathedral radio
  —crocheted table doily
  —delicate handwork as seen on pillows and a cherished platform rocker

—a brass tea-kettle, a cherished family heirloom
—colorfully decorated Christmas cookies
—old, leather-bound volumes

—Smells
    —freshly baked bread
    —spicy smell of pumpkin pies
    —fruity smell of crab-apple jam
    —aroma of hot vegetable soup
    —old "lived in" smell of their house
    —fragrant smell of the hybrid tea roses in the backyard

—Sounds
    —chirping of birds around the bird house
    —familiar sound of the dog barking or canary singing
    —joyful sounds of company (relatives)

—Tastes
    —sweet taste of jelly
    —delicious home-made cooking

—Nursing Home
    —sterile, germicidal smell
    —monotonous dull, pale green walls everywhere
    —cheap, style-less furniture
    —lack of personal picture portraits on the walls
    —common, huge, impersonal dining room
    —cold, unfriendly sitting room
    —lack of privacy
    —bland food
    —impersonal care
    —complaining, irrasible companions
    —lack of variety of age group

DYNAMIC VIEW

—Grandmother's
    —peacefulness settles over the house every evening at dusk
    —grandchildren noisily playing in the yard
    —the elderly people are doing light chores for themselves such as
      cooking, sewing, cleaning, etc.
    —they are chatting with neighbors over the fence
    —trees and flowers in their backyard are blossoming and changing
      colors with each new season

—they are digging up their son's and daughter's old electric trains and baby dolls while reminiscing about days gone by
  —quiet nights are spent silently reading a book or magazine or viewing T.V.
  —they are reminiscing over a freshly brewed cup of coffee
  —they are anticipating calls from children or letters from grandchildren

—The Nursing Home
  —elderly people's senses are idle, nothing new to see, nothing pleasant to hear, time hangs very heavy
  —some old people are holding dolls while rocking back and forth in a rocker, obviously regressing backward to childhood
  —some old people are whining and crying during the day
  —physical therapy "jars" these people into exercising
  —most of these people are hard to handle because they don't want to be there, they are just put there in many cases

RELATIVE VIEW

Analogy

My grandparent's house vs a nursing home is like going away for college vs staying home. When a person goes away to college, he finds himself living in a dorm. All of the rooms are the same dull color, with 2 beds, 2 desks and 2 dressers which have been used for years. You are with the same people all year who are all your age. You become just another person. Some of your individuality and your personality are left at home in your bright room, with posters on the wall.

When an elderly person leaves his home, he leaves alot of his personality there in the furniture, handworks, etc. and just becomes another person in the nursing home in an environment where every room is the same.

Comparison

An old person who is able to care for himself and is put in a nursing home is like a child who is confined to an apartment. A child needs room to grow, to play in a backyard on the swings, to have a pet dog and to make a little noise now and then. Just as an old person needs to be in their own home and do their own cooking, cleaning, sewing and to generally care for themselves.

Commentary The writer records good concrete details of his grandmother's home. The account of the nursing home, however, seems stereotypical, as if the writer had never visited one, nor does he examine the public controversy over care for the aging. The writer presents a sensitive description of the activities of the elderly, but shows no knowledge of the history of this issue. Although this paper does not require research, he might have questioned his parents about care for their grandparents. The analogies and contrasts will work well.

EXPLORATION

Writer 5

THE LEGAL DRINKING AGE

STATIC VIEW

Students' physical appearance
—short, 17 year-old, brown-haired girl's breath smelling of wine after lunch
—staggering a little down the halls but making it look like a joke
—feeling very warm & hot
—flushed cheeks
—opening windows because they are hot
—drinks enough to feel good but not enough to be drunk
—mixes up words but blames it on being tired or just a joke
—dizziness
—sways just a bit when standing up—barely noticeable
—depends on alcohol very much
—responds slower than normal
—swears when normally they won't say anything like that
—acts very friendly, usually much more than normal

Students' attitudes
—laughing very loud in class for no reason
—spending free time to drink—not doing homework
—think they are very mature by drinking
—guys who are not athletic drinking to show their masculinity
—very moody & unfriendly towards friends
—uncooperative in class—won't answer teacher's questions
—try to match their friends by drinking as much or more
—fast, tall, muscular guys kicked out of track because drinking has slowed them down
—doesn't pay attention in class
—barely passes the different classes
—skip class because of too much to drink
—skips class—loss of interest
—skips class—drinking much more important
—mixes beer & pills
—16 & 17 year-olds getting drinks from 18 year-olds
—stealing beer out of a party store because of being a minor
—hiding beer, wine, etc in thermos bottles in hall lockers

—uncontrolled giggling in class
—becoming silly—mocking teacher or classmate
—taking easy classes—just show up in class & get a passing grade—no learning
—sneaking bottles of beer & wine under their bulky coats at dances, football, & basketball games

Damages to health
—drinking after other people—mononucleosis, etc.
—brain damage
—liver damage—cirrhosis
—dependency on alcohol
—becoming an alcoholic
—losing control—beating people up
—depresses the person—could make that person suicidal
—led to mental diseases & depression
—kill themselves by mixing pills & booze
—if bad enough—hallucinate & paralysis

Reasons for drinking
—social acceptance—be part of a certain group
—low grades—can't cope at school
—parents nagging about low grades, school work
—non-understanding parents—no time for their child
—can't decide what to do in life—feels useless
—takes pressure & tension away at exam time
—relationship with girl or boyfriend broken up—drinking makes everything livable

DYNAMIC VIEW

—falling from an A or B student to C or lower
—friendly, outgoing person to a withdrawn, uninterested person
—losing good friends because of only care about drinking
—being involved on committees then dropping out
—don't graduate because of failing—reduced graduating class in June

RELATIVE VIEW

Comparison
—drinking at my high school to another one like Kimball or Ferndale High School
—the high school 4 years ago when drugs were in & now when drinking is in
—their drinking to their parents drinking
—having a high school education & diploma to not have one because of dropping out—job-wise especially

Analogy
Drinking eats into you & destroys you like acid. Drinking is harmful like acid if not handled very carefully.

Although the writer records numerous characteristics of student drinking that he groups under workable headings, the precise nature of the public issue remains unclear. The dynamic view shows a few changes in his peers caused by drinking, but does not trace the history of the issue. The entire exploration remains one-sided, suggesting that the writer is collecting ideas for a preconceived judgment or focus and, hence, is not open to new understanding.

1. Study the Explorations of Writers 3 and 4.
   - What features distinguish their issues from others like them?
   - What personal experience with the issue do they cite?
   - What sides of the issue are explored? What other sides could have been considered?
   - What historical knowledge do they evidence?
   - What kinds of changes in the issue have they noted?
   - How have they classified the issue? In what other groups could they have put their issues?
   - Why have the writers chosen the comparisons or contrasts and analogies? How will these lead to focuses?
2. Explore the issue you chose as a class.
   - Use the Exploratory Guide to record (on the board or on paper) ideas the class gathers with the static, dynamic, and relative views.

EXPLORATION

Writer 3   WOMEN'S MOVEMENT

STATIC VIEW

—watching a countless stream of feminists on the Phil Donahue Show talk about options—and then say in a patronizing tone "Well if you knew all your options and that's what you chose to be—a housewife. . . ."
—feminists talking about how boring and degrading housework is, how unfulfilling—
—feminists talking about universal day care—picturing my daughter at Sugar and Spice or some other day care center herded about with 30 or 40 other kids by 2 or 3 or 4 adults who can't possibly spend enough time with her
—Congress passed initial tax deduction for child care expenses which excluded relatives from being eligible to babysit
—telling someone at a cocktail party what you do & watching their eyes glaze over at the word "housewife"

—feminists calling volunteerism a bad thing which allows society to take unfair advantage of women's labor
—feminists talking about shared parenting—watching the satisfaction and joy my husband has with Mary Sharon

DYNAMIC VIEW

—in the past—women lauded and praised for raising children, baking bread, being "supermom"
—today—emphasis on career women or the women who can do it all—house that looks like a picture in Better Homes & Gardens, well-behaved, beautiful, intelligent, planned-for 2 children, and rising career (she takes Geritol to make it all possible)
—modern books & movies—seldom show a mother with young children in a new role; no images except those of the past on television or in movies which portray this
—frequent movies and TV shows which picture women with older children finding themselves often after a divorce precipitates things, ex. *One Day At A Time, An Unmarried Woman* (movie), *See How She Runs*
—future—some integration of new freedoms that will bring forth books, movies, TV shows which can show women with husband, and babies coping with life, making choices in a more free way
—increased acceptance of woman who chooses to stay home

RELATIVE VIEW

1. Classify
—women's movement is a social movement which had its greatest impact through changes in attitudes, values of society; is also political leading to changes in laws

2. Compare/contrast

—women's movement started in Friedan's book, media coverage & tv changed attitudes and gradually tv changed laws
—left housewives feeling disoriented, women with large families feeling undervalued

—black movement started in the main with changes in laws & then moved (or is moving) slowly toward changes in attitudes
—in some areas left the early blacks who'd had to adapt a certain way to survive feeling younger ones felt they were "Uncle Toms", a term of derision

3. Analogy
Being a housewife today is like rolling logs in water. You move your feet as fast as you can in order to maintain your balance while the water and the log move swiftly under your feet constantly changing like the society in which we live.

Writer 4   NORTHERN IRELAND

STATIC VIEW

—essentially a working class struggle between the Catholics & the Protestants, intensified by the involvement of different political factions
—groups in the war: IRA—Protestant Provisional Army—British government (British soldiers)—Northern Irish—Southern Irish—indirectly
the British middle class
—the cities of the war: dreary, grimy, ugly Irish industrial towns contain
the fighting   Londonderry, Belfast, Dublin, lately London
—fighting has been continuous for over 50 years
—N. Ireland torn with internal hatred   Southern Irish afraid fighting
will spill over the border
—people: one reason they fight is because they do not have anything else
to do; most Americans would reject this argument, however the boredom of a city such as Belfast cannot be described
—often the average, middle-class Englishman really hates the Irish
—an economic-political-social-religious war

Economic
—for years the poor Catholic factory workers were prevented from
working in Protestant factories; the same was true for the Protestant
workers & Catholic factories
—the hate intensified so much that to both sides the only recourse was
violence
—other economic situations affecting the struggle: England has always
accepted Irish labor, supplied the jobs. Some English say: "They take
our jobs & shoot our boys"
—the general economic situation of N. Ireland is very dismal
—the lower classes of Catholics & Protestants work in factories
—menial jobs, inflation is high & creeping higher

Political
—should N. Ireland be a separate country? Many N. Irish still dream of
a united Ireland
—House of Commons—London   scene of the political debates
—Ian Paisley—hateful Protestant leader
—B. Devlin—Catholic Crusader. Both prejudiced due to their backgrounds
—should England have soldiers in N. Ireland or not?
—English soldiers get killed & it's an Irish war
—England's alternatives: withdraw, do not accept Irish immigrants, la-
borers or refugees stop all trade with Ireland
—other alternatives: intensify military pressure. Harsh sentences for all
people involved in anyway with unlawful groups

Social
—the hatred in N. Ireland is a social disease, has infiltrated the schools, affected & finished old friendships between C & Protestants. military victory is not the solution because the problem is within the people

Religious
—religious leaders (Ian Paisley for ex.) have done nothing to help ease the problem. They do not preach love & reconciliation
—In Ireland you choose what you want to read in the Bible
—the church has a medieval stranglehold on the average N. Irish person
—the religious leaders of Ireland today are a disgrace to their religions
—the C & P are fanatics   many people go to church daily & at night are the hooded faces with the tar & feathers N. Irish bigots
—the bombings: senseless cruel   sickening   the people responsible should be punished without mercy
—bombings have intensified over the past two years   both sides responsible
—the particular incident that stands out in my memory is the bomb that went off in downtown Dublin during rush hour   killed almost only women & children   small kids killed, maimed
—the children: famous picture of the children stoning the British soldiers   a war of children
—many kids have nervous breakdowns along with their mothers
—children are indoctrinated by their families to hate the opposite group
—the children of N. Ireland today will be the IRA members of tomorrow   they are brought up in hatred & cannot escape it
—I pity the children   those who have been disfigured & maimed and mentally warped by their parents

Personal experience
—Went to S. Ireland (Cork) two years ago, during the time of the internment & supposed British tortures.
—Saw no evidence of the war except an occasional IRA spray painted on walls
—the people I stayed with were very old & super Catholic
—turned ferocious when you mentioned the fights in the North
—they hated the British & the Protestants
—I know the ugly cities the people of N. Ireland live in & I can understand what is happening & why, better than can a lot of people
—My uncle in London has a girlfriend from Belfast. Eileen told me a lot about how her life has changed in Belfast & how her family lives with the fighting
—Eileen's best girlfriend & this girl's boyfriend were murdered last Christmas   no reason   Her sister (12 yrs. old) has suffered one nervous breakdown & is on the verge of another. Her little brother can tell who is fighting (the IRA & the Protestants or the British & the

IRA) by the sound of the gunfire. He can distinguish between the different sounds the automatic weapons make.

—On my second trip to England I really came face to face with the Irish bombings. My uncle & Eileen & Vito & I decided to visit the Visitors' Gallery in the House of Commons. We started out early in the morning & on the way Eileen said that she had seen a newspaper that said the House of Commons had been bombed. Didn't believe her but when we arrived in central London there really had been a bomb. Bobbies, fire & firemen all around. Scared me to think we could have all been hurt. I have slides of the scene & every time I see them I get upset.

—Many places in London that were not previously guarded were guarded the second time I went. Huge fences had been up in places where people could possibly throw bombs

DYNAMIC VIEW

—as the standard of living in N. Ireland has been raised, the fighting has increased
—the last two years have shown an increase in senseless killings, bombings, shootings & murders
—the P & Cs have completely separated themselves, barricaded themselves into their own ghettos
—political tension not quite as high. England still does not have a strong position
—buildings have been bombed & never rebuilt
—families have been bombed out. Some families have left, some have stayed.
—the hatred has increased over the years
—some women have united & formed political groups
—small children have lost legs, arms & eyes

Changing attitudes toward the struggle
—the increase in bombings happened when the word "bomb" was everyday language in the newspapers, airport-bombs, Vietnam bombs, Arab-Israeli bombs
—Americans do not pay much attention to the Ireland issue
—Ireland has always been torn with fighting
—the green grass has always been stained red
—Ireland is just a tiny isolated spot of hatred in the world today that is filled with hatred
—the fighting has always been more or less confined to the island itself, except recently with the London bombings
—Ireland's war is very small compared to the larger, more flammable situations like the Mid-East
—the fighting in N. Ireland does not really affect the people of the U.S. except perhaps the old Irish immigrants & their children

Future
—the bloodshed could get worse, bombings could increase, considering the problem from a cynical point of view, hopefully they will all kill each other off; not realistic; the fighting will always be there in isolated areas, the P & Cs will completely segregate themselves from each other
—doubtful that England will ever instigate a major policy change, the fruitless debates in Parliament will continue

RELATIVE VIEW

Comparison & contrast
—strife in N. Ireland compared to the Civil Rights Struggle of the 60's in the U.S.
    —both issues involve senseless lynchings & bloodshed
    —the two problems each took different courses. In the South the blacks & whites were originally separated & are now slowly moving together. In N. Ireland the P & Cs at one time coexisted together, now they are segregated
    South   N. Ireland

    —both struggles hurt the children with the racial issue of the South, the scars are beginning to heal, in N. Ireland they are still being made
    —both issues have (or had) political, social & economic dimensions
    —the third parties that were (& are) involved in both fights really got hurt, the social workers & civil rights people from the North & the British soldiers from England
    —perhaps the reason why the fighting has continued in Northern Ireland for so long is because international pressure has never come down really hard, with the racial issue in the South, eventually the national outcry became strong & brought govt. pressure on the situation

Analogy
—the struggle in N. Ireland is like an hereditary disease
—the hatred in N. Ireland has been perpetuated because parents have transmitted their hatred to their children like a disease
—sometimes diseases become immune to the treatments that are given, perhaps the fighting in N. Ireland has reached that "immune stage" & new, harsher medicines must be discovered
—the hatred has affected all levels of society in N. Ireland just like a diseased organ of the body can poison other organs & systems
—some hereditary diseases fade as the generations continue
—hopefully the fighting will fade as a new generation of children grows up & totally rejects the values of their parents

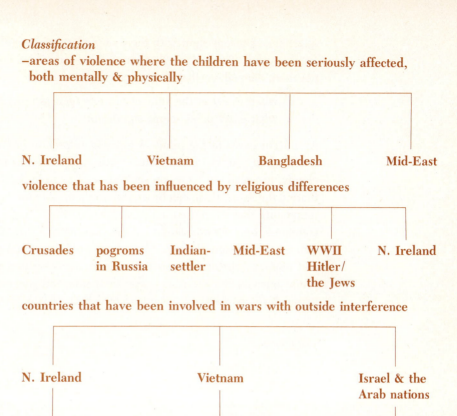

Classification
—areas of violence where the children have been seriously affected, both mentally & physically

| N. Ireland | Vietnam | Bangladesh | Mid-East |

violence that has been influenced by religious differences

| Crusades | pogroms in Russia | Indian-settler | Mid-East | WWII Hitler/the Jews | N. Ireland |

countries that have been involved in wars with outside interference

| N. Ireland | Vietnam | Israel & the Arab nations |
| G. Britain | U.S. | USSR & USA |

ASSIGNMENT

Stage 2 Toward a Paper on an Issue: Exploring

1. **Explore the question you formulated, discovering as many personal and public facets as you can.**
2. **Record those ideas in the most vivid words you can find.**
3. **Seek comments on your exploration from your instructor.**

DISCOVERING AND STATING THE FOCUS

INCUBATING

Incubation occurs during all stages of composing, but its function before focusing remains crucial. Allow sufficient time for it because a good focus never arises directly from the exploration.

STATING THE FOCUS

Remember the distinction between *insight* and *focus*. Insights are the potential answers that the mind discovers during incubation. Some of these, under closer scrutiny, appear less useful responses to the writer's original questions or inconsistent with the writer's larger sense of experience. They are discarded. The insights that sound most promising, however, have to be polished, shaped, so that writers can see clearly:

1. what aspect of the subject has emerged as crucial
2. what exact point seems significant

An insight exists in the mind. A focus is its precise formulation in writing. Often when you try to formulate a focus, you discover that your insight was cloudy, not ready yet. Or you see the need to go back to further exploring. Stating the focus, then, can be a good predictor for you, helping you to avoid judgments that exceed your explorations or those that are merely facts or commonly held generalizations. If the focus merely summarizes the information about the issue, the paper is in danger of becoming a restatement of data and opinions already argued better in newspapers and popular or professional journals. Such writing wastes your time and your reader's. But if your paper develops a strong, original focus, both of you have gained.

FOCUSES

	SUBJECT	POINT OF SIGNIFICANCE
Writer 1	ADC ———————————	is either a trap or a ladder, depending on one's need and attitude.
Writer 2	Older people ———————	should spend their declining years at home.
Writer 3	The women's movement ————	makes the role of housewife difficult to understand.
Writer 4	The conflict in Northern Ireland ——	is a social disease perpetuated by learned bigotry and ignorance.
Writer 5	High school students who drink ——	are denying themselves an education for success in the future.

Commentary Writer 1's judgment seems reasonable because her exploration adequately supports it. The point of significance concentrates on the ways of coping, a focus that the writer can develop. To have concluded "ADC is mismanaged" would have been beyond this writer's investigation. Writer 2's Focus moves a little beyond opinion to probability, supported by his experience. Because he did not examine the other side of the issue—reasons for putting the elderly in nursing homes—his focus is not as balanced as it might have been. His statement is also too generally applicable for his evidence. A revision would place the subject in the first part of the focus and limit the judgment to what the writer can develop. Writer 2's revised Focus read: "Spending their declining years at home is a better way for some older people to age gracefully."

CLASS EXERCISES

1. Discuss the Focuses of Writers 3, 4, and 5.
   - What aspects of the subject have been selected? If the whole subject has been included in the focus, to what does this commit the writer?
   - How are the points of significance responses to the starting questions (pp. 153–154)?
   - Have the writers avoided focuses that are facts or common generalizations or overly ambitious claims? Why or why not?
2. Discuss possible focuses for the issue the class explored.

ASSIGNMENT

Stage 3 Toward a Paper on an Issue: Discovering and Stating the Focus
1. **Allow sufficient time for incubation.**
2. **Formulate a focus stating**
   a. **the aspect and**
   b. **the point of significance**
3. **Get an evaluation of your focus from your instructor.**

PLANNING FOR AIM AND AUDIENCE

THE PERSUASIVE AIM

Writers in this chapter will again be working with a persuasive aim, as will you. Recall that this aim, which emphasizes the audience, involves writers in

1. establishing their credibility in the eyes of the audience
2. convincing the audience of the plausibility of the argument
3. appealing to the audience's emotions

For the fuller discussion of these persuasive goals, see pp. 127–137.

When you do your audience analysis, therefore, be sure to analyze the audience's emotions, plan the role it will play, and the voice that will establish your credibility.

CHOOSING AN AUDIENCE

Issue papers are usually addressed to an audience that either is undecided or that disagrees with the writer's position; that is to say, to a hesitant or hostile audience. In principle your position on a controversial issue will be useful especially to those who do not already hold that position.

In a sense, then, your position selects the audience. And then the subject further narrows the audience in that you can assume that you only write for readers interested in the subject, because if the audience already has an opinion on the subject or has not reached a final judgment on the subject, its members are *interested* in the subject or they wouldn't have given it much thought. An audience that is interested and partially informed will know something of both sides (or the three or four sides) of the issue. Any informed, interested audience will be skeptical of any judgment, if only because it has some glimpse of the complexity of the issue.

It follows that you have to assume that the audience will be hostile to your conclusions and require convincing. The undecided, informed audience is not really neutral; it is simply waiting for the convincing argument that will overcome its skepticism.

You, then, in this case, do not so much choose your audience as you have your audience chosen for you. Then you must still analyze that audience.

ANALYZING THE AUDIENCE

It may seem that if you already know that your audience is interested, partially informed, and hostile, audience analysis is a superfluous step in the writing process. Not so. Crucial in issue papers is the knowledge of what roles you and your audience are to play in your paper, and that can only be answered by using the full Audience Guide (p. 124) to determine why and in what respects the audience is hostile. In other words, you have to find a common ground on which you can address your readers. A hostile audience can be converted into a receptive audience, but that conversion can only be achieved if you know enough about why an audience holds its present position. With such knowledge, you can then create a less threatening role for the audience so that it will *listen*. You can also reduce the threat that a hostile audience feels if you know enough about the audience to find bridges over which the communication can travel.

AUDIENCE ANALYSIS

Writer 1   AUDIENCE: ADC PARENTS

A. Audience in itself
   1. The audience will have had almost exactly the experiences I have had with welfare agencies.
   2. The audience, like me, will value the health and security of their families and, therefore, justice under the regulations.
B. Audience in relation to the subject
   I can combine this answer. The audience will hold a very strong opinion, that getting aid due you is very hard, and they will be very willing to act on any real solution to this problem.

This is a very emotional issue for ADC people; after all, it deals with their survival. One of my tasks will be to channel their anger into constructive channels.

C. The role of audience and writer

I can offer a solution to a problem that the audience and I share if I take on the voice of an equal. I must not sound preachy or superior, because that's the way the agency people speak to them.

Commentary This is a good analysis, after careful selection of audience. The other possible audiences would have been the agency personnel or people higher in the bureaucracy, audiences with whom the writer has little in common. By choosing as audience those served by ADC, the writer has elected to deal not with reforming the system but with coping with the system.

The writer has apparently decided to channel the anger and hostility of the audience toward the agency and away from herself, a wise move. It will be interesting to see if she can deal with her own anger, which was implied in her exploratory list.

AUDIENCE ANALYSIS

Writer 5 AUDIENCE: JUNIOR AND SENIOR HIGH SCHOOL STUDENTS

A. Audience in itself

1. These kids will be going through what I went through in the last five years, so we'll have the same experiences, but they won't see the significance.
2. These kids are most interested in having fun and being cool in the eyes of others. They are sensitive to criticism, easily turned off.

B. Audience in relation to subject

1. The audience probably thinks what I thought when I was their age: no sweat over drinking.
2. Very strongly or they wouldn't act the way they do.
3. They act on their opinion all the time—that's their problem.

C. I will tell them the truth, as someone who lived through what they are living through and knows now what's right.

Commentary Probably too large an audience; it would seem that the message—which is shaping up into a sermon—should be addressed only to those students in danger, and the exploration suggests that this is a relatively small part of junior and senior high school students.

The analysis is puzzling, since the exploratory list seems to indicate that the writer in fact never fell into the trap he is going to describe. Therefore, he did *not* share the same values and opinions. He is assuming a similarity that does not exist. This may cause trouble.

CLASS EXERCISES

1. Discuss Writer 3's Audience Analysis.
   - In what ways will the audience's background allow the writer to find bridges to them?
   - To what values and emotions can the writer appeal?
   - How will the voice the writer has chosen help to establish credibility?
2. Select an audience for the issue explored by the class.
   - Using the Audience Guide, analyze the audience.

AUDIENCE ANALYSIS

Writer 3 **AUDIENCE: ACTIVE FEMINISTS AND WOMEN WHO BASICALLY ACCEPT FEMINIST VIEWS**

A. 1. –varies across all classes, income levels
      –believe in equal pay for equal work, equal opportunity
      –leadership—by and large—middle-class working women; frequently college educated, rarely working in dead-end waitress or other such jobs
   2. Values of great freedom, choices, power, intellectual growth organizations—stated emphasis usually begins with (1) ERA (2) abortion (3) universal day care and then varied other concerns including increased part-time jobs, decrease in volunteerism, shared parenting & housework in family
B. 1. Audience feels strongly that they are opening choices for all women. They often feel the lack of support from many housewives is result of bad press and ignorance of housewives as to what the women's movement stands for. They are very willing to act on what they learn, on their opinions.

ASSIGNMENT

Stage 4 Toward a Paper on an Issue: Planning for Aim and Audience
1. Choose an audience for your own issue and explain your choice.
2. Analyze your audience.
3. Get an evaluation of your choice and analysis from your instructor.

DEVELOPING, ORGANIZING, AND REFINING THE PAPER

DEVELOPING THE PERSUASIVE AIM

In Chapter 3, we discussed developing a paper with a persuasive aim. Briefly, you are called upon to establish your credibility and the plausibility of your argument and to appeal to the reader's emotions. You can prove your focus through induction, deduction, and analogy. (See pp. 127–135.)

1. Discuss Writer 3's First Version.
   - What parts of the larger persuasive pattern are present?
   - How does the writer's voice establish credibility?
   - To what emotions does the writer appeal?
   - What kind of proof is used?

FIRST VERSION

Writer 3   THE BALANCE POINT

The decade of the 60's is commonly referred to as a turbulent era in this country, gorged with social and political movements that sought to make radical changes in our laws, attitudes, values and lifestyles. While many of these movements were here and gone quickly, leaving in their wake only memories, others such as the women's liberation movement left behind changes so complete and yet so subtle that we are just beginning to be aware of what they mean to us. Perhaps the major residue of these movements of the 60's is our belief that anything which frees people from rigid roles, stereotypes and limited options is to be applauded.

The women's liberation movement was intended to free women, to open up options for them, to give them more choices, yet for many housewives the result has been a lessening of choices. In trying to demolish the necessity for women to be "supermom," the woman who could raise perfect children, bake bread, cook gourmet meals, and sew all her own clothes in a spotless house, feminists unintentionally belittled the role of housewife and mother. A countless stream of feminists on *The Phil Donahue Show* spoke about how boring, degrading, and unfulfilling it is to be a housewife. Those of us who found satisfaction in this work felt defensive or wondered what was wrong with us. Feminists argued on behalf of universal day care centers adding that it's not the quantity but the quality of time that is important to children. While they described the Israeli kibbutzim, we pictured our children in Sugar and Spice or some other day care center, herded about with 30 or 40 other kids by three or four adults who could not possibly spend enough time or give enough love to them. Feminists talked about mental stagnation that was inevitable with being home all the time but added that volunteerism, which for many of us was a way of getting out, was bad since it allowed society to unfairly exploit women's labor. At the end of these talk shows some woman would inevitably get up and explain that she freely chose to be a housewife and that she was very happy. The answer was always the same, the feminist would say in a patronizing tone, "Well if you knew all your options and that's what you chose to be—a housewife . . . OK." The message that came across to us was that we could not possibly have known all our options. Instead of enjoying the additional option of working outside the home we sensed that society now believed we *should* be working.

The "supermom" image became unfashionable, but was not really replaced. Instead, a new image was superimposed on it which required even more of women. The new heroine, the supercareerwoman, was the woman who could do it all. She had two intelligent planned-for-children, lived in a *Better Homes and Garden* house, was married to a loving supportive man and was a full-time worker with a rising career. If we took Geritol, the commercial said, then we could do it too. Modern books, movies, and magazine articles were filled with these new superwomen, but very few of them had pre-school children. In fact, pre-school children almost vanished from popular media, but when they were present mothers filled the same role they always had. Television series like *One Day At A Time* and movies like *See How She Runs* and *An Unmarried Woman,* show a woman unable to break free from the restrictive, self-sacrificing, traditional role until a divorce precipitates things.

What all of this means to us is difficult to measure. Most of us approve of equal pay for equal work, welcome our husband's participation in parenting, encourage our daughters to build with erector sets, and allow our sons to play with dolls, but it is our own role that is most difficult to understand. There are few images on television or in movies and books that we can look to for advice. There are few women who have gone before us that we can emulate. We must integrate these new ideas with nothing to guide us but our own common sense. We feel like we are rolling logs in water, moving our feet as fast as we can to maintain our balance while the water and log move swiftly beneath us, constantly changing like the society in which we live.

ORGANIZING A PERSUASIVE PAPER

Recall that a persuasive essay has one pattern within another. The large framework includes:

1. introduction
2. proof
3. refutation (not always present)
4. conclusion

The proof can be arranged by any of several modes: The descriptive, the narrative, the evaluative. That is, you can divide your issue into parts or aspects of the issue (the descriptive mode); you can trace the evolution of your issue (the narrative mode); you can establish a criterion and then measure your issue against that standard (the evaluative mode).

In this chapter, we will introduce another possibility, the fourth mode: classification.

THE CLASSIFICATION MODE

Issue papers can adopt any of the modes; a common choice is classification. Classifying is grouping. You put things in groups by ignoring the differences between things and emphasizing the similarities. In order to do that, you establish some principle by which you either exclude or include things from your group. Hence, a part of classifying involves *definition*. When you put something in a class, you must define the class, identifying the basis for inclusion and exclusion. Writer 1 grouped ADC recipients into askers and demanders. She then had to define what constituted an asker, what a demander. What make a system of classification legitimate and therefore acceptable to the reader are (1) a principle of classification that does not depend on some quirk of the writer and (2) a thorough and logical application of the principle to the subject under discussion. (An eighteenth-century writer classified the characters in one of his novels as Men, Women, and Italians, thus violating both rules of classification.) In this chapter, Writers 1 and 3 chose to use the classification mode of organization.

Whole papers can be organized by the mode of classification. Here we are simply organizing *proof*, since the total organization of the paper is determined by the persuasive aim—the proof will be preceded by an introduction and followed often by a refutation section and always by a concluding section.

The ordinary pattern of classification contains three stages, one of them optional:

1. a statement of the class and definition of it

   or

   an account of characteristics of the class
2. development of the subject in relation to the class—an account of the ways in which the subject meets the definition worked out in stage 1 above or has the characteristics of the class
3. comparison or contrast of the subject with other members of the class; this is an optional step, useful for emphasis or for classification when the writer feels the need for refining the account

If the writer places the subject in more than one class, this pattern is repeated. For example, Writer 1 has divided ADC people into two classes: askers and demanders. The three-stage development above needs to be applied twice. The danger for the writer unfamiliar with the classification mode is the temptation to rig the categories by selecting an artificial basis of classification so that the classes emerge as good, bad, and indifferent, or some variant of those. You should not confuse the evaluative mode with the classification mode. Categories should be able to stand alone on a logical basis apart from your opinion. It's possible to write a paper on "Types of Professors" that divides them into Bright, Mediocre, and Stupid, but, unless you have subjected the professors to a battery of tests, that is an evaluative paper masquerading as classification.

Coherence in the classification mode

Coherence is easier to achieve in the narrative, evaluative, and descriptive modes than in the classification mode because of the conventional thought patterns the first three follow. We saw earlier how any object can be classified in various ways, depending on what you choose as a basis of classification. The classes, the categories, exist only as abstractions, as subgroups that depend on a way of looking at the whole group of objects. With a reasonable basis of classification, you can create acceptable groups, but how do you connect them so that your account of the groups makes sense to the reader? The simplest signals of classification to the reader are numbers, because numbers themselves suggest an orderly sequence. So you label your categories numerically: first, second, third; or the first class, the second class, the third class. This is a very common practice, but frequently it does not work very well, because while it signals a change of direction, it does not meet the second requirement of a *transition*, providing a reason for the change of direction. Why is class one first and not second or third? Why is third third? That is, what is the relationship of first to second to third? Importance? Is the third the most important because it comes last, or is the first the most important because it comes first? Consider that wonderfully confusing phrase that so many writers attach to their final category: "Last, but not least." If it is not least, then what is it? Most? Equal? Somewhere in between?

Transitions indicate to the reader the connections between verbal pieces of a composition and the relationship of the pieces. In the classification mode, you have to supply the reader, quickly and accurately, with the connections and relationships that exist—in your mind. If, for example, you are classifying rocks by their origin and your first category is igneous, the most common type of rock, you have three obvious choices of transitions:

1. *first*—poor
2. *most common*—good
3. *first and most common*—useful for the inattentive reader

CLASS
EXERCISE
1. Reread Writer 3's First Version (pp. 173–174).
   • What classifications does she use?
   • How do these organize her proof within the larger persuasive structure?
   • What transitions does she use?

Diction: connotation and denotation

The persuasive writer must be unusually sensitive to the connotation of words. Words have two sides of meaning: denotative and connotative. (There aren't, incidentally, any purely denotative words or purely connotative words; some words simply have more denotative or connotative content than others.) A word in its *denotative* function points to the object, situation, or perception that it names. A *house*, for example, is a building intended for human habitation. Every word has that kind of meaning because every word points to something it represents. But words also accumulate other meanings by the way they are used; they accumulate overtones, associations that linger in the backs of our minds (or wherever those things live) that affect our attitudes toward the thing the word denotes. That cluster of associations, conscious and unconscious, is the *connotation* of the word.

No one can chart the connotations of words—dictionaries don't even try—but you have to be aware of them because they affect an audience's response. Roughly speaking, *dirt* and *soil* are interchangeable because they have approximately the same denotation and connotation. But there is a great difference between *frugal* and *penny-pinching*, *slim* and *skinny*, *police officer* and *cop, fuzz,* or *pig.*

**CLASS
EXERCISE**

1. Read Writers 1 and 5's First Versions that follow and examine their diction.
   - What connotations are used by each writer?
   - Are they useful in appealing to the audience's emotions? If not, why not?
   - What words with better connotations could have replaced some of the diction?

FIRST VERSION

Writer 1

DON'T ASK—DEMAND

When one needs help to subsist, and seeks it at a public helping-place, one can go about it in basically two ways: asking and demanding. The askers predominate, ranging from the pleaders and weepers to the matter-of-fact apologizers, to the chronic welfare recipients who vocationally spend their energy waiting and convincing. Among the askers are those who do not choose ADC, but fall into it as the only viable means of support. Unskilled single parents of children too young to be put into day care can get into a demeaning narrow state of mind on

ADC, as it provides only enough to subsist on and creates a penny-pinching, rather-spend-time-than-money way of living. For instance, when one has an irregular need, like a new pair of glasses or an appliance, he must get an estimate, take it personally to his case worker, who sends it along with innumerable other forms to the state capital, and wait several weeks for the request to be evaluated. Similarly, a thorough health examination plan had been offered by social services for clients under 21 ("When you've got your health, you've got everything"); nine months after the notice went out, they were just about ready to schedule appointments. The mass of the askers sit and wait for their time to come. The demanders have the upper hand: those who choose ADC may need to get out of a temporary financial depression so they can straighten out their lives and begin again from a more hopeful point. They approach the system without awe, intent on getting what they need. For example, a single father of a school-aged boy, skilled in electronics but unemployed for a year and barely escaping starvation, meekly inquired if he were eligible for ADC. "No, you are able-bodied, go find a job." All job offers he had pursued required personal transportation, and he had no car. After observing the bureaucratic procedures and the demeanor of the askers, he resolved to take another tack, went back and said, "Look, we are starving, I have all of these bills I've been unable to pay, I need help; it is my due." Through logic and intimidation—"I happen to know my rights, and if you don't handle this fairly I'll go above you," not hesitating to create intimidation—power where there was none, as in "What! The unemployment office was sent that document days ago," when he himself had forgotten it, and walking almost belligerently into managerial areas where askers fear to tread, he quickly obtained payment to creditors who had been in pursuit of him for months, was assured that his mortgage and utility payments would be maintained and that he would henceforth receive food orders on demand until his regular aid began, enrolled in a training program in the field of ceramics, and somehow got cab fare to get home.

The difference in attitudes is quite striking, as are the results. The demander in the example got what he needed, and more, will not fall into inertia, because he knows what he wants and how to get it, and will soon be on his own again without trauma. He can look for a suitable job now at his leisure. The asker is likely to shuffle along indefinitely, aimless because he has enough, but not creating his own incentive to get more out of life.

Writer 5   DRINKING IN HIGH SCHOOL

In junior high, we saw film and film strips on the evils of drinking
and taking drugs. These films stated that drinking caused brain
damage, cirrhosis, and the person who drank heavily was doomed to
become a condemned alcoholic. The description of these films may
seem a little dramatic but in essence this is the message that came
across to us, the students. Unfortunately, what these films didn't convey
was that students who drank were denying themselves the education
that could help them in the future. Many of you would dispute that fact
very strongly but it may be because you haven't stopped and thought
about it. We are aware of the health problems involved such as brain
damage, cirrhosis, alcoholism, and severe depression. But do you realize the effect drinking has on a student and that student's performance
in school?

Drinking has always been a big thing in our high school and about
a third of the students drink heavily. By heavy drinking, I mean a student who has to go out for a beer almost after every class. Getting a
drink at our high school is no problem at all. It's almost as easy as getting a drink of water from the water fountain. Some people hide their
beer or wine in a thermos bottle and say it's coffee or pop. Others who
drive to school stash beer in their cars and always have to crawl out to
their cars between classes. If a student is under 18, you can be sure
they have a very good friend who's 18 and will gladly buy beer for
them. You can try and hide your drinking from the teachers but you
can't fool us. If your breath doesn't give you away, your flushed cheeks
definitely will. Or maybe it's when you open the windows when it's 30°
outside because you feel warm. But the definite give away is when
you're on the floor, doubled over in a fit of laughter, while your chemistry teacher is describing the molecular structure of butane.

Besides your appearance, the worse thing is what happens to your
attitude and performance in school. By skipping classes to stagger out
and get a can of beer or not doing chapter 6 in Algebra, how do you
except to get anything out of school. Believe it or not, schools were
built for your benefit, not as a punishment. I'll agree that some of the
homework is busy work and usually nothing is gained by doing it. Not
every class can be geared to your specific level, and even with the busy
work, you get the same amount of knowledge out of a class compared to
the effort you put into that class.

The education that you're suppose to get from school may not seem
so important now, but wait untill you try and find a job. Without that
diploma, the chances of finding a good job with decent pay is next to
nothing. At least with a diploma you've got a 50/50 chance. The big

question that you have to answer is if you do get a job, will you be able to stay sober and go without a drink? It won't be like high school where you can sneak out between classes. Ray Smith, a 19 year-old guy that I went to school with, got a job tightening bolts on an assembly line at the Chrysler plant. He said that it almost drove him crazy tightening bolt after bolt, hour after hour. It was just so monotonous he needed a lot of beer to help him get through the day. Yet he didn't have the knowledge for a higher paying job because he had goofed around in high school. Realizing he was in a rut and his drinking was crippling him, Ray stopped drinking and is now taking night classes in business management. It dawned on him that he didn't want to depend on his drinking for the rest of his life. Stopping wasn't easy for him, but he was determined to do it and he did.

A good job and making good money isn't everything in life but it may be one of the most important. Each of you can become as successful or unsuccessful as you want. Life isn't easy, no one ever said it was. All of us have different problems, home life, social or peer pressures, insecurities, etc., and we each have different ways of coping with them. What you have to decide is how you personally want to cope. If deep down you are unhappy with your drinking, you might want to try something else. There are different areas of education like learning to be a carpenter, artist, or welder that might interest you. But you won't know what you dislike or like untill you try. And that decision is strictly your own. It doesn't hurt to give things a try and then, if you don't like it, you can always give it up. But the important thing is you tried. The same can apply to drinking. If you try and give it up, you may like the results. Yet if you can't do it, you know the beer will still be there. The decision is still yours.

Sentence-combining

1. Study the following phrasal expansion patterns. Combine the sets of sentences into one which imitates the pattern above it.
2. Scan Writers 1 and 5's First Versions, identifying the use of any of these patterns. Indicate places where such structures could have been used. Combine those sentences.

III. PHRASAL EXPANSION PATTERNS

Pattern A Along the creek and in logged areas, deciduous trees leaf out in late spring to create the green shade of summer, the fiery brilliance of autumn, the desolation of winter.

1. It happens on every campus.
2. It happens in surrounding areas.

3. Students arrive.
4. They are university students.
5. They arrive in early fall.
6. Their arrival is to experience reunions.
7. The reunions are with friends.
8. The friends are old.
9. The arrival is to experience long lines.
10. The long lines are of registration.
11. Their arrival is to experience the challenge.
12. The challenge is of classes.
13. The classes are new.

---

1. This happens throughout the delta.
2. It happens in places.
3. The places are irrigated.
4. Sweet corn and beans burgeon.
5. The burgeoning is in the sun.
6. The sun is hot.
7. It is the summer sun.
8. The burgeoning is to yield work.
9. The work is backbreaking.
10. The work is for farmers.
11. The burgeoning is to yield a feast.
12. The feast is movable.
13. The feast is for insects.
14. The burgeoning is to yield meals.
15. The meals are flavorful.
16. The meals are for consumers.
17. The consumers are fortunate.

Pattern B **The low-flying jets broke the sound barrier,** shattering windows and creating panic.

1. His ace won.
2. It was a service ace.
3. It was his final one.
4. The winning was of the match.
5. The ace defeated his opponent.
7. The opponent was exhausted.
8. The ace thrilled the fans.

---

1. The monster attacked.
2. The monster was frighteningly real.
3. The attack was of the city.
4. The monster pulverized buildings.
5. The monster snapped railway cars in two.
6. He did this easily.

Pattern B1 Held every four years in Moscow, the International Tchaikovsky Competition is among the world's most demanding and prestigious tests of musical talents.

1. It was torn by division.
2. The division was ideological.
3. The women's liberation movement proliferated.
4. The proliferating was into groups.
5. There were dozens of these groups.
6. They were splinter groups.
7. They were competing groups.

1. He was grazed.
2. The grazing was by a ball.
3. The ball was wild.
4. It was fast.
5. The pinch-hitter flung a curse.
6. The curse was sizzling.
7. The flinging was toward the mound.

Pattern B2 The alligator attacked his prey, stunning it, and carried it into the water.

1. The fans mobbed the superstar.
2. The fans were frantic.
3. The fans terrified the superstar.
4. They tried to grab pieces.
5. The pieces were of the star's clothes.

1. The man uncrossed his legs.
2. The man was stricken.
3. The man pulled his legs under him.
4. He lunged out of his seat.
5. He lunged into the aisle.

Pattern B3 Moving delicately through the changing patterns of their long scarlet strands of silk, the dancers glide across the stage, costumed as lotus flowers.

1. One searches.
2. This was through layers.
3. The layers were of artifacts.
4. The artifacts were ancient.
5. The archaeologist studies every fragment.
6. The archaeologist is convinced of the significance.
7. The significance belongs to the site.

1. It lounged.
2. This was done in the waters.
3. The waters were deep.
4. The waters were green.
5. The salmon ignores the hook.
6. The hook is baited.
7. The salmon is sated.
8. This is from his meal.
9. The meal was of small fry.

Pattern C Going on fad diets **doesn't mean that you will lose weight.**

1. One invests in stocks.
2. This can lead to pleasure.
3. It can lead to profit.
4. We all dream of this profit.

---

1. One watches TV.
2. This can take up time.
3. It can do so often.
4. The time is valuable.
5. The time cannot be recaptured.

Pattern C1 The beginning of reflexive consciousness in the brain of our remotest ancestor must surely have coincided with the dawning of the sense of time.

1. The reading is of printed works.
2. The reading is by men.
3. The reading is also by women.
4. The men and women are ordinary.
5. Their reading can be traced.
6. The tracing is in general.
7. The tracing is to the inventing.
8. The inventing is of the press.
9. The press is a printing one.

---

1. The advertising is for cereals.
2. The cereals are sugar filled.
3. The advertising is also for foods.
4. They are junk foods.
5. The advertising is on shows.
6. The shows are TV shows.
7. The shows belong to children.
8. This should be banned.
9. The banning should happen at the beginning.
10. The beginning is of the season.
11. The season is the coming one.

Pattern C2 **Shy people might try** joining clubs and participating in small group ac-
tivities.

    1. The cryptographers continued.
    2. They decoded.
    3. The decoding went into the night.
    4. It went far into the night.
    5. They also searched.
    6. The searching was for the message.

            ———————————

    1. The Green Knight kept up the following.
    2. He laughed.
    3. He also challenged everyone in the Hall.
    4. The Hall was King Arthur's.

Pattern C3 **In backgammon the player throws the dice and,** after studying his posi-
tion, planning his strategy, and anticipating the probabilities that his
next throw involves, **makes his move.**

    1. The following happens at Disneyland.
    2. A vacationer enters the gates.
    3. He buys his tickets.
    4. He stands in lines.
    5. He jostles.
    6. The jostling is for a seat.
    7. The seat is in the auditorium.
    8. The auditorium is crowded.
    9. He settles down to enjoy the show.

            ———————————

    1. This happens during the show.
    2. The interviewer introduces her guest.
    3. She breaks the ice.
    4. She elicits funny stories.
    5. She baits the guest.
    6. The baiting is with questions.
    7. The questions are leading.
    8. The questions are calculated to get a laugh.
    9. She captivates the audience.
  10. The captivating is with her own charm.

Stage 5 Toward a Paper on an Issue: Developing, Organizing, and Refining the Paper

1. **Write a first version of your paper with a persuasive aim and a descriptive, narrative, evaluative, or classification mode.**
2. **Refine your diction and syntax.**

Constructively criticizing a paper on issues written in the persuasive aim for a specific audience and in one of four modes may seem to require a reader to juggle an impossible number of considerations. Not really. You are still looking for the components of any effective paper: consistent focus, development, organization, and style, and a firm grasp of conventions. The reader must simply be more than usually sensitive to two requirements: the credibility of the writer and the plausibility of the argument in the eyes of the intended audience.

With that in mind, let's look again at the First Versions of Writers 1 and 5.

Focus

The paper (pp. 177–178) is almost relentless in its concentration on the focus: ADC is a trap or a ladder, depending on whether you are an asker or a demander. There are no asides, no deviations.

Development

Written for other ADC people, the paper does not insult the audience by telling it what it already knows. The paper tries to *analyze* the situation the audience is caught in, bringing together common experience into classifications of experience (askers and demanders) that the reader may not have considered. The role the audience is asked to play is that of victim, a covictim with the writer, caught in a struggle its members can win as individuals.

The problem is lack of development. There is a serious shortage of proof here. The conclusion rests on one case, "a single father of a school-aged boy," and part of that case is a series of inferences by the writer: that the demander "will not fall into inertia," and so on. On that slim base the audience is asked to accept the conclusion. It is not enough to be convincing.

Organization

The paper follows the classification mode, but not perfectly. The basis of the classification is the way ADC people approach the agency. There are two classes, askers and demanders. Askers comprise several subclasses, which are listed. But the classification goes awry.

To be an asker or a demander implies that a choice has been made; the person has chosen his or her attitude toward ADC procedures. But the paper tries to distinguish between "those who do not choose ADC" and "those who choose ADC." That's a different choice. The first class is said to be askers, the second, demanders. But the reader is also told of "unskilled single parents of children too young to be put into day care" and, presumably as a subclass of this group, those who have an irregular need, like a new pair of glasses or an appliance. These people are askers. But common sense tells us that "unskilled parents" may choose or not choose ADC, that "irregular needs" may happen to both those who choose and those who do not choose ADC and to askers or demanders, as well as to highly skilled married parents of children too young or not too young to be put into day care. The system of classification breaks down here very early. The breakdown in the classification leads to an organizational problem, to a lack of coherence. Any of the sentences taken alone is excellent, but not many of them lead to or connect with anything else.

Style

Style projects the chosen voice, a voice that should be consistent. Recall that this writer wished to project the voice of a reasonable equal in order to channel the anger of the reader into constructive channels. In other words, she wished to project the voice of one who, having been through experiences similar to that of the audience, had analyzed the problem and come up with a solution.

Given that purpose, the style has some serious weaknesses:

1. The paper consists of two "paragraphs." The first is over 500 words long and does not break up the thought into logical units.
2. The paper is constructed of a mixture of categorical and noncategorical statements that are not connected properly. Consider the second sentence of the last paragraph—four separate ideas in one sentence:
    a. The demander got what he needed. If the example is true, he did.
    b. The demander will not "fall into inertia." It is not clear what that means except perhaps that he will repeat his behavior and again get what he needs from ADC. There is no evidence that he did or did not.
    c. The demander knows what he wants and how to get it. If that means that he knows what he wants from ADC and how to get it and if the example is accurate, the statement is true. But it simply repeats the second statement. Again, there is no evidence.

d. The demander "will soon be on his own again without trauma." We have no idea what "without trauma" means, but that he "will soon be on his own again" is suspect in context. Why should someone who has found a way to cope with and overcome the system now elect to move outside the system, especially since he has found a way to get what he "wants" and "needed"? The sentence doesn't say.

It may be true that learning to demand rights in ADC strengthens character, and, therefore, the person will abandon ADC and, at leisure, find a job. Without trauma. But not, convincingly, in one sentence. Categorical statements must be acceptable statements.

Another sign of the confusion in this paragraph is the mixture of diction, the jargon added on to colloquial language. Notice the difference between

. . . got what he needed, and more   will not fall into inertia

. . . because he knows what he wants
and how to get it and will
soon be on his own again   without trauma

That is a failure in consistency of style.

Conventions
The writer seems to have good control of spelling, grammar, and punctuation.

CRITIQUE: Writer 5

Focus
The writer (pp. 179–180) has decided to narrow the focus to "the effect drinking has on a student and that student's performance in school." But the focus is not maintained. In the second paragraph, for example, only the last sentence deals with the focus; the rest is concerned with the mechanics of drinking in one high school, material that presumably the audience already knows. The third paragraph returns to the focus but wanders off into a defense of homework. The fourth paragraph talks of drinking on the job, not at school. The fifth paragraph deals not at all with the effects of drinking but with a plea to stop drinking, a reasonable idea for a conclusion, if the paper had developed the focus.

Development
The paper does not develop the persuasive aim; it is hard to believe that a high school audience will find the voice of the writer credible or the argument reasonable, for these reasons:

1. The role of the audience changes. In the beginning the writer and reader are equals, having shared a common junior high exposure to

films on alcohol. But in the second paragraph the audience is asked to believe that it knows nothing about drinking habits in its own high school, even though the audience is comprised of drinkers. In the third paragraph, the audience is asked to play the role of high school drinkers.

2. Only in the last paragraph does the writer speak to the emotions of the audience; that material should have been in the introduction.

3. The paper is not divided into clear-cut segments. The writer is still introducing the issue in the last paragraph.

Organization

The proof is scattered, scanty, and unorganized. There is no consistent use of a descriptive, narrative, evaluative, or classification mode. The parts of the proof vary from generalizations ("Life isn't easy, no one ever said it was") to particulars (the instance of the drinker at Chrysler).

The paper is remarkably bare of transitions, possibly because it is difficult to connect pieces that have no logical relationship. The paper is basically incoherent.

Style

The organizational confusion in the paper is reflected in the confused sentences:

By skipping classes to stagger out and get a can of beer or not doing chapter 6 in Algebra, how do you expect to get anything out of school.

The sentence is self-defeating because it sounds as if it had been written by someone who had just staggered out, and so on. There are three ideas in the last sentence of paragraph three unrelated by devices inside the sentence:

1. Not every class can be geared to your level.
2. Therefore, some classes will contain assignments that for you are only busywork.
3. What you get out of a class is proportionate to what you put into it.

It would be difficult to get those three ideas into a single sentence (1) because only the first and second are related, and (2) because while the first and second are generally true, the third is questionable *especially to this audience*, which has apparently rejected preachy truisms such as this.

Conventions

The paper has several problems that will be especially damaging since the writer is trying to project to the reader the image of one who has evaded the trap and become educated. Let us examine the types of problems the writer displays:

1. *Subject-verb agreement:* "the chances of finding a good job . . . is next to nothing."
2. *Comma splice:* "Life isn't easy, no one ever said it was."
3. *Verb form:* "is suppose"
4. *Pronoun agreement:* "If a student is under 18, you can be sure they have a very good friend who's 18 and will gladly buy beer for them."
5. *Spelling:* "untill," "except" for "expect"

This writer should keep track of his problems. Constant attention to the checklists in Chapter 9, Editing, will help him overcome these difficulties.

REWRITING

It might be possible to save this paper, but major revisions will be necessary. Even the one extended anecdote in the paper—the story of Ray Smith—works against the writer. There is no sign in the paper that Ray Smith drank in high school, only that he "goofed off" and then was driven to drink by the tedium of his job at Chrysler. As proof, the story is not relevant.

There is a good focus here waiting to be developed and organized. This first faulty version illustrates the writer's need to concentrate on what the writing process tells him about how he should present his material. Effective writing "isn't easy; no one ever said it was."

REVISED VERSION

Writer 1

ADC: A TRAP OR A LADDER

When one needs help to subsist, and seeks it at a public helping place, one can go about it in basically two ways: asking or demanding.

Take the Aid to Dependent Children program as a typical arena. People run to or fall into this program for a variety of reasons. Some choose it as a way of life. Some drift in and out of it as their fortunes change. Some use it temporarily, out of needs that are both immediate and long-range: right now they need money to survive, but they also need a temporary resting-place, so that they can straighten out their lives and then move onward and upward. For the first two groups, ADC is a trap, for the third group, a ladder. And one can usually tell which group a person belongs to by observing the way they approach the system. An asker will fall into one of the first two groups, but the demander belongs to the third.

To understand this, you have to realize that ADC is a mess—necessary for the survival of many citizens, but poorly designed, badly coordinated, understaffed, overcrowded, and hampered by almost incredible amounts of red tape. Suppose, for example, a child needs glasses. That's an "irregular need." The mother must get an estimate on the cost, submit it in person to her case worker (who may be responsible for 300 other families), wait for him or her to make up the request and send it to the state capital, wait for the request to be evaluated there, wait for the authorization to come back—or not come back. Meanwhile the child can't see to read.

An asker—one who will sit patiently and wait for this system to plod its way to a pair of glasses—will certainly be a party to harming the child, and she will also have accustomed herself to a way of life: waiting for the government to tell her how to live this month and the next, and the next, according to the speed that papers move through offices. She has given up as a person and become whatever a piece of paper says she is. She will be forever an ADC mother, or she will drift in and out of the system. She does not control her life or those of her family.

A demander, on the other hand, approaches the system without awe, intent on getting what he or she needs, recognizing the purpose of ADC and refusing to be intimidated by its organizational shortcomings.

Here is an example of an asker becoming a demander: A single father of a school-aged boy, skilled in electronics but unemployed for a year and facing starvation, meekly inquired at a Social Services center if he were eligible for ADC. "No," he was told, "You are able-bodied; so find a job." After he left the office, he realized that all the jobs he had applied for required private transportation, and he had no car. He went back to the agency as a demander. "Look, we are starving. I have all these bills I've been unable to pay. I need help; it is my due. I happen to know my rights, and if you don't handle this fairly, I'll go above you." Over a period of days, lying only a little—as when he argued that the unemployment office had sent over several days before a document that he himself had forgotten—and by walking belligerently into managerial areas where askers fear to tread, he quickly obtained payment to creditors who had been pursuing him for months. He was also assured that his mortgage and utility payments would be maintained and that he would henceforth receive food orders on demand until his regular aid began. Eventually he was enrolled in a training program in commercial ceramics. ADC didn't buy him a car, but they gave him cab fare to get home.

Demanders create their own momentum. A person with the drive to fight the system and win will not be content with the system. That kind of parent will move onward and upward and take the children along.

CLASS EXERCISES

1. Using the Critical Guide, do a class critique of Writer 3 (pp. 173–174).

2. Using the Critical Guide and working in groups, critique each other's first versions.
3. Compare Writer 1's Revised Version with her First Version (pp. 177–178). How has she responded to the advice of the critic?

Stage 6 Toward a Paper on an Issue: Critiquing and Rewriting
1. **Use the Critical Guide to critique your own paper. (Written or oral critiques from your instructor and classmates will be helpful here.)**
2. **Rewrite your paper, guided by the critiques.**

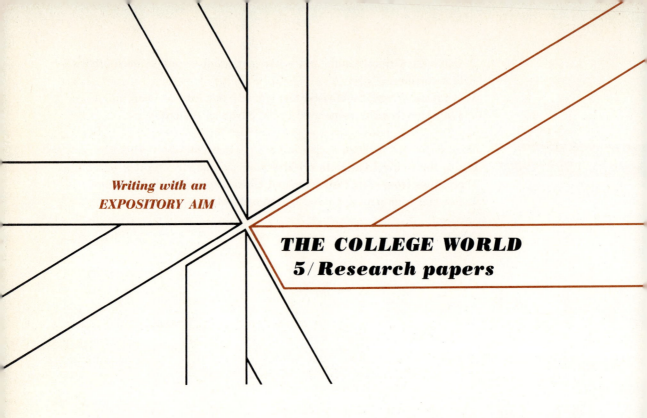

Writing with an
EXPOSITORY AIM

THE COLLEGE WORLD
5/ Research papers

In the past chapters, you have searched for meaning in your private world of persons and places and the public world of the media and issues. Research writing extends your exploration beyond your own experience to the experience of the culture, collected in the library. This treasure is rich with data, experiments, arguments, philosophies, information, but you need training to locate these valuable resources.

FINDING AND EXPRESSING THE STARTING POINT

FINDING THE SUBJECT

Often topics are assigned for research. In classes in which instructors suggest topics, ask yourself the following question: Do I know enough about any of these topics to prefer one over another? If not, you should do some background reading so that you can decide if a topic is worthy of your scrutiny.

If your instructor does not suggest topics, you may profit from selecting *an issue* that intrigues you, perhaps the one you wrote about in the last chapter. Or choose a subject from your intended field of study. Doing research on ideas, theories, movements, major figures in that field will acquaint you with reference materials in that discipline. You must know enough about a subject to formulate a useful starting point. No matter what way you select your subject, unless you make a personal commitment to it, motivated by your intellectual curiosity, the research writing will not be worthy of your time or attention. Until you can ask a question expressing your awareness of dissonance about the subject, you lack a genuine starting point. Writer 1's first choice of subject was "quasars," a topic suggested by the instructor that sounded interesting. But because he knew nothing about the subject, he was unable to formulate a starting question. He instead turned to genetic engineering, a subject that had disturbed him since he saw *The Boys from Brazil*. For his second choice he could articulate his starting point.

EXPRESSING THE STARTING POINT

If you sail into the library with an open-ended topic, you could drift for hours without the compass of a starting *question*. A question helps to chart your search for sources, narrowing your selection. The starting question arises from your dissonance about the subject.

CLASS
EXERCISES

1. Discuss Writer 1's Starting Point.
   • What dissonance does he express?
   • To what research do his questions narrow him?
2. With the class, compile:
   • a list of topics for a research paper in each of the following areas: Humanities, Social Sciences, Natural Sciences, Business, Engineering, Education.
   • Select a few on which to practice articulating starting points.

STARTING POINT

Writer 1

SUBJECT AND MY VALUES: GENETIC ENGINEERING

—one of several "current research topics" suggested in my Biology Course
—In particular, I'm very curious about cloning since I saw *The Boys from Brazil* and saw David Rorvik interviewed on Today. He claims his book *In His Image* documents how the first human clone was produced. My interest leans toward the current gene transplantation experiments rather than toward research into chromsome structure though I know the one depends on the other. I'm not sure how cloning fits with my value of not messing with nature.

Question: Why is genetic engineering, esp. gene transplantation, so controversial? Can this research interfere with nature?

ASSIGNMENT **Stage 1** Toward a Research Paper: Finding and Expressing the Starting Point
1. **Select three possible topics.**
2. **Express the dissonances you perceive in the subjects.**
3. **Articulate three starting questions.**
4. **Get advice on your choice of topic from your instructor.**

PLANNING FOR
AIM AND
AUDIENCE

Your aim will direct the kind of research you do, indicating the amount of material you need, even specifying your method of data gathering. Because you usually do research at this stage of your career for a class, the instructor often specifies your aim.

THE EXPOSITORY AIM

This chapter will demonstrate the use of the *expository aim*, one of the most common aims for research. The expository aim emphasizes the subject rather than the audience. We will distinguish two kinds of expository aims:

1. *the informative,* which relays information *new to the audience*
2. *the scientific,* which proposes a *new hypothesis* on the subject

The scientific aim is more challenging for the inexperienced writer because it demands extensive background and research into a subject. Writers of dissertations pursue this aim. But it may not be beyond you, as we will discuss below. Before we describe these aims, however, let us distinguish two other aims for research expected by professors.

1. Some instructors, especially in writing classes, require that you do research to support a *persuasive aim*. Each focus in Chapter 4 (p. 120) could have been further developed by gathering data beyond the writer's personal experience and general reading knowledge. If you do research for a persuasive aim, the amount you need is limited to whatever will convince the audience. You then use this data in conjunction with personality and emotional appeals to persuade the audience (see pp. 121–122). Emphasis is on the audience, not the subject matter.

2. Research writing sometimes assumes a *pseudo-persuasive aim* when the minimum expectations of the professors are that you will retrieve information familiar to them and organize it in a familiar pattern so that you will persuade them that you understand the subject as they and

others like them understand it. Another type of pseudo-persuasive aim exists when instructors assign research so that you will persuade them that you know how to do research: that you know how to retrieve the appropriate material, organize it well, and come to known conclusions; that you know your way around the library and can construct formally adequate footnotes and a bibliography. Pseudo-persuasive papers approach the status of examinations. Even if your professor has only this minimal expectation, you can plan a more meaningful aim. Because research consumes so much time, why not use the opportunity to discover something more valuable for you and your readers than that you know the research process?

The informative expository aim

With an informative aim, you convey information to readers who lack that information. That statement may seem embarrassingly obvious, but the real embarrassment comes when you labor to tell an audience what it already knows. The informative aim is carried out only when you tell the audience something it does not already know. Even in the hothouse atmosphere of college writing, the principle applies. The student writer who cries out in despair, "What can I possibly tell my history professor about the Civil War that he already doesn't know?" is giving up too soon. Consider two answers to the question: (1) Unless you have an almost supernaturally well-informed instructor, you could probably unearth a lot he or she doesn't know about the Civil War, such as the name of the wife of the Treasurer of the Confederacy or what it cost in dollars for the Union to take Richmond—if you had the time and energy. (2) The name of the Treasurer's wife is trivia. What it cost the Union to take Richmond might, on the other hand, have had serious repercussions on the course of the war and its aftermath. You might find time and energy to research that. You generally find time and energy to discover things that you regard as important or know, in the bargain, are important to others you write for. If you have formulated a significant starting question, you will know what to investigate.

Effective informative research should possess:

1. *Factuality*. You must make sure that your data can be verified. When you read your sources, therefore, check the credentials of the author and the basis for the information (experiments, surveys, and so on). Transfer the information accurately to your notes and then to your paper. The more familiar you are with the subject, the more discerning you can be about the factuality of your information.

2. *Comprehensiveness*. The scope of your starting question and eventually your focus will determine the amount of evidence needed to reasonably inform your audience without distorting its understanding.

Your audience's knowledge and expectations will also affect comprehensiveness. Most instructors do not expect an exhaustive account, given time limitations and your background. You can gain valuable guidance by asking your instructor for comments on your starting point before you begin exploring and then on your focus before you write the paper.

The scientific expository aim

Proving a new hypothesis about a complex academic subject is much more difficult because you need extensive background. As you advance in your professional field, you will develop the power to discover new hypotheses about important subjects. But can your current research writing have such a scientific aim? The answer is a qualified yes. Many academic subjects have unknowns, conflicting theories, vulnerable dogmas. In fact, few systems or theories are closed to further insight. But you have to know enough to recognize a loophole, a contradiction, or a limitation. Sometimes you discover an uncertainty, a controversy when you formulate the starting point. Writer 1's second question (p. 193) suggests one. At other times your early research opens such loopholes. If so, you can attempt a scientific aim. But proving a hypothesis goes beyond the informative aim. In addition to acquainting your audience with new information, you must prove a hypothesis that, as far as you and your audience know, is new in the field.

To prove a new hypothesis, you can take either an inductive or deductive approach, which the persuasive aim also uses, as we have discussed earlier. But remember that the persuasive aim requires only enough proof to convince the audience; the expository aim emphasizes the subject matter, not the audience, and, therefore, requires the use of more material as proof.

If you do not have enough background on your subject to pursue a scientific aim, skip the following section and go on to Analyzing the Audience, p. 197. If you plan to work with a scientific aim, your proof will be either inductive or deductive, a choice which will direct your method of research:

A. *Inductive.* The inductive researcher follows these stages:
1. Formulating a hypothesis and defining all the terms
2. Planning the inductive research design
   a. Reading previous studies that relate to the hypothesis
   b. Devising a way of collecting data to insure that the samples are relevant to the hypothesis, randomly chosen, and large enough for a conclusion to be made
3. Collecting the data, following these principles:
   a. Relevance to the hypothesis
   b. Randomness
   c. Sufficiency

4. Formulating the conclusion(s): verifying, qualifying, or rejecting the hypothesis

Notice that the choice of inductive proof directs the type of research you do.

B. *Deductive*.
    1. Formulating a hypothesis and defining the terms
    2. Establishing a deductive line of reasoning, such as
      a. The categorical syllogism discussed in Chapter 3, pp. 131–133: "Anything that is X is Y. Z is X. Z is Y."
      b. Contradictions: "Something cannot be X and Y. Something is X. Therefore, it cannot be Y."
    3. Setting up the axiom(s) or principles the reader will accept (see pp. 131–133 for examples of such principles)
    4. Connecting the subject with the axiom
    5. Formulating the conclusion: verifying, qualifying, or rejecting the hypothesis

Before beginning research, then, decide whether you will attempt an informative or scientific paper. This chapter will illustrate the informative expository aim.

CHOOSING AND ANALYZING THE AUDIENCE

Because your research papers currently are *academic*, one audience will inevitably be your teachers, but they are not necessarily the primary audience. You may choose to make your classmates or a public group your primary audience. Such a choice, of course, will affect your selection of material, since what will be new information to your classmates may not be new to your teacher.

The expository aim necessitates taking a certain stance toward your audience that reflects a series of assumptions you make about your relationship with them.

1. You assume *one* dissimilarity: that you will know more than they do about the focus you will develop. You are not superior to them in intelligence, character, status, or even general knowledge of the subject.
2. You assume two similarities:
    a. You and they are both interested in the subject.
    b. You and they are equally intelligent. You do not tell the audience what to think about the information or how to respond to it.
3. You assume that the audience understands the role you are playing—a relayer of information, not an advocate.

This last assumption puts on you the burden of factuality and comprehensiveness, the burden of not shaving, exaggerating, or omitting significant facts. The Audience Guide will help you determine what your audience already knows about your subject.

AUDIENCE GUIDE
A. Analyze the audience in relation to itself.
  1. What are the levels and types of experiences that my audience has had (cultural, professional, recreational, educational, and so on)?
  2. What hierarchy of values does my audience possess or profess (money making and power, friendship, security, intellectual growth, and so on)? It is important to distinguish, if possible, between what an audience holds dear and what it *professes* to hold dear, if indeed there is a difference. Does the audience hide one set of values under another? If so, the writer's task grows more complicated.
B. Then analyze the audience in relation to the subject.
  1. What opinion does my audience have on my subject?
  2. How strongly does my audience hold that opinion?
  3. What set of facts about the subject is my audience likely to possess?
  4. How willing to act on its opinion is my audience—if acting is appropriate?
C. Considering what you have learned from your answers to A and B, determine what role your audience should play in relation to your voice as writer (peer, authority, subordinate, familiar, and so on).

Especially important in the Audience Guide is the section that examines the audience's knowledge of the subject. If you are going to give new information, you must estimate what the audience already knows.

AUDIENCE ANALYSIS

Writer 1   AUDIENCE: MY BIOLOGY TEACHER

A. Most important is that my teacher is a professional biologist and, from his lectures, much concerned with the effect of experimentation on the future of the world. His hierarchy of values, therefore, stresses *human responsibility*.

B. Not knowing what opinion my teacher holds on this subject, but knowing his strong concern for subjects of this type, I must assume that whatever opinion he holds he will hold very strongly. He probably already knows most of what I will discover by reading. That means I have to be very careful about my factuality and comprehensiveness.

C. I must show that I share his concern for subjects of this type by coming to a reasonable conclusion. I should try then to talk to him as a peer, even though he's my teacher.

Commentary A and B are excellent; the conclusion in C is a little odd but not dangerously so. A novice trying to talk to an expert as a peer will run some risk, but the point our writer is making here is that he will try to be the instructor's peer in his *involvement* in the subject. That is always a good strategy. Apparently the instructor has deliberately withheld his thinking and feelings about this specific subject, not unusual in the classroom.

CLASS EXERCISES

1. Determine what other audiences would be good for this writer's aim and subject.
2. Do an audience analysis of one of these other audiences.

ASSIGNMENT

Stage 2 Toward a Research Paper: Planning for Aim and Audience
1. **Plan your aim.**
2. **Analyze your audience.**
3. **Get responses from the instructor on your analysis.**

EXPLORING

Library research extends your exploration beyond the search into your own memory and imagination. Because this stage is lengthy and complex, you will profit by following four steps: (1) exploring your own mind, (2) compiling a bibliography, (3) annotating, and (4) notetaking.

EXPLORING YOUR OWN MIND: EXPLORATORY GUIDE

Static view
- What definitions, ideas, theories, information, on my topic do I already know from experience, class lectures, and reading?
- What subtopics are part of my subject?
- What attitudes do I possess about the subject?
- What information do I and my audience need?

Dynamic view
   –What do I know about the history of my subject?
   –What causes or effects am I aware of?
   –What do I need to trace?

Relative view
   –How can I classify my subject now?
   –What comparisons can I now make to further understand my subject?

CLASS
EXERCISE

1. Discuss the Exploration of Writer 1.
   • How much knowledge does he already possess?
   • What other questions under each perspective will help to expand his exploration by research?

EXPLORATION

Writer 1

GENETIC ENGINEERING

STATIC VIEW

–genetic engineering involves replacing one gene by another
–supposedly it would allow for cloning of plants, animals, and even man
   –Cloning is the production of whole organisms from a single body cell.
   –Ira Levin's book *The Boys from Brazil* is about a Nazi scientist's plan to clone Hitler
   –David Rorvik says his book *In His Image* is about how the first human clone, now a fifteen-month-old boy, was produced
   –James Watson, the geneticist, said in a newspaper interview that in no way is Rorvik's claim true
   –What other controversy exists about genetic engineering?
   –What techniques and processes are involved?

DYNAMIC VIEW

–genetic engineering is a recent development, hardly covered in biology textbooks
–need to trace:
   –when did gene transplants begin?
   –who did them?
   –what kinds have been done?
   –how do they work?
   –what do they mean for us?

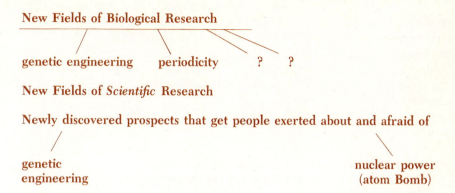

New Fields of Biological Research

genetic engineering   periodicity   ?   ?

New Fields of *Scientific* Research

Newly discovered prospects that get people exerted about and afraid of

genetic
engineering

nuclear power
(atom Bomb)

COMPILING A BIBLIOGRAPHY

After you have recorded your current knowledge, you need a working bibliography (a list of books, journal and newspaper articles, and other sources) to extend your inquiry. Its length should be in proportion to the number of references you need for your paper because this research process is like an inverted pyramid:

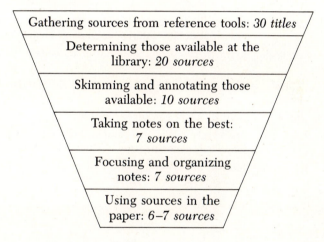

Gathering sources from reference tools: *30 titles*

Determining those available at the library: *20 sources*

Skimming and annotating those available: *10 sources*

Taking notes on the best: *7 sources*

Focusing and organizing notes: *7 sources*

Using sources in the paper: *6–7 sources*

In each phase of the process, some sources will be eliminated; therefore, the broader the start (in proportion to the desired length of the research paper), the better. If you gather a substantial working bibliography, you will not have to retrace steps unnecessarily. Because research is so time consuming, efficiency is important.

Below is a selected list of reference tools that will point you toward titles for your bibliography:

Reference tool	Sources indexed

BOOKS

1) *Card Catalog* — Books available in the library (see sample card, p. 204).

2) *Cumulative Book Index* — New books published each month in English around the world

3) *Essay and General Literature Index* — Chapters or sections of books from 1900, especially on social sciences and humanities

4) *National Union Catalogue* — Works cataloged by the Library of Congress and contributing libraries

PERIODICALS

1) *Readers' Guide to Periodical Literature* — Over 160 widely read magazines (see sample entries, p. 205).

2) *International Index 1907–1965 Social Sciences and Humanities Index 1965–1974 Social Science Index 1974– Humanities Index 1974–* — Journals in anthropology, archeology, art, economics, geography, history, law, literature, music, philosophy, political science, psychology, religion, sociology, theater

3) *Art Index* — Journals and museum bulletins on archeology, architecture, art history, fine arts, industrial design, interior decorating, photography, landscaping

4) *Biology and Agricultural Index* — Journals, pamphlets, bulletins in agriculture, geology, ecology, conservation

5) *Catholic Periodical Index* — Catholic journals published around the world

6) *Consumers' Index* — Journals about consumer interests

7) *Education Index* — Periodicals, books, monographs, bulletins, and reports on education: administration, preschool, elementary, exceptional children

8) *Industrial Arts 1913–1957 Applied Science and Technology Index 1958– Business Periodicals Index 1958–* — Journals in accounting, advertising, chemistry, economics, electronics, engineering, management, math, physics, etc.

9) *Music Index* — Journals in music and related fields

10) *PMLA Supplement* — Journals and books on the major Western and some East European languages and literatures

NEWSPAPERS

1) *New York Times Index* — Copy from *The New York Times*

2) *Times Official Index* — Copy from *The London Times*

ABSTRACTS

1) *Abstracts of English Studies* Summaries of articles from English and American journals on literature

2) *Historical Abstracts* Summaries of articles on cultural, economic, intellectual, political, and social history

3) *Sociological Abstracts* Summaries of articles on sociology

4) *Psychological Abstracts* Summaries of articles, books, and dissertations on psychology

DICTIONARIES

1) *Oxford English Dictionary 1884–1928 Supplements, 1933, 1972 (A–G), 1976 (H–N)* Variant spellings, etymologies, pronunciations, meanings, quotations from English works

2) *Dictionary of American English on Historical Principles* Words originating in America or relating to American history, etymologies, quotations

3) *Dictionary of Americanisms on Historical Principles* Words or expressions originating in the United States, etymologies, quotations

BIOGRAPHIES

1) *Dictionary of National Biography* Biographies of prominent English people

2) *Dictionary of American Biography* Biographies of prominent Americans

3) *Who's Who* Biographies of prominent living English people

4) *Who's Who in America* Biographies of prominent living Americans

5) *International Who's Who* Brief biographies of prominent people throughout the world

6) *Current Biography* Biographies of living international people

7) *Contemporary Authors* Biographies of novelists, poets, playwrights, etc.

OTHER SOURCES OF INFORMATION

1) *Almanacs and Handbooks of Facts* Data, facts, names, dates

2) *Atlases and Gazetteers* Maps, names of towns, cities, mountains and rivers

3) *Bibliographies* Lists of books on subjects or authors

4) *Concordances and Books of Quotations* Sources and wordings of quotations

5) *Encyclopedias* Introductory and summary articles on topics

6) *Yearbooks* Articles and bibliographies on major topics of that year

Card catalog

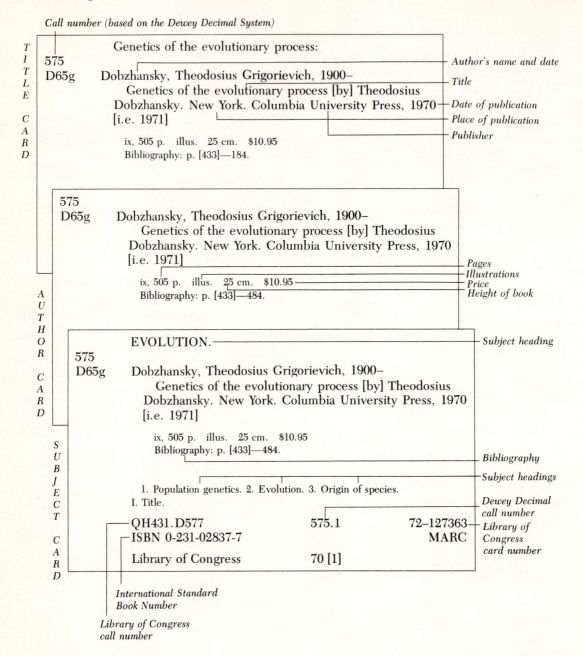

Call number (based on the Dewey Decimal System)

T I T L E C A R D

575
D65g
        Genetics of the evolutionary process:

    Dobzhansky, Theodosius Grigorievich, 1900–
        Genetics of the evolutionary process [by] Theodosius
    Dobzhansky. New York. Columbia University Press, 1970
    [i.e. 1971]

        ix, 505 p.   illus.   25 cm. $10.95
        Bibliography: p. [433]—184.

— Author's name and date
— Title
— Date of publication
— Place of publication
— Publisher

A U T H O R C A R D

575
D65g
    Dobzhansky, Theodosius Grigorievich, 1900–
        Genetics of the evolutionary process [by] Theodosius
    Dobzhansky. New York. Columbia University Press, 1970
    [i.e. 1971]

        ix, 505 p.   illus.   25 cm. $10.95
        Bibliography: p. [433]—484.

— Pages
— Illustrations
— Price
— Height of book

S U B J E C T C A R D

    EVOLUTION.

575
D65g
    Dobzhansky, Theodosius Grigorievich, 1900–
        Genetics of the evolutionary process [by] Theodosius
    Dobzhansky. New York. Columbia University Press, 1970
    [i.e. 1971]

        ix, 505 p.   illus.   25 cm. $10.95
        Bibliography: p. [433]—484.

    1. Population genetics. 2. Evolution. 3. Origin of species.
    I. Title.

    QH431.D577   575.1   72–127363
    ISBN 0-231-02837-7   MARC

    Library of Congress   70 [1]

— Subject heading
— Bibliography
— Subject headings
— Dewey Decimal call number
— Library of Congress card number

International Standard Book Number

Library of Congress call number

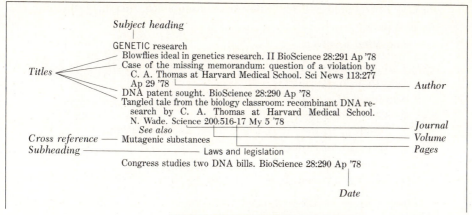

Subject heading

GENETIC research
- Blowflies ideal in genetics research. Il BioScience 28:291 Ap '78
- Case of the missing memorandum: question of a violation by
  C. A. Thomas at Harvard Medical School. Sci News 113:277
  Ap 29 '78
- DNA patent sought. BioScience 28:290 Ap '78
- Tangled tale from the biology classroom: recombinant DNA re-
  search by C. A. Thomas at Harvard Medical School.
  N. Wade. Science 200:516-17 My 5 '78

Titles

Author

See also

Cross reference —— Mutagenic substances

Journal
Volume

Subheading ——————— Laws and legislation

Pages

Congress studies two DNA bills. BioScience 28:290 Ap '78

Date

USING THE REFERENCE TOOLS

For the most efficient use of these indices,

1. Determine the guides that will be most useful by checking the chart of reference tools, which indicates the kinds of subjects indexed.
2. Start with the current volumes and move backward as far as time permits.
3. Record promising titles on separate slips (see sample bibliography cards, pp. 206–207).
4. After using *all* the guides time permits, arrange slips by journal (e.g., all *Time* articles together).
5. Check your library's list of journals or the card catalog:
   a. Record the call numbers of those *in the library.*
   b. Set aside the journal or book titles *not in the library.*

CLASS EXERCISE

1. Consider the five subjects below:
   • What reference tools would you consult for a bibliography on them?
      1. Arab-Israeli conflict
      2. open classrooms
      3. themes in William Faulkner's novels
      4. white-collar crime
      5. preservatives in food
   • How would the reference tools you suggested be useful?

ANNOTATING

After you have determined the titles available in the library, you need to sort out the sources that deserve close reading and notetaking. Because time is a determining factor in your research, a careful skimming of the available sources will help you to identify the most valuable sources for data and ideas.

If you, instead, start taking notes on the first article you have struggled to locate on the shelves, you may waste your efforts taking notes on what turns out later to be the least useful title. As a consequence, time may run out for the best ones.

Annotating involves:

1. Grouping titles from the same journals together so that you may locate them more quickly
2. Skimming the articles or books to determine
   a. Aspects of topics
   b. Depth of treatment and amount of documentation
   c. Authority of author
   d. Focus of the writer
3. Recording impressions on bibliography slips

Step 1 saves needless wandering in the stacks. Step 2 can be done quickly by reading the first and last paragraphs, skimming the subtitles and footnotes. Step 3 aids your memory after you have canvassed the entire list. Below are Writer 1's annotated bibliography cards, on which he intends to take notes as a basis for his paper. He has selected these cards from a potential pool of twenty-eight titles by eliminating some that were not available in the library and rejecting others he deemed superficial or irrelevant.

CLASS EXERCISE 1. Study the annotated Working Bibliography Cards of Writer 1:
   • Which articles promise to be most useful? Why?
   • What kinds of annotations has he made?
   • What bibliographic information was recorded?

WORKING BIBLIOGRAPHY CARDS

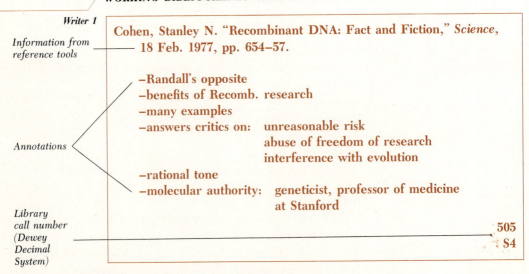

Writer 1

Information from reference tools

Cohen, Stanley N. "Recombinant DNA: Fact and Fiction," *Science*, 18 Feb. 1977, pp. 654–57.

Annotations

–Randall's opposite
–benefits of Recomb. research
–many examples
–answers critics on: unreasonable risk
                        abuse of freedom of research
                        interference with evolution
–rational tone
–molecular authority: geneticist, professor of medicine
                        at Stanford

Library call number (Dewey Decimal System)

505
S4

Galston, Arthur W. "Here Come the Clones," *Natural History,* Feb. 1975, pp. 72–75.

  —new genetic engineering techniques:
      cloning, nuclear transplantation, chromosomal insertion, single-gene insertion
  —detailed example of gene insertion to cure genetic disease
  —fairly technical
  —author: teaches biology at Yale

570.5
N213

Grobstein, Clifford. "The Recombinant-DNA Debate," *Scientific American,* July 1977, pp. 22–33.

  —policy change we face with recomb. research
      —need for   —research to determine risks
                  —central research facilities
                  —policies for commercial use, international research and application
  —careful discussion
  —author: credentials unknown

605
S3

Mc Dougall, Kenneth J. "Genetic Engineering: Hazard or Blessing?" *Intellect,* Apr. 1976, pp. 528–30.

  —definition, genetic engineering
  —gene therapy to cure genetic diseases
      —state of research
  —rather technical
  —author: teaches biology at U. of Dayton

370.5
S4

Mc Wethy, Jack. "Science's Newest 'Magic'—A Blessing or a Curse?" *U.S. News and World Report*, 12 July 1976, pp. 34–35.

—overview article
—debate over the safety and value of recomb. research
—some possible benefits and risks
—author: assoc. editor for *U.S. N. & W. R.*

320.5
Un3

Randal, Judith. "Life from the Labs," *The Progressive*, March 1977, pp. 16–20.

—risks —within the research
        —external from   —universities
                         —government
                         —private industry
                         —private individuals
        —many examples
        —some ideas for reducing the dangers
        —loss of info
        —author: covers health and science for N.Y. *Daily News*,
            nat. syndicated

051
C93

Rivers, Caryl. "Cloning: A Generation Made to Order," *Ms.*, June 1976, p. 51.

—1st clonal frog, 1968
—human cloning
        —state of research
        —consequences of it
—author: cred. unknown

H61101
M55

NOTETAKING

Notetaking begins with the close reading of the articles you have selected as important. The ultimate quality of your research paper is often determined at this stage in which you record ideas and information. Several powers are important here:

1. Understanding and interpreting the source accurately
2. Passing the information through the sieve of your own mind to isolate the relevant material
3. Recording the material
   a. Without distorting it
   b. Without "lifting" the syntax and diction of the writer

Taking notes on cards will help you to develop these powers, allowing you to put similar information together on the same card, a later help in organizing. Notice important features of the notetaking process:

1. The information should be sorted out and organized according to *key words* chosen by you.
2. The information should be recorded in your own words, unless put in quotation marks.
3. The data should be recorded economically.
4. The arrangement should allow you to review the ideas quickly.

SAMPLE NOTE CARDS

Writer 1

Key word *Information in writer's own words* *Author*

Guidelines **Cohen**

656 — NIH
1) prohibits experiments with a known hazard or very bad consequence
2) P-4 containments: experiments (hassa fever virus, Marbury virus, Zaire hemorrhage fever) done with airlocks, filters, safety cabinets, clothing changes, etc.
3) P-3 contain.: labs with double doors, neg. air pressure, air filtration devices—exper. of less risk
4) P-2 unlikely to be serious risk
5) P-1 ordinary biological gene exchange—decontamination work surfaces, mechanical pipetting devices, pest control program, etc.

654 — fearful have different attitudes toward the guidelines
1) fear of unknown
2) fear with some basis in fact

Page no.

655   1)   advancement of fundamental scientific and medical knowledge
             (structure and function of genes, plasmids)

      2)   practical applications (nearer)
          –construction of bacterial strains that can produce antibodies and
            hormones

656   –new types of vaccines—not disease-carrying (E. coli)
         –grain without nitrogen fertilizer
         –pollution-free energy from water

657   "We must examine the 'benefit' side of the picture and weigh the already realized benefits and the reasonable expectation of additional
benefits, against the vague fear of the unknown that has in my opinion
been the focal point of this controversy."

Direct quotation taken because it sums up author's position.

Commentary The key words fit the information collected on each card. The writer has
recorded the material concisely, using only necessary words of his own. He
has also been careful to note the pages from which the information was
taken.

*CLASS
EXERCISES* 1. Read the following article by Judith Randal, one of Writer 1's sources.
2. Compare the sample Note Cards on pp. 218–220 with the article.
   • How accurately has the writer recorded the information?
   • What key words have been used? Why?
   • What other facts or ideas could have been taken?
   • How concisely has the material been recorded?

LIFE FROM THE LABS: WHO WILL CONTROL THE NEW TECHNOLOGY?

Judith Randal

> *As recently as five years ago, almost anyone who suggested that the
> species barrier could be broken much more easily and at far less cost
> than it took to split the atom would probably have been regarded as a
> science fiction buff at best, and more probably as a nut.*

[From *The Progressive*, March 1977]

Today this is no longer fantasy. At the very time, ironically, when thousands of species are threatened by man or already extinct, the tools that will cause entirely unrelated species to exchange hereditary material have become a reality. What now confronts us is the problem of weighing the potential benefits of this new technology against the potential risks—without sacrificing the freedom of scientific inquiry or endangering the world on a previously unimagined scale.

Interspecies hybrids are nothing new, but the issue of such unions— the mule is an example—have always been distinguished by an inability to reproduce. Moreover, those forms of life—bacteria and blue-green algae—which do not have distinct cell nuclei and those which do, have always been autonomous biological kingdoms whose boundaries could not be crossed. With the discovery of enzymes that will fit ordinary bacteria with the genes of any plant, animal, insect, or virus a scientist may choose, and with the evidence that generation after generation of germs will then continue to express the characteristics conveyed by the transplants, such distinctions are fading fast.

As they fade, we suddenly face the prospect that man will be moving genes back and forth across boundaries that many millions of years of evolution have set in place. That prospect now engages the scientific community in a furious debate—one of which most Americans are still unaware, while the rest wonder which biologists to believe.

The dilemma of balancing scientific risks and benefits is, of course, a familiar one. In the case of nuclear energy, both the risks and the benefits are at least familiar and more or less quantifiable. And when physicists have created new elements, they have done so with the knowledge that their behavior will be highly predictable. By contrast, even the experts can only guess what will happen when germs are provided with exotic genetic material and what trade-off this new technology will require. And whereas radiation generally decays, novel microbes might multiply indefinitely in a hospitable environment.

Last June, the National Institutes of Health (NIH) published voluntary guidelines which, in effect, sort proposed genetic experiments according to their estimated risk and then define those which are potentially so hazardous that they should be deferred pending further developments, or completely avoided.

Some biologists, including Nobel laureates David Baltimore and James Dewey Watson of the Massachusetts Institute of Technology and the Cold Spring Harbor Laboratory on Long Island, respectively, are satisfied that the NIH guidelines provide adequate safeguards against the escape into our midst of bacteria that might prove to be drug-resistant. There are others, within and without the Nobel ranks, who think such an "Andromeda Strain" scenario is overblown, and who protest that the NIH has imposed needless limitations on scientific inquiry.

But there are still others—and they, too, include a Nobelist, Professor George Wald of Harvard—who are not at all convinced. They point out that accidents have happened under the best-regulated scientific circumstances, and they would, therefore, have the work go forward only in highly secure facilities and sparsely populated places—if at all.

The bacteria that receive gene transplants are called DNA recombinants. DNA, or deoxyribonucleic acid, is the molecule of heredity (except for some viruses). In the course of the experiments, segments of the DNA of two or more species are annealed. The novel micro-organisms created in this process offer insights into biological mechanisms that are not otherwise easily obtained, thus arousing the scientific curiosity of those who long to unravel the mysteries of cancer and other forms of serious disease. If, indeed, these organisms could be counted on to remain laboratory curiosities—and if reputations and money were not riding on them—there would be little reason to give gene-juggled microbes a second thought.

But this is not the case. In at least one university biology department, opposition to the experiments is already construed as an attempt to block scientific progress. Graduate students who balk at using the technique may find it hard to earn a degree or to find a post at the laboratory of their choice. At the same time, both academia and industry have correctly perceived that programming bacteria to turn out quantities of valuable chemicals and drugs is the stuff of which fortunes may soon be made. Today's fairly modest research project could be the basis of tomorrow's big business deal.

Last October, for example, Dr. Herbert Boyer of the University of California, San Francisco, was a leader of two research groups that reported they had successfully used recombinant technology to induce the production of beta galactosidase, a milk-digesting protein, in Escherichia coli, a species of bacteria whose usual habitat is the human or animal intestine. In this case, the protein was one that E. coli are capable of producing anyway. But Boyer was quick to point out that "we've gone out of the area of basic science into the area of practical application" and to predict that bacteria could be induced to become factories for the manufacture of insulin and other medications and chemicals.

What is important here is that the University of California Institute of Technology, which was also represented on the Boyer team, lost no time in applying for patents on the technique. This means that, while the work was done with NIH funding and therefore adhered to the NIH guidelines, the income generated by it in the future could free both institutions—or for that matter any institution in a like position—from such constraint.

Scientists and the NIH guidelines

Universities, it is true, might be reluctant to incur the displeasure of the NIH. And an NIH regulation (which has never been used) would permit the agency to withhold funding from other projects should a grantee or contractor defy the recombinant guidelines. Nonetheless, the NIH might well be reluctant to discipline the research community. And as universities become more pressed for funds, they are being driven to *engage in projects that may become ethically dubious, though financially rewarding.*

To be fair, there probably would have been no safety guidelines had it not been for the scientists themselves. In mid-1974, eleven prominent molecular biologists—Baltimore and Watson among them—called for and obtained a two-year moratorium on what seemed to be the riskiest gene grafts. It would seem, then, that since scientists initiated and designed the guidelines, they would also have a strong stake in complying with them.

But moral considerations do not necessarily prevail—especially when a recent Federation of American Scientists survey disclosed that 10 percent of those responding thought the guidelines needlessly strict, and when compliance is entirely voluntary.

Under the NIH guidelines, laboratories engaged in the least potentially dangerous studies are designated P-1 (P standing for precautionary). Those somewhat up the line of potential risk are called P-2, and so on. P-4 laboratories have the most elaborate precautions to prevent the contamination of personnel or the escape of bacteria into the environment, and are the only facilities where the potentially most hazardous experiments are sanctioned.

Laboratories at Fort Detrick, Maryland, built for the Pentagon's now-abandoned germ warfare program and now used by the National Cancer Institute, house a P-4 facility. And the multimillion dollar lunar-receiving laboratory at the Johnson Space Center in Houston, designed for the isolation and containment of those "moon germs" that never materialized, would also qualify as P-4. So does the laboratory on Plum Island, off the eastern tip of Long Island, which the Department of Agriculture maintains for the study of hoof-and-mouth disease.

E. coli bacteria are the focus of most of the experiments conducted to date because this species of germ is the most thoroughly studied, and therefore the best understood. Many scientists would feel more comfortable working with a species that does not infect man, though considerable steps have been taken to disarm E. coli.

A special strain, K-12, is used; as far as is known, K-12 will not take up residence in people. And enfeebled substrains of K-12 have been developed that are dependent on an array of special requirements—the presence of certain nutrients, ultraviolet light, and extreme temperatures, for instance—in order to survive or reproduce. The theory is that the needs of such enfeebled strains can be supplied only in the laboratory. One scientist has aptly described the weaknesses that have been bred into the K-12 substrains as "messiah genes."

All this sounds reassuring—more than the facts may warrant. The behavior of bacteria is unpredictable, and the estimates of risk are necessarily crude. And the enzymes that permit scientists to transplant genes from one species to another do not act directly on the bacterial recipients, but on go-betweens. This multiplies the possibilities that something may go wrong.

These go-betweens are viruses known as phages, which naturally infect germs, or tiny, free-floating circles of hereditary material called plasmids, which do the same. Some scientists worry about what might happen if gene-shuffled phages or plasmids came into contact with bacteria that—unlike the enfeebled K-12 substrains—had not been designed to commit suicide in the event of their escape to the outside world.

Exchanges of plasmids, in particular, are known to occur in nature between strains and even between species of bacteria. Proponents of genetic research generally argue that if it happens in nature, there is probably nothing to fear. Critics are not so sure; their concern is that if sufficiently large numbers of these deviants were rapidly introduced, the situation could get out of hand.

Dr. Stanley Falkow, a microbiologist at the University of Washington in Seattle and an expert on E. coli, has questioned the wisdom of introducing certain plasmids even into enfeebled strains of K-12. On the basis of studies he has conducted on calves, he has advised the NIH recombinant DNA Advisory Committee that "it may not be too farfetched to suggest that some DNA recombinant molecules could profoundly affect the ability of this E. coli strain to survive and multiply in the gastrointestinal tract." Another of Falkow's worries is that a recombinant might somehow acquire the ability to reproduce in water, and so pose a massive environmental threat. Whatever the present hazards of E. coli—and it already causes most urinary tract infections and is dangerous to many who are chronically ill—it cannot ordinarily multiply in the presence of oxygen.

These concerns aside, the chemicals that form the basis of the new technology are, in principle, precision instruments that cut specific segments of DNA from one type of cell to be transplanted into others. When they are prepared by sophisticated scientists experienced in recombinant experimentation, restriction enzymes may or may not behave predictably. Such variability contributes to the inherent risk.

The dangers that amateurs could pose

At present, anyone can buy restriction enzymes off the shelf or by mail from such suppliers as Miles Laboratories, and there is nothing to prevent the amateur from dabbling in the technology, nor is there any point in licensing the production of restriction enzymes, since anyone who knows anything about biochemistry can concoct his own from readily available ingredients.

A few years ago, a Massachusetts Institute of Technology undergraduate, having read published reports, demonstrated on paper that he knew how to build an atom bomb. Since DNA recombinant work requires only a meager investment in equipment and can be carried out in limited space, a similarly resourceful high school student could conceivably collect the necessary materials and then simply turn the experimental brew loose on the general environment.

DNA recombinants, like radiation, would not make their presence quickly known to the senses should they escape. They might well prove impossible to trace. Geiger counters will detect radiation; an equivalent device for detecting bacteria has not been invented yet.

Other possible hazards in the process are even more troubling. A Government interagency committee formed by White House directive "to review Federal policy on the conduct of research involving new forms of life" reports that the National Science Foundation, the Energy Research and Development Administration, and the Department of Defense have agreed to observe the NIH guidelines and that the Agriculture Department has indicated its probable willingness to go along. But neither the Occupational Health and Safety Administration, the Center for Disease Control, nor the Environmental Protection Agency—all of which might logically be involved—has assumed any oversight responsibilities for recipients of research grants or contracts, and the NIH, too, has demurred. Such loopholes raise the possibility of reckless mischief.

Furthermore, no one knows how much research is in progress. There is reason to wonder whether the Central Intelligence Agency or its equivalents abroad might not secretly carry out experiments their governments officially decried. And there is, as in nuclear science, the possibility of exploitation by lunatics or terrorists.

There is also the inevitability of exploitation by U.S. private industry. The Pharmaceutical Manufacturers Association, the trade group to which the largest drug firms belong, for example, has told the Senate health subcommittee that it generally agrees with the NIH guidelines, but that its members will want to make larger quantities of DNA recombinants than is permitted under the rules that apply to academic researchers.

Meanwhile, seven of these firms—Miles Laboratories, Eli Lilly, Hoffman-LaRoche, Merck Sharpe and Dohme, Abbott Laboratories, Upjohn, and Pfizer—are already at work with recombinants or are gearing up. There are other such firms that do not belong to the PMA; because they are generally smaller and less visible, they are perhaps even more likely to cut corners in striking out on their own.

What role for private enterprise?

The drug industry is only one of many that has sniffed potential profits in this new technology. While the public interest may dictate full disclosure about recombinant research, private enterprise operates on the principle that if the costs of bringing experimental findings to commercial realization are to justify the investment, trade secrets must be kept.

Thus, at a Commerce Department meeting last November at which several large firms were represented, the consensus was that the private sector should publicly register its projects, but let it go at that. While nuclear reactors must be licensed before they are built, any corporation wishing to build a containment facility for microbes can simply go ahead with no questions asked. In fact, should it decide to perform recombinant experiments at even the P-3 or P-4 level without proper safeguards, it could do that, too.

Dr. Ronald Cape, who heads a biologically oriented California firm called Cetus and who attended the Commerce Department meeting, said later that there was agreement that "the registry would discourage underground or fly-by-night operations because anybody who decided to go into this field would have to stand up and be identified." But Cape obviously had some misgivings, since he also wondered aloud whether this type of enterprise should be in the profit-making sector at all.

Cetus is now doing nothing with recombinants and, according to Cape, is not in a rush to enter the field: "If we go into the business at all, we'll start off with the safe biological containment kinds of things." But the company numbers among its senior consultants molecular biologist Joshua Lederberg, a Stanford University Nobel Prize winner, who is on record as believing the NIH guidelines are too strict.

Lederberg is not the only academic to find himself in a somewhat ambiguous position. One of the most eloquent critics of the entire recombinant movement is Professor Robert Sinsheimer, chairman of the biology division at the California Institute of Technology, who regards the NIH guidelines as "sorely inadequate." Yet people at Cal Tech are engaged in this work, and the institution, which already has a P-2 laboratory, is building a P-3 facility. Sinsheimer says he would not want to be associated with an institution where a department chairman had veto power over his subordinates. And he doubts the public would benefit if the experiments were halted at Cal Tech while they proliferated elsewhere. As he sees it, this would be as meaningless as having a nation unilaterally disarm.

Even if we were to ignore or resolve the danger of catastrophic accident, the emerging genetic technology would raise formidable and frightening problems—many of them similar to, but much more acute than, those already posed by other scientific developments. The production and promotion of antibiotics, and their consequent overuse, has already led to the existence of drug-resistant germs. Now it is being suggested that bacteria can be programmed to manufacture antimicrobials more cheaply. It is not difficult to envision a new surge of highly promoted drugs—and a new health hazard.

General Electric has applied for patents on a technique which will use plasmids to confer on one strain of pseudomonas bacteria some genes endowing it with the capacity to digest more, if not all, of the various hydrocarbons that constitute crude oil. The new species could obviously prove a godsend for cleaning up oil spills. But what would happen if it found its ways into petroleum storage tanks, pipelines, or the wing tanks of a commercial jet aircraft in flight? And what will be the impact on the ocean environment itself? No one knows.

After our experience with antibiotics, pesticides, and many other scientific and technological "advances," we have surely learned that the remedies we devise often create new and acute ailments. An urgent question must, therefore, be asked: Can't at least some of what seems attainable through DNA recombinants be achieved by other, safer means? Perhaps the short-run cost of such alternatives might be higher, but the long-run savings might be immense.

Few people, unfortunately, are even aware that such questions must be raised. But some rearguard actions are being fought. Harvard University, for example, is eager to remodel a floor of its 40-year-old biology building into a P-3 (moderate risk) recombinant research facility, and it has received the approval of the NIH and the promise of some $285,000 of the agency's money. Work has already begun. But some members of Harvard's biology department—notably George Wald and Ruth Hubbard—are convinced that the insect-ridden structure, which by the University's own admission is also subject to floods, is no place for such an endeavor.

When their objections caught the ear of Cambridge's mayor, Albert E. Velluci, and the Cambridge City Council, a classic town-and-gown dispute ensued. Hearings were held, and last July a three-month "good faith" moratorium (which has since been extended) was imposed on P-3 and P-4 experiments at both Harvard and the Massachusetts Institute of Technology.

A citizens' review board appointed at the time has been looking into the situation. Chaired by a former mayor who owns a heating oil firm, the four men and four women—whose occupations range from nurse, social worker, physician, and structural engineer to professor of urban policy and community activists—recommended in January that the experimentation be permitted to resume. But in the belief that "a predominantly lay citizen group can face a technical scientific matter of general and deep public concern, educate itself appropriately to the task, and reach a fair decision," the panel also agreed that the NIH guidelines do not go far enough, and made further safety recommendations of its own. Among these is a proposed city ordinance that would automatically declare any research not in strict conformity to safety requirements to be a public health hazard.

The Cambridge compromise   The Cambridge review board obviously arrived at a political compromise. But its report made an essential point: "Knowledge, whether for its own sake or for its potential benefits to humankind, cannot serve as a justification for introducing risks to the public unless an informed citizenry is willing to accept those risks."

But not every town can be expected to react like Cambridge, and there are limitations to the local-option approach. Scientists, like industries, can readily move on if they don't like what they find in one place. Having already complied with a self-imposed moratorium, recombinant proponents are not likely to stand still indefinitely for what they regard as undue interference. They are, in general, an impatient lot, further pressed by what they feel is a need to make up for lost time in the face of competition from abroad.

Scientists of many nations are eager to participate in recombinant research, and some are already doing so with far less disclosure than there has been here. Britain's Official Secrets Act means, for example, that we may know less about what has been going on in British labs than we do about what has been happening in ours. Further, if U.S. firms cannot experiment at home, nothing can stop them from going abroad.

The new genetic technology is seductive—not only because it is cheap, fast, easy, and potentially lucrative, but also because it is intellectually appealing and holds out the promise of impressive benefits in spite of the admitted risks. The opportunity has probably passed, if it ever existed, to impose a total ban on the work—and any such ban would be breached. If there is one nightmare that biologists on all sides of the issue share, it is that Federal legislation might be drawn so inflexibly that it would impede both the progress and the safety of the research.

How, then, will the inevitable compromises be drawn? By making the research unpatentable? By insisting that all experiments be conducted in regional Federal facilities which industry would have to support in order to qualify for profits from the discoveries? By establishing an intricate system of licensure and environmental monitoring?

It is difficult to make even an educated guess. But it is clear that whatever is to be done must have the careful and immediate attention of scientists, and of the rest of us. A population explosion among microbes can occur in a matter of days, or even hours.

SAMPLE NOTE CARDS

Writer 1

Definitions   **Randal**

17   **DNA recombinants: bacteria that receive gene transplants**

       DNA: deoxyribonucleic acid: molecule of heredity

       E. coli: bacteria whose habitat is in human or animal intestines

18   **K-12: strain of E. coli not in humans**

18   **phages: viruses that infect germs called plasmids (free floating circles of hereditary material)**

Controversy   Randal

16   David Baltimore and James Dewey Watson—adequate
         (MIT Nobel Laueates)   guidelines

      George Wald (Harvard)—guidelines not a safeguard

20   Joshua Lederberg (Stanford, Nobel Prize)—guidelines
                                                too strict

      Robert Sheimer (Cal. Inst. of Tech.)—guidelines sorely
                                                inadequate

      George Wald and Ruth Hubbard—against Harvard's renovation of 40 yr.
         old P-4 facility

      —Cambridge City Council: morotorium on P-3 and P-4 at Harvard and MIT

Guidelines (NIH)   Randal

18   1974   eleven molecular biologists (incl. Baltimore & Watson) made two-
                 year moratorium on risky gene grafts

18   —survey of Fed. of Amer. Scientists: 10%—guidelines were too strict

      —NIH   —levels of danger: P-1 to P-4 (precautionary)
                 —P-4   must take precautions of contamination
                 —P-4   places   —Fort Detrick, Pentagon's germ warfare
                                  —Johnson Space Center, Houston,—moon germs
                                  —Plum Island, Long Island,—Hoof & mouth
18   —profits could cause university to defy NIH guidelines

19   —no agency will oversee use
         —not   —Occupational Health & Saf. Admin.
                 —Environmental Protection Ag.
                 —Center for Disease Control

Dangers/Private Enterprise Randal

19 —Pharmaceutical Manufacturers Assoc.: wants to make larger quantities
      than NIH guidelines
   (Miles Lab, Eli Lilly, Abbot Labs, Upjohn)

    —smaller companies are greater threat: "cut corners"

    —trade secrets—against the public right to know

20 —bacteria to manufacture antimicrobials might lead to drug overuse

    —GE plasmids (to clean oil spills) might get into petroleum storage tanks,
      pipelines, wing tanks of jets
    —threat also to ocean environment

Dangers/Academic Randal

17 —graduate students who fear techniques
    —risk diploma and lose lab positions, jobs
    —scientists may take risks to improve their reputations

18 —milk-digesting protein $\longrightarrow$ into E. coli $\longrightarrow$ manufacture of insulin
      $\longrightarrow$ patent $\longrightarrow$ threat to general research

18 —behavior of bacteria unpredictable
    —deviants in nature but if too many too fast $\longrightarrow$ they may get out of
      control

    —enzymes act on go-betweens (phages)
    —if phages contact bacteria, E. coli may survive and multiply in intestines
     (Dr. Stanley Falkow, microbiologist, U. of Wash.)

18 —if recombinants multiply in water $\longrightarrow$ environmental threat

NOTETAKING AND PLAGIARISM

Good notetaking also helps the writer later to avoid *plagiarizing*, the documented use of a source's ideas or style. Several forms of plagiarism are illustrated below, demonstrating *unacceptable* ways of incorporating ideas from a source into a paper.

The original passage, from Randal's article:

The dilemma of balancing scientific risks and benefits is, of course, a familiar one. In the case of nuclear energy, both the risks and benefits are at least familiar, and more or less quantifiable. And when physicists have created new elements, they have done so with the knowledge that their behavior will be highly predictable. By contrast, even the experts can only guess what will happen when germs are provided with exotic genetic material and what trade-off this new technology will require. And whereas radiation generally decays, novel microbes might multiply indefinitely in a hospitable environment.

1. *Paraphrasing*, substituting other words, but retaining the ideas and general word order without documenting:

The difficulty of keeping equal scientific hazards and helps is a normal one. In the instance of nuclear energy, both the disadvantages and the benefits are at least known and more or less measurable. When scientists have found new discoveries, they have done so with the understanding that their actions will be very normal. In opposition, even the authorities can only speculate on what will occur when germs are given unusual genetic substance and what exchanges this innovative technology will demand. While radiation usually diminishes and dies, new microbes might increase continuously in a favorable environment.

2. *Stealing key phrases*, without quoting them:

Genetic engineering is a fascinating new scientific endeavor. Germs are provided with exotic genetic material to discover what the new combinations will produce. Such experiments are different from the work in nuclear energy where the behavior is highly predictable. Radiation generally decays but novel microbes might multiply indefinitely. This potential hazard raises the old dilemma of balancing scientific risks and benefits.

3. *Stealing an entire sentence or section*, without quoting it:

There are many questions raised about new work in genetic engineering. What will happen when germs are provided with exotic genetic material and what trade-off will this new technology require. And whereas radiation generally decays, novel microbes might multiply indefinitely in a hospitable environment.

Proper incorporation of the source

Below is one way of properly incorporating the ideas from the source:

Writer's own words

Author's name — **Another potential disadvantage of genetic engineering is described by Randal, who suggests that, unlike the radiation produced through nuclear energy, which tends to decay, the microbes made through combining new genes may continue to increase in the right atmosphere.[2]**

Endnote number

Notice several features of the above incorporation:

1. It inserts the author's name into the paper at the beginning to signal that the writer is moving from his or her own ideas to a source.
2. It uses the ideas but not the vocabulary and word order of the source.
3. It places an endnote at the end of the source material.

If you work from carefully taken notes, the danger of plagiarizing diminishes, because the notes separate you from the source so that you cannot, even unintentionally, copy the source. Another advantage of good note-taking is that it frees you from being dominated by the *styles* of different sources.

CLASS EXERCISE

1. As a class, take your own set of notes from the Randal article:
   - Create your own key words.
   - Record the information accurately, but in your own words.
   - If you use a quote, identify it by quotation marks.
   - Be sure to include your page numbers.

ASSIGNMENT

Stage 3 Toward a Research Paper: Exploring

1. **Using the Exploratory Guide, explore your prior knowledge of the subject.**
2. **If you have chosen a scientific aim, determine on either a deductive or an inductive approach.**
3. **Using the reference tools, collect a working bibliography.**
4. **Annotate the available titles.**
5. **Take notes on the most promising titles.**
6. **Seek comments on this work.**

INCUBATING

Because research yields such extensive information, you need time to mull over the collected material. Some writers sort through their notes, organizing them, laying them out on tables or transferring key ideas to large "think sheets." Whatever the method, you need to assimilate the material during incubation or you may fall into the trap of some amateur writers who mistakenly assume that the insight is *in* the data. This false assumption ends in the "regurgitation" paper.

Avoiding these traps is not easy, however, because the weight of the material tends to dominate you. If you want to exert control over your paper, your focus becomes the key. Without a focus your paper will probably be a patchwork of materials that could be read better in the sources. Unless you are able to shape the data to accomplish your aim, you have wasted your time and your reader's. But discovering the insight depends on incubation time.

STATING THE FOCUS

Once you have discovered it, you must form your insight into a focus. Each half of your focus makes a commitment to your audience and controls your material. The first half, the aspect of the subject, indicates the scope of your paper. The second half, the point of significance, puts your imprint on the data, your answer to your starting question or a revised one. Your focus will vary according to your aim:

1. A *persuasive focus:* "Genetic engineering should be stopped."
2. An *informative focus:* "Genetic engineering poses severe physical dangers."
3. A *scientific focus:* "Most P-4 genetic research is conducted in inadequate facilities." (This focus will probably require an inductive proof.) "P-4 experiments are actually illegal." (A deductive proof might work here if laws and precedents can be used as axioms.)

Focuses like these will prove unworkable:

1. A *factual idea which conveys no new information:* "Genetic engineering is being done in many universities."
2. An *idea that violates the integrity of the data, by denying a large number of sources and hence violating factuality:* "Genetic engineering is accomplishing nothing."
3. An *idea that goes too far beyond your research:* "Genetic engineering is being done in many countries."

A good focus contributes your unique understanding of the material without distorting or repeating it. Probably you will have to try out a number of possible insights and several alternative ways of expressing them. Do not regret spending time in this stage because a good focus is the key to a good paper. Organizing and incorporating research into a paper is very time consuming. If you have to rewrite an unfocused paper, the task can be lengthier and more difficult than writing the first version. Writer 1 expresses an informative focus:

SUBJECT   POINT OF SIGNIFICANCE
Genetic engineering ———————— is a complex proposition.

The first idea commits the writer to dealing with the entire subject; whether that is workable will depend on the rest of the focus. The second idea seems obvious, offering the reader neither new information nor a new hypothesis.

CLASS
EXERCISE

1. Evaluate the following focuses:
   a. "Genetic engineering started in the U.S."
   b. "The history of genetic engineering."
   c. "I don't agree with genetic engineering."
   d. "Genetic engineering will never succeed in cloning humans."
   e. "Genetic engineering ought to be stopped."
   f. "The changing guidelines of Genetic Engineering show it lacks adequate control."
   • What focuses are workable? Why?
   • To what kind of development does each focus commit the writer?
   • What kind of aim does each focus invoke?

ASSIGNMENT

Stage 4 Toward a Research paper: Discovering and Formulating the Focus

1. **After reviewing your research, allow considerable time for incubation.**
2. **Formulate your focus.**
3. **Seek guidance on your focus from your instructor.**

DEVELOPING,
ORGANIZING,
AND REFINING
THE PAPER

In a good research paper, the facts *as assembled* speak for themselves— which is not the same thing as "the facts speak for themselves." They don't ever, of course, unless put in some kind of order. In research writing, the order the facts are put in should be transparently clear to the reader.

ORGANIZING AN INFORMATIVE PAPER

The nature of the subject material and the focus often dictate the organizational structure, following one of three modes: description, classification, or narration. Organizing according to these modes will help you to control your material. A sentence plan, moreover, keeps your focus alive throughout a long paper, each sentence acting as a minor focus for a section or paragraph. Below are sample plans for the three modes:

DESCRIPTION

SUBJECT   POINT OF SIGNIFICANCE

FOCUS:

Genetic engineering ——————————— has physical dangers.

Organization
¶1. Introduction
¶2. The lack of predictability of ⌐poses a physical danger.
  the genetic material ———————
¶3. E. Coli itself ——————————— is harmful to animals and possibly
  to men.
¶4. The limitations of the experi- ⌐pose possible threats.
  menters ———————————
¶5. The short-sightedness of the ⌐is a potential danger.
  developers ———————————
    Private industry ——————————— is not careful about guidelines.
¶6.   Universities ——————————— are going beyond restrictions.
¶7. The long-range effects ————— could be physically dangerous.
¶8. Conclusion

Notice that this organizational plan divides the first half of the focus into parts and then shows how each part can be dangerous. This paper will probably have eight paragraphs.

CLASSIFICATION

SUBJECT   POINT OF SIGNIFICANCE

FOCUS:

The dangers and advantages of ⌐pose a dilemma for scientists and
genetic engineering ——————————— the general public.

Organization:
¶1. Introduction
¶2. Several dangers ——————————— exist for scientists.
¶3. Other dangers ——————————— threaten the general public.
¶4. Some advantages ——————————— are gained by science.
¶5. Other advantages ——————————— accrue to the general public.
¶6. Conclusion: the dilemma.

Variations on this plan can be devised. Notice that the plan sustains the two parts of the focus throughout, preventing the writer from speaking first of genetic engineering and then later discussing its impact on scientists and the public.

NARRATION

SUBJECT   POINT OF SIGNIFICANCE

FOCUS:

The attitudes toward regulation of genetic engineering ⌐have been in conflict since its beginning.

Organization:

¶1. Introduction

¶2. In 1974, eleven scientists —— self-imposed a moratorium.

¶3. In 1975, the Asimolar Conference ⌐urged stricter guidelines.

¶4. In 1976, the NIH guidelines —— were considered too strict by some and inadequate by others.

¶5. In 1977, a survey of scientists — showed different ways of adhering to the guidelines.

¶6. Conclusion

CLASS EXERCISES

1. Determine what mode of organization the following focuses suggest:
   a. All categories of DNA research have potential hazards.
   b. Much of the research on genetic engineering promises to benefit man.
   c. Scientists have escalated DNA research in the seventies.
2. Using the following minor focuses as paragraphing guides, create organizational plans for the focuses above.
   a. P-2 experiments pose several risks for personnel.
   b. Bayer used recombinant techniques to produce a milk-digesting protein in *E. coli* in 1976.
   c. Research on plasmids may clean up oil spills.
   d. Work with *E. coli* has potential for vaccines and insulin.
   e. P-1 experiments contain dangers for the researchers.
   f. Sanger worked out the complete nucleotide sequence for the DNA in ϕX174 in 1977.
   g. P-4 research holds severe threats for the environment.
   h. Work on bacterial strains may yield useful antibodies.
   i. Agarwal chemically synthesized the gene for yeast alanine transfer RNA in 1970.
   j. P-3 experiments could contaminate the surrounding area.
   k. Gurdon produced a clonal frog.
   l. Recombinant techniques may correct genetic diseases like diabetes.
3. From the sample notes you took on the Randal article, formulate alternative focuses and organizational plans.

Information and evidence consist of:

1. fact—what is commonly known or what is not commonly known but can be quickly verified by referring to an authority both the reader and writer will accept
2. an inference made by a writer—what results from connecting one fact with another

A critical difference between the two is that a fact is held to be true, an inference only conditionally true. For example:

1. It is a fact that Henry Ford said, "All history, as written, is bunk." For most literate audiences that statement is a fact so widely known that it does not require documentation (i.e., an endnote).
2. It is not a fact that "All history, as written, is bunk." The fact is that Henry Ford said it. Ford's saying it does not, of course, make the content of his statement a fact; it remains an inference of Ford's. You cannot count on finding an audience that would accept Henry Ford as an acceptable authority on all history, as written.

1. It is a fact that in World War II, American armies halted at the Rhine River in the invasion of Germany. That is commonly known.
2. It is a fact that the American armies halted at the Rhine River by order of General Dwight D. Eisenhower. That is probably not universally known; in a paper designed for some audiences, establishing it as a fact would require an endnote.
3. It is a fact that Dwight D. Eisenhower blamed the separation of Berlin and of Germany on the occupation of Berlin by the Russians, and on the fact that the American armies halted at the Rhine and did not press on when they could themselves have easily occupied the capital city of Germany. Again, these are widely known facts, but for some audiences they would require documentation. The concept contains an inference made by Eisenhower, which is not universally acceptable.
4. It is a fact that Eisenhower after the war blamed the halting of the American armies at the Rhine on orders he received from President Roosevelt, dead when Eisenhower blamed him. That fact would require documentation for most audiences other than historians. And the documentation would still only prove that Eisenhower said that Roosevelt had issued such orders, not that Roosevelt had.
5. It is a fact, in need of documentation for almost any audience, that a respected historian has recently published a book informing the public that he can find no record of any such orders from Roosevelt and that Eisenhower issued the order on his own authority. The only fact here is that the historian said what he said.

The point of these examples is that, given the unspoken agreement between writers and readers of research writing, you will be able to hold and convince the reader only so long as you carefully sort out fact and inference in your sources and in what you yourself are asserting. That "sorting out" convinces the reader not only of your impersonality and objectivity but of your command of the material.

CLASS
EXERCISE

1. Identify the followng statements as either facts or inference. Refer to the first two pages of Judith Randal's "Life from the Labs: Who Will Control the New Technology?," pp. 210–218.
    a. "Randal says that most Americans are still unaware of the debate among serious scientists about gene transplants."
    b. "Man will be moving genes back and forth across boundaries that many million years of evolution have set in place."
    c. "The mule cannot reproduce."
    d. Judith Randal is a woman.

ORGANIZING AND DEVELOPING A SCIENTIFIC PAPER

If you chose the scientific aim, your organization and development should duplicate the stages of your research (see p. 222):

A. Inductive
  1. Introduction
      a. Statement of the problem
      b. Hypothesis with definitions
      c. Survey of opinion
  2. Discussion of the method of data gathering organized by description, narration or classification
  3. Data
  4. Conclusions
B. Deductive
  1. Introduction
      a. Statement of the problem
      b. Hypothesis with definitions
      c. Survey of opinion
  2. Discussion of the deductive line of reasoning
  3. Presentation of the axioms
  4. Connection between the hypothesis and the axioms
  5. Conclusion

REFINING THE EXPOSITORY STYLE

The style of a research paper should suggest the objectivity and impersonality of your investigation. That is to say, the voice projected should be that of a disinterested (not the same as an uninterested) observer—one vitally concerned with the subject matter but unbiased, a researcher so interested as to have investigated all of the available literature on the subject (given limitations of time) and so interested in arriving at the truth of the matter that he or she has set aside all personal interests, even though personal interests may explain why the researcher is so vitally interested. Precision, exactness, honesty are necessary. Disinterestedness is established by being open with the audience—no disguises, no trimming of facts, little humor, few flourishes of style, as little metaphor as possible. The first-person pronoun tends to disappear. The writer uses the most concrete diction possible; if a high level of abstraction or technical language is necessary, the writer provides whatever definitions and examples are required by the audience. Sentences tend to be declarative. The reader is not addressed directly. Rhetorical questions disappear.

The style of research writing strives for authenticity, to gain the conviction on the part of the reader that the researcher is telling the truth as far as he or she knows the truth. Authenticity, as we illustrated earlier, is established by conveying to the reader that researcher and reader have the same purpose: to discover the truth. And earlier we discussed the implications of that purpose as they affected development and organization. At the stylistic level, authenticity manifests itself in what may be called the Gesture of Honesty and the Gesture of Knowledge.

The Gesture of Honesty requires that you reveal the sources of all information or inferences that you did not arrive at independently. The Gesture of Knowledge requires that, in addition to revealing all sources that support your position, you list the other sources that you read that did *not* agree with you, or that you did not see fit for any reason to use in your presentation. They were part of your preparation, but not of your presentation.

The formal differences between these two gestures is, of course, the difference between endnotes and bibliography. Endnotes document what you used in the presentation; bibliography records what you consulted and, therefore, what presumably went into your total thinking. Since both are encompassed in the note and bibliography cards you took in the exploratory stage, there should be no problem in recording either. But you may be unclear about two kinds of endnotes; *citations* and *quotations*.

Citations and quotations

When you *cite* an authority, you simply summarize that authority's statement or information in your own words. When you *quote* an authority, you give the exact words of the authority. In any piece of research writing, citation ought to be more frequent than quotation, for these reasons:

1. The paper belongs to you; the center is your focus. You introduce authorities only as illustration or evidence. Your style must, therefore, dominate. Quotation introduces conflicting styles.

2. In exploring others' writing, you are looking for concepts, ideas, and information that can be phrased in different ways, depending on your exact focus and what you find useful.

3. You can convince the reader that you command your material only if you have assimilated that material to your own purposes. Summary and citation suggest assimilation. Quotation suggests raw data, unassimilated. If you cannot say in your own words, appropriate to your purpose, what the source has said in his or her words, it's a pretty good guess that you do not control the material in the source. Notice the difference between the two in Writer 1's paper:

a. Citation (information in the writer's own words):

People wanted to know, especially in places like Cambridge, where Harvard was conducting P-3 and P-4 experiments in a questionable place, was the research safe?[8]

b. Quotation (the exact words of the source):

This science is genetic engineering, "the directed intervention in the genetic material of an organism for the purpose of changing inherited characteristics."[4]

CLASS EXERCISES

1. From the notes you took on the Randal article, write one paragraph that includes citations and at least one quotation. Include a reference to your source (see p. 222) and avoid the forms of plagiarism (pp. 221–222).

2. Seek commentaries on your incorporations from your instructor and classmates.

Documentation forms

A. Endnotes—first note references: The forms for endnotes are conventions established by scholars as a code for recording sources of information. Here are some standard forms.

1. Published books:

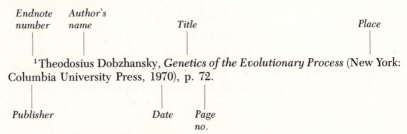

[1]Theodosius Dobzhansky, *Genetics of the Evolutionary Process* (New York: Columbia University Press, 1970), p. 72.

2. Periodicals:

a. With no continuous pagination:

   [2]Clifford Grobstein, "The Recombinant-DNA Debate," *Scientific American*, July 1977, p. 30.

b. With continuous pagination:

   [3]Stanley N. Cohen, "Recombinant DNA: Fact and Fiction," *Science*, 195 (1977), 654.

   Volume number

B. Endnotes—second note references may be documented as follows:

   [4]Dobzhansky, p. 87.
   [5]Grobstein, p. 32.

All endnotes should be typed on a separate sheet at the end of paper (see student example on p. 235). For complete coverage of documentation forms and alternative ways of documenting, see *MLA Handbook* (New York: Modern Language Association, 1977).

C. A bibliography records the sources that form a basis for the paper. Normally, the bibliography is roughly coextensive with the endnotes, unless you have relied heavily on a few sources that are not endnoted. A lengthy bibliography with a short number of endnotes indicates a lack of proportion in your documentation. The form for the bibliography is different from that of the endnotes:

1. Published books:

Dobzhansky, Theodosius, *Genetics of the Evolutionary Process*. New York: Columbia University Press, 1970.

2. Periodicals:

Grobstein, Clifford. "The Recombinant-DNA Debate." *Scientific American*, July 1977, pp. 22–33.

Notice that in the bibliography:

1. The sources are alphabetized, with the last name of the writer appearing first.
2. The publication information is not in parentheses for the book.
3. The second line is indented.
4. The total pagination is given for articles; no pagination is given for books.

See student example for the format (pp. 235–236).

Writer 1

ENGINEERING OUR OWN EVOLUTION: COMPLEXITIES IN AN UNCHARTED FIELD

It has been called "one of the most promising—and at the same time most hazardous—new fields since creation of the atom bomb."[1] It has been hailed as "science's newest 'magic,'"[2] and its technology has been labelled "a sorcerer's apprentice."[3] This science is genetic engineering, "the directed intervention in the genetic material of an organism for the purpose of changing inherited characteristics."[4] Such intervention which has been going on for years in plants and animals is called hybridization. But between 1971 and 1973, molecular biologists, particularly Paul Berg and Stanley Cohen at Stanford University and Hubert Boyer of U. of C., developed means of putting *any* two kinds of DNA together in order to cross the species barrier.

The kind of research called recombinant-DNA "is not a single entity, but rather . . . a group of techniques that can be used for a wide variety of experiments."[5] One technique of cloning, for example, is used to create a number of genetically identical individuals. Yale biologist Arthur Galston explains that individual blastula cells that are not differentiated are separated by chemical and mechanical techniques from the blastula of a developing fertilized egg. They will be able to produce whole new organisms when they are cultivated in the right medium (for lower animals) or are implanted in a substitute mother (for mammals). With the technique of nuclear transplantation, just the nucleus of either a fertilized egg or just an ordinary body cell is destroyed mechanically or by radiation. Then the nucleus from another body cell is injected, and the receptor cell develops into a normal embryo that will be a carbon copy in one generation. The complicated techniques of inserting chromosomes and single-gene involves going into cells on even smaller levels.[6]

Recognizing the implications of recombination, scientists imposed a temporary ban on certain experiments considered the most dangerous until they met in February, 1975 at the Asimolar Conference to urge the National Institute of Health to write research guidelines. In June, 1976 the NIH upheld the ban on hazardous experiments and ordered four levels of containment (lab facilities of varying requirements— airlocks, filters, etc.) for experiments ranging from lowest (P-1) to highest (P-4) categories of possible risk.[7]

Ordinarily, news of scientific developments reaches the public slowly through science magazines and science columns in newspapers. But the fantastic potential of these recombination techniques was quickly learned. People wanted to know, especially in places like Cambridge where Harvard was conducting P-3 and P-4 experiments in a questionable place, was the research safe?[8] What would genetic engineering mean for our futures—a cure for genetic diseases like diabetes and sickle cell? a world-wide epidemic owing to some laboratory mistake? a society of clones?

This possibility of engineering our own evolution—of actually controlling and/or creating plant, animal, and human life on this planet—is a complex proposition.

The complexities are not merely technical. There are dangers in doing the research itself. According to scientists, says *New York Daily News* science writer Judith Randal, the behavior of bacteria itself is unpredictable. Add to this the fact that the chances of error increase because the enzymes involved in gene transplants act on virus go-betweens called phages, rather than directly on the bacteria. Although genetic deviations occur in nature, too, some scientists fear that if too many of them are introduced too fast, the changes could get out of control.[9] The enzymes themselves may or may not act predictably. Moreover, most experiments use the popular *E. coli* bacteria, which can infect animal and human intestines, even though a special strain of *E. coli* called K-12 has been developed which will not infect man. But Dr. Stanley Falkow, a microbiologist expert on *E. coli*, fears that DNA recombinant molecules even in weakened strains of K-12 could increase the ability of this *E. coli* strain to survive and multiply[10] causing chronic diarrhea and bladder infections in livestock or humans.[11] Dr. Falkow also fears that if this strain reproduces in water, it could be an environmental threat.[12]

The results of genetic engineering become so entangled that it is practically impossible to separate and group them. For instance, if by some laboratory accident or mistake a dangerous bacteria escaped and infected people outside, there is both a medical problem and a legal one. Or consider this. According to Kenneth McDougall, a biology professor at the University of Dayton, recombinant techniques hold hope for correcting genetic diseases—especially those caused by single-gene defects, like diabetes, PKU, gout. Rather than treatment by diet or drugs, which some genetic diseases don't even respond to, it will be better just to replace the defective gene. Laboratories have already been able to isolate certain genes related to specific diseases and to produce them in bulk. Then the genes must be put into the right cells of the organism. Two processes for doing this, called transformation and transduction, have been perfected in bacteria but have not been proven in mammals. Another problem is gene regulation—getting a gene to produce the right amount of a substance at the right time.[13] Once these obstacles are overcome, the practice of this genetic therapy could be open to malpractice suits like any other medical procedure—perhaps more so, as long as it is new and controversial.

There are also safety and social problems. Randal suggests that prestige and profit from the new research might bring outside dangers: daring scientists may take greater risks to improve their reputations; a biology student who questions the techniques might risk his degree or be kept from certain professional labs, as supposedly has already happened in at least one university.[14]

Unbelievably, the NIH guidelines for experiments are still voluntary. The penalty for breaking a rule is having your NIH research funding reduced or cut off. Randal wonders whether general research will be prevented if techniques such as the production of insulin from bacteria are patented. Will enough profits be made so as to take all the power out of the NIH sanction?[15]

Thus, the economics of private enterprise further complicate the picture. Pharmaceutical companies have been quick to produce cheaper and better drugs. Companies including Miles Laboratories, Eli Lilly, Abbott Laboratories, and Upjohn have already told a Senate health subcommittee that they want to make greater quantities of DNA recombinants than NIH rules now permit for academic research. And, as Randal points out, smaller firms may actually be a bigger threat because they may "cut corners" and not take the right precautions.[16]

Randal sees other difficulties with private enterprise: 1) the emphasis on trade secrets goes against what many consider the public's right to know about such controversial research; 2) once bacteria can be created to produce antimicrobials cheaply, there might be an overuse of drugs. GE is trying to patent a procedure for cleaning up oil spills. But what would happen if the bacteria found its way into petroleum storage tanks, pipelines, or the wing tanks of a commercial jet? There might even be an impact on the ocean environment itself.[17]

Amateurs pose still more complexities. Right now, anybody can order the enzymes through the mail. Once harmful recombinants got loose, we would probably not find out about it until they showed up in some negative way. They would also be practically impossible to track.[18]

These kinds of possibilities bring genetic engineering into the political arena. As all writers covering the field seem to agree, some agency must have charge of regulating research done in universities, by industry, and by government, and also the application of that research, commercial or otherwise.

But maybe the greatest complexities in genetic engineering are moral. Cloning of amphibians has been an accomplished fact since 1968.[19] Now, human cell nuclei have swollen in size "as much as a hundredfold" in experiments by J. B. Gurdon at Oxford where they were inserted into frog eggs.[20] Rivers estimates that human cloning will be achieved inside ten years and says:

> The consequences of human cloning are almost impossible to imagine. Widespread human cloning would alter human society beyond recognition.

The family would no longer exist, sexuality would have no connection with reproduction. The idea of parenthood would be completely changed. The diversity of human beings provided by sexual reproduction would vanish. One could imagine entire communities of people who looked exactly the same, whose range of potential was identical. Some scientists have suggested that "clones and clonishness" could replace our present patterns of nation and race.

The misuses of cloning are not hard to predict. . . . Would women and men project their egos into the future by producing their own "carbon copies"? Would society choose to clone our most valued citizens?[21]

Thus, the new capabilities that the field of genetic engineering gives to us obviously involve considerations beyond science alone. The complexities are not merely technical. They are legal and medical, economic and political. They have to do with ecology; they are concerned with personal safety and national security. They are, above all, social and moral on an international scale. When we assume the responsibility for the direction of life on our planet, we must determine priorities and make value judgments about the quality of life in our futures.

ENDNOTES

[1] Jack McWethy, "Science's Newest Magic—A Blessing or a Curse?" *U.S. News & World Report*, 12 July 1976, p. 34.
[2] McWethy, p. 34.
[3] Clifford Grobstein, "The Recombinant-DNA Debate," *Scientific American*, July 1977, p. 30.
[4] Kenneth J. McDougall, "Genetic Engineering: Hazard or Blessing?" *Intellect*, 104 (1976), 529.
[5] Stanley N. Cohen, "Recombinant DNA: Fact and Fiction," *Science*, 195 (1977), 654.
[6] Arthur W. Galston, "Here Come the Clones," *Natural History*, 84 (1975), 72–73.
[7] Cohen, 656.
[8] Judith Randal, "Life from the Labs," *The Progressive*, March 1977, pp. 16–20.
[9] Randal, p. 18.
[10] Randal, p. 18.
[11] McWethy, p. 34.
[12] Randal, p. 18.
[13] McDougall, pp. 529–530.
[14] Randal, p. 17.
[15] Randal, p. 18.
[16] Randal, p. 19.
[17] Randal, p. 20.
[18] Randal, p. 18.
[19] Caryl Rivers, "Cloning: A Generation Made to Order," *Ms*, June 1976, p. 51.
[20] Rivers, p. 51.
[21] Rivers, p. 51.

BIBLIOGRAPHY

Cohen, Stanley N. "Recombinant DNA: Fact and Fiction." *Science*, 195 (1977), 654–57.
Galston, Arthur W. "Here come the Clones." *Natural History*, 84 (1975), 72–75.
Grobstein, Clifford. "The Recombinant-DNA Debate." *Scientific American*, July 1977, pp. 22–33.
Mc Dougall, Kenneth J. "Genetic Engineering: Hazard or Blessing?" *Intellect*, 104 (1976), 528–530.

McWethy, Jack. "Science's Newest 'Magic'–A Blessing or a Curse?" *U.S. News and World Report*, 12 July 1976, pp. 34–35.
Randal, Judith. "Life from the Labs," *The Progressive*, March 1977, pp. 16–20.
Ribers, Caryl. "Cloning: A Generation Made to Order," *Ms*, June 1976, p. 51.

CLASS EXERCISES

1. Study the material used by Writer 1 for support.
   - What sections of information lack endnotes as citations?
   - What purpose do the direct quotations give? Should the material have been put into citations instead?
2. Contrast the endnote and bibliography pages of Writer 1.
   - What are the basic differences?
   - What errors, if any, in form are present?

ASSIGNMENT

Stage 5 Toward a Research Paper: Organizing, Developing, and Refining the Paper

1. Organize your ideas and notes, according to your focus.

2. Write the first version of your paper, endnoting your citations and quotations.

3. Refine your style.

4. Include a bibliography.

CRITIQUING AND REWRITING

CRITIQUING RESEARCH PAPERS

The central question in critiquing a research paper is "Who is in control?" The sign of the good paper is that the authority of the writer comes through clearly. The writer's voice dominates. The writer controls the material; the material does not control (and thus defeat) the purposes of the writer. That control will be most clearly evidenced in:

1. *the proportion of citation to quotation:* too many quotes = too little control
2. *the organization:* Does the paper fit together in an easily discernible order?
3. *transitions:* Does the writer move easily from one event to another, from one category to another? Does the writer move easily out of his or her own ideas into borrowed material and back again?

The Critical Guide will again help in critiquing the research paper:

CRITICAL GUIDE

1. Focus
   What is the writer's focus?
   In what ways has the writer maintained the focus?
   Where has the unity been broken?

2. Development

What kind of support—facts, inferences, ideas—has the writer provided?

Does it give new information to the audience?

Does it possess factuality and comprehensiveness?

Has it been properly cited or quoted?

3. Organization

What mode of organization has the writer used?

Has it been followed? If not, where has the writer left the pattern?

What coherence devices has the writer used?

4. Style

How has the writer kept to an expository style?

What kind of diction is used?

What sentence patterns are effective? Which not?

5. Conventions

In what places in the paper has the writer failed to follow the conventions?

Where has the writer failed to use proper endnote and bibliography form?

CRITIQUE:
Writer 1

We note in the beginning that Writer 1 has a command of the conventions of Standard Written English. If one were critiquing this paper only on style and coherence—that is, on the ability to choose words accurately, write efficient sentences, and construct coherent paragraphs—this would be a good research paper. However, command of the conventions and good style do not guarantee success.

Focus

We remarked earlier that the focus as stated seemed a little shaky, a little thin. That genetic engineering is complex may be so obvious a statement as not to require discussion.

What emerges in the paper is a confusion about the key word, "complex." "Complex" means to consist of interconnected or interwoven parts. A writer who deals with a stated complexity must

1. isolate the aspect of complexity
2. break down the complexity to show the parts and their relationship

Past the first, introductory paragraph of definition, the reader is led to believe that the complexity of genetic engineering lies in one aspect—its mechanics. But the third paragraph destroys this notion. The fourth paragraph introduces no new aspect but poses a series of questions about the *future* of genetic engineering. The fifth paragraph says that genetic engineering "is a complex proposition"—something we hardly need to be told and a little puzzling, since, at this point, calling the field a complex *proposition* simply confuses the issue further. The next paragraph tries to make a distinction between "technical complexity" and "dangers in doing the research itself," a not very helpful distinction, because doing the research *is* a technical matter.

Succeeding paragraphs only multiply the confusion. In paragraph seven, to take only one more example, the writer in the first sentence confesses his inability to handle the subject. "Complexity" does not mean "beyond logical discussion" or "beyond analysis." Quite the opposite. The paper has, therefore, a problem with unity because it does not maintain its focus, largely because the focus proves to be no focus at all. Hence, the paper will not show the reader any evidence that the student has mastered the material. To gather material and list it in graceful prose is not to show mastery.

Development

The biology instructor for whom this paper was written is going to be unimpressed. The paper probably tells him little in its details that he does not know. The writer in revising might consider shifting his primary audience and write for his classmates.

More important, there is not enough material in the paper to support the large and somewhat vague focus. If the subject is "complex," it has to seem complex to the *reader*. This paper demonstrates only that the material is too complex for this writer to handle adequately.

Furthermore, the writer has not properly incorporated citations, and paragraphs and major sections of the paper *begin* with quotations. Quotation (and citation) are methods of proof. The writer himself should control his major statements and use quotations and citations for support.

A careful reader—and we assume his biology instructor is a careful reader—will be bothered also by the lack of documentation for long sections of the paper. Every quotation has its proper endnote, but there are stretches of summary that bear no documentation.

Organization

Our comments on the lack of focus imply the critique: there is little organization in this paper. The first paragraph, for example, in its last sentence, seems to suggest that a narrative pattern will emerge. But the second paragraph moves in the first sentence into a classification pattern, then shifts into a descriptive pattern. The third paragraph shifts back into narrative, which ends abruptly in the first sentence of the fourth paragraph.

Style
The writer obviously is at home with the language. Only infrequently does the style of the sources clash with the somewhat more sensational style of the writer—"fantastic potential," "Unbelievably, the NIH guidelines . . . ."

Conventions
More than competent, but in vain.

REWRITING
The paper can be repaired, but only with a considerable investment of time and effort. The writer needs:

1. a narrower focus more in harmony with the scope of his material
2. a clear and consistent pattern of organization
3. perhaps a different audience, because the writer has at least demonstrated that he cannot, as he set out to do, write as a peer of his biology instructor

REVISED VERSION

Writer 1   ENGINEERING OUR OWN EVOLUTION: THE RISKS

Genetic Engineering is the popular term for recombinant DNA research, "the directed intervention in the genetic material for the purpose of changing inherited characteristics."[1] Such research ranges from long-established and relatively innocent experiments in producing hybrid varieties of plants and animals to cloning, the creation of a number of genetically identical individuals. Experiments in cloning have brought GE into the public eye recently and have created a storm of controversy. That controversy tends to center on the moral and social aspects of GE often overlooking the actual physical dangers that lurk in the experiments.

Scientists recognize the dangers. Those engaged in the research imposed a temporary ban on certain experiments considered the most dangerous until they met in February 1975, at the Asimolar Conference to urge the National Institute of Health to write research guidelines.[2] In June, 1976, the NIH upheld the ban on hazardous experiments and ordered four levels of containment (lab facilities of varying requirements—air locks, filters, etc.) for experiments ranging from lowest (P-1) to highest (P-4) categories of risk.[3]

What are those risks?

First, there is the lack of predictability of the genetic material itself. Most recombinant research utilizes bacteria. The behavior of bacteria itself is unpredictable. The enzymes used in gene transplants act on virus go-betweens called phages rather than directly on the bacteria. Since the action of the enzymes and the behavior of the phages is unpredictable at present, the chances of error increase.[4] The experimenter quite simply does not know what will happen.

Second, the bacteria commonly used—the *E. coli*—is harmful to humans and animals. Even though a special strain of *E.coli* called K-12 has been developed which will not infect man, one microbiologist, Dr. Stanley Falkow, an expert on *E.coli*, fears that DNA recombinant molecules even in weakened strains of K-12 could "profoundly [increase] the ability of this *E.coli* strain to survive and multiply in the gastrointestinal tract,"[5] causing chronic diarrhea and bladder infections in livestock or humans. Since *E.coli* is also common in fish, insects, and plants, Dr. Falkow worries "that a recombinant might somehow acquire the ability to reproduce in water, and so pose a massive environmental threat."[6]

Third, there is always the possibility of human error. Suppose that in advanced research a scientist were attempting to correct a genetic disease—like diabetes, sickle-cell anemia, or gout—by replacing the defective gene. Laboratories have been able to isolate certain genes related to specific diseases and to synthesize them in bulk. Then the genes must be inserted into the right cells of the host organism. Two processes for doing this, called transformation and transduction, have been perfected in bacteria but have not yet been proven in mammals, although that next step is surely only a matter of time.[7]

Gene transplanting obviously involves a series of complicated tasks in which, to put it simply, the right material must be inserted at the right time into the right cell. Suppose just one step went wrong and dangerous DNA were inserted. Nobody knows what would be created. The threat has been present since 1973, when molecular biologists developed means of putting *any* two kinds of DNA together, crossing the species barrier.

Fourth, there is the danger posed by human shortsightedness, ambition, and greed. Pharmaceutical companies have been quick to pick up on "bacterifacture" to produce cheaper and better drugs; it is entirely possible, for example, that we will soon have insulin-producing bacteria because of GE.[8] Companies including Miles Laboratories, Eli Lilly, Abbott Laboratories, and Upjohn have already told a Senate health subcommittee that they want to make greater quantities of DNA recombinants than NIH rules now permit for academic researchers.[9]

Judith Randal, science writer for the *New York Daily News*, points out that smaller firms may pose an even larger threat, since they may "cut corners" and not take proper precautions.[10] Even if such firms were to take adequate precautions—and no one knows what "adequate precautions" are—much more recombinant material would be in circulation, available to the research amateur. Right now, anybody can order the enzymes used in recombinant research through the mail.[11]

Even the pursuit of seemingly noble ends by private enterprise poses dangers. General Electric, for example, is trying to patent a procedure for creating a strain of bacteria that can break up the hydrocarbons composing crude oil. As Randal says, this would be a "godsend for cleaning up oil spills. But what would happen if [the bacteria] found its way into petroleum storage tanks, pipelines, or the wing tanks of a commercial jet aircraft in flight?"[12] And what will the bacteria do to the ocean environment?

Fifth, there is the danger of the absolute unknown, the long-range effect of stepped-up evolution. Genetic deviations, of course, occur in nature. GE allows mankind not only to engineer its own evolution but to speed up the process a thousand, even a million fold. What impact that will have on the earth, nobody knows.

At present, the only control over genetic engineering is a set of NIH guidelines. Compliance with those guidelines is voluntary. In view of the unpredictability and infectiousness of the raw material, the possibility of human error, the probabiliy of human short sightedness, and the present ignorance of the long-range effects of experimentation, a policy of voluntary compliance seems at best dangerous and at worst foolhardy.

ENDNOTES

[1] Kenneth J. McDougall, "Genetic Engineering: Hazard or Blessing?" *Intellect*, 104 (1976), 529.
[2] Stanley N. Cohen, "Recombinant DNA: Fact and Fiction," *Science*, 195 (1977), 656.
[3] Cohen, p. 656.
[4] Judith Randal, "Life from the Labs," *The Progressive*, March 1977, p. 18.
[5] Randal, p. 18.
[6] Randal, p. 18.
[7] McDougall, pp. 529–530.
[8] Randal, p. 18.
[9] Randal, p. 19.
[10] Randal, p. 19.
[11] Caryl Rivers, "Cloning: A Generation Made to Order," *Ms.*, June 1976, p. 51.
[12] Randal, p. 18.

The bibliography remains the same as in the first version.

CLASS
EXERCISES
1. Using the Critical Guide and working in groups, criticize your first versions.

2. Read the Revised Version of Writer 1 (pp. 239–241).
   - What changes have been made? Are they improvements?
   - Why or why not?

ASSIGNMENT

Stage 6 Toward a Research Paper: Critiquing and Revising

1. **Do a self-critique based on the criticism from your instructor and classmates.**
2. **Revise your paper.**

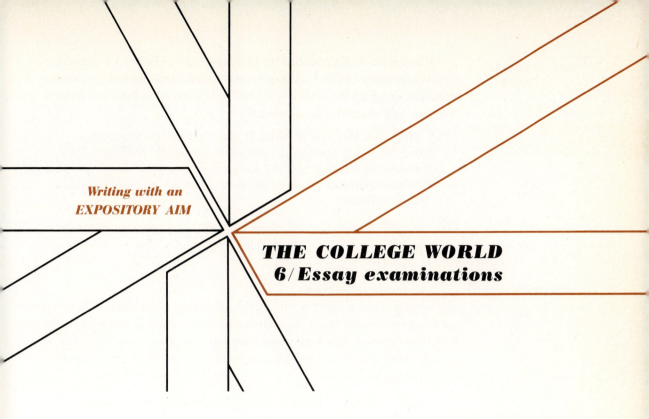

THE COLLEGE WORLD
6/ Essay examinations

Essay examinations test not only your ideas and information but also your writing skills because exams speed up all the stages of the composing process. Exam week is not the time to acquire writing skills but rather the time to display them. Is there any purpose, then, in devoting a chapter to essay exam writing? Perhaps, depending on your type of problem with exams. If you find a discrepancy between the quality of your writing in composition courses and your writing on exams for other courses, you might have one of three types of problems. (1) You may believe that other instructors expect only a demonstration of mastery of content. Or (2) you may not know how to transfer your skills to a pressure situation. Or (3) you may lack experience in exam writing. This chapter cannot help you if you have the first problem, but it does offer assistance if you have the other problems, because it demonstrates how a writer functions during exam taking and provides practice, giving criticism not only on content but also on writing skills.

Essay exam writing has two starting points: at the beginning of a course and at exam time. The first starting point is a long-range one—a questioning attitude throughout the academic course. As you attend lectures and analyze readings, you should continuously ask:

1. How does this new material fit into my previous learning?
2. Are there any conflicting viewpoints among the readings or between the readings and the lectures?
3. What seems significant in this material to my instructor, my future audience?

Keeping track of important questions not only helps you prepare for eventual exams but also aids you in learning itself.

TYPES OF QUESTIONS

The second starting point occurs at the beginning of an exam, when you must determine what kinds of questions are being posed. If you fail to make this determination, you may waste your answers. Below are four general types of questions often asked on essay exams. Notice their implications for your thinking and writing:

1. *Questions that ask you to Define or Identify:* Such questions demand concise and accurate answers. Long, padded paragraphs not only reveal fuzzy thinking but also waste valuable test time.

2. *Questions that ask you to Explain:* These questions expect you to expand an answer, giving a full account, examples, important background material. Short answers here are not sufficient. To handle such questions well, you need to have a thorough understanding of the subject.

3. *Questions that ask you to Compare and Contrast:* Such questions are more demanding because they require not only a good understanding of two or more subjects but also the ability to detect points of likeness or difference quickly and to infer generalizations.

4. *Questions that ask you to Evaluate:* Evaluating is often the most difficult task demanded by an essay question. Even though such a question expects you to know only one subject well, you must quickly isolate significant criteria against which to measure the subject. Sometimes the instructor has given these criteria during the course. Other times you must look for them in your own experience.

TIME PLANS

In addition to identifying the kinds of questions being asked, another task of the starting point is to plan *timing*, because one of the pitfalls of essay exams is uneven time distribution. The type of question suggests the percentage of time you should allow for it. Explanations require more time than definitions. Comparisons and evaluations usually demand the most time. Many instructors guide your planning by weighting the questions with points. If your instructor doesn't give you this guidance, ask for it. A minute's foresight can prevent you from running out of time before you get to the most challenging (and often highly weighted) question.

CLASS EXERCISE

1. Read the following sample essay exams:
   - Determine the kinds of answers that the questions require, and
   - Plan the time you would allow for each question within a 50-minute period.

Essay Exam 1
1. *Define expository, expressive, and persuasive aims.*
2. *Distinguish writing in the private, the public, and the college worlds.*
3. *Discuss the stages and strategies of the writing process.*
4. *Determine the value of the Audience Guide or of the Critical Guide.*

Essay Exam 2
1. *Some urban scholars have pointed out that "cities stand at the center of the currents and cross-currents of broad-scale change that alter and reconstitute societies."*
   Discuss this idea as it applies to any three of the following:
   a. Ancient Rome   b. The Middle Ages
   c. Renaissance cities   d. Egypt and Mesopotamia
   e. London or Paris in the industrial era

2. *Repeatedly in this course we have stressed that urbanization must be studied from a variety of perspectives or, in other words, by examining a number of interrelated variables. By using at least four specific examples of cities, urban civilizations or eras (such as the Middle Ages or Renaissance), explain why this approach is so important.*
   Note: *Only one of your examples may be from the period before the Middle Ages.*
3. *In depth and detail, compare and contrast any two of the following:*
   a. Urban life in the Middle Ages
   b. Urban life in the Renaissance
   c. Urban life in the industrial age

ASSIGNMENT

Stage 1 Toward an Essay Exam: The Starting Point
1. **Take notes on readings (and lectures) on the subject selected by your writing instructor for an essay exam.**

245 THE STARTING POINT

2. **Ask yourself:**
   - **How does this new material fit into my previous learning?**
   - **Are there any conflicting viewpoints among the readings and the lectures?**
   - **What seems significant in this material to my instructor?**
3. **Note questions that come to mind.**

EXPLORING

For an essay exam, you do two kinds of exploring: (1) while studying for an exam, and (2) during the examination itself. The Exploratory Guide you have been using works well to help you review your readings and lectures. If you study the material, organizing it under the three views, you will more easily perform the kinds of thinking required on tests:

1. recalling known material, required for all four types of questions
2. discovering new relationships, required for the comparison and evaluation questions

EXPLORATORY GUIDE FOR STUDYING

Static view
   –What are the key *terms, ideas, theories, persons, dates,* or *events* studied?
   –How would I define or identify them?
   –If asked to explain any of them, what important information and understanding do I need?
   –What examples or instances of them can I recall?

Dynamic view
   –Did any of the above change, develop, or go through stages? If so, what, how, why?
   –What causes or effects do I know about these changes or movements?

Relative view
   –How would I classify any of the above?
   –Are there obvious comparisons or contrasts between ideas, movements, theories, procedures?
   –Are there contrasting viewpoints in the readings? Between the readings and the lectures?

We will present the Exploration of Writer 1 on white-collar crime, a subject on which he was to be examined. The content is taken from a cluster of articles he was assigned. After reading these articles, he organized the information using the three views. We include his full set of notes in the Exploration below so that you can compare them with his later essay answers.[1]

CLASS EXERCISES

1. Study the Exploration of Writer 1
   - What key ideas has he summarized under each view?
   - In what ways will the visual organization of this material aid him in remembering it?
2. As a class, organize under the three views the information you have learned in this book on writing, including material on
   - stages of the process
   - aims
   - modes
   - strategies for each stage
   - worlds of writing

EXPLORATION

Writer 1 STATIC VIEW

Terms and definitions
—white-collar crime (Edwin Sutherland, 1939): "a crime committed by a person of respectability and high social status in the course of his occupation" (popular—Webster): "a crime . . . committed by a person in business, government, or a profession in the course of his occupational activities
—types of white-collar crime (popular vs. academic definition)
—fraud

—insurance	—investment—Ponzi
—check & credit card	game (see notes)
	—tax
—land sales	—shell corporation (see notes)

—stock—examples:
  1) mutual fund mgr. buys heavily from Broker X, who repays favor by tipping mgr. on "hot" issues for mgr.'s personal purchase

---

[1]Articles used by Writer 1: Tom Alexander, "Waiting for the Great Computer Rip-off," *Fortune,* 90 (July, 1974), 142–146, 148, 150; "A $40-Billion Crime Wave Swamps American Business," *U.S. News & World Report,* 21 February 1977, pp. 47–48; J. Taylor De Weese, "The Trojan Horse Caper—and Assorted Other Computer Crimes," *Saturday Review,* 15 November 1975, pp. 10, 58–60; Harry E. Graves, "White Collar Crime: Are New Laws Necessary?" *Vital Speeches,* 15 June 1977, pp. 525–527; "New Style in Public Enemies—the White Collar Criminal," *U.S. News & World Report,* 12 March 1973, pp. 53–55; Gerald D. Robin, "White-Collar Crime and Employee Theft," *Crime and Delinquency,* 20 (July, 1974), 251–262.

2) accs. & execs falsify earnings potential in reports $\longrightarrow$ raises
    stock prices $\longrightarrow$ participants sell at big personal profit
3) execs learn of development that will raise/lower value of their
    co.'s stock, then buy/sell before public knows
   –mail–"scam" operation: take over long est'd business, order big on
      credit, sell mdse, fast, abandon business before paying sup-
      plier
    –bankruptcy fraud
    –housing—FHA officials plotted with accs./appraisers to falsify buy-
    er's $ status and inflate home values
  –embezzlement
  –bribery
  –kickbacks, payoffs
  –computer theft
  –counterfeiting
–employee theft (Robin): middle-class theft within "large businesses and
  industrial complexes: supermarkets, department stores, factories and
  manufacturing plants"
–occupational crimes (Robin): "all violations that occur during the
  course of occupational activity and are related to employment"
–computer crime (Robert Courtney, IBM comp. safety)
 –clerical errors, employee dishonesty, fires, employee sabotage, water
  damage, outside ("remote") manipulation
–losing the "paper trial"—Equity Funding swindle
–accidental nature of detecting computer crime
–Donn Parker (Stanford comp. researcher)
examples computer crime:
1) program bank computer to ignore overdrafts
2) teller pockets most deposit $ then later types false info into computer
  or transfers $ into customers' accts. from any long-inactive accts.
3) bank customer replaces blank deposit slips with his own encoded slips
4) burglar checks computer credit reports to locate rich victims
5) Jerry Schneider, Pacific T&T scandal (see notes)
6) "Trojan Horse" caper: fraud is programmed into *memory* of computer, dormant for a time, then triggered; or, second dormant program covers tracks of first
"tiger teams" test computer safeguards by attacking "on-line" computer
  system—central computer that stores & processes data is connected directly to remote terminals by telephone lines
"spoofing"—mimicking a legit. terminal, for eavesdropping
"piggybacking"—intercepting and *changing* computer messages tapped,
  e.g., insert additional credit transfers to accts.

DYNAMIC VIEW

–Change in Southerland definition needed (Robin):
 –classify white-collar crime and employee theft in separate categories

          –current definition does not include persons in lower classes
        –effect: –underestimates amount of crime
                      –distorts frequency of types of crime
                      –gives wrong impression of char. of criminals
     –white-collar crime growing rapidly
    proofs: –fraud-embezzlement arrests up 86% 1960–71
                                up 70% 1971–76

           –forgery & counterfeiting arrests up 50% 1960–71
           –1972 SEC found 1000+ violations in 900 inspections
           –1972 HUD land deal complaint up from 50/wk. to 300 wk/
             in 8 mos.
           –crackdown on tax cheaters: 1971, 35% of guilty imprisoned;
             1972, 44% of guilty imprisoned
           –crimes against business up 10%/yr.
           –1973–77, white-collar conviction up 100%

    causes: –unsuspecting mgmt.
           –careless security (e.g., honor obvious forgery)
           –risk of getting caught slight
           –victims embarrassed at being "taken" & don't prosecute
           –society's attitude (white collar crime as normal business
             practice) dictates token punishment, if prosecuted at all
           –decline in ties with family, church
           –our hedonistic lifestyles
  –social effects of white-collar crime:
     public cynicism—double std. in courts, token punishment for stock
     manipulators
    costs—consumers—in higher prices
                    in lost tax revenues
     investors, who rely on possibly falsified reports
     citizens—credit info invasion of privacy
  –computer manufacturers continue work to make systems more secure
  (e.g., use separate minicomputers to control access and manage user
  ID)
   –a losing battle
  –changes needed to halt white-collar crime
    –educate users to understand computer capabilities and limits
    –reform not laws themselves but administration of them by judges &
     juries
    –need specific criteria for sentencing
    –change social attitude that white collar criminal is too good to go to
     prison
  –not let-up in growing white-collar crime wave and crime costs foreseen
  –total cost for crimes against business up 75% (to $21.7 billion from
   $12.4 billion) from 1971–77

–Robin's characteristics of
white-collar crime/criminals   *& employee theft/thieves*

1. violations of industrial laws	not
2. violations of regulatory laws (criminality debatable)	violations of criminal laws
3. committed by upper class persons	committed mostly by middle class persons
4. misdemeanors	felonies
5. relatively recent origin	not
6. persistent & deliberate	(no comparative statistics available)
7. wide range of sanctions, criminal/civil, harsh/mild	no such range
8. relative immunity from prosecution	
9. few previous criminal records	
10. lenient treatment by courts	
11. involves a violation of trust	
12. victim is diffuse	
13. corporations and executive management seen as one and the same, i.e., corporations seen as individuals	not
14. crimes are highly skilled & technically complex acts	generally not
15. criminal does not lose status among business associates	generally does
16. criminal contemptuous of law & government	criminal supports conventional legal structures
17. criminals don't see themselves as criminals	
18. criminals learn from others practicing such crime, in relative isolation from those opposed to it	probably not committed due to this "differential association"
19. significance–requires changes in theories of criminal behavior	does not

–popular vs. academic definition of white-collar crime

Crime

Occupational Traditional

     White-Collar Crime   Employee Theft
    (not personal violence)
Non-Computer   Computer Crime-average take per hit = $1,000,000
–average take per hit = $100,000

Exploring during the exam

The second type of exploring, during the examination, is very limited but essential. Before you begin to answer each question, pause to select the relevant information quickly. This rapid overview permits you to focus and organize your answers.

ASSIGNMENT

Stage 2 Toward an Essay Exam: Exploring

1. **Study the material you took notes on for your essay exam.**
2. **Organize the information, ideas, and so on, using the three perspectives.**

PLANNING FOR AIM AND AUDIENCE

THE EXPOSITORY AIM

In essay examinations, almost always your primary aim is expository, your secondary aim persuasive. You attempt to persuade your examiners that you have mastered the material by, first of all, demonstrating your mastery of the material—and that should be done by concentrating on the subject matter, not the audience. That is, you will try to inform the examiner of two things:

1. that you have learned the material
2. that you have learned from the examiner

It's possible to oversimplify this second principle dangerously. Demonstrating that you have learned from the examiner does not imply that you must *agree* with the examiner, and it certainly does not mean that you should only put into an answer what the examiner said about the topic in lecture or discussion. [You may disagree with the examiner, putting contrary information into the answer.] Simply regurgitating what the examiner has said may demonstrate that you have listened to the examiner but not that you have mastered the material, since in any course the material available on any topic exceeds what the examiner has said.

ANALYZING THE AUDIENCE

The audience for an essay examination is obviously the examiner. You have had an opportunity to analyze this audience throughout the course. As with exploration, analysis of the audience should take place *before* the time of examination; you should go into examinations sure of the role you are to play and of the role the examiner will play. In order to do that, you can use the same Audience Guide our writers have used through five chapters of this book—and use it with great profit, since you should by the time of the examination have a rather full dossier on the examiner's attitudes, not only toward the subject matter but toward the students.

The disadvantage of writing for this audience lies in the seemingly artificial writing situation. The essay examination is one of the few kinds of writing in which you pass along information that the audience already possesses and in which the purpose of the writing is not to benefit the audience but to benefit the writer. You have to retune your mind to cope with this paradox.

AUDIENCE GUIDE

A. Analyze the audience in relation to itself.
  1. What are the levels and types of experiences that my audience has had (cultural, professional, recreational, educational, and so on)?
  2. What hierarchy of values does my audience possess or profess (money-making and power, friendship, security, intellectual growth, and so on)?
     It is important to distinguish, if possible, between what an audience holds dear and what it professes to hold dear, if indeed there is a difference. Does the audience hide one set of values under another? If so, the writer's task grows more complicated.
B. Analyze the audience in relation to the subject.
  1. What opinion does my audience have on my subject.
  2. How strongly does my audience hold that opinion?
  3. How willing to act on its opinion is my audience—if acting is appropriate?
C. Considering what you have learned from your answers to A and B, determine what role your audience should play in relation to your voice as writer (peer, authority, subordinate, familiar, and so on).

AUDIENCE ANALYSIS

Writer 1   AUDIENCE: MY CRIMINAL JUSTICE INSTRUCTOR

A. 1. He is a black, ex-policeman who supported himself through graduate school by working as a cop. He knows street crime from experience and probably white-collar crime from books.
  2. Justice seems a passion with him; equal justice. He respects the law, although he is sarcastic about the way it's applied in the courts.
B. 1. He thinks most white-collar crime goes unpunished.
  2. He holds that opinion doggedly.
  3. I think maybe the reason he's teaching the course is that he holds that opinion so strongly.
C. I can't compete with him in his knowledge of crime, street or white

collar, so I had better just try to speak as a subordinate—which is what I think a student is anyway—and show him that I understand where he's coming from and that I agree with him. I do anyway.

Commentary The analysis in A and B is excellent; the writer knows the audience well. The answer to C, while truthful, may not be very helpful to the writer. It suggests that he is intimidated by the examiner and will simply try to agree with the examiner's opinions. It is never a good idea to try to give back to an examiner exactly what he gave you. In the first place, it's impossible. In the second, it says little to the examiner about you or the subject matter or your command of the subject matter.

The primary aim of an essay answer is, as we have said, expository, not persuasive. A good expository answer *is* persuasive.

*CLASS
EXERCISE*
1. Do an audience analysis of an instructor for a course in which you take essay exams.

ASSIGNMENT

Stage 3 Toward an Essay Exam: Planning for Aim and Audience
Using the Audience Guide, do an audience analysis of your writing instructor, who will be the audience for your essay exam.

*DISCOVERING
AND STATING
THE FOCUS*

INCUBATING
Incubation for essay examinations occurs mainly between your study period and the exam. Allow enough time for ideas and information to settle. If you cram until the second before the test starts, you will never be as successful as you could have been with a good night's sleep.

FOCUSING DURING THE EXAM
Focused answers are the delight of instructors because they signal that you have control and direction in your answer. Here are some sample focuses for different types of questions:

1. DISCUSS/EXPLAIN QUESTIONS

SUBJECT	POINT OF SIGNIFICANCE
World War II	had five main causes.
Wallace Stevens' poetry	deals with three major themes.

2. COMPARE/CONTRAST QUESTIONS

SUBJECT	POINT OF SIGNIFICANCE
Desdemona and Ophelia	are alike in three ways, but have one significant difference.
Women's Liberation and the Black Civil Rights Movement	share five important characteristics.

3. EVALUATE QUESTIONS

SUBJECT   POINT OF SIGNIFICANCE

The Panama Canal Treaty ————— is an unsuccessful compromise for two reasons.

In order to write from such focuses you need to pause, quickly explore, and incubate for a moment. If you plunge into the answers with handfuls of information, you will likely waste time and leave the reader in doubt as to the precise answer.

CLASS EXERCISES

1. Reread the questions for *Essay Exam 1* (repeated below).
2. Formulate focuses for answers to questions 2, 3, and 4.

Essay Exam 1
1. *Define the expository, expressive, and persuasive aims.*
2. *Distinguish writing in the private, the public, and the college worlds.*
3. *Discuss the stages and strategies of the writing process.*
4. *Determine the value of the Audience Guide or the Critical Guide.*

DEVELOPING, ORGANIZING, AND REFINING THE ESSAY ANSWER

DEVELOPING AND ORGANIZING THE ANSWER

The inescapable fact about any answer to a question on an essay examination is that you never have time to write the answer you really want to develop. Hence, brevity and precision are all important. Brevity and precision are achieved by selecting a mode of organization before writing. The organization of an answer is usually determined by the question, almost always by the verb in the question: *define, explain, compare and contrast, evaluate, agree or disagree.*

Define

All definition questions are classification questions. Definition is a matter of

1. stating the term to be defined
2. putting the term into a class (e.g., a pencil belongs to the class of writing instruments)
3. distinguishing the term from all other members of the class—hence, creating a subclass

For example, define a pencil:

term   *large class*   *subclass*

A pencil is a writing instrument made of a wooden cylinder with a graphite core.

When Writer 1 encountered his first question, "Define white-collar crime and briefly identify several practices," he needed to know how to organize an extended classification:

1. Definition: "White-collar crime is . . ."
2. Identification (i.e., accounts of subclasses)
   a. Class I
   b. Class II
   c. Class III

Notice that a, b, and c are not *examples;* they are generalized classes.

Explain

Questions that demand explanations as answers are generally organized by description or narration, signaled by the words in the question itself. Fortunately, questions that begin with "Discuss" usually go on to suggest a mode of organization, almost always by means of a noun: "Discuss several factors contributing to the difficulty of combatting white-collar crime" invites a *descriptive* organization with the word *factors.* "Discuss the history of . . ." calls for the *narrative* mode. "Account for" questions generally require the *narrative* mode, whether the question asks for a simple chronological sequence or a cause-and-effect relationship. The alert writer, unless there is good evidence to the contrary, always assumes that "Account for" means "Show me cause and effect"; the writer, therefore, constructs a narrative account showing that not only did one event follow another but it occurred *because* the other had happened.

Compare and contrast

Comparing and contrasting are complementary activities; they rest on discovering similarities and differences between two (or three, four, or more) items or concepts. A list of similarities and differences, located in the exploratory stage, can be organzied in several ways. Suppose, as with Writer 1, the two things to be compared and contrasted are white-collar crime and street crime. You could say everything you had to say about white-collar crime and then everything you had to say about street crime. But no comparison or contrast has happened; the reader is left to make the comparisons. You could, after isolating the similarities and differences, organize the paper by pointing out, first, all the similarities and then all the differences—or vice versa. If you wanted to emphasize the similarities, that account should come last; similarly with the differences.

Or you could organize the paper on the basis of similarities alone, that is, compare the elements the two have in common. If, for example, you were comparing and contrasting two automobiles, you might well organize your paper by writing about the initial price of one and then the other, the styling of one and then the other, the frequency-of-repair record of one and then the other, the mileage of one and then the other, and so on.

Generally the best organization in an essay exam, when two things must be compared and contrasted, is an account, first, of the similarities and, second, of the differences, a simple two-part organization that requires, however, a good deal of forethought in order to generate the similarities and differences.

Evalulate, or agree or disagree

Questions containing these verbs call for the *evaluative* mode. You must set up a standard of judgment, give an account of the actuality, and then reach a judgment by measuring the actuality against the standard. If Writer 1 were asked, for example, "Agree or disagree: White-collar crime can produce more social damage than street crime and traditional offenses," he would have to set up both a definition and a standard for measuring "social damage."

REFINING THE EXPOSITORY STYLE

The style of an essay answer is determined by the style of the examiner. Most examiners take their subjects seriously; a few do not. For the first audience, a breezy, informal style, replete with large generalizations, is wrong. Most examiners see their subjects as disciplines, that is, areas of subject matter approached systematically and logically. A style that leans heavily on impressions or personal estimates (as evidenced in phrases such as "I feel" or "I believe") is wrong for that audience; most essay examinations do not call for expressions of feeling or belief but for a logical synthesis of material. Most examiners see their function as teachers (as opposed to their function as repositories of fact) to be that of showing students how to *relate* bits of factual material—to get from *A* to *B* by seeing a chronological sequence, a cause-and-effect relationship, a contradiction, and so on. For that audience, transitions become very important: *because, since, therefore, on the other hand;* transitions show the direction in which a mind is moving.

Finally, most examiners realize that no one can set down in a brief examination time all the facts that lie behind a generalization. But they expect to see both a generalization and the *representative* facts that validate the generalization. Given a large question and short time, the best stylistic practice is to make heavy use of conventional qualifiers (*for example, for instance, such as, like*) and follow the qualifier with one or two representative items. Because you do not have time to revise your sentences, you must rely on your acquired syntactic fluency and your command of conventions. If possible, allow a little time for rereading your answers.

1. *Define white-collar crime and briefly identify several practices.*
2. *From both a technical and nontechnical viewpoint, account for the vulnerability of computer systems to criminal penetration.*
3. *Discuss several factors contributing to the difficulty of combating white-collar crime.*
4. *How may white-collar crime and employee theft be contrasted as sub-categories of occupational crime?*
5. *Agree or disagree: White-collar crime can produce more social damage than street crimes and traditional offenses.*

The writer, faced with these questions, first determined the nature of the questions: question 1 asked for a precise definition with some identification; questions 2 and 3 called for more developed answers; question 4 involved contrasting, and question 5 required evaluating. These determinations helped him to plan his time. With an hour for the test, he allocated the following time: question 1—5 minutes; questions 2 and 3—10 minutes apiece; question 4—15 minutes; and question 5—15 minutes.

Commentary Writer 1 has assessed wisely both the types of answers required and the timing. His plan indicates that he is prepared for each question. If, however, he felt less able to answer certain questions, he should have planned to proceed first to those he could handle.

EXAM ANSWERS

Writer 1 1. White-collar crime can be defined in two ways: popular—crime committed by workers in their occupations, and academic—crime committed by upper class people, according to Sutherland.

   The following are some examples of white-collar crime:
   1) stock fraud, like when company management gets inside dope about something that will lower the price of their stock and so these insiders dump their personal stocks before the price falls;
   2) the "scam" operation, like when some unscrupulous outfit takes over a reputable business, orders big on credit (the creditors don't realize the business has changed hands), then quickly sells the goods at a discount and disappears before paying the creditors;
   3) embezzlement by computer, like when an employee programs his bank's computers to ignore his overdrafts;
   4) theft by computer, like when Jerry Schneider tapped into Pacific Bell's supply computer, ordered equipment and had it delivered to

places where he picked it up and then later sold it right back to PBT to fill the shortages he himself had created.

Also included would be things like tax evasion, bribery, kickbacks, and even counterfeiting.

2. From a technical viewpoint five factors make computer crime possible. The "time-sharing" set up allows a lot of different people at a lot of different places to use the same computer data banks at the same time by just identifying themselves to the machine. This makes impersonating a user possible if you can find out his ID password.

Since computer communication is by telephone lines, wiretapping is possible to eavesdrop on your competitors, and "piggybacking" is possible—eavesdropping and then impersonating a user to sabotage his operations.

The fact that computers have memories makes the Trojan Horse trick possible. The fact that equipment and programs and codes are all pretty standard makes all these crimes easier. Also, there is the fact that computers work with electronic speed, and can be programmed to neatly erase the dirty business they were first programmed to do.

From a nontechnical viewpoint computers are vulnerable mainly because of poor security. Companies don't guard their terminals and office people give out passwords or leave important printouts lying around in garbage cans.

3. Combatting crime is difficult for three reasons.

White-collar crime in general is hard to fight mainly because of society's attitude toward it. A lot of businessmen consider bribes and payoffs expected practice. Likewise, taking advantage of inside info to buy or sell your stocks isn't criminal to a lot of people.

Judges and juries share this attitude. They just can't get used to the idea of an upper class criminal. They think, this guy is too good to go to jail, he just made a mistake. So white-collar criminals only get token punishment, which doesn't deter them much.

Another reason is that the victims are too embarrassed at being "had" to even admit they have been, or they don't want to lose the public's confidence, or tarnish their image by publicizing a crime. The thing is, officials can't fight crime they don't know about.

Computer crime is a special case. Because electronic records can be erased instantaneously, there's no paper work, say, for suspicious auditors to go over. Experts estimate only 1 in 100 computer crimes will be found out. Because of the nature of computers, it's practically all chance.

4. Though they share some characteristics, white-collar crime and employee theft can be distinguished on several counts. The most obvious difference is that white-collar crime is committed by members of the middle class. White-collar crime usually involves a lot of technical

know-how, whereas simple employee theft doesn't. White-collar crime is thus fairly new on the scene; employee theft has probably been around as long as capitalism itself.

   While white-collar crimes, like collusion and stock fraud and computer cheating, are usually only misdemeanors, employee theft is generally a felony. If an alleged white-collar criminal is convicted, he could get anything from a slap on the wrist to a few years in jail, but he's more likely to get the light sentence because of society's attitudes that favor his class, and are down on giant corporations and take business cheating for granted. And he isn't likely to lose much status with his peers. On the other hand, if an alleged employee thief is convicted, he faces harsher, more consistent and prescribed punishment, and he *does* lose face with his fellow workers.

5. Whether I agree or disagree depends on what is meant by "social damage." If "social damage" means injury to or loss of property or life, then I disagree. Murder, rape, even muggings and robberies do the worst damage. There is no physical harm involved with fraud or embezzlement, (unless you're dealing with the Mafia). But if "social damage" means damage to the moral fiber of society, then I will agree, because white-collar crime *can* corrupt extensively in the long run, more so than isolated street crimes can. White-collar crimes are sneaky and greedy. White-collar criminals want their piece of the action in ripping off the System. If Nixon, if politicians, if businessmen can play dirty games, so can they. This leads to a general mood of distrust and crafty competition where everyone is out to take advantage of the next guy in secret. And if good people continue to see white-collar criminals getting off so lightly in the courts, they will get more and more disgusted. White-collar crimes can contribute much more to creating cynicism in society than even murder or rape can.

CLASS EXERCISES

1. Read Answer 2 of Writer 1 (p. 258).
   - What is the focus?
   - What mode of organization is used?
   - How much from Writer 1's Exploration (pp. 247–251) has he managed to use?
   - How well do his answers develop the question?
2. For practice, answer the questions for *Essay Exam 1* (p. 245).

ASSIGNMENT

Stage 4 Toward an Essay Exam: Focusing, Developing, and Organizing the Essay Exam Answer

1. **Review the questions on the essay exam provided by your instructor.**
   a. **Determine what type of questions are asked.**
   b. **Plan your time.**

c. Quickly explore your memory, recalling the ideas and information needed to answer your questions.

d. Focus and organize your answers.

e. Develop your answers, maintaining an expository style.

CRITIQUING

Essay examinations do not generally produce deathless prose because the answers are written under the pressure of time and usually in a physical setting that inhibits concentration. Even the advice intended to offset atrocities in answers—"Save the last ten minutes to reread and edit"—has a drawback: anyone who has ever tried to read an "edited" essay answer with its crossings-out and writings-over, its carets and arrows pointing to afterthoughts in the margins, and its despairing postscript—"Ran out of time!!!"—knows what a bad impression editing can sometimes leave.

An essay answer should be critiqued with major criteria in mind. An adequate answer requires

1. A clear focus
2. A development of that focus by
   a. Generalizations, supported by representative facts
   b. In a recognizable pattern of organization
3. Phrased in a style appropriate to the examiner's attitude toward the subject matter

In other words, the reader looks for reduced proficiency in the list of powers we have used through six chapters of this book in critiquing papers.

It is reasonable to suppose that an examiner does not require pinpoint accuracy in the fine points of Standard Written English, but that, on the other hand, the examiner is going to be mightily disappointed by a student who writes on the causes of the Civil War and cannot spell "Lincoln" or "Confederacy," or who cannot, by the use of transitions, relate a cause to an effect.

Answer 1

1. The focus is clear: "White-collar crime can be defined in two ways . . . ." Since the two definitions are complementary, the writer need not choose between them.

2. The focus is developed well—four generalizations, each accompanied by an illustration. The writer has chosen to use only four items for illustration, but he has indicated that he is aware of others: "Also included would be. . . ."

3. The style wavers. The answer begins in Standard Written English but lapses into "like when" as a connective in all four examples, and

such phrases as "inside dope," "big on credit." Here, as in other answers, the writer neglects the hyphen: "upper class," "set up," and so on.

Answer 4

1. The focus is clearly announced in the first sentence. The writer has understood the question, which asked only for contrast; the focus statement refers to similarities, but puts the emphasis on differences.

2. The focus is developed well. The differences between white-collar crime and employee theft emerge through a series of categories based on common elements:

    a. which classes commit these crimes
    b. what technical knowledge is necessary
    c. which is newer
    d. what the legal categories are
    e. what the legal penalties are
    f. what the social penalties are

3. As in Answer 1, the style is uneven, perhaps as a result of the writer losing sight of his audience. The answer begins in relatively formal Standard Written English but then shifts to phrases such as "a lot of technical know-how," "new on the scene," "are down on."

CLASS EXERCISES

1. Read Answers 3 and 5 of Writer 1's exam (pp. 258–259).
   - What are the focuses?
   - What information has the writer used? Is it accurate (see notes, pp. 247–251) and adequate? Why or why not?
   - What is the organization used?
   - What style is used?
2. Working in groups, critique each other's answers.

ASSIGNMENT

Stage 5 Toward an Essay Exam: Critiquing and Rewriting
1. **Do a self-critique based on group and teacher criticism.**
2. **Although revision is not normally permitted in essay exams, revise your answers in order to profit by your mistakes.**

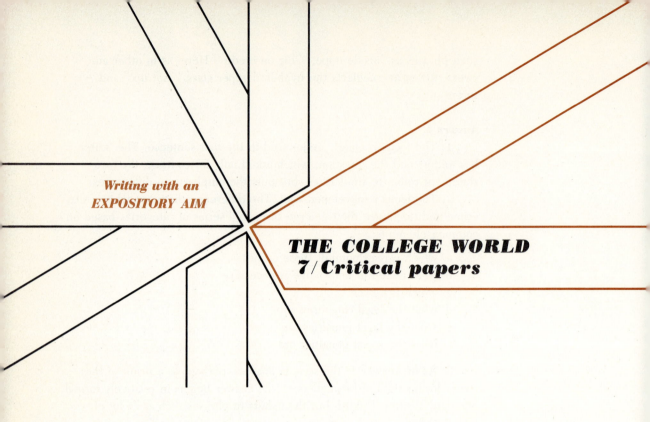

THE COLLEGE WORLD
7/Critical papers

After finishing a novel or reading a poem, have you ever asked, "What was the writer getting at?" Have you and friends ever argued over a play or a movie? These attempts to understand the creations of others, to find more satisfying interpretations, are critical acts. Writing is one of the best ways to penetrate the complexity of novels, poems, plays, and essays. This chapter will show you how to use your writing powers to interpret poetry and essays.

**FINDING AND
EXPRESSING
THE STARTING
POINT**

A good way to begin is with your initial raw response to an essay or poem—"Wow" or "Ugh" or "So?" Look beneath this reaction to identify some general feature of the essay or poem that may have provoked your reaction. Examine how these features relate to your expectations of a good essay or poem or how they jar some of your values. State this dissonance and formulate a question.

Below is the poem "Wires" by Philip Larkin, on which Writers 1 and 2 wrote critical papers:

WIRES

The widest prairies have electric fences,
For though old cattle know they must not stray
Young steers are always scenting purer water
Not here but anywhere. Beyond the wires
Leads them to blunder up against the wires
Whose muscle-shredding violence gives no quarter.
Young steers become old cattle from the day,
Electric limits to their widest senses.[1]

STARTING POINTS

Writer 1	MY VALUES OR EXPECTATIONS	ASPECTS OF THE POEM
	—I feel that free spirits are beautiful	—the reduction of energetic young steers to docile beasts by means of electric wires
	—I hate total confinement	—fencing in of steers
	—It's a painful way for an animal to learn he can never venture beyond	—the steers are unable to detect the electric wires until they actually feel the shock

Question: Why does the fate of the young steers make me so angry? What do the steers and the wires stand for?

Writer 2	MY VALUES OR EXPECTATIONS	ASPECTS OF THE POEM
	—young men becoming old men through their experiences	—young steers becoming old through experience with fence
	—young person wanting to do new things	—young steers' impatience to explore
	—old people's lack of movement	—old age's reluctance to disobey
	—society's fence against people	—steers' violence against the wire

Question: Why does this poem cause me to have a feeling of anger against society?

ESSAYS

Below is an essay from one of the writers in Chapter 4, on which Writer 3 chose to write a critical paper.

[1]Philip Larkin, "Wires," *Today's Poets*, ed. Chad Walsh (New York: Scribner's, 1964), p. 284.

THERE'S NO PLACE LIKE HOME

The last years—they should be spent in happiness and serenity. Does a nursing home provide the happiness and peacefulness that a mobile, self-relient, and competant elderly person deserves, or is institutional living depressing and saddening to older people? My grandmother's house makes me realize that elderly people should spend their declining years in their own home as long as possible.

When I visit my grandma, the smile on her face and the sparkling gleam in her eyes are a sight to behold. As she welcomes me in, the charm and elegance of her little old house overwhelms me. The old, faded, picture portraits hanging on the wall speak to me, telling me all about my grandmother's family, and her worn, but beautifully carved antique furniture relates to me a unique part of her personality. She serves me tea from her brass tea-kettle, which is a cherished family heirloom, as we talk to each other about the happenings in our daily lives. In the background the grandfather clock ticks loudly, as grandma's toy french poodle plays happily with his squeaky toys. The whole atmosphere is one of peacefulness. I ask alot of questions because I find myself so fascinated with her stories. She brings out a dusty box filled with old electric trains, books, and "ancient" science experiment kits that belonged to her son, my dad, and reveals aspects of his youth that I'd never known before. My eyes roam around some more, admiring the delicately embroidered afghan on the old Victorian loveseat and wondering whether that old cathedral radio on the shelf still works, as my grandma busies herself in the kitchen.

The aroma of her own homemade, hot vegetable soup, prepared from a recipe that she says has been in the family for years and freshly baked bread fill the house and suddenly I'm very hungry. Spicy pumpkin pie and beautifully decorated sugar cookies for dessert top off a delicious lunch. After lunch I find I don't have to go far before I am surrounded by beauty again.

Her backyard is filled with many varieties of trees and multicolored blossoms, obviously very carefully tended to. Her hybrid tea roses are very fragrant, and she bid me goodbye after giving me a beautiful bouquet to enjoy at home. As I am leaving I notice the peacefulness and serenity that settle over her house at dusk. She says she spends her nights quietly reading a book or a magazine or watching T.V., but mostly anticipating a call or the next visit from her relatives. She seems so happy and content with her life that I could never imagine her living in a nursing home.

My experience with nursing homes includes several visits to a great aunt whose family put her there a few years go. I find myself so depressed in the atmosphere of a nursing home. The sterile, germicidal smell hits me almost immediately, and the monotonous, dull, pale green walls seem endless. The cheap, style-less furniture in the patients' rooms and the lack of personal pictures on the walls give me no inkling of the occupant's personality. As I pass the huge, impersonal sitting room the patients just stare blankly at me, giving me a cold, uneasy feeling. One elderly lady sits rocking back-and-forth, holding a stuffed baby doll tightly in her arms. Some old people can be heard whining and crying during the day. When I leave the nursing home I feel that the elderly lack privacy here, their care is impersonal, the food is bland and the activity is limited.

I am convinced that young adults who truly love their parents and grandparents should make every effort to let them stay in their own homes by lending a hand with the more strenuous house work. The older persons' own possessions in their homes define and maintain their personality, and the light housework that they do keeps them active and healthy. The reward is two fold—happiness for the elderly person and that unexplainable feeling that a young person has inside when he helps to bring some joy to another.

After a careful reading of the essay, Writer 3 formulated his Starting Point:

STARTING POINT

Writer 3 MY EXPECTATIONS
—good reasons and examples
—emotional appeal

—writer's credibility

ASPECTS OF THE ESSAY
—good focus
—a good example of grandmother's house
—didn't persuade me

Question: Why didn't the essay's good example persuade me despite the fact that I felt the focus was good?

CLASS
EXERCISES

1. Discuss the Starting Points of Writers 1, 2, and 3 (pp. 263–265).
   • What dissonances do they express?
   • To what kinds of interpretations or evaluations of the poem and essay will the questions lead?
   • In what better ways could the questions have been formulated?
2. Read the following poem:

   FINDING A TEACHER
   W. S. Merwin

   In the woods I came on an old friend fishing
   and I asked him a question
   and he said Wait

fish were rising in the deep stream
but his line was not stirring
but I waited
it was a question about the sun
about my two eyes
my ears my mouth
my heart the earth with its four seasons
my feet where I was standing
where I was going
it slipped through my hands
as though it were water
into the river
it flowed under the trees
it sank under hulls far away
and was gone without me
then where I stood night fell

I no longer knew what to ask
I could tell that his line had no hook
I understood that I was to stay and eat with him[2]

3. As a class, discuss your initial feelings about the poem.
4. Identify the aspects that puzzle you or delight you or conflict with your expectations about poetry.
5. Make a list of questions you would like to answer about the poem.

ASSIGNMENT

Stage 1 Toward a Critical Paper: Finding and Expressing the Starting Point

1. **Determine the essay, poem, or other type of literature on which you will do your critical writing.**
2. **Identify some feature of the work that causes an initial reaction in you and that either surpasses or falls short of your expectations or clashes with your values.**
3. **Formulate a question.**
4. **Seek commentary on your starting point from your instructor.**

PLANNING FOR AIM AND AUDIENCE

Writing about man-made creations, especially literature or other arts, usually has one of two aims:

1. the persuasive
2. the expository

Book, film, and play *reviews* usually have a *persuasive* aim and are not, therefore, strictly speaking, critical papers. They differ fundamentally from

[2] W. S. Merwin, "Finding a Teacher," *The New Naked Poetry,* eds. Stephen Berg and Robert Mezey (Indianapolis: Bobbs-Merrill, 1976), p. 266.

critical papers in that the reviewer does not assume that the audience has already seen or read the object, and he or she generally advises the audience whether to do so or not. That is, the reviewer and the audience emphatically do not share equal knowledge or exposure or interest in the work. Writing in Chapter 3, on the media, was persuasive writing in that it aimed at convincing an audience to react in some way. This chapter will *not* concentrate on the persuasive but rather on the expository aim.

THE EXPOSITORY AIM

Critical writing has an expository aim: it attempts to explain the meaning of a poem, play, short story, or essay by examining the language and organization of a work in detail. It attempts, in other words, to enable the audience to see in what it has read something that it did not see before. If the interpretation is new to you and the audience, the aim leans toward the informative. If the interpretation is new to scholarship itself or if you evaluate the work, the discourse leans toward the scientific. (If you need a refresher on the difference between informative and scientific expository aims, see Chapter 5, pp. 194–197).

CHOOSING AN AUDIENCE

Critical writing here is writing about writing. In the beginning you assume that the audience has read the essay, poem, play, or whatever object you are discussing. You and the reader share common *knowledge* of the essay or poem and presumably a common interest in it. Your choice of audience is, therefore, narrow in the beginning: the audience must be one that was interested enough to read the original work. Your task is not to cajole an audience into reading it.

Who might that audience be? There are three possibilities:

1. It might be anyone attracted to the essay or poem by the name of the author, the topic, or the form: Some people like to read, for example, E. B. White's work, no matter what he writes about. Some like to read essays, no matter what essayist. Some like to read about death or sex or butterfly collecting. Other people like to read the poetry of Galway Kinnell. Still others enjoy reading poetry itself.

2. It might be anyone who read the essay or poem out of an interest external to personal preference—as when a student is assigned the reading of a poem, essay, short story, and so on. The interest in the audience in that case may not be so much in the essay or poem as in meeting a class assignment.

3. It might be a teacher or some superior who has assigned the essay or poem.

All three are possible audiences.

ANALYZING THE AUDIENCE

Your Audience Guide, repeated below, will help you think about that audience.

AUDIENCE GUIDE

A. Analyze the audience in relation to itself.
   1. What are the levels and types of experiences that my audience has had (cultural, professional, recreational, educational, and so on)?
   2. What hierarchy of values does my audience possess or profess (money making and power, friendship, security, intellectual growth, and so on)?
      It is important to distinguish, if possible, between what an audience holds dear and what it professes to hold dear, if indeed there is a difference. Does the audience hide one set of values under another? If so, the writer's task grows more complicated.
B. Analyze the audience in relation to the subject.
   1. What opinion does my audience have on my subject? This will include an estimate of the knowledge the audience has of the form. Is it casual or is it expert?
   2. How strongly does my audience hold that opinion?
   3. How willing to act on its opinion is my audience—if acting is appropriate?
C. Considering what you have learned from your answers to A and B, determine what role your audience should play in relation to your voice as writer (peer, authority, subordinate, familiar, and so on).

AUDIENCE ANALYSES

Writer 1   AUDIENCE: MS. SMITH—12TH GRADE LITERATURE TEACHER

A. 1. High school English teacher, master's degree, Advanced Placement English instructor, single
   2. Values
      a. Education/learning
      b. Individuality
      c. Maturity

B. Appreciates literature, feels it is important to pass this appreciation on to students.

C. She will play the role of teacher, literary critic. I will also play the role of critic.

Writer 2

AUDIENCE: MS. BROWN AND MRS. JONES; ENGLISH 160 TEACHERS

A. Audience has knowledge of the poem, college teachers, desire other opinions on poem, value clarity, good understanding of the poem.

B. The audience has knowledge of the subject and their attitude is that of expecting a critical paper on a poem to enhance their understanding of it.

C. I want the audience to read the poem with an open mind, with the possibility of discovering something new about the poem from my writings.

Writer 3

AUDIENCE: TEACHER OF THE WRITING CLASS

A. Audience in itself.
  1. With essays she has had wide experience. She has a deep interest in writing and in teaching her students to write.
  2. She seems to believe that the ability to write essays well is a key to success.

B. Audience in relation to subject.
  1. Her mother is dead—she has mentioned that in class. She has never mentioned nursing homes.
  2. I doubt she is interested in the subject.
  3. I doubt she would do anything about nursing homes.

C. She will be the teacher, I the student. I must show her that I understand the *construction* of the essay and its strengths and weaknesses. She is not interested in the subject or even in the essay, but in my showing that I can write a good critical paper on that essay.

Commentary Writer 3's Audience Analysis is shrewd and exact. He knows exactly what the reader expects and what roles the two will play. He also knows that the content is less important than the form in the eyes of his audience.

CLASS EXERCISES

1. Study the Audience Analyses of Writers 1 and 2.
   - How successful are their choices of audiences?
   - What uses can the writers make of their analyses?
   - What voices will the writers assume?
2. Choose a high school literature teacher as an audience.
   - Using the Audience Guide, analyze your audience.
   - Share your analysis with the class.

Stage 2 Toward a Critical Paper: Planning for Aim and Audience
1. Choose your audience.
2. Use the Audience Guide on p. 268 to analyze your audience.
3. Seek comments on your audience analysis.
4. Keep your expository aim in mind.

In order to explore an essay or poem, you have to know something about its form. You should have no trouble with the essay because by now you have a strong background on what constitutes a good essay, whether expressive, persuasive, or expository. You may, however, require help exploring a poem.

EXPLORING A POEM

To illustrate some of the terms you will need for the analysis of a poem, we will explore the following poem by William Stafford:

BESS

Ours are the streets where Bess first met her
cancer. She went to work every day past the
secure houses. At her job in the library
she arranged better and better flowers, and when
students asked for books her hand went out
to help. In the last year of her life
she had to keep her friends from knowing
how happy they were. She listened while they
complained about food or work or the weather.
And the great national events danced
their grotesque, fake importance. Always

Pain moved where she moved. She walked
ahead; it came. She hid; it found her.
No one ever served another so truly;
no enemy ever meant so strong a hate.
It was almost as if there was no room
left for her on earth. But she remembered
where joy used to live. She straightened its flowers;
she did not weep when she passed its houses;
and when finally she pulled into a tiny corner
and slipped from pain, her hand opened
again, and the streets opened, and she wished all well. [3]

One significant difference between poems and essays is that poems tend

[3] William Stafford, "Bess," *The New Naked Poetry*, eds. Stephen Berg and Robert Mezey (Indianapolis: Bobbs-Merrill, 1976), p. 445.

to make fuller use of the resources of language. The terms that are important to know, then, are simply terms for possibilities that exist in language.

Imagery

One of the primary functions of language is to convey *images*. An image is an imitation in the mind of something that exists outside us, and the kind of language that performs that function has come to have the name of *imagery*. Imagery has several varieties:

1. Direct imagery consists of references to things that can be directly encountered by our senses:
   a. sight—streets, Bess, library, students, flowers, books, hands, friends
   b. sounds—"complained about food or work or the weather"
2. Indirect imagery consists of figures of speech (a fuller list of these appears in Defining Terms), ways of using language that convert things that cannot be directly encountered by our senses into things that can be or that convert things that can be directly encountered into concepts. Here are some of those ways:
   a. *Personification:* turning abstractions into persons

      met her cancer
      Pain moved where she moved.
      The great national events danced.
      where joy used to live

   b. *Metonymy:* using one term for another it suggests

      The word *hand,* for example, recurs in Stafford's poem, but it stands for more than a physical hand. In "her hand went out to help" more than Bess's hand was used to help, and in "her hand opened again," more than her hand relaxed in death.

   c. *Symbol:* using an object or action that can be directly encountered by our senses to represent something more abstract

      pulled into a tiny corner
      The streets opened,
      no room left for her on earth
      secure houses

Diction

The poet also pays close attention to diction, the choice of words. Stafford's poem is composed almost entirely of simple, ordinary words, appropriate to the simple, ordinary person he is describing (who did something complex and extraordinary). The exception occurs in one statement in the first stanza: "And the great national events *danced their grotesque, fake importance.*"

The contrast between the importance of what Bess achieved and the relative insignificance of national events is made plain by this single act of language.

Persona

Acts of language are created by writers. And this leads us to one more term that the critical writer dealing with poetry should command: *persona*. By this time, the concept of a writer choosing a role to play in relation to the audience should be well established. In critical writing, which is writing about writing, the writer is first of all a reader; as a reader, the writer must bear in mind always that the author of the poem has created a voice and is, therefore, not necessarily identical with the voice that speaks in the poem. The created voice that speaks in the poem is called the *persona*, and the characteristics of the persona are discovered from the poem, not from the biography of the author.

Technics of language

Poets also pay closer attention than most prose writers to the *technical* resources of the language.

All writing has divisions of thought. The paragraph of prose becomes the *stanza* of poetry, the physical division on the page of units of thought. Stafford's poem contains two stanzas. The first centers on Bess's relationships with others, neighborhood and national. The second centers on her relationship with her own problem—which she treated in the same fashion as all else.

Within the stanzas, the poet arranges his words with extreme care. Notice these features:

1. *Rhythm:* the pace and pattern of movement in a statement. The first stanza contains longer lines and fewer pauses than the second, causing the reader to slow his pace in the second stanza. The two stanzas are quite different in several technical respects, most notably in the kinds of *repetition* the writer has used.
2. *Sounds:* the poet in the first stanza makes heavy use of repetition of consonants. Notice the repetition of the *s* sound in "Ours are the streets where Bess first met her cancer," and again (with the repetition of *w* added) in "She went to work every day past the secure houses." The pattern does not appear strongly again until the concluding clause of the poem: "and she wished all well."

   Rhyme is, of course, a repetition of sounds—usually at the end of lines. Not all poems rhyme: "Wires" does; "Bess" does not. When a poem rhymes, it generally does so for a reason that may vary, from providing the simple musical pleasure of a recurrent sound to suggesting a pattern of thought in the poem. Repetition, after all, both connects and emphasizes. An examination of the rhyme scheme of "Wires," for example, will suggest to the reader a connection between the stanzas that might otherwise be missed.

3. *Sentence structures:* the first stanza contains almost no repetitive structures. But the second stanza is built on them:

Pain moved where she moved.
She walked/ahead, it came.
She hid; it found her.
No one ever . . ./no enemy ever
her hand opened again, and the streets opened

Exploring a poem means, then, first identifying its distinctive features and structural pattern and then determining what each of these elements *means* in the poem. In addition, you can compare the poem to other poems, classify the poem as to type—sonnet, lyric, ballad, and so on (if you know these types)—and even create analogies for the poem.

This brief survey of terms does not attempt to deal in any depth with *prosody,* the science of sound in poetry, beyond what is said in the short section above headed "Sounds." Your instructor may wish to go further into the study of sound effects—meter, types of rhyme, stanza forms, assonance, consonance, and so on. Certainly if your previous study has equipped you to analyze the technical design of a poem, you should put that knowledge to use. Only one of the writers in this chapter used such knowledge.

EXPLORATORY GUIDE: FOR A POEM
The Exploratory Guide will help direct your analysis of poetry.

Static view
> –What are the major images (direct and indirect) in the poem? What do they mean?
> –Who is the persona in the poem? How does this choice of persona affect the poem?
> –What kind of diction is used? Why?

Dynamic view
> –What kind of stanzaic structure is used? Why?
> –What kind of rhythm does the poem have? Why?
> > Word and sound lengths?
> > Line length?
> > Sound repetitions, echoes?
> > Pauses?

Relative view

   –How can the poem be classified?

      What more does this classification tell about the poem?

   –With what other literature can this poem be compared?

   –What analogies can be created for the poem?

   –What is the central meaning of the whole poem?

      How do the parts relate to this meaning?

EXPLORATION

Writer 1   "WIRES"

STATIC VIEW

1. *Images (direct)*

	Meaning
–wide prairies	–freedom of the young
–old "tamed" cattle	–people who have learned from experience
–young adventurous steer	–young people
–stretches of electric wires	–controls of society
–physical affects of electric shock	–punishments for going against society
–torn flesh muscles	–lures of adventure
–smell—fresh water	

2. *Figures of speech*

   –wires whose violence gives no quarter $\longrightarrow$ personification

   –young steers become old cattle $\longrightarrow$ metaphor

    not old in years but in behavior

3. *Persona* $\longrightarrow$ speaker   possibly author

   animals are silent/noncommunicative

4. *Diction*

   quarter $\longrightarrow$ mercy

   widest $\longrightarrow$ expands   wires

   electric $\longrightarrow$ connotative   confining

   young steers $\longrightarrow$ old cattle (not steer)

   cattle $\longrightarrow$ grouping of blindly following creatures

   steer $\longrightarrow$ carries with it strength, grace, spirit, variety or individuality

DYNAMIC VIEW

1. *Rhythm*–1st & 3rd lines   11 syllables   1st stanza

             2nd & 4th lines   10 syllables

             1st & 3rd lines   10 syllables   2nd stanza

             2nd & 4th lines   11 syllables

   not a smoothly flowing poem

Sounds

widest (long ī) electric (long ē) are the two strong contrasting sounds
though, old, know (assonance)—draggy feeling of old cattle
electric limits—harsh sound

2. *Stanzas*

–two stanzas   —two worlds inside fence & outside
–first stanza paints a sort of still life of prairie
–second presents a picture in motion of the violent encounter with
  electric wires and eventual taming/killing of the young steer's spirit
–the second stanza is sort of a mirror reflection or reversal of the
  first stanza

Both

11 syllables line 4	2nd stanza	*senses*	rhymes with line 1	1st stanza	*fences*
10 syllables " 3	"	"	*day*	"	"	" 2	"	"	*stray*
11 syllables " 2	"	"	*quarter*	"	"	" 3	"	"	*water*
10 syllables " 1	"	"	*wires*	"	"	" 4	"	"	*wires*

line 4(2)   ideas are contrasting
with 1(1)   (1)–from wide prairies (physical) with electrical fenced con-
              finement to vast thoughts, desires (mental) stifled by
              electric shock (memory of)

line 3(2)   (2) line two gives an early description of the tamed "old
with 2(1)   cattle" and in line three the young steers become the
              nonstraying "old cattle"

line 2(2)   The rather pastoral picture of "young steers" "scenting
with 3(1)   purer water beyond is in sharp contrast by the
              "muscle-shredding violence" of the fence

line 4(1)   What is "anywhere" "Beyond the wires" leads the steer
with 1(2)   to venture toward the wires
–one encounter with the wire made a memory strong enough to
  tame an adventurous young steer

RELATIVE VIEW

Compare/contrast

–"Wires"—by Larkin
–feeling: anger
–relatively short
–young steers' attempt to do
  something different
–animals become docile

–poem makes you feel as though
  you should take some action

–"The Calf Path" by Foss
–feeling: helpless
–5 or 6 stanzas
–creatures simply follow blindly

–creatures have never thought to
  stray from the crooked path—
  docile by their own choice
–after reading poem you just sort
  of nod and say "Yeh. That's how
  it is."

–poem makes me think of humans   –poem starts with calf and actually
  but uses only cattle   moves to modern day humans
                                       on expressways

Classifications

Poems that move from a lighter note to a more serious one

"Wires"   "Richard Cory"   "The Highwayman"

Poems which deal with suffering animals

"Stray dog"   "Wires"   "The Legacy of the Loggerhead"

Poems/Literature which deal with fencing in/confinement

"Wires"   *The Stranger*   *The Plague*

Literature in which something/someone had to suffer for going against society

The Scarlet Letter   "Wires"   *Crime and Punishment*

Violent means for changing behavior

war   "Wires"
       street fights   electric shock therapy

Analogy
"Wires" is like the student government in my high school.
1. You couldn't go beyond the boundaries set by the administration.
2. New enthusiastic people would try to do something different only to come up against numerous spirit-weakening barriers.
3. The easiest way to get along was by not making waves.

"Wires" is like a nightmare mental hospital
1. people who don't conform to the rules are given shock treatment/ lobotomies till they no longer possess different, aggressive personalities

This idea popped into my head this morning & I would really like to explore it further.

2. society groups "insane" people together much like cattle
   two worlds—much like the inside & outside of mental hospital
   looking glass

Central meaning: Bitter confrontations sometimes result from originally positive, well-meaning, adventurous objectives

The questions below will guide your analysis of a prose essay.

EXPLORATORY GUIDE: FOR A PROSE ESSAY

Static view
   –What are the focus, aim, and audience of this essay?
   –What kind of diction does the writer use?
   –What kind of syntax is used?

Dynamic view
   –In what mode is the essay organized?
   –How is the essay developed?
   –Is the essay coherent?

Relative view
   –What are the characteristics (criteria) of a good essay with the
    aim and mode of the one you are critiquing?
   –How does this essay relate to those characteristics?
   –What analogy captures your reaction to the essay?

EXPLORATION

Writer 3   "THERE'S NO PLACE LIKE HOME"

STATIC VIEW

Focus: The writer says that older people should be kept at home and
   not put in nursing homes.
Aim: To persuade the reader of this and to provoke action.
Audience: Peers like me because we will understand best the writer's
   experience and be able to do something
Persuasive appeals: The writer appeals to emotion by using a lot of sensory words about the grandmother's house. He appeals to reason
   with two examples from his own life. He shows his own credibility
   by presenting himself as one who has first-hand knowledge of the
   issue and who is sensitive and considerate of his grandmother.

Diction: —good sense words:

> *sight:* "brass tea-kettle," "toy french poodle," "Delicately embroidered afghan"
>
> *taste:* "spicy pumpkin pie"
>
> *smell:* "aroma of hot homemade vegetable soup," "Hybrid tea rose"
>
> *sound:* "grandfather's clock ticks"
>
> *some cliches:* "Sparkling clean," "sight to behold," "little old house," "eyes roam around," "stare blankly," "there's no place like home"

Syntax: majority of the sentences are varied; most are complex

DYNAMIC VIEW

Mode: narrative except in the first and last paragraphs

Order: Question/Answer: first paragraph
> Narrative of grandmother's house: paragraphs two-four
> Narrative about nursing home: paragraph five
> Generalizations: last paragraph

Coherence: maintains tense but account of visit to grandmother's is a single time while the visit to the nursing home seems over a period of years

Transitions: mainly repetitive words

RELATIVE VIEW

Requirements for a good essay of this type
1. Persuasive Aim
    —keep audience foremost
    —appeal to reason, personality, emotions
    —language: concrete, connotations
    —refute if necessary
2. Narrative Mode
    —chronological order
    —coherence: same person and number, transitions

Evaluation of this essay in relation to the ideal

—aim: —last paragraph irritates audience
> —*appeals:* good example in the grandmother account
> nursing home account sounds impersonal
> good emotional and personality appeals
> concrete diction in account of grandmother's but not in nursing home account: the first and the last paragraphs

—mode: —good narrative of grandmother's
> —first, last, and nursing home paragraphs break the chronology
> —*coherence:* transitions needed between first paragraph and

grandmothers, between grandmothers and nursing homes, and before the last paragraph

person and number—ok

–focus: –maintained but not developed well

Analogy: reading the essay is like coming out of a disappointing Academy Award Film

CLASS EXERCISES

1. Study the Explorations of Writers 1 (pp. 274–277) and 3 (pp. 277–279).
   - How complete is the list of the distinctive features of the poem (images, persona, diction) or of the essay (focus, aim, audience)? What could have been added?
2. For those doing a critical paper on poetry:
   a. Read the following poem:

   LOSING TRACK
   Denise Levertov

   Long after you have swung back
   away from me
   I think you are still with me:

   you come in close to the shore
   on the tide
   and nudge me awake the way

   a boat adrift nudges the pier:
   am I a pier
   half-in half-out of the water?

   and in the pleasure of that communion
   I lose track,
   the moon I watch goes down, the

   tide swings you away before
   I know I'm
   alone again long since,

   mud sucking at gray and black
   timbers of me,
   a light growth of green dreams drying.[4]

   b. Using the Exploratory Guide, do a class analysis of the poem.
3. For further practice in exploring poetry, complete the exploration on "Bess" (p. 270).
4. For those doing a critical paper on a prose essay, use the Exploratory Guide to examine any student paper in this book (or an essay provided by your instructor).

[4] Denise Levertov, "Losing Track," *The New Naked Poetry*, eds. Stephen Berg and Robert Mezey (Indianapolis: Bobbs-Merrill, 1969), p. 127.

Stage 3 Toward a Critical Paper: Exploring

1. **Explore either the poem or essay you will write on. (In order to gain your own power in exploring, we suggest that you use poems or essays that have not been explored in class.)**
2. **Seek comments from your instructor on your exploration.**

DISCOVERING
AND STATING
THE FOCUS

THE CRITICAL FOCUS

Allow time for incubation to prompt an insight that will either interpret or evaluate the poem or essay. A critical focus for an expository paper creates a synthesis of your mind with the work. It does not retell or paraphrase the work. Nor does it project the work into your own private world. A critical essay on *The Scarlet Letter*, for example, does not paraphrase the plot nor does it recount the adultery of the critic's Aunt Lucy.

FOCUSES

	SUBJECT	POINT OF SIGNIFICANCE
Writer 1	All of the elements of "Wires"———	contribute to a looking-glass image for society.
Writer 2	"Wires" ———————————	grieves over the frustration experienced by the young attempting to develop their human capabilities.
Writer 3	"There's No Place Like Home"———	is a good attempt to persuade with disappointing flaws in mode.

Commentary   Writer 3 avoids the two pitfalls mentioned above. The subject commits him to discussing the whole essay, not dangerous here because the essay is relatively short. The point of significance promises an evaluation of the aim and mode. His exploration supports the focus.

CLASS
EXERCISES

1. Discuss the Focuses of Writers 1 and 2.
   • What new interpretation of the poem do the focuses propose?
   • Which focus promises to be the more workable one?
   • What pitfalls (paraphrasing or projecting into their personal world) do the focuses avoid or fall into?
2. Discuss the following alternative focuses for Writer 3.
   a. The essay is against nursing homes.
   b. The essay compares nursing homes to staying at home.

c. The essay reminds me of my grandfather's situation.

d. A critique of "There's No Place Like Home."

e. The essay is a satire on life in outer space.

f. The structure of the essay reveals that it is a modern fairy tale.

• Which will lead to expository papers?

• Which are weak? Why?

ASSIGNMENT **Stage 4** Toward a Critical Paper: Discovering and Stating the Focus

1. **After incubating, state your focus in two parts.**
2. **Make sure it avoids the pitfalls of paraphrasing or personalizing.**
3. **Seek comments on your focus from your instructor.**

DEVELOPING, ORGANIZING, AND REFINING THE PAPER

DEVELOPING THE CRITICAL PAPER

Critical papers with an expository aim must always refer to the work, using examples from the essay or poem to support the focus. Here is an example from a student paper on John Donne's Holy Sonnet X, "Batter My Heart":

The opening lines of the sonnet personify God as a metalsmith; that is an appropriate metaphor, since the theme of the poem deals with the need for reshaping, even remaking the sinful speaker.

The sentence itself has two components:

1. *reference to the work:* "The opening lines of the sonnet personify God as a metalsmith"
2. *statement relating a detail of the work to the focus of the work:* "that is an appropriate metaphor since the theme of the poem deals with the need for reshaping, even remaking the sinful speaker."

Notice that these two components can appear in any order with a little rewording. Below is a sentence from Writer 3's paper illustrating how he refers to the work in the first half of the sentence and then relates that information to his focus ("No Place Like Home" is a good attempt at persuading . . .) in the second half:

The afghan, the home-made food and the flowers speak with sensitivity of the active life she still leads at home.

Not every sentence of a critical paper, of course, must contain both components. But no topic sentence of a paragraph should lack both and no single sentence should lack one or the other. The expository aim demands relentless concentration on the subject matter.

CHOOSING A MODE OF ORGANIZATION

Since you assume that the audience has already read the poem or essay, a narrative organization tends to rehash the surface of the original—and that is knowledge the audience already possesses. That leaves the descriptive, classification, and evaluative modes. Critical papers using the *descriptive mode* will outline the major parts, by breaking down the work into its component parts:

Essay	Poem
focus	images
development of the aim	persona
organization by mode	stanza structure
audience	diction
diction	rhythm
syntax	

Papers using the *classification mode* will organize by

classifying the work
defining the class or genre or type of writing
demonstrating how the essay or poem has the characteristics of the class

Papers using the *evaluative mode* will include the following parts:

criteria for a good essay or poem
judgment about the essay or poem in question
information from the essay or poem related to the criteria

FIRST VERSION

Writer 1   "WIRES"

While not everyone has the time to mentally reflect upon his life, practically everyone has seen a carbon copy of himself in a mirror, making it a universal image. In Philip Larkin's "Wires," all of the elements contribute to a "looking glass" image for society.

The two stanzas which make up the poem are like the outside and inside of the mirror. The first stanza deals with the pastoral dream-world of the young steer. The land of "purer water" is much like the wonderland world inside the mirror, a world that can only be dreamt of. The second stanza is the painfully real world, accurately reflected by the mirror with the impact of "muscle-shredding violence." The difference between the two stanzas is the difference between realities and dreams, between what people wish they looked like and what they see in the mirror. The young steer, desiring and attempting to enter the freer more beautiful world inside the mirror, encounters an electric barrier like the glass that separates the two worlds of the mirror. Defeated, the young steer becomes one of the "old cattle," his dreams shattered.

The rhyme scheme and syllabication between the two stanzas give the effect that one stanza is a one-hundred-and-eighty-degree angle mirror reflection of the other. Thus, line one of the first stanza rhymes with line four of the second, "fences, senses"; and line four of stanza one is coupled with line one of stanza two, "wires, wires," the pattern continued throughout the entire poem. The ideas of the paired rhyming lines are inverse in meaning much like the reverse reflection given by the looking glass. The poem moves from physical limits, "fences," for the steer's movement to psychological "electric limits," the memory of electric shock. The physical difference between the "old cattle" and the "young steers" becomes secondary to the psychological unity created by their common memory of the electric shock. The steer's dream for "purer water" is killed by the physically merciless wires. The thought of what lay "beyond the wires" prompted the steers to action, "to blunder up against the wires." Each psychological idea in stanza one is reversed to something physical in stanza two, and a physical idea in one becomes psychological in two.

The images in the poem are a reflection in the likeness of animals, steers of a human experience: dreaming and seeking a better existence only to be chastized by society for not conforming to norms. Much like the electric fence in "Wires," electric shock has been used on "insane" people to alter behavior. Nursing homes are filled with many old people who, like the "old cattle," no longer possess dreams for the future. The young steers enclosed by "wire" are like the thousands of "radical" youth behind bars. Each time a formerly free spirit has been battered to the point of defeat, one more person joins the "crowd" and becomes one of the "old cattle." "Wires" is Larkin's illustration of the two-sided world. Reality, the reflection in the mirrors, and dreams, what exists inside the mirror, can never cross each other, and anyone seeking to reach their dreams will encounter barrier after wearisome barrier.

REFINING THE EXPOSITORY STYLE

Diction

Since in a critical paper you assume in the beginning some knowledge and interest in the work on the part of your audience, you must project a voice that gives serious attention to the work. That voice generally expresses itself in relatively formal diction. Since you are writing about writing and are posing yourself as a judge of writing, you must pay particular attention to the technical quality of your own prose. Critical papers begin with dissonance; the finished paper deals with the poem or essay. Hence, the first-person pronoun tends to fade, and statements of feeling and belief disappear. The writer concentrates increasingly not on what is happening inside himself or herself but what has happened in the work. In order to concentrate in that fashion, the writer must use the appropriate terms for aspects of the work.

SENTENCE PATTERNS

Because many of the sentences in a critical paper include both a reference to the poem or essay and a support of the writer's focus, their structures include embedded sentences. In previous chapters you have practiced simple, clausal, and phrasal expansions. In this chapter we introduce a few more phrasal patterns for your scrutiny. Pattern F offers you one of the most sophisticated structures for expressing complex relationships between ideas.

CLASS
EXERCISES

Sentence-combining: additional phrasal expansion patterns

1. Study each phrasal pattern. Practice combining the sets of sentences into ones that match the pattern above it.
2. Examine the papers in this chapter and locate examples of these patterns. Rewrite and group sentences that could be effectively combined into these patterns.

Pattern D **To ignore the warnings of air traffic controllers that their equipment is inadequate is to endanger the lives of millions of passengers.**

    1. One dismisses the complaints.
    2. The complaints belong to the farmers.
    3. The complaint is the following.
    4. Their profits are too low.
    5. This dismissing bites the hand.
    6. The hand is of our feeder.

    1. One eats the following.
    2. The food is full.
    3. The fullness is of preservatives.
    4. The preservatives are unnecessary.
    5. They are chemical.
    6. One eats in vain.

Pattern D1 **The scrambling quarterback searched for his receivers, knifed back to the line of scrimmage, and fell on the ball to avoid being tackled by two oncoming linebackers.**

    1. The river meanders.
    2. The river is mighty.

3. The meandering is through the valley.
4. The river swells.
5. It does so as it enters the gorge.
6. The gorge is narrow.
7. The river rushes.
8. The river is to cascade.
9. The cascading is over a falls.
10. The falls is spectacular.
11. The falls is 80-foot.

---

1. The comedian muffed his opening.
2. He was young.
3. He lost his composure.
4. The loss was momentary.
5. He went on.
6. He wins the audience.
7. He did so with his humor.
8. The humor was subtle.

Pattern D2 **The student employment office tries** to help students find jobs by introducing them to prospective employers.

1. Cicero managed.
2. He regained his inheritance.
3. He outwitted his guardian.
4. The guardian was deceitful.
5. The outwitting took place at a trial.

---

1. Muhammad Ali hoped.
2. He caps his career.
3. He wins the title.
4. The title is the heavyweight one.
5. The winning would be for a third time.
6. The third time is unprecedented.

Pattern D3 **Black authors such as W. E. B. DuBois, Eldridge Cleaver, Frederick Douglass, and Booker T. Washington have used autobiography** to examine their lives and cultures.

1. The fighters demanded.
2. They were fire fighters.
3. The demand was for an engine.
4. The engine was additional.
5. The engine backs up their old one.
6. The old one is outdated.

---

1. Men stole a car.
2. The men were armed.
3. There were two men.
4. The car was abandoned.
5. They escape.
6. The escape is with $8 million.
7. The $8 million is in securities.
8. The securities are negotiable.

Pattern E An accomplished guitarist and banjo player, Roy Clark can also play eight other instruments with ease.

1. He was winner of the Kentucky Derby.
2. He was winner of the Preakness.
3. Affirmed went on to capture the crown.
4. The crown was the triple crown.
5. The crown is coveted.
6. The capturing was in the Belmont Stakes.

---

1. He was a consummate wordsmith.
2. Vladimir Nabokov was one of the authors.
3. The authors are great.
4. The authors are of the twentieth century.

Pattern E1 Noam Chomsky the influential MIT linguist, believes that children are born with a potential knowledge of grammar.

1. Jose Ortega y Gassett described.
2. He was a philosopher.
3. He was Spanish.
4. The describing was of "the look."
5. "The look" comes.
6. The coming is direct.
7. The coming is from some people.
8. The people are charismatic.

---

1. Jacques Tati walks.
2. He is French.
3. He is a movie actor.
4. He walks loosely.
5. He walks as though the parts of his body were somehow disconnected.

Pattern E2 In the early seventeenth century, Sir Robert Bruce Cotton collected the relics of ancient pre-Christian Britain—coins, medals, inscribed stones, and manuscripts.

1. The following happened at 9:00 A.M.
2. My brother began.
3. The beginning was of his day.
4. The beginning was with breakfast.
5. The breakfast was his favorite.
6. It included Big Macs.
7. There were three of them.
8. It included fries.
9. There was a double order of them.
10. It included Coke.
11. There was a half-gallon of this.

---

1. The following happened in a dash.
2. The dash was to the North Pole.
3. Robert Peary faced hardships.
4. His companion also faced hardships.
5. The hardships were excruciating.
6. One hardship was cold.
7. The cold was extreme.
8. One hardship was frostbite.

Pattern F The film presents an image of three peasant women, all three facing front, their faces stolid, their hands spread open on their knees.

1. Her sister waved.
2. The sister is Dawn.
3. The waving is to her.
4. One hand made an arc.
5. The arc was slow.
6. Her voice faded.
7. The fading was quick.

---

1. Mick Jagger appeared.
2. The appearing was onstage.
3. The appearing was sudden.
4. His suit was trimmed.
5. The suit was tight.
6. The suit was white.
7. The trimming was with a sash.
8. The sash was red.
9. His sandals were studded.
10. The studding was with rhinestones.

Pattern F1 Parking areas and loading zones clogged with cars, terminals besieged by distraught passengers, the major airport was hit by unprecedented numbers of snafus and snarls.

1. Their profits were dwindling.
2. Their costs were soaring.
3. The soaring was steady.
4. The cattlemen cut their herds.
5. The cutting was by thirty percent.

1. Its mood turned surly.
2. This happened suddenly.
3. The legislature voted.
4. The voting was against cloture.

CLASS
EXERCISES

1. Study Writer 1's First Version.
   • What sections both refer to the work and support the focus (see p. 280)?
   • What mode of organization is used?
   • What elements of style support the expository aim?
   • Notice how the writer has enclosed exact references to the poem in quotation marks. Point to some examples of this convention.
2. Read the First Versions of Writers 2 and 3.

FIRST VERSION

Writer 2

FREEDOM AND FRUSTRATION

The poem Wires is symbolic of the "electric fences" or restrictions in society. The young steers would be the youth, maybe the hippies of the sixties, who are trying to go past society's boundaries, but eventually "blunder up against the wires," a confrontation with the law, and then become old from that day. The old cattle are the complacent elders of society who have become wary through their experiences and therefore live within the restrictions. The eight lines are very compact and get the main point across well. Wires is a poem that grieves over the frustration experienced by the young attempting to develop their human capabilities.

In line one the "widest prairies" are freedoms, possibly the large freedoms U.S. citizens enjoy, but the line also warns that even with all these freedoms their are restrictions, like laws in the U.S. Lines two through four set up the situation that will be resolved in the last stanza. The old cattle or people have learned through their encounter with the electric fence not to make waves, but the youth are impatient and aggressive and want to explore new lifestyles beyond the wires or laws, similar to pot-smoking or other activities frowned on by authorities.

In the final stanza, the question of what will happen to these restless youngsters, posed in stanza one, is answered. Their quest to try new things leads them into a confrontation with the law. The "muscle shredding violence" could be likened to the teenager getting busted for marijuana possession, a drug who's harmful effects are still debated, be thrown in jail and given a stiff sentence. The poem then goes on to say that this violence "gives no quarter." My understanding of this phrase would be no mercy is given to anyone going beyond societies restrictions. So saying this violence gives no quarter seems absurd because given the present condition of our judicial system, a rich kid caught with drugs would probably get a lesser electric limit than a poor black brought before the bench on the same charges.

The above complaint aside, the poem finishes up by saying that after the offenders confrontation with the electric wires, they change from young to old that day on. This is true in a way because once experiencing the brutality of a jail sentence, for example, one is less likely to want to explore beyond the wires again and therefore becomes more complacent. These lines seem overly general, though, because many who are "shocked" once return to their old vices as evidenced by the number of repeat offenders in jail.

This critic finds the poem "Wires" to contain several flaws but in the end still it still creates a strong impression of frustration experienced by the youth in their struggle to try new things. The questions raised about the poem in the above paragraphs may not be so to another reader, as of course poetry is very personal, but, to the authors credit, the main theme of youth attempting to develop their human capabilities probably shines through to most readers.

FIRST VERSION

Writer 3   FLAWED PERSUASION

Finishing "There's No Place Like Home" is like coming out of a disappointing Academy Award film. There were plenty of good parts with some flaws. Even though the writer strengthened my conviction that keeping older people at home is better than putting them in nursing homes, I was irritated by some parts of the essay.

The account of the visit to grandmother's was the most convincing. The faded picture portraits, antique furniture, grandfather clock, and dusty box of trains impress the reader with the personal tradition that surrounds the grandmother. The afghan, the home-made food and the flowers speak with sensitivity of the active life she still leads at home. The diction gives the reader a full participation in the visit, engaging the senses: sight—"brass tea kettle" and "toy french poodle," sound—"grandfather clock ticks," taste—"spicy pumpkin pie," and smell—"aroma of homemade vegetable soup." Even the few cliches, like "sparkling clean," "little old house," and especially the title are forgotten in the vividness of the other details. Although it is unclear why the account is divided into three relatively short paragraphs, the organization supports the diction, taking the reader chronologically from the grandmother's welcome through the meal to the bouquet at the departure. All of these features combine to make the writer's point about the healthiness of remaining at home.

The persuasiveness of the writer's paper, however, is marred by the first paragraph which explains too much, not allowing the reader to discover the conclusion through the narrative. The last paragraph also irritates because it again translates what the reader has already discovered and goes on to state directives about the reader's responsibility, oversimplified into: "lending a hand with the more strenuous house work."

The most flawed aspect of the essay is the account of the nursing home visit. Although the writer starts with sight and smell impressions, "pale green walls" and "germicidal smell," the majority of the details seem taken from stereotypical descriptions, not from the writer's visit. No mention is made of the aunt who was visited. The patients are generalized. The whining and crying comment seems to go beyond the time of the visit itself. The last sentence summarizes aspects which could have been persuasively developed, "impersonal care, bland food, and limited activity."

Perhaps the expectations set up by the grandmother narrative cause the nursing home account to contrast more negatively. In any case, this essay is partially convincing, winning me to feel more strongly about the writer's focus, but disappointing and irritating me because the writer failed to maintain the vivid narrative mode.

ASSIGNMENT **Stage 5** Toward a Critical Paper: Developing, Organizing, and Refining the Paper
1. **Plan your organization.**
2. **Write the first version of your critical paper.**

CRITIQUING AND REWRITING A critical paper is, as we have noted, writing about a piece of writing to which the writer and reader have equal access. The reader will hold the writer responsible for certain things that would not apply if this were a paper dealing with a person, place, or thing known only to the writer.

1. The reader expects the writer to use the proper technical terms for components of the work, whether those terms are *image, metaphor,* and *stanza* or *focus, aim,* and *mode.*
2. The reader expects the writer to illustrate the analysis by referring to the work, pointing to the details being discussed.

3. The reader expects the writer to avoid the two pitfalls of critical writing: paraphrase and projection.
4. The reader expects the writer who evaluates to state clearly a set of acceptable criteria on which the evaluation will be based.
5. The reader expects the writer to show in the development of the paper an acceptable understanding of the work—not just a reaction but a total grasp of the work.

As usual, and in addition, the critical paper must show the features set out in our Critical Guide, adapted here to the special demands of criticism:

1. A clear focus
2. A development of that focus by
   a. Interpretation, supported by
   b. Representative facts
3. A recognizable pattern of organization: description, classification or evaluation
4. A style appropriate to the audience's attitude toward the subject matter
5. A maintenance of the conventions of Standard Written English

CRITIQUE:
Writer 2

Focus

The focus is not clear. "The poem Wires is symbolic of the 'electric fences' or restrictions in society" indicates that the writer is not in control of the terminology he needs to discuss the poem. Language in a poem may symbolize various abstractions; but a poem can't symbolize anything. Possibly what the writer meant was "In the poem 'Wires,' the electric fences symbolize restrictions in society." But even that would be a focus dealing only with a portion of the poem. The real focus is the last sentence of the first paragraph, but it is not developed.

Development

There is no consistent development of a focus. The writer has apparently started with a pseudo-mathematical equation ("electric fences" = restrictions in society) and has then attempted to give phrases in the poem exact restrictive equivalents, larger or narrower than the original, according to the feeling of the writer.

The paper does not deal with the poem but lands in one of the pitfalls we mentioned earlier. It speaks of the writer's opinions about equal justice under the law, pot-smoking, and the effects of incarceration. Nowhere does the paper try to deal with the poem. The emphasis falls on the writer, not on the subject matter, as the writer confesses: "The questions raised about the poem in the above paragraphs may not be so to another reader, as of course poetry is very personal . . . ."

Organization

Through the first three paragraphs of this five-paragraph paper, the mode is descriptive, a movement from the whole to the parts. The first paragraph is a summary interpretation; the following two paragraphs approach the poem as if it had three parts: "In line one . . . . Lines two through four . . . . In the final stanza . . . ." But the last sentence of the third paragraph shifts into evaluation. The first sentence of the fourth paragraph shifts back to description ("the poem finishes up by saying") and then shifts again to evaluation. The fifth paragraph begins with evaluation and ends with a puzzling sentence: its first half seems to be a possible focus for another, different paper; its second half is a broad evaluation supported by nothing in the paper.

Style

Since the paper is radically defective, a discussion of its style would be inappropriate.

Conventions

The hard truth is that an audience will not take seriously a paper on a literary topic from a writer who cannot demonstrate conventional literacy. The errors in conventions that litter this paper would destroy its credibility even if it had a clear focus, a logical development, and so on. Consider the first paragraph. In the first sentence, "Wires" is a title; it should appear in quotation marks. In the second sentence either the punctuation or the diction is faulty. What may be intended there is "the youths of the sixties, perhaps the hippies," but then the tense sequence would break down: "are trying" would have to become "were trying." Even that correction would blunder up against the tense of the quotation, "blunder up against the wires." The phrase "societies boundaries" should, of course, be "society's boundaries" or, even better, "the boundaries of their society."

CRITIQUE:
Writer 3

Focus

The focus is maintained throughout the paper.

Development

The writer uses many examples from the essay. He speaks of "aims," "modes," "diction," "cliches," and "organization" in order to speak the language of his audience, the teacher. His major problem with development lies not in the sufficiency of support but in the accuracy of the analysis. In paragraph three, the writer claims that "the first paragraph which explains too much, not allowing the reader to discover the conclusion through the narrative" is a flaw in the persuasive aim. The flaw is in the narrative mode.

Because the writer is evaluating the paper for its persuasiveness, he should also have commented on its appeals to emotion, reason, and personality.

Organization

The writer has committed himself to the evaluative mode. Unfortunately, he never makes the transition from his initial reaction to a set of criteria by which the essay can be evaluated. The criteria here seem to be personal and secret. We know that the writer was either *irritated* or *convinced* by parts of the work; but the reader wants to know what prompted and therefore justified the irritation or conviction. Since the criteria are not set forth clearly in the beginning, no "convincing" pattern of organization emerges.

Style

The style needs some repair. In the second sentence, for example, the diction fluctuates: "plenty of good parts" is down-home, chatty conversation; "some flaws" is more sophisticated, less personal, more objective. Yet both phrases occur in the same sentence. In the fourth paragraph, the second sentence is sophisticated, except for the phrase, "the majority of the details." The writer means "most." "Majority" means one more than half: impressions should not be disguised as statistics.

The syntax is sound, except in a few places such as the first sentence of the second paragraph. "The account . . . was the most convincing"—as opposed to what? If the reference is to the account of the nursing home, then the account of the visit to grandmother's is *more* convincing than the other. But it's not clear that the writer intends that meaning only.

Conventions

Obviously the paper contains some typographical errors—and they are clearly typographical, not conventional. Nevertheless, they will alienate a reader because poor typewritten copy always conveys to the reader that the writer takes little pride in his or her work.

REWRITING

REVISED VERSION

Writer 2   FREEDOM AND FRUSTRATION

The poem "Wires" is symbolic of the electric fences or restrictions in society. The young steers are the youth, maybe the hippies of the sixties, who are trying to go past societies' boundaries, but eventually "blunder up against the wires," a confrontation with the law, and then become old from that day. The old cattle are the complacent elders of society who have become wary through their experiences and therefore live within the restrictions. The eight lines are very compact and get the main point across well. "Wires" is a poem that grieves over the frustration experienced by the young attempting to develop their human capabilities.

In line one of the poem the "widest prairies" are freedoms, possibly the large freedoms U.S. citizens enjoy, but the line also warns that even with all these freedoms there are restrictions, laws. Lines two through four then proceed to set up the situation that will be resolved in the second stanza, namely the inevitable fate of the young steers. The old cattle have learned through their encounter with the electric fence not to make waves, but the youth, though, are impatient and agressive and want to explore new lifestyles beyond the wires or laws, similar to teens' pot-smoking or other activities frowned on by authorities.

In the final stanza the question of what will happen to these restless youngsters, posed in stanza one, is answered. Their quest to try new things leads them into a confrontation with the law. The "muscle-shredding violence" could be likened to the teenager getting busted for marijuana possession, thrown in jail and given a stiff sentence. The poet appears to be grieving over the constant cycle of generations blundering up against the fence. After the electric limit people keep quiet and become indifferent. They follow the accepted ways without questioning.

"Wires" creates a strong impression of frustration experienced by the youth who struggle to live differently. The new generation doesn't seem to be given the freedom to develop their human capabilities. The boundaries which are imposed upon the young would limit their sensory development and in turn their imagination and as a result their creativity.

REVISED VERSION

Writer 3   FLAWED PERSUASION

Finishing "There's No Place Like Home" was like coming out of a disappointing Academy Award film. The aim and the execution were laudable, but something was lacking in consistency and completeness.

The account of the visit to grandmother's is consistent and complete. The faded picture portraits, antique furniture, grandfather clock, and dusty box of trains suggest the personal tradition that surrounds the grandmother. The afghan, the home-made food and the flowers speak with sensitivity of the active life she still leads at home. The diction gives the reader a full participation in the visit by engaging the senses: sight—"brass tea kettle" and "toy French poodle"; sound—"grandfather clock ticks"; taste—"spicy pumpkin pie"; smell—"aroma of homemade vegetable soup." Even the few cliches, like "sparkling clean," "little red house," and especially the title are forgotten in the vividness of the other details. Although it is unclear why the account is divided into three relatively short paragraphs, the organization supports the diction, taking the reader chronologically from the grandmother's welcome through the meal to the bouquet at the departure. All of these features combine to make the writer's point about the healthiness of remaining at home.

The first half of the paper is marred only by the first paragraph—which explains too much, not allowing the reader to discover the conclusion through the narrative—and by the last paragraph—which translates what the reader has already discovered and goes on to state the reader's responsibilities, oversimplified into "lending a hand with the more strenuous housework."

The account of the nursing home visit, however, which should balance the account of grandmother's house, is incomplete and, therefore, inconsistent with the method of the earlier description and narration. Although the writer starts with sight and smell impressions, "pale green walls" and "germicidal smell," most of the details are stereotypical, not taken from the writer's visit. No mention is made of the aunt who was visited. The comment on whining and crying goes beyond the time of the visit itself. The last sentence summarizes aspects which could have been persuasively developed: "impersonal care, bland food, and limited activity."

By not maintaining the vivid narrative mode established in the second paragraph, the writer has failed to carry out completely his persuasive aim.

CLASS EXERCISES

1. Using the Critical Guide (p. 291), do a critique of Writer 1's First Version (pp. 282–283).
2. Using the Critical Guide and working in groups, critique each other's papers.
3. Study the Revised Versions of Writers 2 and 3 above.
   • To what extent have they followed the advice of their critics?

ASSIGNMENT

Stage 6 Toward a Critical Paper: Critiquing and Rewriting

1. **Do a self-critique of your first version, guided by criticism from your instructor and classmates.**
2. **Revise your paper.**

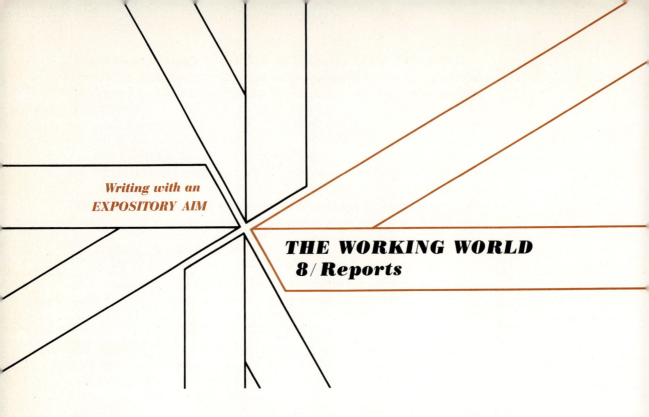

THE WORKING WORLD
8/ Reports

We include a chapter on report writing to demonstrate that you follow the same composing process when you write in the world of work as you do in the other worlds. Therefore, you can readily transfer the power you have developed to this kind of writing.

You may tend to view reports as impersonal, purely technical. But why is one report more successful than another? If a computer could write them, they would be equally effective. Each writer, however, handcrafts a good report, leaving a signature. The chapter will demonstrate one kind of feasibility report which recommends a solution for a problem.

FINDING AND
EXPRESSING
THE STARTING
POINT

FINDING THE SUBJECT

In the world of work, you are usually assigned your subject for a report. In a composition course, if you have a choice, select a subject from your present or past employment or from any institution where you have been an insider. In this chapter, we will present three student reports. Writer 1 chose a problem with her job as a nursing assistant. Writer 2 decided to report about the traffic court system with which he was very familiar. Writer 3 selected a computer-related subject because he had gained extensive background in computers through his high school job.

EXPRESSING THE STARTING POINT

Whether your subject is assigned or chosen, you must still formulate a precise starting point by identifying the exact problem to be addressed by the report. A good starting point pins down the gap between the work situation and the needs, values, and structures of an institution.

STARTING POINTS

Writer 1 ASPECT OF MY NURSING JOB
—the inability of nursing assistants to perform adequately certain responsibilities

VALUES OF THE INSTITUTION
—effective care of patients
—efficiency regulation that NAs work alone

Question: What kind of method could be devised so that the Nursing Assistant could have the help needed for heavy work, yet still remain independent for her individual duties?

Writer 2 ASPECT OF TRAFFIC COURT
—excessive time spent settling business

VALUES OF THE INSTITUTION
—just and efficient system of operation, within alloted budget

Question: How can traffic court be run more efficiently and reduce the confusion it causes for citizens?

Writer 3 ASPECT OF MY COMPUTER JOB
—inefficient, slow and poor-quality printout

VALUES OF THE INSTITUTION
—efficiency, speed, good quality

Question: How could computer print-out turn-around time be sped up?

Commentary Writer 1's question identifies a specific problem to be solved and finds a structure within the institution with which it conflicts.

CLASS EXERCISES

1. Examine the Starting Points of Writers 2 and 3.
   • What gaps do the writers identify between the work situation and the needs and values of the institution?
   • To what kinds of solutions will their questions point?
2. Select a problem in an academic, social, or economic institution where the members of the class are insiders.

- Identify the element(s) that clash with the needs or published values of that institution.
- Formulate questions that seek a solution to the problem.

ASSIGNMENT

Stage 1 Toward Report Writing: Finding and Expressing the Starting Point

1. **Identify the aspect of the job or system that clashes with the needs and values of the institution.**
2. **Form a question to point your exploration.**
3. **Seek comments on your starting point from your instructor and the class.**

PLANNING FOR AIM AND AUDIENCE

THE EXPOSITORY AIM

Although the writers of feasibility, progress, and final reports are anxious for their readers to accept their conclusions and recommendations, the primary aim of any report is expository, not persuasive. Even the simplest kind of report—the letter of application—has an expository aim, whatever the applicant's desperation. The transaction between writer and audience in reports is public and institutional. The question is not how good you will look but how useful your skills and information will be to the institution. The transaction rests on the quality of the information provided.

ANALYZING THE AUDIENCE

In report writing, your audience is given, not chosen. A report will be read by a superior who can act on the substance of the report. This fact makes audience choice irrelevant and audience analysis easy. You write *up*—that is, you write as subordinate to superior. Furthermore, you write for a busy, impatient audience. Part of the subordinate-superior relationship is that the subordinate always assumes (the truth of the matter is another thing) that the superior is busier than the subordinate. This has obvious stylistic implications: reports are written as concisely and exactly as possible. The first commandment of professional writing is that the reader's time is valuable.

In this instance, then, you will not choose your audience but identify him or her. And in the bargain, in using the Audience Guide you will see the audience not as an individual human being but as a link in a chain of command, a box in an organization chart. The audience is composed not so much of persons as of representatives of an institution (a company, a board of directors, a government) who qualify as an audience by being able to think corporately, not individually. Their criterion will not be a personal preference but what is useful to the institution. There is, in a very basic sense, nothing personal in professional readers. The editor of a magazine, for example, does not accept or reject your manuscript because of personal likes or dislikes, but because he or she sees the readership as liking or not liking it.

The difference between an individual audience (like the student on your left) and the corporate audience (like a management superior) is that the corporate audience responds to trends and directives that are easily discoverable. If, for example, you are reporting on the state of equal opportunity at some division of IT&T, you know that IT&T is under federal judgment to hire more minority personnel. This is a *value* they hold by default, and your writing should reflect that imposed value.

AUDIENCE GUIDE

A. Analyze the audience in relation to itself.
  1. What are the levels and types of experiences that my audience has had (cultural, professional, recreational, educational, and so on)?
  2. What hierarchy of values does my audience possess or profess (money making and power, friendship, security, intellectual growth, and so on)? It is important to distinguish, if possible, between what an audience holds dear and what it professes to hold dear, if indeed there is a difference. Does the audience hide one set of values under another? If so, the writer's task grows more complicated.
B. Analyze the audience in relation to the subject.
  1. What opinion does my audience have on my subject?
  2. How strongly does my audience hold that opinion?
  3. How willing to act on its opinion is my audience—if acting is appropriate?
C. Considering what you have learned from your answers to A and B, determine what role your audience should play in relation to your voice as writer (peer, authority, subordinate, familiar, and so on).

AUDIENCE ANALYSIS

Writer 1   AUDIENCE: MS. X, R.N. AFTERNOON NURSING SUPERVISOR

A. 1. Ms. X has a Bachelor of Science in Nursing, was supervisor before she came to Y Hospital from Z hospital. (She was fired from Z's staff.)
  2. My audience believes that rules should not be bent, twisted, or changed. She believes that hospitals set down rules which are perfect and should be followed to the letter. Ms. X is a very private person, so it is very difficult to determine if she has one set of values under another.

B. Ms. X believes that Nursing Assistants should work individually.

C. Role of Ms. X: my superior; my voice: concerned employee who knows the system well.

Commentary Writer 1 has done an excellent though brief audience analysis:

1. She indicates the audience's qualifications for making judgments: the B.S. degree and prior experience.
2. She suggests that she may have had difficulties in the past with her attitudes, although we do not know for sure why she was fired before.
3. She sets her general attitude toward the topic of change.
4. She hints at her view of herself as a "public" person.
5. She sets out her attitude toward this subject in particular.

The writer can assume that this will be a hostile audience.

CLASS EXERCISES

1. Examine the Audience Analysis of Writer 3.
   - What background information and values will the writer be able to employ in the report?
   - What use can the writer make of this knowledge?
   - What other aspects of the audience could have been noted?
   - How will the audience's role and writer's voice work for the report?
2. Identify the appropriate audience for the subject the class chose to practice expressing the starting point.
   - Analyze the audience.
   - Choose a role and voice.

AUDIENCE ANALYSIS

Writer 3 AUDIENCE: MR. Y (VICE-PRESIDENT OF COMPANY A, A SUBDIVISION OF XXX)

A. 1. Nice fellow, good technical background
   2. Tight on company's money, but would want very good product at most reasonable cost
B. Constantly busy and sometimes unaware of company problems
C. Role of Mr. Y: employer; my voice: subordinate but experienced operator

ASSIGNMENT Stage 2 Toward Report Writing: Planning for Aim and Audience

1. Identify your audience.
2. Using the Audience Guide, analyze your audience.
3. Seek comments on your analysis from your instructor.
4. Keep your expository and persuasive aims in mind.

Exploring for ideas, information, evidence, and data constitutes an important stage of recall and discovery for report writing. You need such material not only to prompt a focus but also to develop your report. The Exploratory Guide can again be used to investigate your problem.

EXPLORATORY GUIDE

Static view
　　—What are the significant features of the problem?
　　—What data (statistics, information, related reports) bear on the subject?
　　—Who is involved?

Dynamic view
　　—When and how did the problem begin?
　　—What changes have occurred?
　　—What are the causes of the problem?

Relative view
　　—How would I classify the problem?
　　—How does this problem compare with other problems I have met?
　　—What analogy can be discovered for my problem?
　　—What criteria should an adequate solution meet (e.g., efficiency, inexpensiveness, fairness)?
　　—What alternate solutions can I formulate?
　　—How do these solutions meet the criteria I have posed?

EXPLORATION

Writer 1 　　　　　　　　　　　NURSING ASSISTANTS

STATIC VIEW

—It is very difficult to re-adjust an uncomfortable patient by yourself. It takes at least two to help pull someone up in the bed.
—It is safer to get a patient who has just been operated on up with two people. Often they are dizzy and weak which is too much for a single assistant to handle.
—In order to give good back care to bed-ridden patients, it is necessary to roll them over. This is very difficult to do with only one person.
—Often a patient who finds it difficult to walk will feel insecure if there is only one person available to help them.

—It is more difficult to make a good tight bed by yourself than if there is another person available to assist.

—It is nearly impossible to make an occupied bed well with only one person.

—Comatose patients need alot of care and attention, often more than one person can give.

—Although almost all functions of a nursing assistant are made easier if two are working together, there is no reason two assistants should take temperatures, pulses, respirations, and blood pressures. It also only takes one assistant to run sugar and acetone tests, collect intake and outputs and chart.

—Isolation set up, break down and many functions carried out in isolation are nearly impossible for one person to do.

—It is difficult to get help from another person if they have an equally heavy load and do not feel they have time to offer you help.

—Sometimes two patients of the same assistant will be having a difficult time. This requires that she run all evening while other assistants may have no one in distress.

DYNAMIC VIEW

—Before nursing assistants were so common in X Hospital there would be 1 assistant per twenty patients but the LPN's and RN's would also be available to help for heavy duties.

—There are many more nursing assistants, about 1 per 8 people. Now, however, the nurses are not required to help. So, although there are more aides, there are fewer nurses and very little joint effort.

—Often, two assistants would try to help one another in order to make the job easier and to offer the patient the best, most secure methods available. This was looked down upon by the supervision and regarded as just an excuse to socialize.

—The idea of team work was almost instituted but it was defeatd by Ms X because she felt it would allow the assistants to fool around.

RELATIVE VIEW

—Classification
  —This problem is an administrative problem because they are the ones who determine hospital policies.
  —It is also a problem for the assistants. The work is more difficult and much more demanding if done separately.
  —It is a problem for the patients because they do not receive the best possible care.
—Criteria for a good solution:
  1) allow for efficient individual duties
  2) allow for teamwork.

−Solutions:

Team

Both girls do work that requires 2 people.

Marcy's assignment	Mary's assignment
Rm 319–323	Rm 324–328
Marcy does individual duties for these rooms.	Mary does duties for these rooms.

Working separately *(present structure)* (Rooms, Patients assigned separately)	*Working in teams* (Two people, duties combined)
1 eliminates socializing among workers	1 promotes socializing among workers
2 difficult to treat total-care (comatose) patients	2 much easier to care for comatose patients
3 harder to reassure insecure patient	3 easier to help unsteady patient to walk
4 if there are two problems at one time, one has to wait	4 two problems can be handled at once
5 individual work is handled well by one person	5 individual work is either divided or one person does more than the other
6 each assistant is responsible for her own duties	6 both assistants are responsible for all duties, if one is lazy, the other must make up for it
7 hard to help O.R. patient	7 easy to help O.R. patient
8 difficult to give good back care	8 much easier to give good back treatment
9 because it is so difficult to turn patients by oneself, individual assignments promote bedsores	9 it is much easier to frequently position people with 2 people, discourages bedsores

Commentary Writer 1's Exploration shows a careful consideration of the problem from many angles. The features and criteria provide a good basis for a solution. Her investigation of previous attempts at teamwork should help her avoid unworkable or unacceptable solutions. Her proposed solution seems feasible. But she has not explicitly related it to the criteria, a necessary task before arriving at a conclusion. Her exploration and her eventual report will be stronger if she explores at least one other alternative solution.

CLASS EXERCISES

1. Read the Explorations of Writers 2 and 3.
2. Compare the Explorations of Writers 2 and 3:
   • Which set of static features assesses the problem more thoroughly?
   • Which analysis of causes will be more useful for the report writer?

• Which writer does a better job of relating criteria to solutions?
     Why?
3. Explore the problem the class selected as a subject for a report:
   • Note down the features of the problem.
   • Trace its history and causes.
   • Classify the problem.
   • List criteria for a good solution.
   • Describe at least two alternate solutions.
   • Relate these to the criteria.

EXPLORATION

Writer 2   TRAFFIC COURT

STATIC VIEW

Features of the problem
–Traffic courts deal with about 2700 people a day.
–They are the state's busiest court.
–It takes hours to settle the simplest matter if you want to contest.
–The county owns the buildings.
–The city pays $750,000 a year for the use of the building.
–The county does a poor job of maintaining the building.
–The building is dingy, crowded, and old.
–The court usually starts over an hour late.
–There are three traffic judges.
–The computer system is inefficient.
–Employee morale is low.
–Over 800,000 people deal with the court each year.
–Clerks often have to check records by hand.

DYNAMIC VIEW

–The building was built in 1904.
–The system has remained the same as long as I can remember.
–Causes: Bureaucracy
         Citizen's willingness to put up with the system
         Allocation of funds to other areas
         Judges' attitudes

–Classification

Agencies that operate inefficiently

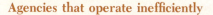

| Income Tax Division | Traffic Court | U.S. Post Office | Department of Transportation |

Places where it takes a long time to transact business

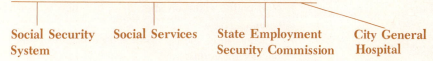

| Social Security System | Social Services | State Employment Security Commission | City General Hospital |

Agencies that need a complete overhaul

| U.S. Postal System | State Mental Health Department | Department of Housing & Urban Development | Department of Transportation |

Firms that operate efficiently

| Eastman Kodak | United Parcel Service | IBM | Greyhound Bus Co. |

–Analogy

Paying a ticket is like buying a house. It is time-consuming and expensive, and frustrating.

–Comparison with banking

Traffic court	*24-hour bank teller*
–It takes several hours to transact business.	–It takes a few minutes.
–You have to wait a long time.	–There is no waiting.
–You have to deal directly with several people.	–Everything is computerized.
–Business is transacted 8 to 5.	–Business is transacted 24 hours a day.
–Transacting business is usually frustrating.	–Transacting business is usually pleasant.
–You have to come into the building.	–You don't have to go inside.
–There is no free parking.	–Free parking is available.

–Criteria for a solution:
  –Speed and simplicity of paying fines
  –Adequate building and computer system
  –Within the budget

–*Alternative solutions*
  1. Update the computer system.
  2. Have lines like those in a bank that allow a person to go to the next available clerk.
  3. Make it possible to pay minor traffic violations at any bank, police station, or neighborhood city hall.
  4. Non-traffic violation should be handled by a division of Recorder's Court.
  5. Traffic Court should be in a building designed to serve its contemporary functions.

–*Relation between solutions and criteria*
  1. Too expensive; partial solution.
  2. Fast but not adequate building.
  3. Bank—can already mail traffic violations in.
     Police stations—meets all criteria.
     City hall—more bureaucracy.
  4. Not that many types of cases—doesn't lessen the referee's caseload
  5. A new building—too costly.

EXPLORATION

Writer 3   **COMPUTER PRINTOUTS**

STATIC VIEW

Features of the problem
–old printers: DATA 100 and DOCUMENTATION
–new proposed printer XEROX 5100

	DATA 100	DOC	X 5100
Speed:	800–10001/m (1/m: lines per minute)	1600–18001/m	5000–54001/m
Size:	4′ × 3′ × 6′ (H × W × L)	5½′ × 3′ × 6′	5′ × 5′ × 7′
Carriage control:	Paper tape	Disc pack	EPROM
no. of:	1	48	00
Special forms:	No	Yes	Yes
No. of printing cards:	1	2	1
Lower case:	No	Yes (with extra printing band)	Yes
Spec. char.:	No	Yes ″	Yes

	DATA 100	DOC	X 5100
Paper stacker:	Drop (inefficient)	Feed (very efficient)	Chute (efficient)
Restruction of FCB:	Not available	45 minutes	5 minutes
Air Cond. Reg.:	Yes 70°↓F	Yes 75↓°F	Yes, 75°F
Cost:	$15,000	$50,000 + disc pack	$100,000
Extra disc pack:	Not needed	$15,000	Not needed
Extra paper tapes:	$500–$1000	N/A	N/A
Total:	$15,000–$16,000	$65,000	$100,000
Cost per 1/m:	$16.00	$36.11	$18.51
No. of employ. to run	2	3	4
No. of printers: for stand. jobs:	7	4	3
Total employ.:	14	12	12

DYNAMIC VIEW

Causes and effects of problem

—*long hours:* turn around time has been slow & quality of work has been poor on NYC, WASA, & SYS OUT A projects

—*additional pay:* programmers have been required to stay overtime to get jobs back

—*add. per.:* more employees required to run DATA 100's than DOC's and X 5100's

—*poor atmosphere:* programmers have been hostile to operators, who have no control over slow speed

Future solution

—*cut time:* turn around time increased 300–400% on big projects

—*cut in prog.:* programmers work standard hours

—*cut in pay & personnel:* just a few operators needed on X 5100 no operators needed after 8:00 p.m.

—*good atmosphere:* programmers will pipe down

RELATIVE VIEW

Classification

Problem is social and management problem

Social

—programmers mad at operators

—operators mad at system because they have to work longer

—steam constantly being let off, causing little work to be done

Management

—company could make more money with better printers

—quality can be increased, drawing more clients

—no. of employees can be cut or dispursed into other areas of research, where they would do more good

Criteria
Speed, Cost, Accuracy

Alternative solutions:
1. phase out DATA 100's and keep DOC's
2. phase all DOC's and DATA 100's out and get new X 5100's
3. replace DATA 100's and DOC's with any other, more efficient printer
4. continue as is, and lose money

ASSIGNMENT

Stage 3 Toward Report Writing: Exploring
1. Using the Exploratory Guide, gather as much information as you can.
2. Seek commentary on your exploration from your instructor.

**DISCOVERING
AND STATING
THE FOCUS**

MAKING A RECOMMENDATION

If you assume that report writing is simply a matter of organizing material and transferring it to paper, consider the conclusions of a workshop held by the management of a leading automotive company. The purpose of the workshop was to determine the cause of communication problems that had been plaguing the company. They concluded that their major problem was a lack of focus in reports: their writers had been sending on information with no significant recommendations.

But such recommendations do not leap from information. They come after careful exploring and incubating. A good recommendation for a report includes (1) a solution, and (2) advice on implementation. The solution is the alternative that best meets your criteria. The advice on implementation is the action that you propose should be taken on the solution. A formulation of a focus would look like this:

X5100————————————————ought to be purchased.
(Solution)   (Implementation)
X5100————————————————ought to be further tested.
(Solution)   (Implementation)

A solution springs from the data available to you. Implementation looks beyond the data. If you were trying to choose between two kinds of radio receivers, A and B, you might conclude from the data that A is cheaper initially, more reliable, equally versatile, equally expensive in repair costs, and then move to the general conclusion that A is a better set than B. But you don't necessarily recommend the purchase of A because you may have any of a series of misgivings:

1. The data were faulty or incomplete; you might recommend more testing.

2. The data were restrictive. You may know of another kind of set, *C*, that wasn't even in his data and that you haven't been able to investigate. You might recommend looking further.

Below are the Focuses (recommendations) of the three writers.

FOCUSES

	SOLUTION	IMPLEMENTATION
Writer 1	Nursing assistants working in teams	should be organized immediately.
Writer 2	Satellite traffic offices	should be placed in five precinct police stations on a trial basis.
Writer 3	Three X5100 printers	should be examined and possibly purchased in the near future.

CLASS
EXERCISES

1. Compare the alternative focuses below with those of the three writers. Determine which versions make the more effective recommendations for the audience.
   A. (1) A new system for nursing assistants ought to be developed.
      (2) The present NA system has problems.
      (3) Nursing assistants working in teams ought to be organized immediately by the supervisor.
   B. (1) Satellite traffic offices ought to be set up.
      (2) Traffic court needs a more efficient way of handling traffic tickets.
      (3) A committee should be appointed to study the inefficiency of the traffic courts.
   C. (1) Management should purchase a more efficient printer.
      (2) Some X5100 printers ought to be studied.
      (3) DATA 100's ought to be junked.
2. Formulate focuses for the problem the class explored.

ASSIGNMENT

Stage 4 Toward Report Writing: Discovering and Stating the Focus
1. **Allow sufficient time for incubation.**
2. **Formulate your focus in two parts: solutions and implementations.**
3. **Seek comments on your focus from your instructor.**

**DEVELOPING,
ORGANIZING,
AND REFINING
THE PAPER**

THE FORMAT OF THE REPORT

Different kinds of reports use different types of organization. Inside most institutions, the format of a definite kind of report is dictated; large companies generally circulate to their employees a manual that outlines the format of different kinds of reports. Reports can use various patterns of organization, depending on the type of report. We will illustrate the feasibility report, which fundamentally uses an evaluative organizaton.

1. A title page, a table of contents, and a list of illustrations (if needed). These parts are guides for the busy reader who may not want to read the entire report. In short reports—those under 750 words—the title page, table of contents, and list of illustrations are usually dispensed with, and the report is cast in the form of a memorandum, with an appropriate heading.
   Date:
   To:
   From:
   Subject:
2. A concise introduction:
   a. Brief statement of the problem
   b. Solution
   c. Implementation } focus (see pp. 308–309)
   This part, a summary of the most important sections of the report, is for those busy readers, usually several job levels above the writer, who need to know only the most important parts of the communication. Notice that what you think of as the meat of the paper—the procedures, the evidence, the reasoning—don't appear here.
3. An overview:
   a. The purposes of the report
   b. The problem to be examined
   c. The scope of the report—an enumeration of the alternative solutions to be discussed later
4. Criteria: a statement of the criteria used to evaluate the alternatives should be given here. The reader needs to know the grounds on which you chose your solution. Criteria for the purchase of a radio receiver might be initial cost, reliability, versatility, and repair costs. Or you might set up the appearance as a criterion. The reader has a right to know.
5. Discussion of alternative solutions in relation to the criteria. This is the lengthiest technical part of the report, an account of whatever research went into selecting the solution judged best. Each alternative is judged in the light of the criteria.
6. A reiteration of the solution and the implementation.

This organization is due to the audience for whom the report is written. Roughly speaking, the very busy reader of reports wants the focus alone—hence, the concise introduction. The busy reader wants a brief overview. Other readers, particularly those who will have to make resource allocation decisions connected to the topic of the report, want the whole story—criteria, evidence, and focus. Your challenge is that the report has to be written for all three audiences.

CLASS EXERCISES

1. Read the following report of Writer 2 and examine its organization. Since this was a short report, the writer chose the memo form.
2. Discuss the following:
   • How has the writer developed each section?
   • How much of this first version was supplied by his Exploration, pp. 304–306?

REPORT

Writer 2   *Date:* October 27, 1979
To: The Honorable James Thin, Presiding Judge, Recorder's Court
From: George Gunther
Subject: Organization of Traffic Court

INTRODUCTION

Traffic Court is confusing, inefficient, inadequate, crowded, and requires several hours to settle the simplest traffic violation. To solve some of these problems, the court should remain in a central downtown location but satellite offices should be placed in five police stations, on a trial basis, by the Michigan State Supreme Court.

OVERVIEW

The purpose of this report is to consider the feasibility of several satellite offices as a promising solution. Several alternative solutions suggest themselves:

1. Traffic Court could be in a building that is designated to serve its contemporary functions.
2. All non-traffic violations, now handled by Traffic Court, could be handled by a separate division of Recorders Court.
3. Minor traffic violations could be paid at any bank, police station, or neighborhood city hall.
4. The lines could be set up to move like those in a bank which allows a person to go to the next available clerk.
5. The computer system could be updated.

CRITERIA

Any effective solution to Traffic Court's problems should be based upon speed and simplicity of paying fines, an adequate facility in which to transact business, an updating of the computer system, all within the budget.

ALTERNATIVES

1. A new building would be too costly without solving any of the other problems except space.
2. If non-traffic violations, which are only heard on Friday, were handled by a division of Recorders Court, the problems would still exist. There are not that many of these type of cases to make much difference. Since these cases can only be heard by a judge, the referee's case load is not lightened.
3. Being able to pay minor traffic violations at any bank, police station, or neighborhood city hall would probably do little good since citizens already have the option of mailing their traffic violations in.
4. If lines were set up to move like those in a bank, which allows a person to go to the next available clerk, it would alleviate congestion immediately. But this would not solve the other problems that the court is plagued with.
5. The purchase of a new computer would be too expensive and would solve just part of the problem because the court usually starts more than an hour late. There are a lot of human errors that a computer could not solve.
6. If Traffic Court had a central downtown headquarters, with several satellite offices placed on trial at five police stations to handle minor traffic violations, it would then be in a position to effectively deal with its problems. This recommendation solves the problems of simplicity and speed of paying fines, the need for an adequate facility in which to transact business, and for an updated computer system. A citizen could come to court at the precinct station in which he received his violation. These offenses could be quickly handled outside the judicial system, through an administrative procedure involving hearings and officers with the right of appeal to the court. The satellite office, which would be located in the precinct station, would have the use of the jail and computers that all precinct stations have at their disposal. The price would not be too great since they would be set up on a trial basis.

RECOMMENDED SOLUTION

The satellite office method should be implemented for a limited period of time at only five precinct stations. This system should be monitored for its effectiveness and cost.

Diction

The diction of reports tends to be relatively formal, although we hasten to add that *formal* does not mean stuffy or inflated. If you mean to say "Radio A costs $4 less per set than Radio B," say so, instead of "Data acquired by this office indicate that, by comparative analysis, there is a differential of $4 in the purchase price of sets A and B in favor of the former." Slang and colloquialisms have no place in report writing, but neither does difficult jargon. The style of report writing aims at conciseness, ease of reading, and precision. Thus, "Data acquired by this office . . ." are bad, but not much worse than Radio A is cheaper than Radio B." How *much* cheaper? The good report is unambiguous, easy to read, and specific in detail.

The style of reports plays down the "I" in an effort to put the emphasis on the subject. There is a difference between "I have discovered that the Xerox 5100 has a printing speed of 5400 lines per minute" and "The Xerox 5100 has a printing speed of 5400 lines per minute." The second sentence removes the emphasis from the writer's discovery of the fact and places the emphasis on the fact.

The distinction between the "I" construction and alternatives becomes very important when you have to draw conclusions and make recommendations. The speed with which the Xerox 5100 prints lines is not a recommendation. It's either a fact or it isn't. But suppose you have to recommend whether your company should buy the Xerox 5100; that recommendation will spring from a consideration of a great many other facts than its speed, such as its initial cost, its frequency of repair, its size, and so on. It is in this stage of the report that the removal of the "I" in any form should be complete—not in order to remove responsibility but in order to indicate that the responsibility rests exactly on your powers of research and reasoning.

Consider these three statements:

I think the 5100 printer should be purchased.

There is reason to believe that the 5100 printer should be purchased.

It is clear that the 5100 printer should be purchased.

All three are the same statement because they are personal (two of them in a disguised fashion), and all three direct attention away from the conclusion itself. The proper statement is clear, unambiguous, and focused on the problem: "The 5100 printer should be purchased."

The first statement is clearly personal because of the "I think." (The question is, What do you know and what have you concluded, and, therefore, what are you recommending?) In the second statement, "There is reason to believe" is a grammatical trick that cannot really hide the statement behind it, "I believe." (Again, the question is not one of belief but of knowledge and judgment.) "It is clear" means "It is clear to me." (Again, the question is, Why is it clear to you?) The statement that needs to be made is simply, "The 5100 printer should be purchased."

CLASS EXERCISE

1. Study the diction of Writer 3's report, which follows.
   • Indicate any words or phrases that would be redundant or inflated *for the audience*.

REPORT

Writer 3 **Date:** December 8, 1979
To: Joseph Deacon, Director of Computer Services, CAS
From: Jason Headley
Subject: Replacement Hardware

INTRODUCTION

The long turn-around time has decreased the quality of work being produced in the computer division of CAS. Replacing old DATA 100 and DOCUMATION printers with more efficient printers would totally eliminate the problem of turn-around time. It is recommended that CAS examine and test new and more efficient printers for possible replacement.

OVERVIEW

Since the addition of the Washington project, the turn-around time at CAS has been increased. Because of this increase in turn-around time they have had to hire new operators to get all of the backed up jobs out. They have also had to increase the number of hours the programmers have to work, causing an unnecessary increase in overtime pay. These long hours have made the programmers very tired and cranky, making the work atmosphere hostile. CAS should look at the possibility of replacing their old printers with either the XEROX 5100 or the IBM 1354.

CRITERIA

The most important criteria for the printer to meet is that it must be faster than their present printers. It must be under $150,000, as the company could only afford two such printers. Lastly, the printer must be very efficient with few errors per print-out. It would also be helpful if the printer could be obtained relatively soon.

Replacing old printers with X5100

The XEROX 5100 printer has a printing speed of approximately 5400 lines per minute, making it three to seven times as fast as CAS' DATA 100 and DOCumation printers. The X5100 is slightly more expensive than their existing printers, making up for these losses with its phenomenal speed and efficiency. Unlike the DOC printers the X5100 requires no diskpack for carriage control, storing them in EPROM. This elimination of the diskpack also eliminates expenses in maintenance, room, and hardware. The reconstruction of the FCB, on the X5100, takes only five minutes, nine times as fast as the DOC reconstruction. The X5100 also has lower case and special characters on the same standard band, eliminating the purchase of an extra band. The chute-type paper stacker on the X5100 is not quite as good as the DOC's feed stacker.

In the long run the staffing would be less. The DOC printer requires only three employees to run it, as compared to the four needed to run the X5100. CAS will, however, need only three X5100s running from 8:00 am to 4:00 pm, as compared to the four DOC printers presently needed to run 24 hours a day. CAS would need only one shift of twelve people a day to run the X5100s, eliminating the extra two shifts of twelve needed now to run the DOCs. CAS would be able to send their programmers home one or two hours earlier every day, because of the increase in efficiency. This cut in pay and personnel will give the company more profit.

The X5100 printers cost $100,000 each (as shown on table 1), making the total for the three needed $300,000. The printers would more than pay for themselves in one year. Cutting programming time will, in one year, give CAS $104,000. The operation cut will give the company $280,320 in just one year. The cut in the cost of maintenance will average $129,540. Totaling the cuts in personnel and payroll will earn CAS a minimum of $513,860 in one year, showing a profit of $213,860 the first year and over half a million each successive year. (Further information on personnel cost and profit can be seen on tables 2 and 4).

Replacing old printers with IBM 1354

The IBM 1354, although it is not quite as impressive as the X5100, should also be considered as an alternative to the problem of turn-around time. Printing at a speed of 3200 lines a minute the IBM 1354 is two to four times as fast as CAS' present printers. It, like the DOC, will require a diskpack to control carriage, representing additional expenses in hardware, room and maintenance. The additional expenses will be cheaper than those of the DOC printers. Reconstruction of the FCB on the IBM printer takes 10 minutes, four and a half times as fast as the reconstruction procedures for the DOC printers. The IBM 1354 is very much similar to the X5100 in most aspects, except for speed it has most of the other qualities.

As with the X5100 staffing would also be cut with the IBM 1354. The three IBM 1354 printers would require a staff of 24 operators working in two shifts to get the work done. The programmers would be able to go home an hour earlier almost every day. This cut in pay and personnel is slight, but would still be beneficial to CAS.

Purchasing the IBM 1354 printers will represent an initial cost $255,000. These printers will, in one year, pay for themselves, just as the X5100 printers will. They will show a profit of not quite $2,000 the first year, but over a quarter of a million each succesive year. (Refer to tables 2 and 4 for more information).

RECOMMENDED SOLUTION

CAS should examine and test the X5100 printer and look at the possibility of purchasing three in the near future. The purchase of three of these printers would increase the quality of work at CAS. The progammers and operators would, once again, be at peace. Most importantly, the company will profit in dollars and cents from not only cuts in staffing but from new clients impressed with CAS' work and efficiency.

Specifications of Printers (table 1)

	DOC	X5100	IBM 1354
Speed	1600–1800 1/m	5000–5400 1/m	3000–3200 1/m
Size (H × W × L)	$5\frac{1}{2}' \times 3' \times 6'$	$5' \times 5' \times 7'$	$5' \times 5' \times 6\frac{1}{2}'$
Carriage control	Diskpack	EPROM	Diskpack
No. of carriage controls	63	0	255
No. of print bands	2	1	2
Paper stacker	Feed	Chute	Chute
Reconstruction of FCB	45 min	5 min	10 min
Special forms	Yes	Yes	Yes
Lower case	Yes[1]	Yes	Yes[1]
Special char.	Yes[1]	Yes	Yes[1]
Air condition	Yes 75°F	Yes 75°F	Yes 70°F
Printer cost	$50,000	$100,000	$70,000
Diskpack cost	$15,000	Not needed	$15,000
Total cost	$65,000	$100,000	$85,000

Personnel Cost (table 2)

	DOC	X5100	IBM 1354
Operation[2]	$420,480 (3)	$140,160 (3)	$280,320 (2)
Programming[3]	$520,000 (2)	$416,000 (0)	$468,000 (1)
Maintenance[4]	$518,160	$388,620	$453,390
Total	$1,458,640	$944,780	$1,201,710

Printer Cost (table 3)

	DOC	X5100	IBM 1354
No. needed	4	3	3
Price each	$65,000	$100,000	$85,000
Total	$260,000	$300,000	$255,000

Profit (table 4)

	DOC	X5100	IBM 1354
First year	$0	$213,860	$1,930
Each successive year	$0	$513,860	$256,930

[1] on separate printing band
[2] figures represent average pay scale; numbers in brackets are no. of shifts
[3] figures represent averages; numbers in brackets are no. of hours of overtime expected
   daily from each programmers (also averages)
[4] figures represent averages

SENTENCE PATTERNS

There is nothing special about the sentence patterns of reports except that they tend to be shorter than they would be in more relaxed prose. The reason for that is simply that shorter sentences are easier to read by people in a hurry. The shorter sentence also tends to give the impression of concise, clear statement.

The syntax does tend to be more formal than in prose in the expressive aim, and that formality is expressed in several ways. Embedded clauses tend to come before the sentences to which they are attached: "Although Radio A has a better appearance, it does not operate as well . . . ." Prepositions tend to lead, not follow, their nouns: "The men with whom I worked," not "The men I worked with." What this formality expresses, of course, is the roles you and the reader play: subordinate and superior. The prose reflects the same protocol that you would observe, for example, if you were being introduced to a person of higher authority. Finally, professional writing demands Standard Written English, typed on a good quality paper with few or no erasures, and no mistakes in grammar or spelling. Since style is the major means by which you project a personality to the audience, it is imperative that the personality projected be professional: competent, efficient, educated to the level of the position.

Sentence-combining

CLASS
EXERCISES

1. As a last exercise, study the following combined patterns. Practice combining the two sets of sentences according to the pattern above them.

2. Examine the reports in this chapter, identifying combined patterns.

3. Rewrite any sentences that should be combined.

IV. COMBINED PATTERNS

Pattern A **All the newspapers seem to be running wine columns these days, and more and more people are going in for wine tasting, wine one-upmanship, and other forms of recreation that are connected with the juice of the noble grape.**

1. All of Britain bubbled.
2. The bubbling was with celebration.
3. The jubilee was commemorated.
4. The jubilee was marking the reign.
5. The reign is a 25-year one.
6. The reign is of Elizabeth.
7. The commemoration was by a carriage procession.
8. The procession was dazzling.
9. The commemoration was by a "Royal Progress."
10. The progress took place on the Thames.
11. The commemoration was by bonfires.
12. There were hundreds of these.
13. The bonfires were on beacon hills.
14. The hills are all over the United Kingdom.

1. The war hit even harder.
2. It was the Second World War.
3. Tennis courts were torn up.
4. The tearing was to make way for patches.
5. The patches were vegetable patches.
6. Eggs seemed to disappear.
7. The disappearing was by magic.
8. Our leaders encouraged us.
9. The encouragement was to eat pemmican.

Pattern A1 **We checked into the Westwind Hotel, which had neither log fires nor a bar, but effective central heating, unnecessary hot-water bottles in the cupboards, a bath as big as a boat, and an affable welcome.**

1. Kerry decided.
2. The decision was for the time being.
3. The decision was on an essay.
4. The essay would not challenge her.
5. It would not teach her anything.
6. The essay would satisfy the instructor.
7. The essay would be painless to write.
8. It would get a sure C.

1. We made an offer.
2. The offer was on the property.
3. The property was island property.
4. The property did not have power.
5. The power was electrical.
6. The property did not have a water pump.
7. The property did have a cabin.
8. The cabin was tiny.
9. It was made of logs.
10. The property had a waterfall.
11. The waterfall was 60 feet.
12. The property had a stand of hemlocks.
13. They were towering.
14. The property had a view.
15. The view was of the sound.

Pattern A2 **On any weekend, Jack can quite easily sleep all day or, if he is particularly energetic, arise before noon.**

1. This takes place in the wild.
2. Caribou may pose.
3. They may do so endlessly.
4. The posing is for the camera.
5. The caribou may streak away quickly.
6. The streaking happens if the caribou sense nervousness.
7. It also happens if they sense fear.

---

1. This happens at the planetarium.
2. Visitors can enjoy.
3. The enjoying is of the displays.
4. The displays are weekly.
5. This happens when conditions are favorable.
6. The conditions are atmospheric.
7. Visitors can view the planets.
8. They can view the stars.
9. The viewing is through the telescope.
10. The telescope is mounted.
11. The telescope is refracting.

Pattern B **The SALT talks began two days early, catching the chief negotiators off guard, and moved quickly to a stalemate, quashing hopes for a settlement and leaving both participants and observers stunned.**

1. The four-wheeler sped.
2. It was tough.
3. It was a Cherokee.
4. The speeding was up the road.
5. The road was abandoned.

(sentence set continues on next page)

6. It was a logging road.
7. The four-wheeler kicked up dust.
8. There were clouds of dust.
9. The four-wheeler turned off.
10. It went into open country.
11. It negotiated the terrain.
12. The terrain was rocky.
13. The negotiation was with ease.
14. The four-wheeler headed toward the summit.
15. The summit was round.
16. It was the summit of the hill.

---

1. Bird watchers usually keep lists.
2. The bird watchers are amateur.
3. The lists are species lists.
4. Bird watchers note as many details as possible.
5. The details are specific.
6. Bird watchers become more and more curious.
7. This happens gradually.
8. The curiosity is about their data.
9. Bird watchers conjure up hypotheses.
10. The hypotheses are provocative.
11. Bird watchers plan for more observations.
12. The observations are extensive.

Pattern C **Professor Williams calls the kind of writing that he advocates in his lectures "textured," writing that goes beyond the simplest communication of the simplest ideas, beyond the plainest of the plain styles.**

1. Artists created forms.
2. The artists were black.
3. The artists were jazz artists.
4. The artists were such as Charlie Parker, Eubie Blake, and Duke Ellington.
5. The forms were musical.
6. They were forms that were new.
7. The newness was dynamic.
8. The forms established them as masters.
9. The masters were of their own craft.
10. The forms established them as legends.
11. The legends were in their own times.

---

1. The introduction led.
2. The introduction was of DDT.
3. The leading was to consequences.
4. The consequences were largely unforseen.

5. The consequences touch on the preservation.
6. The preservation is of wildlife.
7. The consequences touch on the preservation.
8. The preservation is of man himself.

D. Free Exercises in Combined Patterns *Combine the following sets of sentences in the most effective way you can find to do so.*

1. A hill was nearby.
2. The hill was steep.
3. We swung off the hill.
4. We did so sometimes.
5. We swung from ropes.
6. The swinging was like Tarzan.
7. The ropes were tied.
8. The tying was to branches.
9. They were tree branches.

————————

1. The following is on television.
2. The walls are painted.
3. The walls are in a cell.
4. It is a jail cell.
5. The paint is white.
6. The white is brilliant.
7. The white is glowing.
8. The walls are in a real jail cell.
9. These walls are filthy.

————————

1. He made one last attempt.
2. The attempt was vain.
3. The attempt was to make out what I had written.
4. He shook the page loose.
5. He crumpled the page up.
6. He tossed the page.
7. The tossing was in the other direction.
8. The tossing was casual.

ASSIGNMENT **Stage 5** Toward Report Writing: Developing, Organizing, and Refining the Paper
1. **Organize your material.**
2. **Write a first version of your report.**
3. **Refine your style.**

CRITIQUING THE REPORT

The unique property of report writing is that an ultimate and unassailable judge exists. If you submit a report to a superior, you get a simple, definitive answer. The recommendation of the report will be followed, or it will not be followed.

In critiquing, therefore, the critic should try to play the role of the intended audience as thoroughly as possible. And what the audience is looking for is an organization, developed adequately in its parts, that follows this pattern:

1. Title Page or Heading
2. Introduction
3. Overview
4. Criteria
5. Discussion of Alternative Solutions
6. Recommended Solution

REPORT: FIRST VERSION

Writer 1 *Date:* November 12, 1979
To: Betsy Bratteng, R.N., Supervisor of Nursing
From: Elizabeth Holliday, Nursing Assistant
Subject: Assignment of Nurses

INTRODUCTION

The current method of assigning individual duties to Nursing Assistants on the medical-surgical units at X Hospital does not allow the aides to deliver the best care possible to total care patients. This problem could be remedied by assigning workers in teams rather than singly.

OVERVIEW

It is very difficult for a single person to give good care to a patient who requires a lot of attention. It is impossible for a worker to individually turn comatose patients as frequently as necessary, give them adequate decubitis care, and align them properly. These duties require two people joining energy, perhaps working as a team sharing all duties or as two workers with individual duties working together on their most difficult patients. These are the solutions to be discussed in this report.

CRITERIA

In order for a system of assigning duties to Nursing Assistants to successfully fill the needs of all patients it must—

a) allow the Assistant to carry out specific duties including taking blood pressures, temperatures and pulse rates, charting and other individual jobs effeciently,

b) make it possible for the workers to join efforts in the care of total-care patients, O.R. patients, and comatose patients.

DISCUSSION OF ALTERNATIVES

There are two team work alternatives to review. The first involves two Nursing Assistants being assigned one set of patients. This method would allow the two aides together to help those patients who need more help than one worker alone can provide. This solution requires that the individual duties be shared among the workers rather than having these jobs evenly divided between workers or in one worker carrying the load of another. For example, the taking and charting of vital signs is an individual job which has to be divided, as do sugar and acetone tests, ambulation of patients, blood pressures and cleaning duties. Leaving the division of these duties to the workers themselves would lead to arguments concerning who does what and as a result, does not allow the assistant to carry out individual tasks efficiently.

The second team work approach is the better combination of strict individual duties and the team work method previously mentioned. The individual duties for specific patients would be assigned to each assistant. Along with these assignments, each worker would be a part of a two worker team who would combine efforts to care patients of either aide who require more care than one person can give. Using this format, a Nursing Assistant would be able to perform his/her specific individual duties (vital signs, charting) efficiently and would receive assistance to give the best possible care to comatose patients, O.R. patients and other total care patients.

RECOMMENDED SOLUTION

The combination team work-individual duty method of assignment of Nursing Assistant duties should be initiated into the procedures at X Hospital.

CRITIQUE:
Writer 1

Focus

The focus is announced in the introduction and then maintained throughout the paper, although one element, as we shall see, seems to have dropped out of part of the overview.

Development

The difficulty surfaces here. There is a logical and a psychological aspect to the difficulty, since the writer is dealing with a hostile audience. Logically, the "problem" the paper addresses is not the present system but, as the writer admits, "to deliver the best care possible to total care patients." There are, then, not "two team work alternatives" to be considered (because that excludes the present system) but three:

1. individual assignments
2. team work assignment—model 1
3. team work assignment—model 2

Psychologically, this logical division is preferable because the writer's version ignores that Nurse X's system is a possibility, thereby running the risk of making her even more hostile. Her system is not only a possibility, it's a fact, while the other two are suggestions.

Any reasonable person would, after reading the analysis, conclude that the central issue is that it takes two people to lift, shift, and reposition one person who is almost inert. That is not an arguable issue, given the laws of physics, unless the job description of a nurse's assistant includes the requirement of more than normal male strength.

But that central issue is hidden because the nurse's assistant who wrote the paper tries to fight her superior on her own battlefield, where the supervisor is the expert. Corporals don't defeat generals, but civilians sometimes win over or win out over generals. A nursing assistant is unlikely to win out over a nursing supervisor when she asserts that she is a better nursing supervisor than the present one, who is also her audience. But a nursing assistant can possibly turn her supervisor around if she argues the simple principle that one nursing assistant cannot lift twice her own weight once every three hours. That's the issue.

Organization

The overall organization follows the order of a feasibility report. The headings are faithful to that outline. But the contents are not organized properly. The third alternative is missing. In addition, the alternatives are not clearly set out. In the discussion of alternatives, the first team work alternative is set up so as to oppose the present system, but the present system then appears not as one system but as two: "This solution requires that the individual duties be shared among the workers rather than having these jobs evenly divided between workers or in one worker carrying the load of another." That sentence implies that under the present system two contradictory situations exist:

1. jobs divided equally between workers
2. jobs divided unequally between workers

If that is so, then the "system" is no system at all, in which case the writer has a strong argument that she is not using effectively. Or is it that the system does *in theory* divide jobs equally between workers, but *in practice* one worker has to carry the load of another? In that case, the system doesn't work. But the reader has no way of knowing the truth, because the alternatives are not set out clearly and coherently.

Furthermore, there is a hidden principle of division of duties that for some reason doesn't surface here. What produces this paper isn't so much that some patients require a "lot of care" and others do not, but, instead, that some patients require a *kind* of care that others do not. Two quite different types of care appear in the report:

1. light, technical duty, that ranges from taking blood pressures to cleaning
2. heavy physical duty that involves constant lifting, shifting, and positioning of patients

The first can be done individually; the second requires a team. Yet that point—the crucial one in the paper—is never stated. A writer cannot organize material that has not been divided into logical units.

Style

The writer deserves credit for trying to be concise. But the desire for brevity leads her astray at critical points. And, as is so often the case, problems with diction, for instance, occur in this sentence from "discussion of alternatives":

For example, the taking and charting of vital signs is an individual job which has to be divided, as do sugar and acetone tests, ambulation of patients, blood pressures and cleaning duties.

Something is drastically wrong with that sentence:

1. How can an "individual job" be "divided"? Does that mean that the two tasks have to be assigned to one person? Or that one task has to be assigned to two persons? Or that, as in some hospitals, nursing assistants take the "vital signs" but may not chart the results, that task being reserved to the R.N.?

2. What does "as do sugar and acetone tests" mean? Nursing assistants (or for that matter, R.N.'s and doctors) do not do sugar or acetone tests: they simply draw the samples and the lab runs the tests; in some hospitals, only R.N.'s can draw the samples. More exactly, why is this a duty to be divided in the writer's situation?

3. What does it mean to say that "blood pressures" have to be divided? The taking of blood pressure? The assigning of who takes blood pressure?

Conventions

The conventions are generally observed. A word or phrase was dropped from the third sentence of the second paragraph on "discussion of alternatives."

REVISED REPORT

Writer 1 *Date:* November 17, 1979
To: Betsy Bratteng, R.N., Supervisor of Nursing
From: Elizabeth Holliday, Nursing Aide
Subject: Assignment of Nurses

INTRODUCTION

The current method of assigning duties to Nursing Assistants on the medical-surgical units at X Hospital does not allow the assistants to help deliver the best care possible to total-care patients because assistants are assigned as individuals to individual tasks. This problem could be remedied by assigning workers in teams rather than singly.

OVERVIEW

It is very difficult for one assistant to give adequate care to a patient who requires frequent attention, especially when that attention requires frequent lifting and turning of the patient. It is impossible for one female aide to turn comatose patients as frequently as is necessary. A duty such as this requires two aides, working as a team in all their duties or as two workers with individual duties that can be performed singly and joint duties that can only be performed by the team.

CRITERIA

In order for a system of assigning duties to Nursing Assistants to meet the needs of all patients, it must

1. Allow the Assistant to carry out individual duties efficiently: taking blood pressures, temperatures, and pulse rates and charting them; obtaining samples for sugar and acetone tests; ambulation of patients; cleaning; and changing linen,
2. permit Assistants to join efforts in duties beyond the strength of individual aides: turning and positioning total-care, O.R., and comatose patients,
3. avoid waste of time.

DISCUSSION OF ALTERNATIVES

There are three alternatives:
1. Assigning individual assistants to individual patients. This is the present system. It has the advantage of being easy to schedule and it meets the first criterion, since any of the tasks listed can be performed by a single aide. It does not, however, meet the second or third criterion. Few aides possess the strength to lift, turn, and position unconscious or otherwise helpless patients. The aide struggles to

do the work properly, not only wasting time but endangering the condition of the patient and the aide herself.

2. Assigning two Nursing Assistants as a total team. All work would be shared by a team of two aides, rather than having the work evenly divided between aides. This method would meet the first and second criteria, but not the third. There is no need for two people to take blood pressures, temperatures, etc.; that would waste time. Supposing the aides attempted to divide those duties on their own, there is the possibility of argument and ill-will and consequent further waste of time.

3. Assigning Nursing Assistants on a modified team system. Individual duties for specific patients would be assigned to each assistant. But each aide would also be a part of a team of two who would combine efforts to care for patients who require more care than one person can give. This method would satisfy all three criteria. It has the slight disadvantage of requiring the supervisor to draw up a slightly more complex schedule.

RECOMMENDATION

The modified team system of assigning Nursing Assistants should be initiated at X Hospital.

CLASS
EXERCISES

1. Using the Critical Guide, do a critique of Writer 3's Report (pp. 314–317).
2. Compare Writer 1's Revised Report with her first Report (pp. 322–323).
3. Using the Critical Guide and working in groups, critique each other's reports.

ASSIGNMENT

Stage 6 Toward Report Writing: Critiquing and Rewriting

1. Do a self-critique of your report based on criticism from your instructor and group.
2. Revise your report.

II/GUIDE TO EDITING
AND
SENTENCE-COMBINING

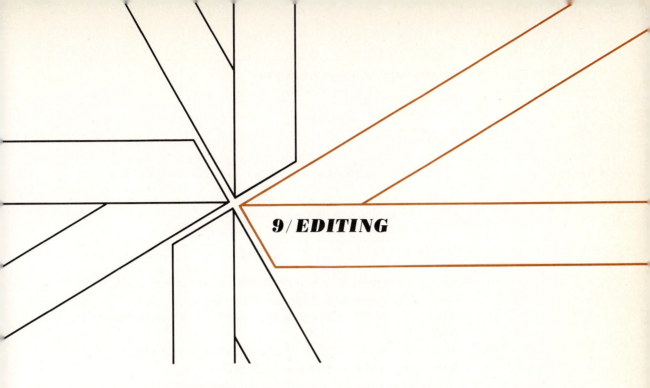

9/EDITING

Most of the writing we do is meant to be shared, to be presented or published. Once we mail a letter or send a piece of writing off to a journal or submit it to a professor, we are usually unable to make further changes: the piece of writing, for better or worse, represents us. As editors of our own work, therefore, we examine every word, every sentence, with a "fine-tooth eye," assuring ourselves that what we have written will be accurate and worthy. This chapter will help you refine your editing skills through a series of checklists for reference as you edit your work. Each checklist treats a particular grammatical, punctuation, spelling, or mechanical *convention* (that is, a widely accepted and established practice).

Editing a paper is one of the last stages in the process of writing. As such, it comes at a time when you are ready to turn your attention from the major substance of a paper to its conventional or surface features (spelling, punctuation, and so on). You probably know from experience that your audiences (professors, employers, business associates) expect adherence to the conventions of edited American English, and that you are often judged by your ability to produce writing that meets such standards.

Conscientious use of the following editing checklists can help you to achieve conventional correctness. But we do not mean to suggest that you should work through the entire set of checklists for every paper you write. Different writers have different editing problems, and by now, with the help of your instructor and classmates, you have discovered your own major problems. We suggest, then, that you concentrate on the checklists that apply to your editing difficulties. And as you strive to create conventionally correct pieces of writing, remember that *all* writers make errors. Poor writers often view errors as failures, as dead ends. Good writers, on the other hand, view their errors as practice in learning how not to make the same errors again!

GRAMMATICAL CONVENTIONS

A. NUMBER

Checklist

√ Does the word in question refer to one (*singular*) or more than one (*plural*)?

√ If the word is plural, is its ending correct?
  - Add *s* if the word ends in a vowel plus *y*. (boys; keys)
  - Change *y* to *i* and add *es* if the word ends in a consonant plus *y*. (dictionaries)
  - Add *es* if the word ends in a consonant and the plural ending is pronounced as a separate syllable. (sandwiches)
  - Add *s* if the plural ending is NOT pronounced as a separate syllable. (books; papers)
  - Add *s* if the word is a proper name and ends in *y*. (Careys)
  - If the word ends in *o*, check your dictionary.

√ If the word is a number or letter, is the plural formed by adding *'s*? (straight A's; a pair of 4's)

√ Can you detect any unnecessary shifts in number?

UNEDITED	EDITED
1. Rest <u>home's</u> are seldom restful.	1. Rest <u>homes</u> are seldom restful.
2. Newton, Locke, and Leibniz were famous <u>contemporarys</u>.	2. Newton, Locke, and Leibniz were famous <u>contemporaries.</u>
3. Most students are unhappy when they receive <u>Ds</u>.	3. Most students are unhappy when they receive <u>D's</u>.
4. The <u>banjoes</u> seemed almost alive in the skilled hands of Roy Clark and Buck Trent.	4. The <u>banjos</u> seemed almost alive in the skilled hands of Roy Clark and Buck Trent.
5. How many <u>lunchs</u> have you missed lately?	5. How many <u>lunches</u> have you missed lately?
6. The <u>Henries</u> have asked me to join them at the concert.	6. The <u>Henrys</u> have asked me to join them at the concert.

B. TENSE

Checklist

√ Is the tense of each verb accurate?
  - If the tense is *present*, the action is happening now. (People <u>talk</u>.)

–If the tense is *past*, the action happened before now and is completed. (People <u>talked</u>.)

–If the tense is *future*, the action will happen later. (People <u>will</u> <u>talk</u>.)

–If the tense is *present perfect*, the action began in the past and may continue into the present. (People <u>have</u> <u>talked</u>.)

–If the tense is *past perfect*, the action happened in the past before another past time or event. (People <u>had</u> <u>talked</u>.)

–If the tense is *future perfect*, the action will be completed in the future before another time or event in the future. (People <u>will</u> <u>have</u> <u>talked</u>.)

–If the tense is *present progressive*, the action is ongoing in the present. (People <u>are</u> <u>talking</u>.)

–If the tense is *past progressive*, the action was ongoing at an earlier time. (People <u>were</u> <u>talking</u>.)

–If the tense is *future progressive*, the ongoing action will take place at a later time. (People <u>will</u> <u>be</u> <u>talking</u>.)

✓ If the verb is in one of the three perfect tenses, is it formed by using the auxiliary verb *has, had,* or *will have* with the past participle?

✓ Are unnecessary or confusing shifts in tense avoided?

✓ If direct discourse is used, are the verbs in the tense that the speaker used?

UNEDITED

1. A suburban homestead that <u>was</u> solar-powered and produc<u>ed</u> food all year long in both an outside garden and a solar greenhouse begins to make self-sufficiency possible.

2. The great Russian weightlifter has broke_ seven records this year.

3. The frightened child asked, "Who <u>it was</u>?"

4. Jody has studied so many hours that <u>he forgot</u> what sleep is like.

5. In the latest incoherent thriller flick, long passages of cinematic exposition alternate with gory bits, which <u>were</u> frequently presented in slow motion to extend the violence.

EDITED

1. A suburban homestead that <u>is</u> solar-powered and produc<u>es</u> food all year long in both an outside garden and a solar greenhouse begins to make self-sufficiency possible.

2. The great Russian weightlifter has brok<u>en</u> seven records this year.

3. The frightened child asked, "Who <u>is it</u>?"

4. Jody has studied so many hours that <u>he has forgotten</u> what sleep is like.

5. In the latest incoherent thriller flick, long passages of cinematic exposition alternate with gory bits, which <u>are</u> frequently presented in slow motion to extend the violence.

C. AGREEMENT BETWEEN SUBJECTS AND VERBS

Checklist

✓ If the subject is singular, is its verb also singular?

✓ If the subject is plural, is its verb also plural?

✓ If the subject is third person and singular (<u>he</u>, <u>she</u>, <u>it</u> or a noun that <u>he</u>, <u>she</u>, or <u>it</u> can be substituted for, as in <u>Janet</u>, <u>Gordon</u>, or <u>the game</u>), does the form of the present tense verb end in *s*?

✓ If the verb is a form of *to be*, does its form agree with the subject? (I <u>am</u>; you <u>are</u>; he, she, or it <u>is</u>; we <u>are</u>; you <u>are</u>; they <u>are</u>.)

✓ If two singular subjects are joined by *or* or *nor*, is the verb singular? (Either Dave or Cathy <u>is</u> <u>willing</u> to pick you up.)

✓ If two plural subjects are joined by *or* or *nor*, is the verb plural? (Either first-year or second-year students <u>are</u> <u>enrolled</u> in this course.)

✓ If one singular and one plural subject are joined by *or* or *nor*, does the verb agree with the nearer form? (Neither Ruth nor her classmates <u>want</u> to do the assignment.)

UNEDITED

1. The dolphin brain resemble the human brain in being very large and very wrinkled.

2. Carrie Chapman Catt and Elizabeth Cady Stanton was women's rights leaders.

3. Dr. Powell be my best instructor this term.

4. Each of the boys tend to imitate his hero.

5. Neither a biographical section nor a gazetteer section appear in *Webster's Third New International Dictionary.*

6. The name *opossum,* along with *moose, terrapin,* and *caribou,* are of Indian origin.

7. A bird or a bee or a crab communicate information, emotions, and warnings.

8. Neither he nor his roommates eats in the cafeteria.

EDITED

1. The dolphin brain resembles the human brain in being very large and very wrinkled.

2. Carrie Chapman Catt and Elizabeth Cady Stanton were women's rights leaders.

3. Dr. Powell is my best instructor this term.

4. Each of the boys tends to imitate his hero.

5. Neither a biographical section nor a gazetteer section appears in *Webster's Third New International Dictionary.*

6. The name *opossum,* along with *moose, terrapin,* and *caribou,* is of Indian origin.

7. A bird or a bee or a crab communicates information, emotions, and warnings.

8. Neither he nor his roommates eat in the cafeteria.

D. AGREEMENT BETWEEN PRONOUNS AND THEIR ANTECEDENTS

Checklist

√ If the antecedent is singular, is the pronoun singular?

√ If the antecedent is plural, is the pronoun plural?

√ If the antecedent is first person, is the pronoun first person?

√ If the antecedent is second person, is the pronoun second person?

√ If the antecedent is third person, is the pronoun third person?

√ If the antecedent is *everyone, everybody, each, either, neither, nobody, one,* or *anyone,* is the pronoun singular?

√ If the antecedent is two nouns joined by *and,* is the pronoun plural?

√ If the antecedent is two singular nouns joined by *or* or *nor,* is the pronoun singular?

√ If the antecedent is two plural nouns joined by *or* or *nor,* is the pronoun plural?

UNEDITED

1. Nuclear reactors create the potential for disasters so severe that it could change the whole course of human history.

2. Each student should bring their book to class.

3. Although the members complained, the president ignored him.

4. When a student begins to write an essay, you need to have a clear focus.

5. William Aide and Robert Aitken will perform his arrangement of Mozart's "Flute Quartet."

6. Either Groucho or Harpo loses their pants in the final battle scene of the Marx Brothers' *Duck Soup.*

EDITED

1. Nuclear reactors create the potential for disasters so severe that they could change the whole course of human history.

2. Each student should bring his or her book to class.

3. Although the members complained, the president ignored them.

4. When a student begins to write an essay, he or she needs to have a clear focus.

5. William Aide and Robert Aitken will perform their arrangement of Mozart's "Flute Quartet."

6. Either Groucho or Harpo loses his pants in the final battle scene of the Marx Brothers' *Duck Soup.*

E. PRONOUN REFERENCE

Checklist

√ Is the referent or antecedent for every pronoun present in the sentence?

√ Is the referent or antecedent for each pronoun clear?

√ If the pronoun is *this*, as in "this perplexed me," is the word *this* followed by a specifying noun? (This stubbornness perplexed me.)

√ If the pronoun *this*, *that*, *such*, or *which* stands for a preceding statement, is the relationship between the pronoun and the preceding statement absolutely clear? (<u>Sara missed all her classes today, which shocked me</u> should be edited to read <u>I was shocked that Sara missed all her classes today</u>.)

UNEDITED	EDITED
1. Both his father and mother are in the hospital, and his sister is home alone. <u>This</u> caused Jim to withdraw from school.	**1.** Both his father and mother are in the hospital, and his sister is home alone. <u>This unexpected emergency</u> caused Jim to withdraw from school.
2. Since the strike ended at midnight, <u>they</u> say production should resume within twenty-four hours.	**2.** Since the strike ended at midnight, <u>union spokesmen</u> say production should resume within twenty-four hours.
3. Barbara shouted to Sue while <u>she</u> waited in line.	**3.** While Barbara waited in line, <u>she</u> shouted to Sue.
4. <u>It</u> says in the paper to expect the first snowfall before Thanksgiving.	**4.** <u>The paper</u> says to expect the first snowfall before Thanksgiving.
5. After Carlos attended Dr. Smith's class and Dr. Freeman's class, he decided to enroll in <u>it</u>.	**5.** Carlos attended both Dr. Smith's and Dr. Freeman's lectures before he decided to enroll in Dr. Smith's class.
6. Helen's voice was low and mellifluous, <u>which</u> pleased her.	**6.** Helen's low and mellifluous voice pleased her.

F. CASE (SUBJECTIVE, OBJECTIVE, POSSESSIVE)

Checklist

√ If a pronoun is the subject of a verb, is the pronoun in the subjective case? (*I; we; he; she; they; who*)

√ If a pronoun is the object of a verb, is it in the objective case? (*me; us; him; her; them; whom*)

√ If a pronoun is the object of a preposition, is the pronoun in the objective case?

√ If the pronoun is the subject OR object of an infinitive, is the pronoun in the objective case?

√ If the pronoun is part of a compound, is it in the case that it would be in if it stood alone?

√ If the pronoun or noun comes before and modifies a gerund (an *ing* word used as a noun), is the pronoun or noun in the possessive case? (Joe's leaving disappointed him.)

√ Are singular possessive nouns formed with *'s*? (Mary's coat is here. The Jones's house was sold today.)

√ Are plural possessive nouns formed by adding *s'*? (The boys' coats are over there. The Joneses' houses were sold today.)

UNEDITED

1. <u>Nelson and him</u> were going over some difficult technical problems when we arrived.

2. The snowballs hit <u>he and I</u> squarely between our shoulders.

3. The responsibility must rest on <u>she and I</u>.

4. Professor Foster asked <u>he and I</u> to lead the class discussion.

5. <u>Him and the umpire</u> debated the call until the ump threw him out of the game.

6. <u>Sheila</u> asking the question surprised all of us.

7. <u>Ramonas</u> sister called to say that Ramona will be home tonight.

8. I wish the professor had chosen someone <u>elses</u> paper to discuss in class.

9. The <u>womens'</u> room and the <u>mens'</u> room in the old railway station have been closed for repairs.

10. The two <u>violinist's</u> performance was well received by the audience.

11. The victory is <u>theirs</u>, not <u>your's</u>.

EDITED

1. <u>Nelson and he</u> were going over some difficult technical problems when we arrived.

2. The snowballs hit <u>him and me</u> squarely between our shoulders.

3. The responsibility must rest on <u>her and me</u>.

4. Professor Foster asked <u>him and me</u> to lead the class discussion.

5. <u>He and the umpire</u> debated the call until the ump threw him out of the game.

6. <u>Sheila's</u> asking the question surprised all of us.

7. <u>Ramona's</u> sister called to say that Ramona will be home tonight.

8. I wish the professor had chosen someone <u>else's</u> paper to discuss in class.

9. The <u>women's</u> room and the <u>men's</u> room in the old railway station have been closed for repairs.

10. The two <u>violinists'</u> performance was well received by the audience.

11. The victory is <u>theirs</u>, not <u>yours</u>.

The following passage contains errors in *number, tense, agreement between subjects and verbs, agreement between pronouns and antecedents, pronoun reference,* and *case.* Edit the passage carefully, correcting every error you can find.

The student's I usually encounter on campus have graduated from high school recently and were attempting to cope with the new experience of going to a large university. Many of these are confused and frustrated by the impersonal treatment he or she received in classes of 100 or more and by the sometimes apparently backward educational system with which they must deal. Consequently, its easy for those in his or her first year to find fault with almost everything, from poor food service and high prices to incompetent professor's, in order to release some of their frustrations'. But this was as far as most bothers to go, and only those students who chooses to be involved with council and committees for change seems to have ideas for solutions to them.

G. 1. SENTENCE FAULTS: FRAGMENTS

Checklist

√ Does the sentence have both a subject and a verb that can change tense? If not, the sentence is a fragment.

√ Is an *ing* word used as the only verb? If so, the sentence is a fragment.

√ If the subject is *who, which, whose,* or *whom,* is the sentence a question? If not, the sentence is a fragment.

✓ If the subject and verb are introduced by a subordinating word such as *although, since, when, after, because,* or *while,* is this clause connected to a main clause? If not, the sentence is a fragment.

✓ Can the sentence be turned into a question without omitting any words? If it cannot be, then the sentence is a fragment.

✓ If a fragment appears in your finished essay, is it used purposely to achieve emphasis?

UNEDITED

1. Sidney recently saw the revue *Ain't Misbehavin'*. <u>Which is a delightful tribute to Fats Waller.</u>

2. Mozart's *Mitridate Re di Ponto* is a tremendous achievement. <u>Showing Mozart's uncanny gift for characterization through music and his incredible understanding of what the human voice can actually do.</u>

3. The convicted murderer recanted his confession as soon as the sentence was passed. <u>Although he originally pleaded guilty.</u>

4. Thirty-five million Americans have high blood pressure. <u>Including one out of four persons over age 18 and growing numbers of children.</u>

5. Your muffler emits nerve-jarring, scraping sounds as it drags down the road. <u>Because the exhaust system has suffered a breakdown.</u>

6. Coleus, impatiens, and geraniums are the easiest plants to grow from cuttings. <u>Especially if the stems are dipped in a rooting hormone.</u>

7. How can we become better writers? Only by immersing ourselves in the entire writing process.

EDITED

1. Sidney recently saw the revue *Ain't Misbehavin'*, <u>which is a delightful tribute to Fats Waller.</u>

2. Mozart's *Mitridate Re di Ponto* is a tremendous achievement, <u>showing Mozart's uncanny gift for characterization through music and his incredible understanding of what the human voice can actually do.</u>

3. <u>Although the convicted murderer originally pleaded guilty</u>, he recanted his confession as soon as the sentence was passed.

4. Thirty-five million Americans, <u>including one out of four persons over age 18 and growing numbers of children,</u> have high blood pressure.

5. <u>Because the exhaust system has suffered a breakdown,</u> your muffler emits nerve-jarring, scraping sounds as it drags down the road.

6. Coleus, impatiens, and geraniums are the easiest plants to grow from cuttings, <u>especially if the stems are dipped in a rooting hormone.</u>

7. (Intentional fragment. Leave as is.)

G. 2. SENTENCE FAULTS: FUSED SENTENCES

Checklist

√ If the sentence contains two or more main clauses, are they joined by *and, but, or, nor, for, yet, so,* or by a semicolon? If not, the main clauses are fused sentences.

UNEDITED	EDITED
1. Everything on the Mediterranean has been strained beyond limit by the hoards of sunworshippers as a result, the pollution of the sea is worse than ever.	**1.** Everything on the Mediterranean has been strained beyond limit by the hoards of sunworshippers; as a result, the pollution of the sea is worse than ever.
2. Start with this 10¢ coupon then get details at your store on how to save $1.00.	**2.** Start with this 10¢ coupon, and then get details at your store on how to save $1.00.
3. Wine industry people tend to rate a winery's size by annual production in cases storage capacity in gallons can also indicate physical size.	**3.** Wine industry people tend to rate a winery's size by annual production in cases, but storage capacity in gallons can also indicate physical size.
4. John left for classes Tim went to work.	**4.** Tom left for classes, and Tim went to work.
5. I might stay I might go I'll have to wait and see.	**5.** I might stay, or I might go; I'll have to wait and see.

G. 3. SENTENCE FAULTS: COMMA SPLICES

Checklist

√ If the sentence contains more than one main clause, are the clauses joined by only a comma? If so, the sentence is a comma splice.

√ Are two main clauses joined by a comma plus a word such as *therefore, however,* or *although?* If so, the sentence is a comma splice.

UNEDITED	EDITED
1. To test a turkey for doneness, make a small cut in the thickest part, no pink should show.	**1.** To test a turkey for doneness, make a small cut in the thickest part; no pink should show.
2. We had a Dante's *Inferno* among my father's books, such books were common in rural districts at the time.	**2.** We had a Dante's *Inferno* among my father's books. Such books were common in rural districts at the time.

3. The long, white beaches on Barbados are warm year round, therefore tourists flock there in every season.

3. The long, white beaches on Barbados are warm year-round, so tourists flock there in every season.

4. The quarterback held onto the ball, however he was sacked by two blitzing linebackers.

4. The quarterback held onto the ball, but he was sacked by two blitzing linebackers.

OR

Although the quarterback held onto the ball, he was sacked by two blitzing linebackers.

OR

The quarterback held onto the ball; however, he was sacked by two blitzing linebackers.

H. DANGLING AND MISPLACED MODIFIERS

Checklist

√ Does each modifier in the sentence *clearly* refer to the word(s) it describes?

√ Could the modifier possibly describe *either* the word before it or the word after it? If so, the modifier is *squinting* (it looks both ways at once).

√ If the modifier is an introductory phrase such as "Walking down the road," does it modify the subject of the main clause? If not, the modifier is *dangling*.

√ Is each modifier placed as closely as possible to the word(s) it modifies? If not, the modifier is *misplaced*.

UNEDITED

1. Properly pickled, no one can resist a mushroom.

EDITED

1. Properly pickled, a mushroom is irresistible.

OR

No one can resist a properly pickled mushroom.

2. Students who practice writing often will begin to improve their styles.

2. Students who often practice writing will begin to improve their styles.

OR

Students who practice writing will often begin to improve their writing.

3. <u>Riding my bike peaceably</u> the gas-guzzling Chrysler almost ran me down.

3. <u>Riding my bike peaceably,</u> I was almost run down by a gas-guzzling Chrysler.

4. New sports-medicine clinics have sprung up to care for people <u>all over the nation</u> <u>wounded in the pursuit of physical fitness.</u>

4. New sports-medicine clinics have sprung up <u>all over the nation</u> to care for people <u>wounded in the pursuit of physical fitness.</u>

5. The beloved maestro waved to the audience with his baton <u>filled with expectancy.</u>

5. The beloved maestro waved with his baton to the audience <u>filled with expectancy.</u>

6. The man with the dog <u>who was asking questions</u> startled us.

6. The man, who had a dog, startled us with his questions.

I. PARALLEL OR GRAMMATICALLY EQUAL STRUCTURES

Checklist

✓ In a series of words, does each item in the series have the same form—a noun followed by a noun, a gerund by a gerund, a participle by a participle, and so on? (The garden was filled with <u>rhododendrons</u>, <u>azaleas</u>, and <u>hydrangeas</u>.   My favorite sports are <u>swimming</u>, <u>hiking</u>, and <u>bicycling</u>.   <u>Gasping</u> and <u>coughing</u>, the diver emerged from the water.)

✓ In a series of phrases, does each item in the series have the same form—a prepositional phrase followed by a prepositional phrase, an infinitive phrase followed by an infinitive phrase, and so on? (The true gourmand delights not <u>in the cooking</u> but <u>in the eating</u>.   Sylvia's coach wants her <u>to work out</u>, <u>to diet</u>, and <u>to sleep</u> nine hours a night for the next two months.)

✓ In a series of clauses, does each item in the series have the same form—a relative clause followed by a relative clause, a noun clause followed by a noun clause, and so on? (Most of us want a partner <u>that we can love</u> and <u>that we can trust</u>.   <u>What we aim for</u> and <u>what we achieve</u> coincide more often than not.)

UNEDITED

1. During pre-registration week, we are usually concerned with <u>choosing good courses</u> and <u>that we can find an inexpensive place to live</u>.

EDITED

1. During pre-registration week, we are usually concerned with <u>choosing good courses</u> and <u>finding an inexpensive place to live</u>.

2. The architectural features responsible for most accidents in buildings are <u>stairs</u>, <u>running into doors</u>, and <u>windows</u>.

2. The architectural features responsible for most accidents in buildings are <u>stairs</u>, <u>doors</u>, and <u>windows</u>.

3. Unscrupulous landlords often force tenants <u>to move out on short notice</u> or <u>make them</u> pay <u>exorbitant rents</u>.

3. Unscrupulous landlords often force tenants <u>to move out on short notice</u> or <u>to pay</u> exorbitant rents.

4. Most men now know <u>that their skin is vulnerable to the elements</u> and <u>taking special care of it</u>.

4. Most men now know <u>that their skin is vulnerable to the elements</u> and <u>that it requires special care</u>.

5. Dr. Land's 1947 development of Polaroid's instant photography was <u>for children</u>, <u>for adults</u>, and <u>not fiddling</u> with the details of camera use.

5. Dr. Land's 1947 development of Polaroid's instant photography was <u>for children</u>, <u>for adults</u>, and <u>for anyone</u> who didn't want to fiddle with the details of camera use.

CUMULATIVE EDITING EXERCISE The following passage contains errors in sentence structure: *fragments, fused sentences, comma splices, dangling and misplaced modifiers*, and *nonparallel structures*. Edit the passage carefully, correcting every error you can find.

As an upper-middle-class citizen, it is difficult to imagine the hardships others, such as the characters in *The Grapes of Wrath*, have had to endure. Not until I read that novel did I experience what I would consider the worst situations anyone could live through. Outcasts from their own land, forced from the family home, starving, penniless, and with little hope. The novel shows a family illtreated by those they turned to for help. We all hope such circumstances will never recur in the United States, they should not be forgotten for that reason. A work such as Steinbeck's ensures that life in the late 1920's was not the cozy, being comfortable existence most of us now enjoy. Were it not for such pieces of literature which enable us to see not only the very best of life, whether luxury or loving, along with the opposite extreme of squalor and degradation, we would be much shallower people. Thus Steinbeck enriches us as we experience his words the readers can adapt them to their own lives.

A. PERIODS, QUESTION MARKS, AND EXCLAMATION POINTS

Checklist

✓ If the sentence is a statement, does it end with a period?

✓ If the sentence poses an indirect question, does it end with a period? (She wondered if I would pick up her papers.)

✓ If the sentence poses a direct question, does it end with a question mark? (Will you pick up my papers?)

✓ If the sentence makes an especially emphatic command or statement, does it end with an exclamation point? (Keep away from the fire!)

✓ If a term is an abbreviation, month, title, or degree, is a period used appropriately? (Sept., Dr., M.D., etc.) If in doubt, check the dictionary. See p. 363 for abbreviations without periods.

✓ If part of a quotation is omitted, does an ellipsis (three periods in a row) take the place of the omitted passage? (The visiting ambassador said: "I will meet with the press . . . at 4:00.")

✓ If the omission of part of a quotation occurs at the end of a sentence, do four periods mark the omission as well as the end of the sentence? (The visiting ambassador said: "I will expect newsmen to refrain from harassing me. . . .")

UNEDITED

1. Could an increasing accumulation of carbon dioxide in the atmosphere significantly raise global temperatures by early in the next century or even alter our way of life.

2. The critic asked whether the film was in any way fresh or innovative?

3. According to Lance Morrow, "After centuries of racks, gougings, hangmen and unspeakably inventive tortures, much of mankind adopted the lockup as its principal instrument of punishment . . ."

4. "Save my baby" screamed the woman as she leaped from the burning balcony

EDITED

1. Could an increasing accumulation of carbon dioxide in the atmosphere significantly raise global temperatures by early in the next century or even alter our way of life?

2. The critic asked whether the film was in any way fresh or innovative.

3. According to Lance Morrow, "After centuries of racks, gougings, hangmen and unspeakably inventive tortures, much of mankind adopted the lockup as its principal instrument of punishment. . . ."

4. "Save my baby!" screamed the woman as she leaped from the burning balcony.

5. Rachel's sister recently received an <u>MS</u> degree.

5. Rachel's sister recently received an <u>M.S.</u> degree.

B. COMMAS

√ If the sentence contains two main clauses, are they joined by a semicolon or a comma followed by *and, but, or, nor, for, so,* or *yet?* (It's summertime, and the livin' is easy.)

√ If the sentence opens with an introductory word, phrase, or clause, does a comma follow the introductory element? (The preceding sentence offers an example of an introductory clause followed by a comma.)

√ Are words, phrases, or clauses in a series separated by commas? (Deliver us from goblins, ghosts, long-legged beasts, and things that go "bump" in the night.)

√ Are commas used to set off the name of a person spoken to? (Dr. Jones, would you step this way?)

√ Are commas used to set off dates, addresses, and places? (Vladimir Nabokov died in early July, 1977 at his home in Montreux, Switzerland.)

√ Are interrupting expressions set off by commas? (The assignment, he argued forcefully, was too time-consuming.)

√ If a modifier follows the word(s) described and is *not* essential to the meaning of the sentence but rather supplies *extra* information, is that modifier set off by commas? (Willie Nelson, who wrote "Red Headed Stranger," has three hot-selling albums.   The steelworkers, who accepted the arbitrator's ruling, returned to work today.   Julia Child, TV's culinary star, launched a new series last year.)

√ If a modifier follows the word or words described and *is* essential to the meaning of the sentence, is that modifier *not* set off by commas? (The man who first walked on the moon recorded his sensations in detail. Salmon smoked over an open alder fire has a unique flavor.   He who laughs last laughs best.)

UNEDITED

1. Subscribers will have no minimum number of books to buy_and they may cancel subscriptions at any time.

2. Of course_I have always been a football fanatic.

3. Historian Barbara Tuchman's description of the fourteenth cen-

EDITED

1. Subscribers will have no minimum number of books to buy, and they may cancel subscriptions at any time.

2. Of course, I have always been a football fanatic.

3. Historian Barbara Tuchman's description of the fourteenth cen-

tury is exciting_artistic_and schol-
arly.

4. Larry_will you give me a hand?

5. April 1_1978 was a day I will
never forget.

6. The composing process is_as we
noted earlier_a complex one.

7. The court's statement was_as we
expected_inconclusive.

8. Boccaccio's Doctor Simon_who
was a proctologist_had a chamber
pot painted over his door.

9. Men, who have very poor eye-
sight, should not qualify as aircraft
pilots.

tury is exciting, artistic, and schol-
arly.

4. Larry, will you give me a hand?

5. April 1, 1978 was a day I will
never forget.

6. The composing process is, as we
noted earlier, a complex one.

7. The court's statement was, as we
expected, inconclusive.

8. Boccaccio's Doctor Simon, who
was a proctologist, had a chamber
pot painted over his door.

9. Men_who have very poor eye-
sight_should not qualify as aircraft
pilots.

C. SEMICOLONS

Checklist

√ If two main clauses have *not* been joined by a coordinating conjunction
(*and, but, or, nor, for, so, yet*), have they been joined by a semicolon?
(We arrived on campus today; tomorrow we face the long lines of registration.)

√ If two main clauses are linked by a word in the following list, is that
word *preceded* by a semicolon?

accordingly	furthermore	meanwhile	similarly
also	hence	moreover	still
anyway	however	nevertheless	that is
as a result	in addition	nonetheless	that is to say
besides	indeed	on the contrary	then
consequently	in fact	on the other hand	therefore
for example	likewise	otherwise	thus
for instance			

(The rain seeped slowly through the soles of my shoes; consequently, I
caught my first cold of the season.)

√ If a sentence contains a semicolon, does the semicolon have a main
clause before it and a main clause after it (except in the following √)?

√ If a sentence contains a series which contains commas, are the items in
the series separated by semicolons instead of by additional commas? (The
crowd in Tehran included angry students in jeans; women in the black

chador, the traditional veil; peasants and merchants, whose clothing marked them immediately; and the black-robed mullahs, the leaders of the Shi'ite branch of Islam.)

UNEDITED

EDITED

UNEDITED

1. The last known case of smallpox occurred recently in London, hence the disease has not yet died out.

2. Socrates taught by asking questions, Plato apparently could answer many of them well.

3. Mary's courses included English 402, History of the English Language, Psychology 204, Introduction to Cognitive Psychology, and Philosophy 210, Logic for Nonmajors.

4. Conference participants attended large morning lectures, then they formed small discussion groups every afternoon.

5. Smokers should be more considerate of nonsmokers, for instance, they should never smoke in elevators.

EDITED

1. The last known case of smallpox occurred recently in London; hence the disease has not yet died out.

2. Socrates taught by asking questions; Plato apparently could answer many of them well.

3. Mary's courses included English 402, History of the English Language; Psychology 204, Introduction to Cognitive Psychology; and Philosophy 210, Logic for Nonmajors.

4. Conference participants attended large morning lectures; then they formed small discussion groups every afternoon.

5. Smokers should be more considerate of nonsmokers; for instance, they should never smoke in elevators.

D. COLONS

Checklist

√ If a sentence introduces a list, series of explanations or illustrations, or other specifying material, does a colon precede this material? (Lynda's writing is characterized by three elements: sound logic, careful attention to detail, and wry humor.)

√ If a sentence contains a colon, is the colon *preceded* by a main clause?

√ If a sentence introduces a quotation, is the quotation preceded by a colon?

UNEDITED

1. As the experienced climber attempted to climb Everest, she said "I may indeed reach the summit, but I will never conquer this mountain."

EDITED

1. As the experienced climber attempted to climb Everest, she said: "I may indeed reach the summit, but I will never conquer this mountain."

2. During the first cooking class, we practiced using these tools, a paring knife, a butcher knife, a cleaver, a wire whisk, and a mortar and pestle.

3. Dawn's preferred class hours are: eight-thirty, nine-thirty, and ten-thirty.

4. Ainsley has recently developed a new interest, collecting rare treatises on magic.

5. Everyone who owns a McDonald's restaurant attends "Hamburger U" and receives a degree in QSC, quality, service, and cleanliness.

2. During the first cooking class, we practiced using these tools: a paring knife, a butcher knife, a cleaver, a wire whisk, and a mortar and pestle.

3. Dawn's preferred class hours are eight-thirty, nine-thirty, and ten-thirty.

4. Ainsley has recently developed a new interest: collecting rare treatises on magic.

5. Everyone who owns a McDonald's restaurant attends "Hamburger U" and receives a degree in QSC: quality, service, and cleanliness.

E. DASHES

Checklist

√ Are all dashes made with two unspaced hyphens with no space either before or after them? (Walk—don't run—to the nearest exit.)

√ Is the dash used to emphasize an unexpected element, or to mark off a summary word, phrase, or clause at the end of a sentence? (When Ivan wants to be alone, he whistles nervously to himself—a habit his friends have come to recognize and respect.)

√ Are pairs of dashes used within the sentence to mark an abrupt parenthetical element or interruption in thought? (Often a favorite children's story—like *Goodnight, Moon*—contains no obvious moral or lesson at all.)

√ Are commas omitted before and after dashes?

UNEDITED

1. Some psychologists believe that in our society the biggest thrill and sense of power comes from our biggest killer the automobile.

2. The poet William Blake was a complex combination of innocence and experience, fantasy and practicality, a man behind a mask.

EDITED

1. Some psychologists believe that in our society the biggest thrill and sense of power comes from our biggest killer—the automobile.

2. The poet William Blake was a combination of innocence and experience, fantasy and practicality—a man behind a mask.

3. Some Western medical practitioners have always believed,— without knowing why,—that they achieved spectacular successes with acupuncture.

3. Some Western medical practitioners have always believed— without knowing why—that they achieved spectacular successes with acupuncture.

F. PARENTHESES AND BRACKETS

Checklist

√ Are parts of sentences that add incidental explanatory, illustrative, or specifying information enclosed in parentheses?

√ Are any special directions to the reader enclosed in parentheses?

√ When parentheses fall within other parentheses, are brackets used for the "inner" parentheses? *For example:* But others oppose the plan (see Hugh Jones, *The Weight of Power* [Princeton, 1968], pp. 72–84).

UNEDITED

1. Light beer contains less than half the calories, 68, and half the alcohol, 2.5 percent, of regular beer.

2. The word *hypnosis,* from the Greek, meaning "put to sleep," was coined in the nineteenth century by Scottish physician James Braid.

3. Six companies are currently competing for the right to sell fighter aircraft, (see illustration on opposite page).

4. Please note the exceptions to this rule (see page 42 of *A Guide to Writing,* New York, 1975).

EDITED

1. Light beer contains less than half the calories (68) and half the alcohol (2.5 percent) of regular beer.

2. The word *hypnosis* (from the Greek, meaning "put to sleep") was coined in the nineteenth century by Scottish physician James Braid.

3. Six companies are currently competing for the right to sell fighter aircraft (see illustration on opposite page).

4. Please note the exceptions to this rule (see page 42 of *A Guide to Writing* [New York, 1975]).

G. APOSTROPHES

Checklist

√ Is the apostrophe plus *s* used to mark possessive nouns which do not end in *s*? (boy's; girl's)

√ Is the apostrophe used alone to mark possessive nouns that do end in *s*? (boys'; girls')

✓ In a contraction, does the apostrophe appear in the space of the omitted letter(s) or number (s)? (don't; we'd; it's)

✓ Does the possessive pronoun its omit the apostrophe? (The boat lost its anchor.)

UNEDITED	EDITED
1. The rampaging rhino trapped <u>it's</u> prey.	**1.** The rampaging rhino trapped <u>its</u> prey.
2. The evening paper advertised <u>ladie's</u> coats at half-price.	**2.** The evening paper advertised <u>ladies'</u> coats at half-price.
3. Jack doesn't mind cleaning up after the store closes; <u>its</u> all in a <u>days</u> work.	**3.** Jack doesn't mind cleaning up after the store closes; <u>it's</u> all in a <u>day's</u> work.
4. If you <u>were'nt</u> there to hear him tell the story, then you probably <u>wont</u> think <u>its</u> funny.	**4.** If you <u>weren't</u> there to hear him tell the story, then you probably <u>won't</u> think <u>it's</u> funny.
5. An excellent article on ways to prevent high blood pressure appeared in the October <u>78</u> issue of *Health.*	**5.** An excellent article on ways to prevent high blood pressure appeared in the October <u>'78</u> issue of *Health.*

CUMULATIVE EDITING EXERCISE

The following passage contains errors in the *conventions of punctuation.* Edit the passage carefully, correcting every error you can find.

I was rummaging in my purse for a pen when he took the chair next to mine tossing a confident "Hi" in my vicinity. Most of the students in my psychology class know Mike by sight now. He's an extrovert; the kind of person who likes to draw attention to himself; to be noticed by others. Its important to him that strangers know he is sports-minded or "very athletic" as he thinks of himself. Education, is not as important to Mike as are the social benefits school offers. He thinks no party is complete or successful unless he is on the guest list. A self-centered person Mike has numerous but, not close, friends. He tends to use rather than to enjoy his buddies?

While others arrive on time for class, Mike is invariably late. He begins conversing with a friend over other student's heads (we all learn that he scored three goals in last nights' game. Later the professor asks a question which requires a vote, then Mike raises his hand for both enjoying the snickers his action receives. Unselfconsciously he sneaks sips from a can of Old Fashioned Lemonade which the friend naturally fetched for him. We have been told that Mike the athlete does'nt smoke but he does enjoy other habits, cracking his knuckles frequently is the most annoying of them.

A. *IE/EI*

√ Does *i* come before *e*

EXCEPT after *c*

OR when sounded like *a* as in *neighbor* or *weigh*

OR in exceptions like *weird* and *efficient?* *

UNEDITED

1. Being <u>decieved</u> was not the worst of it, since his neighbor was also a <u>theif.</u>

2. The <u>peir</u> <u>wieghed</u> nearly <u>ieght</u> tons, but the hoist <u>weilded</u> it like a toy in its <u>feirce</u> grip.

3. <u>Sieze</u> the day, or <u>forfiet</u> your <u>consceince.</u>

4. Although he had <u>niether</u> his opponent's <u>hieght</u> nor his <u>wieght</u>, Mike's skill at karate ensured his victory.

EDITED

1. Being <u>deceived</u> was not the worst of it, since his neighbor was also a <u>thief.</u>

2. The <u>pier</u> <u>weighed</u> nearly <u>eight</u> tons, but the hoist <u>wielded</u> it like a toy in its <u>fierce</u> grip.

3. <u>Seize</u> the day, or <u>forfeit</u> your <u>conscience.</u>

4. Although he had <u>neither</u> his opponent's <u>height</u> nor his <u>weight</u>, Mike's skill at karate ensured his victory.

*****OTHER COMMON EXCEPTIONS:** *counterfeit, either, neither, height, weight, seize, forfeit, foreign, leisure.*

B. *UNPRONOUNCED E*

√ 1. Does the word end in an unpronounced *e*?
√   Does the suffix you are adding begin with a consonant?
    –If the answer to each question is yes, KEEP the *e*. (direful; discouragement)

√ 2. Does the word end in an unpronounced *e*?
√   Does the suffix you are adding begin with a vowel or a *y*?
    –If the answer to each question is yes, DROP the *e*. (writing; lovable; hazy)

√ 3. Does the word end in a soft *ce* or *ge*?
√   Is the word followed by any suffix except *ing*?
    –If the answer to each question is yes, KEEP the *e*. (manageable; disadvantageous; pronounceable)

1. The <u>carless</u> driver is often <u>completly</u> responsible for an automobile accident.

2. The gifts were <u>gratfully</u> accepted.

3. We were <u>hopeing</u> for sound <u>guideance</u>, but we actually got less-than-<u>desireable</u> advice.

4. <u>Continueal</u> <u>encouragment</u> kept them from getting <u>shakey</u>.

5. His <u>resourcfulness</u> in studying for examinations was <u>immediatly</u> <u>noticable</u> to his classmates.

1. The <u>careless</u> driver is often <u>completely</u> responsible for an automobile accident.

2. The gifts were <u>gratefully</u> accepted.

3. We were <u>hoping</u> for sound <u>guidance</u>, but we actually got less-than-<u>desirable</u> advice.

4. <u>Continual</u> <u>encouragement</u> kept them from getting <u>shaky</u>.

5. His <u>resourcefulness</u> in studying for examinations was <u>immediately</u> <u>noticeable</u> to his classmates.

C. DOUBLING CONSONANTS

Checklist

√ 1. Is the final vowel in the word a *long* vowel?
 –If so, DON'T double the consonant. (sleeping; biting)

√ 2. Does the word contain only one syllable?
√   Does the word end in one consonant preceded by a single vowel?
√   Does the suffix you are adding begin with a vowel?
   –If the answer to each question is yes, DOUBLE the consonant. (throbbed)
   –If the answer to any question is no, DON'T double the consonant. (raining)

√ 3. Does the word have more than one syllable?
√   Does the word end in one consonant preceded by a single vowel?
√   Is the last syllable in the word accented?
√   Does the suffix you are adding begin with a vowel?
   –If the answer to each question is yes, DOUBLE the consonant. (occurrence)
   –If the answer to any question is no, DON'T double the consonant. (listening)

√ 4. Is the last syllable of the word accented?
√   If you add a suffix, does the accent shift to the *first* syllable of the word?
   –If so, DON'T double the consonant. (infér; ínference)

1. The <u>traveller</u>, given her <u>preference</u>, would have gone to Italy.

1. The <u>traveler</u>, given her <u>preference</u>, would have gone to Italy.

2. The <u>growlling</u> continued through the night. <u>permiting</u> no one to sleep.

2. The <u>growling</u> continued through the night, <u>permitting</u> no one to sleep.

3. <u>Sailling</u> can be fun, even for the <u>beginner.</u>

3. <u>Sailing</u> can be fun, even for the <u>beginner.</u>

4. She spent most of the morning rolling out dough and <u>bakking</u> bread.

4. She spent most of the morning rolling out dough and <u>baking</u> bread.

D. SEDE, CEED, CEDE

Checklist

√ If the spelling is *sede*, is the word *supersede*?

√ If the spelling is *ceed*, is the word *exceed*, *proceed*, or *succeed*?

√ Are all other words ending with that syllable spelled *cede*? (*precede*)

UNEDITED

1. In order to <u>succede</u> at her job, the president of the company refused to allow any authority to <u>superceed</u> hers.

EDITED

1. In order to <u>succeed</u> at her job, the president of the company refused to allow any authority to <u>supersede</u> hers.

2. Those who <u>procede</u> with care will never <u>exsede</u> the speed limit.

2. Those who <u>proceed</u> with care will never <u>exceed</u> the speed limit.

3. The star of the rock show was <u>preceeded</u> by a second-rate local group.

3. The star of the rock show was <u>preceded</u> by a second-rate local group.

E. WORDS THAT SOUND ALIKE BUT HAVE DIFFERENT SPELLINGS

Checklist

√ Have you checked each use of the following pairs of words to make sure you have made the correct choice?

1. accept (I will be happy to <u>accept</u> your invitation.)
   except (My niece will eat anything <u>except</u> spinach.)
2. affect (usually a verb: Her resignation <u>affects</u> all of us.)
   effect (usually a noun: The movie won an Academy Award for special <u>effects.</u>)
3. already (The meeting was <u>already</u> over when I arrived.)
   all ready (It isn't often that we are <u>all</u> <u>ready</u> on time.)
4. choose (present tense: I <u>choose</u> you.)
   chose (past tense: I <u>chose</u> you yesterday.)
5. cite (verb: Always <u>cite</u> your references.)
   site (noun: The homes were built on the <u>site</u> of an old churchyard.)

6. its (possessive: The dog hid <u>its</u> bone.)

   it's (contraction of *it is*: <u>It's</u> snowing heavily today.)

7. lead (adjective: He uses a <u>lead</u> pencil.)

   led (verb: He <u>led</u> his horse across the river.)

8. lose (verb: We must be careful not to <u>lose</u> our tickets.)

   loose (adjective: These slacks are too <u>loose</u>; they will have to be altered.)

9. principal (main: Her <u>principal</u> objection was to the high price of the stereo.)

   principle (basic truth, rule, or standard: Sir Thomas More was a man of <u>principle</u>.)

10. their (possessive: The children lost <u>their</u> mittens.)

   there (like *here*: Put the paper over <u>there</u>.)

   they're (contraction of *they are*: <u>They're</u> joining us for dinner.)

11. to (preposition: I went <u>to</u> the movie.)

   too (adverb: The oven is <u>too</u> hot for baking bread.)

12. weather (Our <u>weather</u> has been unusually cool this year.)

   whether (like *where, when, why*: <u>Whether</u> or not she gets to the party on time depends on the number of friends she picks up.)

13. who's (contraction of *who is*: <u>Who's</u> sorry now?)

   whose (possessive: <u>Whose</u> coat is on the floor?)

14. you're (contraction of *you are*: <u>You're</u> next.)

   your (possessive: May I borrow <u>your</u> pen?)

F. MISCELLANEOUS SUFFIX AND PREFIX PATTERNS

Checklist

√ 1. Does the word end in *c*?

√   Does the suffix you are adding begin with *e, i,* or *y*?

   –If the answer to both questions is yes, ADD *k* before the suffix. (panicky; frolicking)

√ 2. Are the last letters of the stem word and the first letter of the suffix the same?

   –If the answer is yes, KEEP BOTH LETTERS. (fatally; rottenness; roommate; cannot)

√ 3. Are the last letter of the prefix and the first letter of the stem word the same?

   –If the answer is yes, KEEP BOTH LETTERS. (disservice; dissection; irremovable; misstep; overrate)

UNEDITED	EDITED
1. Opening leaf buds are perfectly <u>mimiced</u> by the caterpillar's green-and-yellow markings.	**1.** Opening leaf buds are perfectly <u>mimicked</u> by the caterpillar's green-and-yellow markings.

2. The <u>suddeness</u> with which the death scene ended startled even the most <u>imovable</u> members of the audience.

2. The <u>suddenness</u> with which the death scene ended startled even the most <u>immovable</u> members of the audience.

3. My <u>roomate</u> and I are both <u>disatisfied</u> with our landlord.

3. My <u>roommate</u> and I are both <u>dissatisfied</u> with our landlord.

G. SPELLING INVENTORY

Checklist

√ Have you made a spelling inventory sheet on which you list all words which you have misspelled?

√ Have you grouped your misspellings into the following categories?
–*ie/ei*
–long vowel sound
–short vowel sound
–unpronounced *e*
–last-letter consonant
–double consonant
–sound-alike words
–prefix
–suffix
–letter reversals
–omitted letters
–words whose spelling differs markedly from your pronunciation of them

√ Have you studied the checklists on the preceding pages that apply to the categories your misspellings fall into?

√ Have you thought of special ways to remember the spellings of words you pronounce differently from their spelling? For example, do you remember that there is a *cog* in *recognize*, even though you pronounce it *reckanize?* Or a *govern* in *government* even though you don't pronounce the *n*?

√ Do you practice pronouncing words you misspell syllable by syllable?

√ Do you correctly copy words you have misspelled so that your hand will get a "feeling" for the correct spelling?

√ Do you note words you have misspelled so that your eyes will get accustomed to seeing those words spelled correctly?

√ Have you studied your dictionary so that you know how to find the pronunciation, syllabification, grammatical classes, and usage of words?

√ If you have trouble spelling the first part of a word or if you can't find a word in the dictionary, have you asked someone to help you spell it?

The following passage contains errors in the conventions of spelling. Edit the passage carefully, correcting every error you can find.

The five-year periode between 1930 and 1935 marked some of the roughest yeares of the Depression, provideing the best exampals of posative and negative human behavior in times of crisus and uncertanty. During the "Dirty Thirties," newspapers presented glosy views of life, while minoraty groups were blammed for causing all the hardships faced by everyone else. But the survivers of the Depresion were those who made do with what little they had.

North American newspapers choose too present completely unrealistic pictures of life durning the thirties. My reading of microfilm from the period reveailed full-page storys of the World Seres or the Stanley Cup instead of reports on the bredlines or recipes for "depression stew." Human interest storys like those about the Dionne Quintuplets made headlines. The newspapers resolutly avoided the grim starvation of jobbless people. Newspappers painted a rosie picture and stayed clear of the harsh realty. Shirley Temple's movies were very popular during the Depression ara. Perhaps it was somehow desireable for the average person to avoid realty and excape to the foreign land of "The Good Ship Lollipop," while impoverrished people on street corners asked, "Brother can you spar a dime?"

A. PREPARING FINAL COPY

Checklist

√ If the essay is typed, have you used unlined white bond paper?

√ If the essay is handwritten, have you used white, lined loose-leaf paper?

√ Have you allowed one-inch margins at the top, bottom, and both sides of the paper?

√ Is the essay double-spaced throughout, including footnotes and quotations?

√ Is each new paragraph indented five spaces from the left margin?

√ Is each extended quotation (more than four lines) separated from the body of the paper by triple-spacing and indented ten spaces from the left margin?

√ Is the title of the essay centered on the first page of the essay?

√ Is the title written *without* quotation marks or underlining?

√ Does your name, your instructor's name and course number (if appropriate), and the date appear at the top right corner of the first page?

√ Except for the first page, which is unnumbered but which counts as page one, are all pages numbered consecutively in the upper right-hand corner?

B. CAPITALIZING

Checklist

√ Have you capitalized the following items?
   –The first letter of the first, last, and all other words in a title except articles, conjunctions, and prepositions?
   –The first letter of all proper names?
   –The first letter of the first word in every line of verse?
   –The first letter of the first word in a sentence?
   –The first letter of a title or abbreviation of a title that comes before a proper name? (Prime Minister; Ms.)
   –The pronoun *I*.
   –The first letter of months, days of the week, and holidays?
   –The first letter of titles of historical events? (Battle of Cutting Knife Creek)
   –The first letter of the names of languages, peoples, religions, cities, counties, countries, provinces, bodies of water, mountains, deserts, spe-

cific locations, divisions of governments? (English; Rocky Mountains; Third Street; Parliament)

UNEDITED	EDITED
1. Over 150 million cars are now on the roads in <u>n</u>orth <u>a</u>merica.	1. Over 150 million cars are now on the roads in <u>N</u>orth <u>A</u>merica.
2. Derived from the <u>g</u>reek words for house and management, our word *economy* meant simply household management.	2. Derived from the <u>G</u>reek words for house and management, our word *economy* meant simply household management.
3. In <u>t</u>okyo during <u>j</u>anuary, <u>m</u>ay, and <u>s</u>eptember, <u>j</u>apanese wrestlers perform ritualistic fights in the <u>k</u>uramae <u>k</u>okugikan <u>s</u>tadium.	3. In <u>T</u>okyo during <u>J</u>anuary, <u>M</u>ay, and <u>S</u>eptember, <u>J</u>apanese wrestlers perform ritualistic fights in the <u>K</u>uramae <u>K</u>okugikan <u>S</u>tadium.
4. Edgar <u>a</u>llan Poe's "Murders <u>I</u>n <u>T</u>he Rue Morgue" was made into an excellent movie.	4. Edgar <u>A</u>llan Poe's "Murders <u>in</u> <u>t</u>he Rue Morgue" was made into an excellent movie.
5. Prime <u>m</u>inister Begin spoke to the assembled <u>S</u>enators.	5. Prime <u>M</u>inister Begin spoke to the assembled <u>s</u>enators.
6. The <u>u</u>nited <u>s</u>tates <u>i</u>ndependence <u>d</u>ay and the <u>c</u>anadian <u>c</u>onfederation <u>d</u>ay both fall in early <u>j</u>uly.	6. The <u>U</u>nited <u>S</u>tates <u>I</u>ndependence <u>D</u>ay and the <u>C</u>anadian <u>C</u>onfederation <u>D</u>ay both fall in early July.
7. In the nineteenth century, <u>dr.</u> Livingstone first conquered the <u>n</u>ile.	7. In the nineteenth century, <u>Dr.</u> Livingstone first conquered the <u>N</u>ile.

C. QUOTING

Checklist

√ Are all quoted words enclosed in double quotation marks?

√ Is the quotation within a quotation enclosed in single quotation marks?

√ Are titles of articles, chapter of books, essays, lectures and speeches, poems, short stories, songs, and individual episodes of radio and television programs enclosed in double quotation marks?

√ Are periods and commas placed INSIDE the closing quotation mark?

√ Are colons and semicolons placed OUTSIDE the closing quotation mark?

√ When an entire sentence, rather than the part in quotation marks, is a question or an exclamation, is the question mark or exclamation mark outside the closing quotation mark?

√ When the quoted part of a sentence is a question or an exclamation, is the question mark or exclamation point inside the closing quotation mark?

1. French novelist Gustave Flaubert once said: He who plants a vine becomes entangled in its branches.

2. Aristotle defined rhetoric as the faculty of discovering all the available means of persuasion.

3. The chairman of our Energy Conservation Commission recently remarked: "People ask themselves, "How little insulation can I get away with"? when they should be asking "How much insulation should I install to get the most efficient use of energy"? Such attitudes must change."

4. My first boss used to greet us every morning by shouting "Au boulot!;" loosely translated, his greeting meant "To the grindstone"!

1. French novelist Gustave Flaubert once said: "He who plants a vine becomes entangled in its branches."

2. Aristotle defined rhetoric as "the faculty of discovering all the available means of persuasion."

3. The chairman of our Energy Conservation Commission recently remarked: "People ask themselves, 'How little insulation can I get away with?' when they should be asking 'How much insulation should I install to get the most efficient use of energy?' Such attitudes must change."

4. My first boss used to greet us every morning by shouting "Au boulot!"; loosely translated, his greeting meant "To the grindstone!"

D. ITALICIZING (UNDERLINING)

Checklist

√ Are words that are referred to as words italicized?

√ Are foreign words italicized?

√ Are titles of ballets, books, operas, paintings, pamphlets, periodicals and newspapers, plays, films, radio and television programs, sculptures, and names of ships, trains, or aircraft all italicized?

√ Have you avoided the unwarranted use of italics for emphasis?

1. Marni is characterized by exuberant joie de vivre and by the ability to empathize with others.

2. Tonight, the Metropolitan Opera Company will present Verdi's Otello.

3. *Wherever* he goes, the popular rock idol is *adored* by throngs of fans.

1. Marni is characterized by exuberant *joie de vivre* and by the ability to empathize with others.

2. Tonight, the Metropolitan Opera Company will present Verdi's *Otello*.

3. Wherever he goes, the popular rock idol is adored by throngs of fans.

4. The word doubt comes from a
Latin word which meant "to
waver."

4. The word *doubt* comes from a
Latin word which meant "to
waver."

E. NUMBERING

Checklist

√ As a general rule, are the numbers one through ten spelled out?

√ If a series contains numbers both under ten and over ten, are numerals used throughout for consistency?

√ Are arabic numerals used to express dates, page numbers, addresses, identification numbers, and hours of the day when used with A.M. or P.M.? (September 23, 1980; 3721 Princess Avenue; P.O. Box 86773; page 27; Channel 9; 1:00 P.M.)

√ If a number is the first word in a sentence, is the number spelled out? (Seventy-six trombones led the big parade.)

√ In technical or statistical writing, are numerals used consistently to save space?

UNEDITED

1. Tokyo's 775-square-mile metropolitan area, with its <u>twelve</u> million people, contains <u>twenty-six</u> cities, <u>five</u> towns, <u>one</u> village, and the <u>seven</u> islands south of Tokyo Bay.

2. At precisely <u>ten</u> A.M. on <u>September seventh</u>, <u>nineteen twenty-eight</u>, the Chief of Scotland Yard presented himself at <u>ten</u> Downing Street.

3. Channel <u>Nine</u>, a Public Broadcasting Station, reports that <u>seventy-two-and-one-half</u> percent of its budget comes from contributions.

4. The greenhouse, which costs $2,500 to build, is placed on and attached to leveled <u>four-inch by four-inch</u> rough cedar foundation supported by concrete piers; the floor consists of 12″ x 12″ pavers, placed on a <u>two-inch</u>-thick sand bed.

EDITED

1. Tokyo's 775-square-mile metropolitan area, with its <u>12</u> million people, contains <u>26</u> cities, <u>5</u> towns, <u>1</u> village, and the <u>7</u> islands south of Tokyo Bay.

2. At precisely <u>10:00</u> A.M. on September <u>7, 1928</u>, the Chief of Scotland Yard presented himself at <u>10</u> Downing Street.

3. Channel <u>9</u>, a Public Broadcasting Station, reports that <u>72½</u> percent of its budget comes from contributions.

4. The greenhouse, which costs $2,500 to build, is placed on and attached to leveled <u>4″ x 4″</u> rough cedar foundation supported by concrete piers; the floor consists of 12″ x 12″ pavers, placed on a <u>2″</u>-thick sand bed.

5. A bill passed last year lifts the minimum wage from $2.65 an hour to $2.90 this year, to $3.10 next year, and to $3.35 the following year; but some top officials feel that eliminating the increases might open up as many as <u>four hundred and fifty thousand</u> jobs.

5. A bill passed last year lifts the minimum wage from $2.65 an hour to $2.90 this year, to $3.10 next year, and to $3.35 the following year; but some top officials feel that eliminating the increases might open up as many as <u>450,000</u> jobs.

F. ABBREVIATING

√ As a general rule, are abbreviations avoided in formal prose?

√ Are abbreviations used for the following titles and degrees: Mr.; Mrs.; Ms.; Jr.; Sr.; Dr.; M.D.; M.A.; Ph.D.; L.L.D.?

√ Does the abbreviation B.C. *follow* the date and the abbreviation A.D. *precede* the date?

√ If you have used the capitalized initials of a place, organization, or agency (CBS, FBI), will the meaning of those initials be known to your readers?

√ In footnotes or bibliographical citations, are the following standard abbreviations used?

cf.	(compare)	i.e.	(that is)	rev.	(revised)
ed.	(edition or editor)	no(s).	(number[s])	trans.	(translated by)
eds.	(editions or editors)	p.	(page)	vol.	(volume)
e.g.	(for example)	pp.	(pages)	vols.	(volumes)

UNEDITED

1. Dr. Horowitz said he would have our <u>psych. exam.</u> graded by next <u>Fri.</u>

2. The chief spokesman for the <u>PQ</u> recently held a press conference.

3. The years between 55 B.C. and <u>200 A.D.</u> saw the apogee of the Roman Empire.

4. The <u>SCA</u> is currently recruiting students with an interest in the medieval period to join in their first festival here.

EDITED

1. Dr. Horowitz said he would have our <u>psychology examination</u> graded by next <u>Friday.</u>

2. The chief spokesman for the <u>Parti Québecois</u> recently held a press conference.

3. The years between 55 B.C. and <u>A.D. 200</u> saw the apogee of the Roman Empire.

4. The <u>Society for Creative Anachronism</u> is currently recruiting students with an interest in the medieval period to join in their first festival here.

G. HYPHENATING

√ As a general rule, if you are at all uncertain about how to hyphenate a compound word, have you checked your dictionary?

√ Have you hyphenated two words which are working as one unit? (yellow-green shirt; trash-compactors; ninth-century England)

√ Are two-word numbers hyphenated? (twenty-eight pages)

√ Is a hyphen used to link numbers which indicate a range? (pp. 253–297)

√ If fractions are written out, are they hyphenated? (one-half cup vinegar)

√ Are hyphens used to link words you have compounded or coined for a special purpose? (My roommate shot me an I-told-you-so look.)

√ Are words that begin with the prefixes *ex* or *self* hyphenated? (ex-student; self-appointed critic)

√ Is a hyphen used to link prefixes to proper nouns or numbers? (pro-Egyptian; anti-British; pre-1900)

√ If a word has two or more prefixes before it, is each prefix followed by a hyphen? (Our instructor has given us one-, two-, and three-hour examinations.)

√ Are words that might be confused with other words hyphenated? (He needed time to re-create.)

√ Is a word that must be divided at the end of a line hyphenated *between syllables?* When in doubt, check the dictionary.

UNEDITED	EDITED
1. By the time you leave, you will have acquired a taste, perhaps a passion, for the delicacies of <u>smoked</u> fish.	1. By the time you leave, you will have acquired a taste, perhaps a passion, for the delicacies of <u>smoked</u> fish.
2. <u>Old fashioned</u> glasses are making a comeback.	2. <u>Old-fashioned</u> glasses are making a comeback.
3. The detective slipped into a <u>bullet proof steel grey vest.</u>	3. The detective slipped into a <u>bullet-proof steel-grey vest.</u>
4. Luke's <u>brother in law</u> recently bought an expensive <u>self winding</u> watch and a <u>red and white</u> Audi.	4. Luke's <u>brother-in-law</u> recently bought an expensive <u>self-winding</u> watch and a <u>red-and-white</u> Audi.
5. What has brought on such a <u>down at the mouth</u> expression?	5. What has brought on such a <u>down-at-the-mouth</u> expression?
6. The <u>pre Columbian</u> pottery exhibit contained <u>800 to 900 year old</u> items.	6. The <u>pre-Columbian</u> pottery exhibit contained <u>800- to 900-year-old</u> items.

| 7. This reading course offers a number of <u>pre</u> and <u>post tests.</u> | 7. This reading course offers a number of <u>pre-</u> and <u>post-tests.</u> |
| 8. Her boss asked that she <u>recount</u> her expenditures. | 8. Her boss asked that she <u>re-count</u> her expenditures. |

CUMULATIVE
EDITING
EXERCISE

The following passage contains errors in *mechanical conventions*. Edit the passage carefully, correcting every error you can find.

On december second, nineteen hundred and seventy one, a new country, the union of Arab Emirates, was formed. Later named the United Arab Emirates (U.A.E.), the small country lies on the persian gulf, in the strategic position between the East and the West. The events leading up to, and resulting from, its formation show the Emirates' importance in world affairs.

In the 18th-century, france, Britain, and holland were looking for trading centers. The area which is now the U.A.E. was ideal in view of their furtherance of trade with India. By the early nineteenth century, all but the british were gone, but powerful local arab "pirate boats" attacked all trade vessels in the Gulf. The East india company of Eng. retaliated in eighteen twenty and, in economist K. G. Fenelon's words: forced the seven sheikdoms in the 19th-century to end piracy and protect trade routes to India by under-taking defense of that area." The truce thus established led to the country's original name of the Trucial States. Local matters were still the individual rulers' concerns, but all Foreign and navigational policies were controlled by britain.

10 / SENTENCE-COMBINING
Imitating and generating sentences

Whether you are writing for the academic world or for the private world, whether your aim is expressive or persuasive, whether your mode is narration or classification—as you write to explore and create your own particular meanings, you will be doing so with sentences. Because sentences are crucial in helping you to achieve meaning, we have included sentence exercises in many chapters. This portion of the text provides further practice in crafting effective sentences.

Learning to expand and combine sentences allows you to bring ideas together in new ways, creating a variety of relationships, conjunctions, and emphases. As your stock of sentence patterns or syntactic options grows, your writing will become more mature, more varied and interesting. But how can you best increase the number and variety of your sentence patterns? You can best do so not by memorizing rules or by studying grammar but by imitating and practicing these sentence patterns. Even more important than imitating sentences, however, is generating the patterns and assimilating them into your own writing. Imitation may be the means, but internalization of new patterns is your end goal.

The patterns that follow generally increase in complexity, but the basic features of each set remain constant: You are asked (1) to study a sentence pattern; (2) to combine lists of sentences in imitation of the pattern; and (3) to generate your own sentences and a combination of them that imitates the pattern. In Pattern A, which follows below, for instance, the pattern sentence contains the following shorter sentences:

1. The stunt man approached the precipice.
2. The stunt man was lean.
3. He was muscular.
4. The precipice was narrow.
5. It was icy.

These short sentences, when combined, yield "The lean, muscular stunt man approached the narrow, icy precipice." Note that the words *lean, muscular* and *narrow, icy* are highlighted in the pattern sentence to call your attention to their important position in the pattern.

I. SIMPLE EXPANSION PATTERNS

Pattern A **The lean, muscular stunt man approached the narrow, icy precipice.**

1. After studying the sentence pattern, combine each of the following sets of sentences into a sentence that imitates Pattern A.

1. Men marched through the city.
2. They were haggard.
3. They were hollow-cheeked.
4. The city was silent.
5. The city was hungry.

_____

1. Alice met the Queen.
2. Alice was little.
3. She was timid.
4. The Queen was furious.
5. The Queen was crimson-faced.
6. She was Queen of Hearts.

_____

1. The clothing is designed.
2. The clothing is expensive.
3. The clothing is faddish.
4. The clothing is presented by magazines.
5. They are fashion magazines.

6. The designing is for the girl.
7. The girl is tall.
8. The girl is pencil thin.

Note: You may wish to compare your combination of the set of sentences
above with the original sentence in a student essay on p. 134.

1. Businessmen admire.
2. There are many such businessmen.
3. They admire the way the Cowboys play.
4. They play football.
5. The way is cold.
6. It is precise.
7. It is reliable.
8. It is dependable.
9. It is predictable.
10. It is efficient.
11. It is businesslike.

----

*2. Now write a series of at least five sentences and then combine them
into one sentence that imitates Pattern A. Then write at least two more
sentences that imitate the pattern.*

Pattern B **The General Motors assembly line grinds out cars** swiftly, smoothly,
and effortlessly.

*1. After studying the sentence pattern, combine each of the following sets
of sentences into a sentence that imitates Pattern B.*

1. The mass of ice marched.
2. The ice was moving.
3. The marching was down a valley.
4. The marching was slow.
5. The marching was quiet.
6. But the marching was inexorable.

----

1. We tend to use technologies.
2. The technologies are new.
3. Our use is profuse.
4. Our use is unwise.
5. Our use is even harmful

----

1. H. L. Mencken criticized foibles.
2. The foibles belonged to society.
3. The society was American.
4. The criticism was witty.
5. It was sarcastic.
6. It was unmerciful.
7. The unmercifulness occurred often.

---

1. The lecturer droned.
2. The lecturer was nondescript.
3. The lecturer was bespectacled.
4. The droning went on and on.
5. The droning was mechanical.
6. The droning was monotonous.
7. The droning was interminable.

---

2. Now write a series of seven sentences and combine them into one sentence that imitates Pattern B. Then write at least two more sentences that imitate the pattern.

Pattern B1 **She studied diligently so that she could answer the examiner's questions very quickly and very accurately.**

1. After studying the sentence pattern, combine each of the following sets of sentences into a sentence that imitates Pattern B1.

1. The aircraft landed.
2. The aircraft was malfunctioning.
3. The landing was immediate.
4. The landing was so that it could unload the passengers.
5. The passengers were worried.
6. The unloading was quick.
7. The unloading was safe.

---

1. The packhorses were loaded.
2. They were gold rush packhorses.
3. The loading was very careful.
4. The loading was so that the packhorses could negotiate the trails.
5. The trails were steep.
6. The trails were treacherous.
7. The negotiating was confident.
8. The negotiating was surefooted.

---

2. Now write a series of six sentences and then combine them into one sentence that imitates Pattern B1.

3. Now complete the following sentences, being careful to imitate Pattern B1.

a. He dressed . . . .
_____

b. The golden retriever begged . . . .
_____

II. CLAUSAL EXPANSION PATTERNS

Pattern A   **Alfred the Great, who was the most famous king of the West Saxons, reigned in the second half of the ninth century.**

1. After studying the sentence pattern, combine each of the following sets of sentences into a sentence that imitates Pattern A.

1. Joe Morgan is named.
2. He plays second base for the Reds.
3. His naming is usual.
4. The naming is to the Team.
5. The team is the All-Stars.
_____

1. The !Kung survive.
2. They live in the Desert.
3. The Desert is the Kalahari.
4. The Kalahari is harsh.
5. It is unyielding.
6. Their survival is by joining groups.
7. The groups are for protection.
8. The groups are also for shelter.
_____

1. Nicholas Reynolds has discovered the remains.
2. He is an archaeologist working in Scotland.
3. The remains are of the structure.
4. The structure is the oldest one yet found.
5. The finding was in the British Isles.
_____

2. Now write a series of five sentences and combine them into one sentence that imitates Pattern A. Then write at least two more sentences that imitate the pattern.

Pattern A1 **The large folding screens**, which once decorated the houses in Kyoto and Edo, give the most complete visual account of everyday life in old Japan that has come down to us.

1. After studying the sentence pattern, combine each of the following sets of sentences into a sentence that imitates Pattern A1.

1. Horse Creek flows.
2. Horse Creek is a stream.
3. The stream is small.
4. It is unnavigable.
5. It is 25 miles long.
6. It is in the Cascades.
7. They are the Oregon Cascades.
8. The flowing is through mountains.
9. The mountains are timbered.
10. The timber is dense.
11. The mountains are protected.
12. The protection is from loggers.

---

1. The beer provided.
2. The beer was frosty.
3. The beer had been lovingly protected.
4. The protection was from the sun.
5. The sun was hot.
6. The providing was for a reward.
7. The reward was instant.
8. The reward was for the members.
9. The members were of a group.
10. The group was a hiking group.
11. The group had finally arrived.
12. The arrival was at the campsite.

---

1. The house had a stairway.
2. It was a traditional house.
3. The house was simple.
4. The house was infinitely appealing.
5. The stairway was open.
6. The stairway was a symbol.
7. The symbol was one of welcome.

---

2. Now write a series of at least eight sentences and combine them into one sentence that imitates Pattern A1. Then write at least two more sentences that imitate the pattern.

Pattern A2 The man whom we feared made us an offer that we couldn't refuse.

> *1. After studying the sentence pattern, combine each of the following sets of sentences into a sentence that imitates Pattern A2.*

> 1. The chef created a menu.
> 2. We hoped to emulate the chef.
> 3. The menu was innovative.
> 4. The innovation was from beginning to end.

> _____

> 1. The crowds heard a speaker.
> 2. They were fortunate crowds.
> 3. Martin Luther King addressed the crowds.
> 4. The speaker was one that they won't forget.

> _____

> 1. The umpire gave them a warning.
> 2. The players taunted the umpire.
> 3. The warning was stern.
> 4. The warning silenced them.
> 5. It did this immediately.

> _____

> *2. Now write a series of at least four sentences and then combine them into one sentence that imitates Pattern A2. Then write two more sentences that imitate the pattern.*

Pattern B Officials beheaded Mary Queen of Scots after Queen Elizabeth's chief spy intercepted and decoded Mary's letters.

> *1. After studying the sentence pattern, combine each of the following sets of sentences into a sentence that imitates Pattern B.*

> 1. The students ordered pizzas.
> 2. The students were weary.
> 3. There were three pizzas.
> 4. The pizzas were extra large.
> 5. The pizzas were deluxe.
> 6. The students had completed their assignment.
> 7. The assignment was their last.
> 8. It was a lab assignment.

> _____

1. Stephanie savored her cup of coffee.
2. It was her second.
3. She also read the paper.
4. It was the student newspaper.
5. She then went to class.

---

1. Mark returned to the town.
2. The town was rural.
3. His ancestors had lived there.
4. They had worked there.
5. They had done so for centuries.

---

1. Rhonda and I attended school.
2. It was a high school.
3. It was an all-girl school.
4. We met guys.
5. We met them at dances.
6. The dances were held only on weekends.

Note: You may wish to compare your combination of the set of sentences above with the original sentence in a student essay on p. 93.

2. Now write a series of six sentences and then combine them into one sentence that imitates Pattern B. Then write two more sentences that imitate the pattern.

Pattern B1 While his friend sunbathed on a flat rock and the puppy slept beneath the alders, Gene baited a red wriggler on a Number 8 hook and waded into the icy water.

1. After studying the sentence pattern, combine each of the following sets of sentences into a sentence that imitates Pattern B1.

1. Cities have a surplus.
2. The surplus is of physicians.
3. Rural areas need doctors.
4. Their need is desperate.
5. We should follow the lead.
6. The lead is of other countries.
7. We should send every medical school graduate.
8. The sending would be to a rural area.
9. The sending would be for two years.

---

1. Energy boils.
2. The mood intensifies.
3. It is the mood of the dancers.
4. The dancers sweat.
5. The sweating is profuse.
6. Their muscles quiver.
7. The muscles are tired.
8. The quivering is from exhaustion.

---

1. The sky was blue.
2. The blue was brilliant.
3. The sun warmed the grass.
4. The grass was beneath her feet.
5. The freshman picked up her books.
6. The books were chemistry books.
7. She headed for the library.
8. The library was uninviting.

---

1. I was eating.
2. I became aware of the following.
3. The hamburger was turning to dust.
4. It was a McDonald's hamburger.
5. The dust was in my mouth.

Note: You may wish to compare your combination of the set of sentences above with the original sentence in a student essay on p. 89.

2. Now write a series of at least five sentences and then combine them into one sentence that imitates Pattern B1. Then write two more sentences that imitate the pattern.

Pattern C **That the atmosphere of desperate failure grows steadily** makes the **worn-out men and nervous, overworked women old before their time.**

1. After studying the sentence pattern, combine each of the following sets of sentences into a sentence that imitates Pattern C.

1. Our stereo stays on.
2. It does so all night.
3. It does so all day.
4. This may cause friction.
5. The friction will be with our neighbors.
6. They are new neighbors.

---

1. The pilot landed.
2. The piloting was of an aircraft.
3. The aircraft was crippled.
4. The landing was safe.
5. This left the passengers full.
6. They were full of gratitude.

---

1. The discoverer would speak.
2. The discoverer was well known.
3. He discovered DNA.
4. He would speak soon.
5. This filled the audience with expectation.
6. The audience was impatient.

---

1. Computer equipment is fairly standardized.
2. Computer programs are also fairly standardized.
3. Computer codes are also fairly standardized.
4. This standardization makes crimes easier to commit.
5. This standardization makes crimes easier to cover up.

Note: You may wish to compare your combination of the set of sentences above with the original sentence in a student essay on p. 258.

2. Now write a series of six sentences and then combine them into one sentence that imitates Pattern C. Then write two more sentences that imitate the pattern.

Pattern C1 **At bedtime, we crawl into our sleeping bags and hope** that tomorrow's hike will be an easy one.

1. After studying the sentence pattern, combine each of the following sets of sentences into a sentence that imitates Pattern C1.

1. The following has happened for centuries.
2. People have looked.
3. The people are throughout the world.
4. Their looking was at the heavens.
5. The people believed the following.
6. The stars controlled their lives.

---

1. The following would happen in the future.
2. We may leave home.

3. We may leave at 9:00 A.M.
4. We may know the following.
5. Our computer will do the wash.
6. It is a household computer.
7. It will clean the house.
8. It will cook dinner.

---

1. The following happened in junior high.
2. Films and film strips stated the following.
3. Drinking causes brain damage.
4. Drinking causes cirrhosis.
5. Drinking causes eventual alcoholism.
6. The films and film strips were on the evils of drinking.

Note: You may wish to compare your combination of the set of sentences above with the original sentences in a student essay on p. 179.

2. Now compose a series of at least seven sentences and then combine them into one sentence that imitates Pattern C1. Then write two more sentences that imitate the pattern.

Pattern C2 **One of the functions of the wilderness is to teach us that constant activity is not the only way of life.**

1. After studying the sentence pattern, combine each of the following sets of sentences into a sentence that imitates Pattern C2.

1. Thousands failed.
2. The thousands were movie lovers.
3. They were throughout the city.
4. Their failure was to believe the following.
5. The board would be successful.
6. It was a new board.
7. It was a censorship board.
8. Their successfulness would be in the ban.
9. The ban was of a favorite.
10. The favorite was an old one.

---

1. A majority decided.
2. The majority was of workers.
3. The workers were beer workers.
4. They were on strike.
5. Their decision was to agree to the following.
6. They would accept the offer.
7. The offer belonged to management.
8. The offer was for a raise.
9. The raise was for five percent.

---

2. Now complete the following sentences, being careful to imitate Pattern C2:

a. After a tough exam, we all hope . . . .

---

b. Professors should always realize . . . .

---

3. Now compose a series of eight sentences and then combine them into one sentence that imitates Pattern C2. Then write two more sentences that imitate the pattern.

III. PHRASAL EXPANSION PATTERNS

Pattern A **Along the creek** and **in logged areas,** **deciduous trees leaf out** **in late spring** **to create the green shade** of summer, **the fiery brilliance** of autumn, **the desolation** of winter.

1. After studying the sentence pattern, combine each of the following sets of sentences into a sentence that imitates Pattern A.

1. The following has happened throughout the country.
2. It has happened in spite of opposition.
3. The opposition has been vocal.
4. Recycling centers have sprung up.
5. They have sprung up in the last decade.
6. The springing up has been to combat habits.
7. The habits are wasteful.
8. The habits are those of individuals.
9. The springing up has been to combat the ways.
10. The ways are spendthrift.
11. The ways are of big business.

12. The springing up has been to combat spending.
13. The spending is extravagant.
14. The spending is by government.

----

1. The following has happened from 1950 onward.
2. It has happened in every nation.
3. The nations are industrialized.
4. Television has tended.
5. The tendency is to become a babysitter.
6. The babysitter is for children.
7. The children are mesmerized.
8. The tendency is to become a means of escape.
9. The escape is for adults.
10. The adults are bored.
11. The tendency has been to become a friend.
12. The friend is electronic.
13. The friend is one to people.
14. The people are lonely.
15. The people are old.

----

1. The following happens in his albums.
2. It happens in his performances.
3. The performances are public ones.
4. Ry Cooder's sound has continued.
5. Cooder is a guitarist.
6. The sound is jazz-folk.
7. The continuing has been to reveal his respect.
8. The respect is for the past.
9. The past is musical.
10. The continuing has been to reveal his joy.
11. The joy is infectious.
12. The joy is in the present.
13. The continuing has been to reveal his hope.
14. The hope is abiding.
15. The hope is for the future.
16. The future is of music.
17. The music is North American.

----

1. The following happens during the summer.
2. It happens in the early fall.
3. Advertisements leap out.
4. The advertisements are for cars.
5. The cars are new.
6. The leaping out is from pages of magazines.
7. The leaping is to announce features.
8. The features are the newest ones.
9. The features are in design.
10. The leaping is to announce advances.
11. The advances are the latest.
12. They are engineering advances.
13. The leaping is to announce rises.
14. The rises are inevitable.
15. The rises are in costs.

---

2. Now write a series of at least 12 sentences and then combine them into one sentence that imitates Pattern A. Then write at least two other sentences that imitate the pattern.

Pattern B **The low-flying jets broke the sound barrier,** shattering windows and creating panic.

1. After studying the sentence pattern, combine each of the following sets of sentences into a sentence that imitates Pattern B.

1. REM (Rapid Eye Movement) sleep occurs.
2. It occurs roughly every 90 minutes.
3. REM sleep relaxes muscles.
4. REM sleep triggers dreams.

---

1. The Norsemen traveled far.
2. The Norsemen were ninth- and tenth-century men.
3. The Norsemen ravaged Italy.
4. They ravaged Greece.
5. They colonized Greenland.
6. They colonized Iceland.
7. They discovered America.

---

1. The Norsemen invaded England.
2. They were adventuring.
3. The Norsemen injected words.

4. The words were in the language.
5. The words were Norse.
6. The language was English.
7. The Norsemen influenced the sound structure.
8. The structure was of English.

_____

2. *Now write a series of seven sentences and then combine them into one sentence that imitates Pattern B. Then write two other sentences that imitate the pattern.*

Pattern B1 **Held every four years in Moscow,** the International Tchaikovsky Competition is among the world's most demanding and prestigious tests of musical talents.

1. *After studying the sentence pattern, combine each of the following sets of sentences into a sentence that imitates Pattern B1.*

1. It is characterized by the use of sequences.
2. The use is Picasso's.
3. The sequences are nightmare ones.
4. *Guernica* remains a depiction.
5. The depiction is timely.
6. The depiction is vivid.
7. The depiction is of war.

_____

1. It was covered with strawberries.
2. It was covered with whipped cream.
3. A sundae provides relief.
4. The relief is refreshing.
5. The relief is from the day.
6. The day is hot.
7. The day is humid.

_____

1. It was destroyed.
2. The destruction was partial.
3. The destruction was by neglect.
4. There were years of this neglect.
5. The house presented challenges.
6. The house was centuries old.
7. The challenges were frustrating.
8. The house also presented headaches.
9. The challenges and headaches belonged to the owners.
10. They were new.

_____

1. He is widely admired.
2. He is widely recognized.
3. This recognition is as a citizen.
4. The citizen is of all nations.
5. The recluse spends hours a day.
6. He is a sometime recluse.
7. The hours are many.
8. He spends the hours shut away in his room.

Note: You may wish to compare your combination of the set of sentences above with the original sentence in a student paper on p. 140.

2. *Now write a series of eight sentences and then combine them into one sentence that imitates Pattern B1. Then write two more sentences that imitate the pattern.*

Pattern B2 **The alligator attacked his prey, stunning it, and carried it into the water.**

1. After studying the sentence pattern, combine each of the following sets of sentences into a sentence that imitates Pattern B2.

1. Jan picked up her notes.
2. The notes were psychology ones.
3. She clutched the notes.
4. She carried them out of the room,

---

1. The white water caught the canoe.
2. The water swamped it.
3. The water pulled the canoe.
4. The pulling was into the rapids.
5. The rapids were ahead.

---

1. The train lumbered.
2. The lumbering was into the station.
3. The train filled the station with smoke and noise.
4. The train disgorged the passengers.
5. They were disgorged onto the platform.
6. The platform was icy.

---

2. *Now write a series of five sentences and then combine them into one sentence that imitates Pattern B2. Then write two more sentences that imitate the pattern.*

Pattern B3 Moving delicately through the changing patterns of their long scarlet strands of silk, the dancers glide across the stage, costumed as lotus flowers.

1. After studying the sentence pattern, combine each of the following sets of sentences into a sentence that imitates Pattern B3.

1. He combed his memory.
2. He did so for syllogisms.
3. The syllogisms were half-remembered.
4. The student settles.
5. The settling is into his desk.
6. The student is prepared.
7. The preparation is for the exam.
8. The exam is a midterm.
9. It is in logic.

——————

1. They are spurred by the craze.
2. The craze is for fitness.
3. They are fired up.
4. This is as a result of the movement.
5. The movement is feminist.
6. They are buttressed by rulings.
7. These are court rulings.
8. They are buttressed by mandates.
9. The mandates are legislative.
10. Women have been moving.
11. They have moved from cheerleading.
12. The cheerleading is miniskirted.
13. Their moving has been to playing.
14. The play is hard.
15. The play is for themselves.
16. They are convinced of their final victory.

——————

1. He slipped into the booth.
2. The slipping was quiet.
3. The booth was nearby.
4. It was a phone booth.
5. Clark Kent trades his suit.
6. It is a business suit.
7. It is traded for the cape.
8. The cape is familiar.
9. The cape is red-and-blue.
10. Clark Kent is prepared.
11. His preparation is for his battle.
12. The battle is ongoing.
13. The battle is with evil.

---

2. *Now write a series of ten sentences and then combine them into one sentence that imitates Pattern B3. Then write two more sentences that imitate the pattern.*

Pattern C **Going on fad diets lures many who want an easy solution to weight problems.**

1. *After studying the sentence pattern, combine each of the following sets of sentences into a sentence that imitates Pattern C.*

1. One converts to the system.
2. The system is metric.
3. This causes difficulty.
4. The difficulty is for government.
5. The difficulty is for businesses.
6. The difficulty is for citizens.
7. They don't want to give up their ways.
8. Their ways are old.

---

1. One makes paper.
2. One does so by hand.
3. This has become an art.
4. The art is lost.
5. The losing has been in this century.

---

1. One remembers points.
2. The points are major.

3. The points are from lectures.
4. This presents a task.
5. The task is formidable.
6. The task is necessary.
7. The task is for students.
8. The students want to perform well.
9. Their performing is in this course.

---

2. Now write a series of six sentences and then combine them into one sentence that imitates Pattern C. Then write two more sentences that imitate the pattern.

Pattern C1 **The beginning of reflexive consciousness in the brain of our remotest ancestor must surely have coincided with the dawning of the sense of time.**

1. After studying the sentence pattern, combine each of the following sets of sentences into a sentence that imitates Pattern C1.

1. Embarking lures.
2. The embarking is on a round.
3. The round is of adventures.
4. The adventures are gastronomic ones.
5. The luring is of many North Americans.
6. The luring is to the island.
7. The island is Maui.

---

1. Creating was one.
2. The creating was of the Bois de Boulogne.
3. The Bois de Boulogne is in the land.
4. The land is wooded.
5. The land is west of Paris.
6. The creating was one of the plans.
7. The plans were Napoleon III's.
8. The plans were great.

---

1. Our understanding is of the following.
2. It is of the parts.
3. It is also of the functions.
4. The parts and functions are of our bodies.
5. This will result in the following.
6. We will take care of ourselves.
7. The care will be better.

---

2. *Now write a series of seven sentences and then combine them into one sentence that imitates Pattern C1. Then write at least two more sentences that imitate the pattern.*

Pattern C2 **Shy people might try** joining clubs and participating in small group activities.

1. *After studying the sentence pattern, combine each of the following sets of sentences into a sentence that imitates Pattern C2.*

1. Nonvoters should stop.
2. The nonvoters are dissatisfied.
3. They should stop complaining.
4. They should stop shouting.
5. The shouting is at leaders.
6. The leaders are elected.
7. The leaders are political.

    ———————————

1. We enjoy.
2. We walk.
3. The walking is brisk.
4. We exercise.
5. We do these things at every opportunity.

    ———————————

1. The surfers began.
2. They were novices.
3. They practiced.
4. They also trained.
5. They did so with exercises.
6. The exercises were balance ones.

    ———————————

2. *Now write a series of four sentences and then combine them into a sentence that imitates Pattern C2. Then write two more sentences that imitate the pattern.*

Pattern C3 **In backgammon, the player throws the dice and,** after studying his position, planning his strategy, and anticipating the probabilities of his next throw, **makes his move.**

1. *After studying the sentence pattern, combine each of the following sets of sentences into a sentence that imitates Pattern C3.*

1. The following happens at Sun Valley.
2. The skier takes the lift.
3. The skier is a novice.
4. The skier checks his skis.
5. The skier crosses his fingers.
6. The skier holds his breath.
7. The skier heads down the mountain.
8. It is a "baby" mountain.
9. The mountain is for beginners.

---

1. The following happened as a guest in China.
2. I was taken to a restaurant.
3. The restaurant was spacious.
4. I met relatives and close friends.
5. I toasted each person in turn.
6. I ate four courses.
7. The courses were of hors d'oeuvres.
8. I began the serious eating.

---

1. The following happens during spring break.
2. The group heads.
3. Their heading is for the beach.
4. They swim all morning.
5. They sunbathe all afternoon.
6. They dance at parties.
7. The parties last all night.
8. They exhaust themselves.

---

2. *Now write a series of eight sentences and then combine them into one sentence that imitates Pattern C3. Then write two more sentences that imitate the pattern.*

Pattern D To ignore the warnings of air traffic controllers that their equipment is inadequate is to endanger the lives of millions of passengers.

1. *After studying the sentence pattern, combine each of the following sets of sentences into a sentence that imitates Pattern D.*

1. One discontinues negotiations.
2. The negotiations are deadlocked.
3. This destroys the hopes.
4. The hopes belong to the employees.
5. The hopes are for a settlement.
6. The settlement is an eventual one.

---

1. One argues the following.
2. History reflects only the story.
3. The story belongs to the mighty.
4. This ignores the record.
5. The record belongs to people.
6. The people are countless.
7. The people are ordinary.
8. The record is in shaping the course.
9. The course is of events.

---

1. One sits.
2. The sitting is among the monoliths.
3. The monoliths make up Stonehenge.
4. This recaptures the sense.
5. The sense is of the past.
6. The past is distant.

---

2. Now write a series of six sentences and then combine them into one sentence that imitates Pattern D. Then write two more sentences that imitate the pattern.

Pattern D1 **The scrambling quarterback searched for his receivers, knifed back to the line of scrimmage, and fell on the ball** to avoid being tackled by two oncoming linebackers.

1. After studying the sentence pattern, combine each of the following sets of sentences into a sentence that imitates Pattern D1.

1. B. B. King cradled his guitar.
2. B. B. King tilted his head.
3. The tilting was back.
4. B. B. King closed his eyes.
5. B. B. King set the mood.
6. The mood was for his tunes.
7. The tunes were soulful.
8. The tunes were blues tunes.

---

1. Borg matched shot for shot.
2. Each shot was brilliant.
3. The matching was throughout the volley.
4. The volley was long.
5. Borg went to the net.
6. He powered the ball.

7. The ball went past Connors.
8. Borg won the match.
9. The winning was in sets.
10. The sets were straight.

---

1. Paul Kane left his home.
2. He was the nineteenth-century artist.
3. The home was an eastern one.
4. Paul Kane traveled.
5. The traveling was over the prairies.
6. He lived among the Indians.
7. He records the lifestyles.
8. The lifestyles are unspoiled.
9. The lifestyles were of Americans.
10. The Americans were native.

---

2. Now write a series of nine sentences and then combine them into one sentence that imitates Pattern D1. Then write two more sentences that imitate the pattern.

Pattern D2 **The student employment office tries to help students find jobs by introducing them to prospective employers.**

1. After studying the sentence pattern, combine each of the following sets of sentences into a sentence that imitates Pattern D2.

1. Moses tried.
2. He helps his people.
3. He leads them to the land.
4. The land was promised.

---

1. Juanita's roommate promised.
2. The roommate helps her.
3. The roommate gives her a course.
4. The course is a crash course.
5. The course is in calculus.

---

1. Copernicus wanted.
2. He revolutionizes astronomy.
3. He proves his theory.
4. The proving was to his fellow scientists.

---

2. Now write a series of four sentences and then combine them into one sentence that imitates Pattern D2. Then write two more sentences that imitate the pattern.

Pattern D3   **Black authors such as W. E. B. DuBois, Eldridge Cleaver, Frederick Douglass, and Booker T. Washington have used autobiography** to examine their lives and cultures.

1. After studying the sentence pattern, combine each of the following sets of sentences into a sentence that imitates Pattern D3.

1. The band carved.
2. It was an Indian band.
3. The Indians were Nootka Indians.
4. They carve out an area.
5. They call it their own.

1. World War Two was not the war.
2. It ends all war.

1. Gardeners store vegetables and fruit.
2. They are home gardeners.
3. They are many.
4. The vegetables and fruits are enjoyed in the winter months.

2. Now write a series of five sentences and then combine them into one sentence that imitates Pattern D3. Then write two more sentences that imitate the pattern.

Pattern E   **An accomplished guitarist and banjo player,** Roy Clark can also play **eight other instruments with ease.**

1. After studying the sentence pattern, combine each of the following sets of sentences into a sentence that imitates Pattern E.

1. It was a $1 million project.
2. It was a ten-year project.
3. The Kinsey Report is based.
4. The report is the latest.
5. The basing is on interviews.
6. The interviews were with homosexuals.
7. There were 979 interviews.

1. It is a delicate liquid.
2. It is a winey liquid.
3. *Cidre* adds piquancy.
4. The piquancy is special.
5. The adding is to dishes.
6. The dishes are French Canadian.

1. It is steamy.
2. It is a 2226-square-mile sultanate.
3. It is on the north coast of Borneo.
4. Brunei sits on petroleum.
5. The petroleum is estimated.
6. The estimation is at 1.6 billion barrels.

2. *Now write a series of six sentences and then combine them into one sentence that imitates Pattern E. Then write two more sentences that imitate the pattern.*

Pattern E1 Noam Chomsky, the influential MIT linguist, believes that children are born with a potential knowledge of grammar.

1. *After studying the sentence pattern, combine each of the following sets of sentences into a sentence that imitates Pattern E1.*

1. Samuel Johnson lent.
2. He was the compiler.
3. The compiling was of the 1755 *Dictionary of the English Language*.
4. He lent the touch.
5. It was the first touch.
6. The touch was of genius.
7. The lending was to lexicography.
8. The lexicography is English.

1. *Juke* had a meaning.
2. *Juke* is a word of African origin.
3. The meaning originally denoted "disorderliness."

1. Bede wrote.
2. He was an eighth-century historian.
3. The writing was the following.
4. The Jutes came to England.
5. Their coming was in response to a plea.
6. The plea was from the king.
7. The king was Celtic.
8. The king was named Vortigern.

---

1. Ngo Dinh Diem was overthrown.
2. He was the South Vietnamese president.
3. The overthrowing was by a military coup.
4. The overthrowing was in November of 1963.

---

2. Now write a series of six sentences and then combine them into one sentence that imitates Pattern E1. Then write two more sentences that imitate the pattern.

Pattern E2 **In the early seventeenth century, Sir Robert Bruce Cotton collected the relics of ancient pre-Christian Britain—coins, medals, inscribed stones, and manuscripts.**

1. After studying the sentence pattern, combine each of the following sets of sentences into a sentence that imitates Pattern E2.

1. The following has happened since its invention.
2. The laser has been applied.
3. The application has been to fields.
4. The fields are diverse.
5. The fields are many.
6. One field is engineering.
7. One field is medicine.
8. One field is communications.
9. One field is defense.

---

1. The following is as a dancer.
2. Mikhail Baryshnikov has it all.
3. Baryshnikov is Russian.
4. He has strength.
5. The strength is superior.
6. He has grace.
7. The grace is fluid.
8. He has ability.

9. The ability is dramatic.
10. The ability is powerful.
11. He has looks.
12. The looks are good.
13. The looks are boyish.

---

1. The following happened in the early twentieth century.
2. Summer W. Matteson photographed.
3. The photography was of the richness.
4. The richness was of tribes.
5. The tribes were North American Indian tribes.
6. One tribe was Hopi.
7. One tribe was Gros Ventre.
8. One tribe was Sechelt.
9. One tribe was Cree.

---

2. Now write a series of ten sentences and then combine them into one sentence that imitates Pattern E2. Then write two more sentences that imitate the pattern.

Pattern F **The film presents an image of three peasant women**, their faces stolid, their hands spread open on their knees.

1. After studying the sentence pattern, combine each of the following sets of sentences into a sentence that imitates Pattern F.

1. The twins dressed.
2. The dressing was identical.
3. They were at a disco party.
4. Their shirts were crisp.
5. The crispness was with newness.
6. The shirts were short-sleeved.
7. The shirts were plaid.
8. Their pants were bloused.
9. The blousing was at the boot.
10. The pants were olive-green.
11. They were Army pants.

---

1. The couple sat.
2. The couple was elderly.
3. The sitting was in lawn chairs.
4. The chairs were folding ones.
5. The sitting was at a concert.
6. The concert was open air.
7. The couple's shoulders moved.
8. The movement was jaunty.
9. The movement was with the beat.
10. The beat was of the music.
11. The music was lighthearted.
12. The couple's feet tapped.
13. They tapped in unison.

1. The house created.
2. The house was the architect's.
3. The creation was of a sense of openness.
4. The house's spaces were framed.
5. The spaces were large.
6. The spaces were white.
7. The framing was with glass.
8. The glass was smokey.
9. The house's stairway ascended.
10. The stairway was rail-less.
11. The stairway ascended to a balcony.
12. The balcony was immense.
13. The balcony was brightly lit.

1. The dancers evoke.
2. The dancers are precocious.
3. The dancing is in *Quadrille*.
4. The evocation is of themes.
5. A theme is of courtship.
6. A theme is of etiquette.
7. The girls cast glances.
8. The glances are intriguing.
9. The glances are over the shoulder.
10. The boys do grand jetés.
11. They also do pirouettes.
12. They do them a little numbly.

2. Now write a series of 12 sentences and then combine them into one sentence that imitates Pattern F. Then write two more sentences that imitate the pattern.

Pattern F1 Parking areas and loading zones clogged with cars, terminals besieged by distraught passengers, **the major airport was hit by unprecedented numbers of snafus and snarls.**

1. After studying the sentence pattern, combine each of the following sets of sentences into a sentence that imitates Pattern F1.

1. Her hair was coifed.
2. The coifing was neat.
3. Her dress was crisp.
4. Her dress was starched.
5. The dress was a shirtwaist.
6. It was red, white, and blue.
7. The ERA opponent distributed bread.
8. The bread was home-baked.
9. The bread was apricot.
10. The distributing was to the legislators.
11. The legislators were assembled.

1. His arteries were free of obstruction.
2. His angina was gone.
3. Robert left the hospital.
4. He returned to work.
5. The work was at his job.
6. The job was his old one.
7. The job was at the bank.

1. His timing was improved.
2. The improvement was considerable.
3. His fast ball was perfection.
4. The perfection was absolute.
5. Don Gullet fired his shutout.
6. The shutout was his second.
7. The shutout was of this season.

1. Its beds were infested.
2. The infesting was with roaches.
3. Its toilets were clogged.
4. Its showers were out of order.
5. The ship ran into troubles.
6. It was a cruise ship.
7. It was newly refurbished.
8. There were a sea of troubles.

1. Its windows are bricked against bombs.
2. The windows are shop windows.
3. Its streets are barricaded.
4. Its thoroughfares are patrolled.
5. The patrolling is by soldiers.
6. The soldiers are British.
7. Belfast is gripped.
8. The gripping is with fear.

2. Now write a series of eight sentences and then combine them into one sentence that imitates Pattern F1. Then write two more sentences that imitate the pattern.

IV. COMBINED PATTERNS

Pattern A **All the newspapers seem to be running wine columns these days, and more and more people are going in for wine tasting, wine one upmanship, and other forms of recreation that are connected with the juice of the noble grape.**

1. After studying the sentence pattern, combine each of the following sets of sentences into a sentence that imitates Pattern A.

1. Students are working their ways.
2. There are more and more such students than ever before.
3. Their ways are through college.
4. Their employers find them bright.
5. The brightness is remarkable.
6. The employers find them responsible.
7. The responsibility is consistent.
8. The employers find them aggressive.
9. The aggression is confident.

1. Convertibles have always been popular.
2. The popularity has been with the rich.
3. Rolls Royce produces one.
4. It has a roof.
5. The roof is cloth-lined.
6. The roof is snugly tailored.
7. It has an interior.
8. The interior is luxurious.

9. The interior is leather.
10. It also has a body.
11. The body could be described.
12. The description would be as "art on wheels."

1. The place is Old Town's Bazaar.
2. It is famous.
3. The fame is for its musicians.
4. The musicians are strolling.
5. The fame is for margaritas.
6. The margaritas are giant-sized.
7. The fame is for *enchiladas rancheras*.
8. These are special.
9. They are tortillas.
10. The tortillas are dipped in tomatillo sauce.
11. They are stuffed with chicken.
12. They are topped with sauce and melted cheese.
13. They are garnished with refried beans and sour cream.

2. Now write a series of ten sentences and then combine them into one sentence that imitates Pattern A. Then write two more sentences that imitate the pattern.

Pattern A1 **We checked into a hotel which had neither log fires nor a bar, but effective central heating, unnecessary hot-water bottles in the cupboards, a bath as big as a boat, and an affable welcome.**

1. After studying the sentence pattern, combine each of the following sets of sentences into a sentence that imitates Pattern A1.

1. The workers agreed.
2. The agreement was to a contract.
3. The contract was new.
4. The contract did not provide for benefits.
5. The benefits were increased.
6. The contract did not provide for hours.
7. The hours were shorter.
8. The contract provided a raise.
9. It was an across-the-board raise.
10. The contract provided a clause.
11. It was a cost-of-living clause.
12. The contract provided a bonus.
13. The bonus was semiannual.

1. Barbara ordered a banana split.
2. It did not have whipped cream.
3. It did not have cherries.
4. The cherries were maraschino.
5. The split had ice cream.
6. There were six flavors.
7. The split had bananas.
8. There were three of them.
9. The split had toppings.
10. They were fruit.
11. There were four of them.

---

1. The doctor recommended.
2. The recommendation was for an exercise.
3. The exercise would not harm him.
4. The exercise would not tire him.
5. The exercise would strengthen his muscles.
6. The exercise would increase his lung power.
7. The exercise would stimulate his heart.
8. The exercise would improve his circulation.

---

2. *Now write a series of 12 sentences and then combine them into one sentence that imitates Pattern A1. Then write two more sentences that imitate the pattern.*

Pattern A2 **On any weekend, Jack can quite easily sleep all day or, if he is particularly energetic, arise before noon.**

1. *After studying the sentence pattern, combine each of the following sets of sentences into a sentence that imitates Pattern A2.*

1. The gourmet may buy a blender.
2. The gourmet is budding.
3. The following happens if the gourmet's budget is not limited.
4. The gourmet may splurge on a food processor.
5. The processor is a Bosch.
6. It is German-made.
7. It is high-powered.
8. It is expensive.

---

1. Mapmakers would label areas.
2. The mapmakers were early ones.
3. The areas were uncharted.

4. The labeling would be "Terra Incognita."
5. The following happened when the mapmakers wanted to be more decorative.
6. They would fill in the areas.
7. The filling in would be with beasts.
8. The beasts were fanciful.
9. The filling in would also be with monsters.

---

1. This happens during good weather.
2. The hang glider can enjoy a glide.
3. The glide is simple.
4. The glide is easy.
5. The following happens as she becomes more experienced.
6. The hang glider can execute maneuvers.
7. The maneuvers are fancy.
8. The maneuvers are technical.

---

2. *Now write a series of eight sentences and then combine them into one sentence that imitates Pattern A2. Then write two more sentences that imitate the pattern.*

Pattern B **The SALT talks began two days early, catching the chief negotiators off guard, and moved quickly to a stalemate, quashing hopes for a settlement and leaving both participants and observers stunned.**

1. *After studying the sentence pattern, combine each of the following sets of sentences into a sentence that imitates Pattern B.*

1. The government has not curbed inflation.
2. That leaves most voters unhappy.
3. The unhappiness is increasing.
4. The government has, in fact, fueled fires.
5. The fires are of inflation.
6. The government backs an increase.
7. The increase is huge.
8. The increase is in the wage.
9. The wage is minimum.
10. The government promotes increases.
11. They are tax increases.
12. They are Social Security increases.
13. The government forces a settlement.
14. The settlement is expensive.
15. The settlement is of the strike.
16. It is a coal strike.

---

1. Donald surveyed his batch.
2. It was his latest.
3. The batch was of beer.
4. The beer was homemade.
5. He arranges the bottles.
6. The arranging is lovingly.
7. He arranges them on the shelves.
8. He began to label each one.
9. The labeling is careful.
10. He hums to himself.
11. He calculates how much money he has saved.

---

1. The following happened in the first decades of our century.
2. George S. Curtis traveled.
3. The traveling was extensive.
4. The traveling was throughout the West.
5. The traveling was throughout the Northwest.
6. Curtis carries equipment.
7. The equipment is complicated.
8. The equipment is carried on the backs of mules.
9. Curtis photographed American Indians.
10. The photographing was in their habitat.
11. The habitat was natural.
12. Curtis captures the flavor.
13. The flavor is extraordinary.
14. The flavor is of their lives.
15. Curtis preserves images.
16. The images are of our native culture.
17. The preserving is for generations.
18. The generations are future ones.

---

2. Now write a series of 14 sentences and then combine them into one sentence that imitates Pattern B. Then write two more sentences that imitate the pattern.

Pattern C Professor Williams calls the kind of writing that he advocates in his lectures "textured," writing that goes beyond the simplest communication of the simplest ideas, beyond the plainest of the plain styles.

1. After studying the sentence pattern, combine each of the following sets of sentences into a sentence that imitates Pattern C.

1. Anchors often possess credentials.
2. The anchors are highly paid.
3. The anchors are network anchors.
4. The credentials are only skin deep.
5. The credentials are based on the look.
6. The look is handsome.
7. The look is blow-dried.
8. The look is of dolls.
9. The dolls are Ken and Barbie.
10. The credentials are based on the tones.
11. The tones are sonorous.
12. The tones are of Ted Baxter.
13. Ted Baxter belongs to the *Mary Tyler Moore Show*.

---

1. Aristotle fathered the philosophy.
2. It was a type of philosophy.
3. We call the philosophy "empirical."
4. The philosophy bases knowledge on observation.
5. The philosophy bases truth on knowledge.

---

1. A veteran told.
2. The veteran was Soviet.
3. He was a war veteran.
4. The telling was to a crew.
5. The crew was a camera crew.
6. They were a visiting crew.
7. They were a *National Geographic* crew.
8. The veteran told them the following.
9. He hoped Russia would protect the peace.
10. He hoped America would protect the peace.
11. The peace is bread and life.
12. The peace is blood and family.
13. It is these things to those.
14. Those have been to war.

---

2. *Now write a series of 11 sentences and then combine them into one sentence that imitates Pattern C. Then write two more sentences that imitate the pattern.*

DEFINING TERMS

ABSOLUTE PHRASE See *Parts of sentences.*

ABSTRACT DICTION Words or phrases that *do not* refer to things that can be sensed. Usually opposed to *concrete diction.*

Examples goodness; sentimentality; justice; complexity; success; immaturity.

ADJECTIVE See *Parts of speech.*

ADJECTIVE CLAUSE See *Parts of sentences.*

ADVERB See *Parts of speech.*

ADVERB CLAUSE See *Parts of sentences.*

AGREEMENT Subjects and verbs are said to *agree* or to be *in agreement* when they are identical in number (either singular or plural) and person (first, second, or third).

Examples He studies every night. (Both He and studies are singular and third-person).

Long plane trips leave me exhausted. (Both trips and leave are plural and third-person.)

403

ALLITERATION In a phrase or sentence, the recurrence of words that emphasize the same initial sound.

Examples <u>P</u>risoners Make <u>P</u>alace-to-<u>P</u>lane Escape.

The <u>p</u>rime, <u>p</u>roper, <u>p</u>rivate <u>p</u>arlors . . .

<u>C</u>olt Defense <u>C</u>louts the <u>C</u>owboys.

<u>D</u>rowsy and <u>d</u>rugged on <u>h</u>oney and <u>h</u>appiness . . .

ALLUSION A reference to a person, place, event, or work; usually drawn from history, literature, or mythology.

Examples His boss was a perfect <u>Scrooge</u>. (The allusion is to the miserly and bitter old man in Dickens's *A Christmas Carol*.)

The old general had finally met his <u>Waterloo.</u> (The allusion is to the battle at which Napoleon was defeated in 1815.)

Since his appointment, the ambassador has revealed a number of <u>Machiavellian</u> tendencies. (The allusion is to the fifteenth-century political theorist Machiavelli, who held that, for a ruler, any means are justified if they attain the end of political power.)

AMBIGUITY Uncertainty of interpretation, usually because the phrase or passage in question could have two or more meanings.

Examples How did you find your sister? (How did you locate her, or what condition was she in?)

When the Dodgers met the Expos, they emerged triumphant. (Who won?)

No one builds cars like our company builds cars. (Do they build them better or worse than others?)

ANALOGY An extended comparison between two seemingly dissimilar things. In this text, used especially in the planning stages to help a writer gain a new or enlarged perspective on a subject (see pp. 26–32).

Examples Our streams and rivers and lakes are the circulatory system of our nation's body. Their health is intricately linked to our nation's health.

The sixteenth-century English public schools were prisons in which barbarous headmaster/wardens drilled lessons by rote into cold, hungry, stupefied children.

The script for a new movie on the Second World War provides only a comic-strip version of history in which characters are reduced to flat stereotypes with unbelievable dialogue which would easily fit into a bubble.

ANTECEDENT The word for which a pronoun stands.

antecedent pronoun

Examples Elizabeth, who is Jim's youngest sister, arrived at noon today.

antecedent   pronoun

Colleen was in class yesterday, but today she is ill.

ANTONYM A word having the opposite sense of another word.

Examples **Evil** is an antonym for <u>good</u>; <u>light</u>, for **dark**; <u>innocent</u>, for **guilty**, easy, for **difficult**; hate, for <u>love</u>; <u>bravery</u>, for <u>cowardice</u>, and so on.

APPOSITIVE A word or phrase that identifies or extends the meaning of a word that immediately precedes it.

appositive

Examples Bill Reid, <u>Northwest coast Indian artist and author</u>, will speak at our university this week.

appositive

The famous line, "<u>Play it again, Sam</u>," occurs in *Casablanca*.

CASE The form of nouns or pronouns that shows whether they are *actors* (subjective case: <u>I</u>, <u>we</u>, <u>he</u>, <u>she</u>, <u>they</u>), the *receivers of action* (objective case: <u>me</u>, <u>him</u>, <u>her</u>, <u>us</u>, <u>them</u>), or the *possessors of something* (possessive case: <u>my</u> book; <u>his</u> or <u>her</u> coat; <u>their</u> car; <u>Steve's</u> catalog).

CLAUSE See *Parts of sentences*.

CLICHÉ A word or phrase that has been used so often that it has become dull, stale, or stereotyped.

Examples The comedian had them <u>rolling in the aisles</u>.

This product is <u>tried and true</u>.

Let's <u>put our cards on the table</u>.

In big business, power is <u>the name of the game</u>.

Divers who <u>raced against time</u> to free the trapped submarine crew later received <u>a heroes' welcome</u> from thankful family and friends.

CONCRETE DICTION Words or phrases referring to specific things that can be sensed. Usually opposed to *abstract diction*.

Examples <u>Peanut butter and strawberry jam sandwiches</u>; <u>honk</u>; <u>scratchy</u>; <u>red</u>; <u>fractured ankle</u>; <u>damp and mouldy</u>.

CONJUNCTION See *Parts of speech*.

CONNOTATION The suggested or associated meanings that surround a word; opposed to or in addition to the literal or *denotative* meaning of the word.

Examples The word <u>welfare</u> denotes health, happiness, general well-being, or public relief. But the same word often connotes a handout or something for nothing.

<u>Odor</u> denotes only a scent or smell, but it usually connotes an unpleasant or bad smell.

The contractors who say, "We don't build houses; we build homes" are counting on the favorable connotations of the word <u>home</u> to help them sell their product.

DECLARATIVE STATEMENT One which announces or states, as opposed to one which asks a question (*hypothetical statement*) or gives a command (*imperative statement*).

Examples The ability to use language is the most distinctive characteristic of human beings.

Bob had a Big Mac Attack last night.

This month's rate of inflation was 15 percent.

DENOTATION The explicit or literal meaning of a word; see *Connotation*.

DEPENDENT CLAUSE See *Parts of sentences*.

EUPHEMISM An agreeable or inoffensive term that makes an idea or thing more attractive or acceptable to us.

Examples A chubby (instead of a <u>fat</u>) child

The rest room (instead of <u>toilet</u>)

No credit (instead of <u>failure</u>)

A tipsy person (instead of a <u>drunk</u>)

Retrenched teachers (instead of <u>fired</u>)

Blown away (not <u>murdered</u>) opponent

FIGURES OF SPEECH Expressions that create forceful, emphatic images or descriptions. See *Metaphor, Simile, Hyperbole, Understatement, Personification*.

GERUND An *ing* form of the verb that is used primarily as a noun. May be active or passive (as in *driving; being driven*).

Examples
gerund
<u>Curling</u> is a popular sport in cold, icy climates.

gerund
Vic and Stan enjoy <u>dining</u> in gourmet restaurants.

GERUND PHRASE See *Parts of sentences*.

HYPERBOLE A phrase or statement that is exaggerated or extravagant.

Examples Wild horses couldn't keep me away.

My brother will buy <u>anything</u> as long as it is on sale.

The long-distance runner's aching feet were on fire.

The first sip of Martini and Rossi is sheer surprise and every sip after is simply beautiful. A taste like no other on earth.

His cough was tremendous, vibrant, utterly explosive.

IMAGISTIC LANGUAGE Language characterized by the use of figures of speech and vivid descriptions which create pictures in the reader's mind.

Examples Straw-hatted and garden-gloved, she was squatting on her hams in front of a flower bed and pruning or tying something up.

Only the eerie green glow of the Cyalume cylinders marked the swordfish 100 yards to starboard, as he began tearing across the inky water and encircling the boat with line.

He had cafe-au-lait eyes.

The overalls of the workers were white, their hands gloved with a pale corpse-colored rubber.

INDEPENDENT OR MAIN CLAUSE See *Parts of sentences.*

INFINITIVE The *to* form of the verb, as in *to eat, to sleep, to wake.* May be active or passive (*to know; to be known*). May be used in a sentence as noun, adjective, or adverb.

infinitive as noun

Examples <u>To graduate</u> with honors is Marni's immediate goal.

infinitive as adverb

He was too frightened <u>to protest</u>.

infinitive as adjective

The union leaders gave the order <u>to strike</u>.

INFINITIVE PHRASE See *Parts of sentences.*

IRONY The effect created by a deliberate contrast between a literal statement and its often entirely opposite meaning.

Examples To do your best writing, simply write down random thoughts on a scrap of paper as they occur to you; then turn it in as soon as you have filled up one side of the page.

The instructions that come with the build-your-own computer are so simple that a child of 35 or 40 can easily follow them.

Tonight's cafeteria specialty, Mystery Meat, is sure to delight your taste buds.

JARGON The special technical language of a group.

Examples While the base line of the trace is an accurate (0.2° per 1000 cy/sec of audio output) and reproducible (± 0.5 percent) measure of the core temperature of the animal, a transistor alone will not detect rapid change of temperature. (from an experimental psychology report)

In Richard Whately's system, all propositions were considered to be subject-copula-predicate in form. All arguments were held to be reducible to syllogisms and syllogisms to be based on the *dictum de omni et nullo.* (from logic)

The director of instructional resources ordered 20 new self-instructional viewing modules. (from education)

METAPHOR An implicit comparison.

Examples Let your brush be a dancer, twirling lightly on the palette, leaping deftly to the canvas, and there gliding without a falter or a jerk.

Our life is a candy store, and we are its self-indulgent owners.

Television has become a vast electronic desert dotted only by a tiny, occasional oasis.

MODIFIER A word, phrase, or clause that describes or in some way limits another part of a sentence.

Examples
 modifier word modified
Her gold earrings glinted in the sun.

 modifier   word modified   modifiers   word modified
Working hurriedly, the cook assembled an elegant chocolate mousse.

 words modified   modifier
I will meet you after you finish the physics exam.

MOOD The property of verbs that expresses inquiry or fact (*indicative mood*), condition or possibility (*subjunctive mood*), or command or request (*imperative mood*).

Examples I finished the assignment. Did you finish the assignment? (Both verbs are indicative.)

Finish the assignment! (Verb is imperative.)

If I were to finish the assignment, I could go to bed. (Verb is subjunctive.)

NOUN See *Parts of speech*.

NOUN CLAUSE See *Parts of sentences*.

NUMBER The concept of singularity and plurality.

Examples Boat: the number is singular, that is, one boat; boats: the number is plural, that is, more than one boat.

OBJECT A noun or noun substitute that is affected by the action of a verb. Often described as answering the questions "What?" or "Whom?" In the sentence, "Sam hit the ball," the word *ball* (the object) answers the question, "*What* did Sam hit?"

Direct Object The direct receiver of the action of a verb.

Example Mary asked Jim.

Indirect Object The indirect receiver of the action of a verb.

Examples
 indirect object direct object
Jack gave him his notes.

Object of Preposition	The noun or noun substitute that follows a preposition.
	object of preposition
Example	We went to the <u>movie</u>.

Object of Infinitives, Participles, and Gerunds	The noun or noun substitute that follows an infinitive, participle, or gerund.
	object of infinitive
Examples	The author asked her to read his <u>novel</u>.

object of participle

Adding the <u>eggs</u> carefully, the baker assembled his famous gateau.

object of gerund

Smelling fresh-baked <u>bread</u> is one of the joys of Christmas.

PARADOX	An apparently contradictory statement that may, after closer inspection, be at least partially true.
Examples	As Saint Augustine might have said, To know God is to know what He is not.
	To be free is to know the limits of constraint.
	The truly wise man, said Socrates, knows that he does not know.
PARALLELISM	Repetition of the same structure within a sentence.
Examples	Unjustly accused, hurriedly tried, and falsely condemned, he became the first political prisoner of the revolution.
	The perfect wine is neither too dry nor too sweet, too fruity nor too acid, too mellow nor too bold, but a subtle interplay of all these.
	The town, like a dream, had faded, and most of its inhabitants, like chaff, had scattered far and wide.
PARTICIPIAL PHRASE	See *Parts of sentences.*
PARTICIPLE	A form derived from the verb that functions primarily as an adjective. Participles can be present (*ing* forms: *driving; equating*) or past (*driven; equated*). May be active or passive (*coaxing; being coaxed*).

present participle

Examples	The <u>driving</u> rain forced her off the road.

past participle

The path was blocked by a <u>fallen</u> branch.

PARTS OF SENTENCES	Although a sentence can consist of only one word (as in *Help!*), most written sentences contain at least one subject-verb unit. This basic unit, however, may be expanded by adding other subject-verb units (called *clauses*) or groups of words (called *phrases*).
SUBJECT	A noun, or any word, phrase, or clause that can stand in its place, and including all its modifiers. Usually acts as the topic of the verb.

PREDICATE	A verb and all its modifiers. Acts as a *comment* on the subject.
CLAUSE	A group of words containing a subject and a predicate.
Main or Independent Clause	Contains a subject and a predicate and can stand alone as a sentence.

Example

subject   predicate

The batter swung at the ball.

Subordinate or Dependent Clause	Contains a subject and a predicate but cannot stand alone as a sentence. Subordinate clauses can function in a sentence as nouns, adjectives, or adverbs.

Examples

noun clause as subject

That we are on vacation no doubt means we will have bad weather all week.

adverb clause (modifies will have won)

If Josh takes first place in the skating championship tomorrow, he will have won three years in a row.

adjective clause (modifies book)

The book **that I ordered** was out of print.

adjective clause (modifies skater)

The skater, **who had pirouetted beautifully,** suddenly fell.

PHRASE	A group of words that functions as a single part of speech but does *not* contain both a subject and a predicate. The most frequently used phrases include:
Noun Phrase	A noun and all its modifiers.

Example

noun phrase/subject

The red fire engine roared down the street.

Verb Phrase	A verb form that consists of more than one word.

Example

verb phrase

The tourists **are seeing** the sights.

Prepositional Phrase	A preposition, its object, and any modifiers—usually functions as an adjective or an adverb.

Examples

prepositional phrase/adverb

We went **to the store.**

prepositonal phrase/adverb

He swam **across the river.**

prepositional phrase/adjective

He bought a car **with a convertible top.**

prepositional phrase/adverb

He bought a car **with his savings.**

Participial Phrase   A participle, either present or past, and its object and/or modifiers. Functions as an adjective.

present participial phrase prepositional phrase

Examples   <u>Tossing</u> their <u>hats</u> <u>in the air</u>, the band members saluted the victorious team.

past participle phrase   prepositional phrase

<u>Tossed relentlessly</u> <u>by the waves</u>, the small canoe began to give way.

Infinitive Phrase   An infinitive (*to go*; *to do*; and so on) and its subject, object, and modifiers. Functions as a noun, adjective, or adverb.

infinitive phrase as noun

Examples   <u>To hear Isaac Stern</u> is a rare privilege.

infinitive phrase as adjective

Yesterday was a day <u>to remember forever</u>.

infinitive phrase as adverb

Jenny played the song <u>to make him sad</u>.

Gerund Phrase   An *ing* form of the verb, its object, subject, or modifiers. Functions as a noun.

gerund phrase as noun subject of verb

Examples   <u>Teasing Ian and Kristy</u> is Lance's favorite sport.

gerund phrase as object of verb

Greg enjoyed <u>painting landscapes and still lifes</u>.

gerund phrase as object of preposition

Before <u>ordering the pizza</u>, Gary played the guitar for us.

Absolute Phrase   A noun and part of a predicate, most often a participle. Functions independently in that it does not modify a particular word in the sentence.

absolute phrase

Examples   <u>All differences resolved</u>, the two brothers shook hands.

absolute phrase

The dancers leapt onto stage, <u>faces flushed and expectant</u>.

PARTS OF SPEECH   Traditionally categorized as *nouns, pronouns, verbs, adjectives, adverbs, conjunctions, prepositions,* and *interjections.* In addition, words can be categorized according to their *function* in a sentence (*subject; modifier; object of preposition;* and so on) or their *form* (the *ed* of most past tense verbs or the *s* of most plural nouns). One difficulty with systems of classification is that many English words can belong to more than one part of speech and can serve various functions in a sentence. Note the differing uses of *arm,* for example, in the sentences below:

subject/noun

Examples   Her <u>arm</u> was broken at the elbow.

verb

<u>Arm</u> yourself for a tough debate.

modifier/adjective

The yellow <u>arm</u> chair was given to him by his grandmother.

NOUN A word, like *cabbage* or *hat*, that can be made plural (*hats; cabbages*) and possessive (*the hat's owner*).

PRONOUN A word that "acts for" a noun. Pronouns include the following categories:

Personal Pronouns

Subjective	Objective	Possessive
I	*me*	*my, mine*
you	*you*	*your, yours*
he; she; it	*him; her; it*	*his; her; hers; its*
we	*us*	*our; ours*
you	*you*	*your; yours*
they	*them*	*their; theirs*

Reflexive Pronouns *Myself; ourselves; yourself; yourselves; himself; herself; itself; themselves.*

Indefinite Pronouns *All; another; any; anybody; anything; anyone; both; each; each one; either; everybody; everyone; everything; few; many; most; much; neither; nobody; none; no one; one; other; several; some; somebody; someone; something.*

Demonstrative Pronouns *This; that; these; those.*

Interrogative Pronouns Pronouns used to ask direct questions: *who; which; what; whose;* and their combinations with *ever.*

Relative Pronouns Pronouns that introduce noun or adjective clauses: *who; whom; whose; which; that;* sometimes *what;* and their combinations with *ever.* See *Relative clause* under *Parts of sentences.*

VERB A word, like *sing* or *see*, that shows the difference between present (*she sings; he sees*) and past (*she sang; he saw*). If a *verb* can take an object, it is called a *transitive verb.* In "They ate the pizza," *ate* is followed by the direct object *pizza;* hence *ate* is transitive. Some verbs do not take objects, and are called *intransitive verbs.* In the sentence, "She seemed happy," the verb *seemed* could not be followed by an object and is, hence intransitive.

ADVERB A word, like *quickly* or *intensely*, that is often compared by using *more* and *most* (*more quickly; most quickly*) and that is often marked by the suffix *ly.* May modify verbs, adjectives, or other adverbs. This category includes adverbs that answer the questions "When?" (*again; now; soon; immediately; yesterday*), "Where?" (*here; there; everywhere; up; down; inside*), "To what degree?" (*never; only; maybe; possibly; not*), and adverbs that intensify the words they modify (*very; too; quite; extremely; rather; somewhat*).

ADJECTIVE A word, like *small* or *happy*, that can be compared (*small, smaller, smallest; happy, happier, happiest*) and that can modify nouns or pronouns. This category also includes words that limit rather than describe nouns, such as the articles *a, an,* and *the,* the *ordinal* and *cardinal numbers,* such as *first* and *second* or *one* and *two.* Note that demonstrative, indefinite, and interrogative pronouns may *function* as adjectives within a sentence.

CONJUNCTIONS Words that serve to connect words, phrases, or clauses.

Coordinating Conjunctions *And; but; or; nor; for; so; yet.* The coordinating conjunctions are the only words with which two main clauses can be joined; see *Fused sentence.*

Correlative Conjunctions *Both-and; either-or; neither-nor*

Subordinating Conjunctions *When; since; because; if; although; unless; after; before; while; as; until;* and so on. See *Subordinate clause* and *Sentence fragment.*

PREPOSITION A word, like *to* or *with,* that introduces a prepositional phrase. Most frequently used prepositions include *above; across; after; against; around; at; before; behind; below; beneath; beside; between; beyond; by; down; during; except; for; from; in; near; off; out; over; through; toward; under; until; with; without.* See also *Prepositional phrase* under *Parts of sentences.*

INTERJECTION Words like *Oh!; Ouch!; Ah!; No!;* and so on.

PERSONIFICATION A figure of speech that gives human qualities to abstractions or to inanimate or nonhuman objects.

Examples Hunger sat shivering on the road.

Tenderly, the night lay its gentle covers over the tired, sleepy, earth.

What stunning conjuring tricks our magical mechanical age plays with old mother space and old father time.

The black factory chimney vomited forth its refuse.

PHRASE See *Parts of sentences.*

POINT OF VIEW The position in space and time from which the writer, while consistently maintaining first, second, *or* third person stance, views or considers the topic.

Examples Efficient use of time is important for you as a college student. You must arrange class and work schedules so that you have time left over for both study and relaxation. (The use of second person is consistent, as is the present time frame.)

As I walked down the corridor, past closed doors on either side, the point of light at the end became larger and brighter, always brighter. (The use of first person is consistent, as are the past time frame and the spatial relationships.)

PREDICATE See *Parts of sentences.*

PREPOSITION See *Parts of speech.*

PREPOSITIONAL PHRASE See *Parts of sentences.*

PRONOUN See *Parts of speech.*

RELATIVE CLAUSE Adjective clause introduced by a relative pronoun.

SATIRE The use of irony, derision, sarcasm, and wit to expose foolishness or evil.

Examples In *Babbitt*, Sinclair Lewis satirizes Middle America as he depicts an annual convention of realtors: "In the midst of these more diffident invitations, the golden doors of the ballroom opened with a blatting of trumpets, and a circus parade rolled in. It was composed of the Zenith brokers, dressed as cowpunchers, bareback riders, Japanese jugglers. As a clown, beating a bass drum, extraordinarily happy and noisy, was Babbitt . . . . Their coats were off, their vests were open, their faces red, their voices emphatic. They were finishing a bottle of corrosive bootlegged whiskey and imploring the bellboy, 'Say, son, can you get us some more of this embalming fluid?'"

Woody Allen's "The Whore of Mensa," from which the following excerpt is taken, opens with a "private investigator" listening to his "client": "Well, I heard of this young girl. Eighteen years old. A Vassar student. For a price, she'll come over and discuss any subject—Proust, Yeats, anthropology. Exchange of ideas . . . . I mean, my wife is great, don't get me wrong. But she won't discuss Pound with me. Or Eliot. I didn't know that when I married her . . . . Whenever I have that craving, I call Flossie. She's . . . . a master's in comparative lit."

SIMILE An explicit comparison between two typically unlike things.

Examples Like ancient trees, we die from the top.

Phantomlike, he slipped past the waiting soldiers.

He had chirped, like an irate bird, in my ear all day long.

He was as bold as a buck in springtime.

SUBORDINATE OR DEPENDENT CLAUSE See *Parts of sentences.*

SYMBOL The representation of a concept, usually by association, and especially with a material object. For most people, the dove symbolizes peace; the river, time; the sun, life.

Examples During our recent family crisis, my mother was a veritable Rock of Gibraltar. (symbol of permanence)

To many North Americans, the <u>golden</u> <u>arches</u> of McDonald's restaurants symbolize one thing: a fast, reasonably priced meal.

SYNONYM A word that has the same, or almost the same, meaning as another.

Examples <u>Fiery</u> is a synonym for <u>burning</u>; <u>damp</u>, for <u>moist</u>; <u>incredible</u>, for <u>unbelievable</u>; <u>peak</u>, for <u>pinnacle</u>; <u>start</u>, for <u>originate</u>; <u>book</u>, for <u>tome</u>.

SYNTAX The pattern of word order in phrases and sentences. A *subordinate clause* is one syntactic pattern; a *main* or *independent clause* is another

TENSE Although *tense* is a technical term, we will use it loosely here to refer to that property of verbs that allows them to express time (see pp. 332–333).

Examples

Present:	She talks.
Past:	She talked.
Future:	She will talk.
Present perfect:	She has talked.
Past perfect:	She had talked.
Future perfect:	She will have talked.
Present progressive:	She is talking.
Past progressive:	She was talking.
Future progressive:	She will be talking.

UNDERSTATEMENT The deliberate representation of something as of much less magnitude than it really is. Understatement and its counterpart, *hyperbole*, are generally regarded as types of *irony*.

Examples After hurling a million profanities at his opponent, Jack ran mad with spleen, spite, and hatred; in short, here began a breach between the two. (from Jonathan Swift: The first part of the sentence exemplifies *hyperbole*; the second part exemplifies *understatement*.)

In defusing the live bomb, the squad handled a rather delicate situation efficiently.

It isn't very serious. I have this tiny little tumor on the brain. (from J. D. Salinger)

VERB See *Parts of speech*.

VERBAL *Participles*, *gerunds*, and *infinitives*, the three verbal forms, resemble verbs but do not function as verbs.

VOICE The property of verbs that indicates whether the subject of the verb is an *actor* (active voice) or *acted upon* (passive voice).

Examples

	Active voice	Passive voice
Present:	He asks.	He is asked.
Past:	He asked.	He was asked.
Future:	He will ask.	He will be asked.

Present perfect:	He has asked.	He has been asked.
Past perfect:	He had asked.	He had been asked.
Future perfect:	He will have asked.	He will have been asked.
Present progressive:	He is asking.	He is being asked.
Past progressive:	He was asking.	He was being asked.
Future progressive:	He will be asking.	He will be being asked.

INDEX

417

Gerund, 406
  object of, 409
Gerund phrase, 411
Grammatical conventions
  case, 336–337
  comma splices, 340–341
  fused sentences, 340
  modifiers, dangling and misplaced,
    341–342
  number, 332
  parallel or grammatically equal
    structures, 342–343
  pronoun reference, 335–336
  pronouns and antecedents,
    agreement between, 335
  sentence faults, 338–341
  sentence fragments, 338–339
  subjects and verbs, agreement
    between, 334
  tense, 332–333

Hyperbole, 406
Hyphenating, 364–365

Imagery, 271
Imagistic language, 407
Incubating, 42, 72, 119, 167, 223, 253,
  280, 308
Independent clause, 410
Indirect object, 408
Inductive proof, 127, 196
Infinitive, 407. *See also* Verb
  object of, 409
Infinitive phrase, 411
Inflated diction, 86–87. *See also*
  Diction
Informative aim, *see* Expository aim
Insight, 42, 167–168
Interjection, 413
Interrogative pronouns, 412
Introductions, 135–136, 174. *See also*
  Organization
Irony, 407
Issues, *see* Context, the writing
Italicizing (underlining), 361–362

Jargon, 407

Language, *see* Diction; Poetry; Style
Library of Congress cataloging system,
  204
Literary aim, 44

Main clause, 410
Mechanical conventions
  abbreviating, 363–364

capitalizing, 359–360
  final copy, preparing, 359
  hyphenating, 364–365
  italicizing (underlining), 361–362
  numbering, 362–363
  quoting, 360–361
Media, *see* Context, the writing
Metaphor, 408
Metonymy, 271
Modes, *see* Classification mode;
  Descriptive mode; Evaluative
  mode; Narrative mode;
  Organization
Modifier, 408
  dangling and misplaced, 341–342
Mood, 408. *See also* Verb

Narrative mode, 52
  in expository writing:
    essay examinations, 255
    research papers, 226
  in expressive writing, 52–57, 80,
    84–85, 88–90, 99, 101
  in persuasive writing, 127–130, 137,
    174
Newspapers, researching, 202
Notetaking, 209–210
  and plagiarism, 221–222
Noun, 411, 412. *See also* Pronoun
  absolute phrase, 411
  case, 336–337, 405
  gerund, 406
  gerund phrase, 411
  infinitive phrase, 411
  number agreement with verb, 332,
    403
  as object, 408–409
  as subject, 334, 403, 409
Noun clause, 410
Noun phrase, 410
Number, 408
  agreement in, 332, 403
Numbering, 362–363

Object, 408–409
  direct, 408
  indirect, 408
  infinitives, participles, gerunds, 409
  of preposition, 409
Organization, 51–52. *See also*
  Coherence (transitions and
  paragraphing); Classification
  mode; Descriptive mode;
  Evaluative mode; Narrative
  mode